Manchuria Under Japanese Dominion

Encounters with Asia

Victor H. Mair, Series Editor

Encounters with Asia is an interdisciplinary series dedicated to the exploration of all the major regions and cultures of this vast continent. Its timeframe extends from the prehistoric to the contemporary; its geographic scope ranges from the Urals and the Caucasus to the Pacific. A particular focus of the series is the Silk Road in all of its ramifications: religion, art, music, medicine, science, trade, and so forth. Among the disciplines represented in this series are history, archeology, anthropology, ethnography, and linguistics. The series aims particularly to clarify the complex interrelationships among various peoples within Asia, and also with societies beyond Asia.

Manchuria Under Japanese Dominion

Yamamuro Shin'ichi

Translated by Joshua A. Fogel

PENN

University of Pennsylvania Press

Philadelphia

Printed in the United States of America on acid-free paper

10 9 8 7 6 5 4 3 2 1

Published by
University of Pennsylvania Press
Philadelphia, Pennsylvania 19104-6005

Library of Congress Cataloging-in-Publication Data

Yamamuro, Shin'ichi, 1951–
    Manchuria under Japanese dominion / Yamamuro Shin'ichi ; translated by
Joshua A. Fogel.
    [Kimera. English]
        p.   cm.—(Encounters with Asia)
    Includes bibliographical references and index.
    ISBN-13 : 978-0-8122-3912-6
    ISBN-10 : 0-8122-3912-1 (cloth : alk. paper)
    1. Manchuria (China)—History—1931–1945.   I. Title.   II. Fogel, Joshua A.,
1950–.   III. Series
DS784.Y347   2006
951'.8042—dc22   2005042367

Contents

Translator's Preface

Despite the many years it has taken this translation of Yamamuro Shin'ichi's masterful study of Manchukuo, *Manchuria Under Japanese Dominion*, to be completed, it has been well worth it. Originally entitled *Kimera: Manshūkoku no shōzō* (Chimera: A Portrait of Manzhouguo), this English rendering appears roughly at the same time as a Korean translation of the work is due out. It thus raises the scholarly bar elsewhere in Asia and throughout the Anglophone world more or less simultaneously.

Shortly after the original work first appeared in 1993, it was awarded the prestigious Yoshino Sakuzō Prize for that year and simultaneously set off a wide debate. Yamamuro was certainly not the first Japanese scholar to discuss the Manzhouguo period in Chinese and Japanese history, but his book nonetheless opened a debate on this highly contested era in East Asian history and with a much more balanced tone. Yamamuro was not only interested in how the Japanese military conspired to bring about the establishment of a regime on the Asian Mainland that most were prepared to write off as a "puppet state"; he was equally interested in how they brought ordinary Japanese into the master plan, how they worked to get a certain degree of Chinese complicity, and how Puyi, the last emperor of the deposed Qing dynasty, played along with and into their hands. As Yamamuro explains in his introductory chapter, he employs the metaphor of the classical Greek beast, the chimera, to imagine the forces at work in this government sponsored by the Japanese military.

The decade following the initial appearance of the book has been filled with considerable disputation about it and the issues its story tells. A lengthy interview in 2002 with the new journal *Kan* enabled Yamamuro to lay out some of his ideas more clearly for readers. Two years later, in 2004, he had the opportunity to see the work republished. At that juncture he added his own lengthy afterword—also in a question-and-answer format—to elucidate a number of related issues not taken up directly in the book itself. While the book on the whole deals primarily with military and political history of the Manzhouguo years, these appendices contain considerably more information of a cultural nature. Taken as a whole, the entire era of Japanese expansion into what is now Northeast China becomes simultaneously much richer and much more complex. I have included as well a chronology which may help the reader unfamiliar with the major events of the era in China, Japan, and Manzhouguo.

One element of the Japanese original that readers of the English edition may perforce not be able to enjoy is Yamamuro's extraordinary grasp of the written Japanese language. While his use of comparative metaphors from both the traditional East Asian and Western literary and historical arsenals can easily be appreciated, his beautiful prose style may largely be sacrificed in translation. One tends to lament such a shortfall in translations of works of fiction, but it is no less distressing in such finely crafted works of scholarship. My strongest hope in this instance is that the prose does not get in the way of the fascinating ideas Yamamuro has to offer. This is the hardest work of modern Japanese I have ever sought to bring out in English, and I need to thank the University of Pennsylvania Press for seeing it through to fruition. The difficulty in his style may be partially responsible for the fact that, with the exception of an essay by Prasenjit Duara, Yamamuro's work has been all but completely ignored by subsequent scholarship in the West, although this is hardly an uncommon fate.

I have chosen to render all Chinese proper nouns (toponyms, personal names, and the like) according to the *pinyin* system of romanization. Consistency necessitates forgoing "Manchukuo" for Manzhouguo and "Kwantung" for Guandong. The former is an odd amalgam of Wade-Giles romanization and constructed "Manchu" nostalgia; the latter is a relic of the even older Postal Atlas transcription system.

Introduction

The Shadow of Manzhouguo

There was once a country known as Manzhouguo (also rendered Manchukuo). It emerged suddenly in China's northeast on March 1, 1932, and vanished with Emperor Puyi's manifesto of abdication on August 18, 1945, having lasted for just over thirteen years and five months.

For the Japanese who actually lived there, however, this country's final end was only the beginning of their real Manzhouguo "experience." What was Manzhouguo and how did it relate to them personally? They must have asked themselves these questions repeatedly as various images of Manzhouguo later took shape; virtually all of these Japanese went through gruesome experiences in the aftermath of the state's collapse, often lingering between life and death—the invasion of the Soviet Army, their evacuation, and perhaps their internment in Siberian camps—experiences that are exceedingly difficult to describe. Is it now possible for us to see through to the countless fragments of these images of Manzhouguo which continue to live in their memories now strewn through innumerable notes and memoirs?

For the great majority of Japanese who have since lived through more than a half-century longer than the thirteen and one-half years that Manzhouguo existed, that land has become little more than a historical term which conjures up no particular image of any sort. To be sure, the past half-century has been sufficiently long for many matters to pass from experience to memory and from memory into history, long enough perhaps for even the experience of hardship to be refined into a form of homesickness, for the crimes that transpired all around them to be forgotten as if the whole thing had been a daydream. For the Japanese in the home islands with no links to Manzhouguo, whether they have sunk into oblivion or, pent up with their memories, have taken their ignorance of Manzhouguo as commonsensical, today the scars left from Manzhouguo continue to live on in that land, be it as the issue of war orphans "left behind" in China or as that of the wives left behind. Although Manzhouguo has ceased to exist, for the people who continue to live there, and for the dwindling number of survivors of that era, the wounds of Manzhouguo continue to ache and will not heal or disappear.

In fact, the Japanese are by no means the only ones still affected. Indeed, the Chinese and Koreans who lived in Manzhouguo suffered far more and bore far heavier burdens. Certainly for descendants of those "suppressed" as "bandits" who opposed the state of Manzhouguo and Japan and for those who had their lands confiscated by such concerns as East Asian Industry (Tō-A kangyō) and the Manchurian Colonization Corporation (Manshū takushoku kōsha), the shadow of Manzhouguo always lingers close at hand and never leaves for long. So, too, for those who may have participated in Manzhouguo affairs or been pro-Japanese and were subjected to persecution by their fellow nationals, particularly at such times as the Cultural Revolution in China. Furthermore, among those Koreans who, in conjunction with the colonial policy of Japan and Manzhouguo, were forcibly moved there, many were mobilized by the Guandong (also transcribed as Kwantung) Army and taken prisoner in Siberia, and later—after the disintegration of Manzhouguo—wanted to return home but were detained for economic reasons and must have been burning with homesickness for Korea.

Manzhouguo, a Puppet State

The number of people who have no knowledge of Manzhouguo increases with each passing day. However, like a piercing thorn that cannot be removed, the incessant pain it caused has left a residue of bad feelings in the minds of many Japanese, Chinese, Koreans, and others. While the great majority of people now know nothing about Manzhouguo, for those who lived through it, much too short a time has passed for it to be forgotten. Any evaluation of Manzhouguo would be remiss not to stress the extraordinary artificiality of which it smacked.

In Japanese dictionaries and historical encyclopedias, its position has all but become fixed. The general narrative runs as follows: Manzhouguo—in September of 1931, the Guandong Army launched the Manchurian Incident and occupied Northeast China; the following year it installed Puyi, the last emperor of the Qing dynasty, as chief executive (he was enthroned in 1934), and a state was formed; all real power in national defense and government were held by the Guandong Army, and Manzhouguo thus became the military and economic base for the Japanese invasion of the Asian mainland; it collapsed in 1945 with Japan's defeat in the war. Also, most designate Manzhouguo as a puppet state of Japan or of the Guandong Army.

In Chinese history texts and dictionaries, by contrast, Manzhouguo is described in the following manner: a puppet regime fabricated by Japanese imperialism after the armed invasion of the Three Eastern Provinces (also known as Manchuria or Northeast China); with the Japan-Manzhouguo Protocol, Japanese imperialism manipulated all political, economic, military, and cultural powers in China's northeast; in 1945 it was crushed with the victory of the Chinese people's anti-Japanese war. In order to highlight its puppet nature and its anti-popular qualities, the Chinese refer to it as "wei Manzhouguo" (illegitimate Manzhouguo) or "wei Man" for short. They frequently refer to its institutions, bureaucratic posts, and laws as the "illegitimate council of state," "illegitimate legislature," and "illegitimate laws of state organization." This language is not unique to mainland China, but appears in works published in the Republic of China (Taiwan) as well.

In addition to writings of this sort by people involved in the events, narratives of Manzhouguo in English and other Western languages frequently offer explanations such as the following: "Manchukuo" (or Manchoukuo): a puppet state established by Japan in China's northeast in 1931; although Puyi was made nominal ruler, all real power was dominated by Japanese military men, bureaucrats, and advisors; in so doing, Japan successfully pursued the conquest of Manchuria, which had been contested by China and Russia (later, the Soviet Union) for nearly half a century; in spite of the fact that many countries recognized it, Manzhouguo remained essentially a puppet regime; and it was destroyed with Japan's surrender in World War II.

Putting aside for the moment the actuality of who manipulated and ruled whom and in what way, if we consider a "puppet state" one in which—despite its formal independence as a nation—its government rules not on behalf of the people of that nation but in accordance with the purposes of another country, then Manzhouguo was a puppet state. One can scarcely deny that one of the forms of colonial rule was the very form this state took. In particular, for people who were mercilessly stripped of the wealth they had painstakingly saved on the land they worked for many years and who consequently suffered greatly, no matter how often they heard the ideals of this state recounted in elegant, lofty language, they certainly would not have accepted any legitimation for a state that threatened their lives and livelihoods.

Each person is likely to see the level of "puppetry" in Manzhouguo somewhat differently. While the concept of an illegitimate or puppet state may be too strong for many Japanese to accept, once exposed to the Chinese museum exhibits and pictures depicting excruciating pain in such places as the Museum of the Illegitimate Manzhouguo Monarchy in Changchun, or the Northeast China Martyrs Museum and the Museum of the Evidence of the Crimes of Unit 731 of the Japanese Army of Aggression in Harbin, or the Hall of the Remains of the Martyred Comrades at Pingdingshan in Fushun, comfortable images will no longer be acceptable.

Furthermore, it is certainly necessary to investigate the realities behind the "pits of 10,000 men" scattered about at various sites where it is said were buried roughly one million victims to plans for the development of the region from 1939, or the "human furnaces" at which human bodies were roasted on plates of steel to draw off their fat. However, when we realize that in most cases forced labor in general prisons or reformatories led to death and arrest itself was completely arbitrary, it would seem only natural that the horrifying shock this entails would necessitate calling Manzhouguo an Auschwitz state or a concentration-camp state, more than just a puppet state.

Manzhouguo, an Ideal State

In spite of all this, though, Manzhouguo was never simply a puppet state or just a colonial regime. Another view has continued unshakably to persevere even after 1945: Manzhouguo as the site of a movement to expel Western imperialist control and build an ideal state in Asia; its establishment then is seen as an effort to realize a kind of utopia.

Hayashi Fusao (1903–75) once wrote: "Behind this short-lived state lay the 200-year history of Western aggression against Asia. The Meiji Restoration was the first effective resistance against this [onslaught]; Manzhouguo was the continuation of this line of opposition. . . . Asian history will itself not allow us to disregard it by invoking the Western political science concept of a 'puppet state.' Manzhouguo still continues to live in the development of world history."[1] It may take another one hundred years, he noted, to come to a proper evaluation of Manzhouguo.

Kishi Nobusuke (1896–1987), who worked as deputy director of the Management and Coordination Agency of Manzhouguo and became prime minister of Japan after the war, has also noted in a memoir that, in the establishment of Manzhouguo, "the ideals of ethnic harmony and peace and prosperity [lit. the paradise of the Kingly Way] shone radiantly. A scientific, conscientious, bold experiment was carried out there. This was a truly unique modern state formation. The people directly involved devoted their energies to it motivated by their sincere aspirations, and also the peoples of Japan and Manzhouguo strongly supported it; and Mohandas Gandhi, the Indian holy man, offered encouragement from far away. At the time Manzhouguo was the hope of East Asia."[2]

Furumi Tadayuki (1900–1983), who witnessed the last moments of Manzhouguo as a deputy director of the Management and Coordination Agency, firmly believed in it: "The nurturing that went into the establishment of the state of Manzhouguo was a trial without historical precedent. . . . It was the pride of the Japanese people that, in an era dominated by invasion and colonization, our efforts to build an ideal state were based on ethnic harmony in the land of Manchuria. That young Japanese at that time, indifferent to fame or riches, struggled for their ideals remains the pride of Japanese youth."[3] Without the least doubt, he believed that the ideal of ethnic harmony—the founding ideal of the state of Manzhouguo—would continue to shine brilliantly for many years.

Guandong Army Staff Officer Katakura Tadashi (1898–1991), who promoted the establishment of Manzhouguo, saw Manzhouguo as the manifestation of a humanism based on the lofty ideals of peace, prosperity, and ethnic harmony. "In the final analysis," he averred, "as a cornerstone for stability in East Asian, it was an abundant efflorescence."[4] Similarly, Hoshino Naoki (1892–1978), who worked as director of the Management and Coordination Agency, endlessly praised the formation of Manzhouguo: "Not only did the Japanese take a leading position, but all the ethnic groups of East Asia broadly worked together for development and growth. We were building a new paradise there in which the blessings were to be shared equally by all ethnicities."[5]

In one line of his memoirs, Hoshino attached to Manzhouguo the heading "Atlantis of the twentieth century."[6] (By "Atlantis" he was referring to the ideal society of the distant past, as described in Plato's dialogues, *Timaeus* and *Critias*, said to have been to the West of the Straits of Gibraltar.) It is unclear in what sense Hoshino was himself dubbing Manzhouguo the "Atlantis of the twentieth century," because he simply suggests this heading and says nothing about the content of Atlantis itself. However, the plot of a visionary state—beyond the Straits of Gibraltar, with an orderly, well-planned city and strong military organization, based on a national structure of harmony and single-mindedness, which having attempted the conquest of Asia and Europe now faced retaliation by Athenian warriors, and had sunk into the sea in a single twenty-four-hour period of great earthquakes and floods—remains eerily imaginable even now, corresponding in great detail to Manzhouguo. Like the tale of Atlantis as a dreamlike paradise, Manzhouguo would be passed down over the centuries, and perhaps a day would come many generations hence when it might occupy a kind of resuscitated historical position, such as that given Atlantis by Francis Bacon in his *New Atlantis* (1627).

Be that as it may, even if it cannot compare to the myth of Atlantis, which is said to have produced a wide assortment of books in excess of 20,000 volumes, Manzhouguo has continued to be portrayed in the image of such an ideal state. A good part of the reason for this is the exceedingly tragic experience that followed its dismemberment and the great suffering that ensued. One can readily imagine that an act of psychological compensation—not wanting that pain to go for naught—has been invested in this now defunct state.

All this notwithstanding, the examples given by these and other leading figures cannot sustain the view that Manzhouguo alone, in its search for coexistence and coprosperity among all ethnic groups, was qualitatively different from other colonies. This view would undoubtedly be the sentiment shared by those people who were on the spot as local officials or members of cooperatives, as well as those who were directly connected with them; so, too, among most Japanese who were linked to the formation and management of Manzhouguo in one form or another, such as the Japanese emigrants there and the Manchurian-Mongolian Pioneer Youth Corps. There were many who, supported by a sense of personal pride in the accomplishments of Manzhouguo, survived down into the postwar era. This being the case, we have to redouble our efforts to listen to the low, strained voices behind the loud, booming voices propounding the idea of an ideal state and try to ascertain the realities of this "ideal" in which not only Japanese but Chinese, too, gambled their lives.

Must we heed the view repeatedly put forward that one should rightfully look not only at the aspect of the Japanese invasion of the mainland leading to the creation of Manzhouguo but also at the aspect of its accomplishments? In other words, it has been emphasized that despite its short history a "legacy of Manzhouguo" has contributed greatly to the modernization of China's Northeast in such areas as the development and promotion of industry, the spread of education, the advancement of communications, and administrative maintenance. These attainments, the argument continues, cannot only withstand scrutiny from our perspective today—when ethnic harmony has become an important ideal in politics—but they also warrant significance as an "experiment for the future"—namely, what may be possible in the arena of cooperation among different ethnic groups in years to come. Can this argument be justified?

How would this argument about an ideal state, stressing the positive factors and legacy of Manzhouguo, echo among people from countries other than Japan? The issue of Manzhouguo refuses to leave us—not only must we evaluate its results but the "seeds it planted" as well. In fact, one may recognize its distinctive qualities as being surpassingly pregnant with contemporary implications.

Manzhouguo, a Chimera

On reflection, there may be nothing that spurs on human dreams and emotions quite like the reverberations of such words as "state-founding" or "nation-building," as hinted at by Goethe in *Faust*. Especially in the early Shōwa years, the Japanese empire towered overwhelmingly above the individual, and people were seized by a sense of being closed in and unsettled. When he committed suicide in 1929, Akutagawa Ryūnosuke (b. 1892) left behind the expression: "bakuzentaru fuan" (a sense of being unsettled). For Japanese of that time, words such as "state-founding" or "nation-building" may have borne a distinctively seductive power offering an impression of liberation stirred up by a sense of mission hidden within. Thus, for many Japanese, the notion that "what drew them to Manchuria was neither self-interest nor fame, but a pure aspiration to participate in the opening up of a new realm and the building of a new nation"[7] cannot be completely denied as false consciousness. That they firmly believed this in their own subjective minds would scarcely be strange, but selfless, unremunerated, subjective goodwill does not necessarily guarantee good deeds as a final result, especially in the world of politics. Also, no matter how pure the emotions behind one's actions, in politics responsibility for ultimate results is an issue, and one cannot elude the blame that one deserves. One individual's ideal may for one's counterpart be an intolerable hypocrisy, indeed a form of oppression.

In the final analysis, in what sense was Manzhouguo a Japanese puppet or colonial state? Should we instead recognize that this is merely a distortion, an arbitrary understanding dictated by the victor nations, the "historical view of the Potsdam Declaration" or the "Tokyo Trials view of history" which echo it; and insist that the historical reality of Manzhouguo was the creation of a morally ideal state in which many ethnic groups would coexist? As Kagawa Toyohiko (1888–1960) has noted: "In the invasion carried out by Japan, only Manzhouguo possessed a mixture of dreams and lofty ideals."[8]

Before rushing to any conclusions, we need to begin by asking why Manzhouguo was established in the first place and then follow its traces where they lead us. Why in the world did this state of Manzhouguo have to have been created under Japanese leadership in China's Northeast? What was the process of its formation, and how were Japanese and Chinese involved in it? Furthermore, what actually were the ruling structural and national ideals of the new state? Also, what were the mutual relations among Manzhouguo, China, and Japan in political institutions and legal systems, policy and political ideas? In sum, what was the distinctive nature of Manzhouguo as a state, and what place should it occupy in modern world history? Portraying this state of Manzhouguo through an analysis of these questions is the principal task of this book.

I set the task in this way because one reason the evaluation of Manzhouguo remains unsettled lies in the fact that each of the opposing views of this state that I have outlined stresses only one side of the issue. From the perspective that sees it as a puppet state, the organization and ideals of Manzhouguo are belittled as merely camouflaging its essence as one of military control by Japan; from the perspective that sees it as an ideal and moral state, its essence lies more in the lofty state principles it professed than in the background to its founding, and the actual mechanisms of rule are of scant interest.

Although Manzhouguo enjoyed a short life, still portraying the features of this state as a whole in more or less the correct proportions remains an exceedingly difficult task. Although the quantity of memoirs and reminiscences about Manzhouguo written since the end of World War II is absolutely immense, there is nonetheless a dearth of official government sources, as much of the "primary historical documentation" from the Manzhouguo era itself was destroyed by fire or disappeared during the period when the state was in the process of destruction.

In considering all this, there may simply be no way to avoid the abundance of material in one arena and the rough and uneven quality of it in another, but by focusing on Manzhouguo as a state, I hope in this book to offer a portrait of Manzhouguo as I have come to understand it. I have attempted here to portray Manzhouguo by likening it to the Chimera, a monster from Greek mythology. Thomas Hobbes used the Leviathan, a beast that appears in the Book of Job, to symbolize the state as an "artificial being." Similarly, Franz Neumann (1900–54) used the name of the monster Behemoth to characterize the Third Reich of the Nazis. Drawing inspiration from these cases, I offer for Manzhouguo the Chimera, a beast with the head of a lion, the body of a sheep, and the tail of a dragon. The lion is comparable to the Guandong Army, the sheep is the state of the emperor system, and the dragon the Chinese emperor and modern China. What is implied here will be become clear as the argument of this book develops.[9]

Chapter One
Japan's "Sole Road for Survival"
The Range of Views Within the Guandong Army
over the Seizure of Manchuria and Mongolia

In the 1920s, Japan's notion of its "special interests" in Manchuria and Mongolia clashed violently with the rising tide of Chinese nationalism. The urgent need for a resolution of the issue of "Manchuria-Mongolia"[1] was linked to Japan's life or death. In October 1928 when the fires from the explosion that killed Zhang Zuolin (1875–1928) still smoldered, Ishiwara Kanji (1889–1949) was sent to the Manchuria-Mongolia region as a Guandong Army staff officer in charge of operations.

From his studies of the history of warfare ever since his years as a student in Germany and his understanding of the principles of Nichiren Buddhism, Ishiwara had developed a unique conception of an ultimate world war. On the basis of this distinctive point of view, he harbored in his heart of hearts a plan for the resolution of the Manchuria-Mongolia issue.

With Ishiwara's rise, Japanese policy with respect to Manchuria and Mongolia became part of an extension of the operation to turn geographical areas into special regions and, in its objective and its means, this marked a radical transformation of Japanese policy. The resolution of this particular regional issue was not to be accomplished at the level of Japan's "special interests in Manchuria and Mongolia" and how they could be preserved. Instead, the issue was reconceived at the level of why Manchuria and Mongolia were necessary and what were the most effective means of meeting this necessity. Earlier efforts to resolve this issue had been based on international treaties and by the political situation at home and abroad; they invariably made Japanese leaders feel as if they had been forced into impasses leaving no room for movement. However, Ishiwara cleverly made use of the fact that the centralization of power in the Three Eastern Provinces (as the Chinese called Manchuria) following the murder of Zhang Zuolin put Japan in a desperate situation to respond to the Manchuria-Mongolia issue and required a reconceptualization of terms contrasting sharply with the most recent turn of events in the world. His plan for its resolution was the annexation of the region of Manchuria-Mongolia itself.

Although this view in favor of the annexation of Manchuria and Mongolia provoked the Manchurian Incident, his own project was never ultimately realized; instead, events took the form of the founding of Manzhouguo. No matter what form it would take, however, the intentions of the Guandong Army which built the frame of the Manzhouguo chimera are clearly laid out in Ishiwara's ideas. It is thus no exaggeration to say that this plan essentially fixed the nature of the state of the future Manzhouguo.

In the chapter that follows, I want to examine the meaning of the Guandong Army's founding of Manzhouguo by looking at the structure of the idea, advocated by Ishiwara, of annexing Manchuria-Mongolia and the range of views at which that idea was aimed. This will provide the most direct answer to the questions of why Manzhouguo was founded and what its raison d'être was intended to be.

Manchuria-Mongolia: A Gordian Knot

The Korean peninsula and the terrain of Manchuria and Mongolia beyond it have been compared to a dagger thrust into the side of the body of the Japanese archipelago. Thus, gambling its national future, Japan was to fight two wars, one with China (1894–95) and one with Russia (1904–5), and narrowly attain victory. Manchuria and Mongolia were seen as irreplaceable terrain that could be purchased with "100,000 lives and two billion in cash from the national treasury." Their development and management were considered a mission of the Japanese people in continuance of the "legacy bequeathed by the great Meiji Emperor."[2] As an area contiguous with Japan's borders ever since the annexation of Korea in 1910, here was land deemed necessary to the national defense. In addition, the great natural resources lying idle in this soil were viewed as something that promised economic development for Japan, and thus Manchuria-Mongolia came to be recognized as a special region which would determine Japan's life or death.

Manchuria and Mongolia, however, were at this time lands under Chinese sovereignty, of course. For the Chinese as well, this was terrain tied to hopes for economic improvement in their lives, and virtually every year in the early 1920s between 800,000 and 1,000,000 Chinese crossed the Great Wall and settled in the region. From 1923 to 1930, there was a net population increase of roughly 2,780,000 in the region, and the number of Chinese there reached 30,000,000. By contrast, the number of Japanese in Manchuria in 1930 was at most, including the Guandong Leased Territory, only 240,000. In economic competition with the Chinese as well, the Japanese were losing. The situation was further complicated by the presence of

Koreans, Russians, Mongolians, and other ethnic groups, who formed rival forces in politics, economics, culture, religion, ideology, and the like. British and American interests were intertwined in the mix, making it a cockpit of divergent and competing ethnic groups. It was dubbed at various times the crossroads of ethnic problems, the Balkans of Asia, the Alsace-Lorraine of the East, and the powder keg of the Far East.

According to the American China scholar Owen Lattimore, in the 1920s it was China and Japan which, needless to say, faced off on radically opposed sides in Manchuria-Mongolia, the area he dubbed a "Cradle of Conflict." The reason was that the policies the Japanese government undertook there were an effort to separate Manchuria and Mongolia as a special zone from China proper and have Japan's exclusive interests in this region recognized. The Chinese nationalist movement which rapidly arose following the May Fourth Movement aimed at bringing about national unity domestically and recovering national sovereignty vis-à-vis the foreign powers. Japan's separatist operation ran head on into China's national unification efforts, and the expansion of Japanese special interests directly conflicted with Chinese demands for the return of sovereignty. The only form China's national unification and recovery of sovereignty seemed able to assume so as to reach fruition was the exclusion of Japan from the Manchuria-Mongolia area. Thus, the anti-Japanese movement as a nationalist Chinese effort with regard to the Three Eastern Provinces—primarily, Manchuria and Mongolia—rose in a crescendo from the efforts to recover Lüshun (Port Arthur) and Dalian (Dairen) in 1923, to the struggle for the return of jurisdiction over the Guandong Leased Territory and educational rights in lands attached to the South Manchurian Railway (S.M.R.) in 1924, to the Guandong Army's warnings concerning the preservation of order and the dispatch of troops into the Three Eastern Provinces at the time of the Guo Songling Incident of 1925 and the withdrawal from Beijing of Zhang Zuolin in 1928. However, the flames of this movement first raged in a significant way within the Three Eastern Provinces only after Zhang Zuolin's death that year.

When the Nationalist government under Jiang Jieshi (Chiang Kai-shek) based in Nanjing achieved a degree of success in the Northern Expedition, it announced on July 7, 1928 a revision of the unequal treaties and on July 19 the abrogation of its commercial treaty with Japan. As the Nanjing regime began the recovery of national sovereignty on the diplomatic front, plans for the centralization of power over the Three Eastern Provinces took shape with the appointment of Zhang Xueliang (1900–2001), son of the recently murdered Zhang Zuolin, to be commander-in-chief of public security over the region. In December 1928, Zhang Xueliang took the bold step of switching sides by linking forces with the Nationalist government and flying the Nationalist flag. In so doing, Japan's operation to turn Manchuria and Mongolia into a special area met with total failure. The

Political Affairs Council of the Northeast, set up in January 1929 by Zhang Xueliang after his volte-face, underwent the ceremony of entering the Nationalist Party (Guomindang), and in March 1931 the Northeast Branch of the Guomindang was founded. Although this did not necessarily mean that a monolithic party had been formed, for the time being the task of unifying the Chinese state had been accomplished. In so doing the recovery of national sovereignty became the pressing political task in the Three Eastern Provinces. Beginning with the National Diplomatic Council of Liaodong Province, founded in July 1929, groups involved in the recovery movement emerged one after the next in the Three Eastern Provinces, and developed an anti-Japanese movement calling for such things as boycotts of Japanese goods. Along with it anti-Japanese textbooks based on the Three People's Principles of Sun Zhongshan (Sun Yat-sen) inundated the Three Eastern Provinces.

What became a point of contention in the effort to recover Chinese sovereignty was the Treaty Concerning Southern Manchuria and Eastern Mongolia signed in May 1915 on the basis of the Twenty-One Demands. Since it was a treaty forced on the Chinese by undue pressure, from the moment it was concluded there were incessant public calls for its invalidation and abrogation in China. May 9, the day that the government under Yuan Shikai accepted final notification of the Twenty-One Demands, became a day of national humiliation, and a National Humiliation Anthem was sung with the following words:[3]

1. May Ninth, May Ninth, alas, it's our national humiliation,
   They demand the impossible of us and force us to accept the Twenty-One Demands.
2. May Ninth, May Ninth, what great pain is this national humiliation!
   They're using on us the means they used to destroy Korea, and, oh, shall neither of us rise again?
3. May Ninth, May Ninth, we must wash ourselves clear of this national humiliation.

Although the first section of this treaty had stipulated a ninety-nine-year extension of the Japanese leasehold in Lüshun and Dalian, if the treaty were nullified this leasehold inherited from Russia would expire in March 1923. It was from this base that the movement for the restoration to China of these two cities grew.

In addition, the second article of this treaty accorded Japanese the right to lease land commercially in southern Manchuria, and the third article gave them freedoms of residence, movement, and commercial pursuit there. The movement to abrogate these rights, though, was becoming ever more acute. To begin with, the Chinese and Japanese understandings of the concept of the "right to sell or rent land" differed; while the Japanese took it to mean a right enabling them to lease land in perpetuity—namely, actual landownership—the Chinese understood it as leasing based on the voluntary consent of landlords and hence merely the right to use and earn profit on land. As the Japanese saw it, this agreement meant that they had acquired the right to live as they wished throughout southern Manchuria, but the Chinese objected that this move was a Japanese means of invading China—aimed at violating China's territorial sovereignty—and they adopted measures to punish persons who leased land to Japanese as crimes of selling out their country and misappropriating national terrain through its sale. Concretely, this began with the application of the Rules for Dealing Severely with Traitors (promulgated in June 1915), followed by the Nationalist government's Ordinance Strictly Prohibiting Misappropriation through Sale of Land (February 1929) and the Jilin provincial government's Order Prohibiting Sale or Lease (of Land) (officially announced in January 1929). In all some sixty legal measures were enacted in an effort to bring an end to commercial leasing of land and homes and to recover previously leased parcels and houses. This movement on the part of the Chinese to end Japanese leases and to recover land and homes brought about numerous confrontations with the Japanese, such as the incident at the Sakakibara Farm in June 1929. Those who suffered the most as a result of such instances, though, were Koreans living in Manchuria, and bringing relief to them became one of the grounds justifying Japanese dominion over Manchuria.

Furthermore, the movement to recover national sovereignty in the Three Eastern Provinces extended to the core of Japanese interests in Manchuria-Mongolia with the repudiation of such rights as cutting timber and mining, demanding the withdrawal of troops by abrogating the treaty stipulation giving the Guandong Army the right to station forces in the Three Eastern Provinces, and seizing the S.M.R. The Northeast Committee on Communication, established in September 1929, began actively pursuing plans to eviscerate Japanese interests in Manchuria-Mongolia with the building of a provincial-run Chinese railway network encircling the S.M.R. and the construction of a harbor at Hulu Island near Jinzhou to replace the port at Dalian. Japanese interests in the region were gradually to be held at bay and reduced. As the feeling of crisis deepened among Japanese living on the land in question, a sense that armed force would be necessary to break through this distressing situation began to envelop the Japanese army, especially the Guandong Army.

As long as the Gordian knot of the Manchuria-Mongolia issue in which various treaty and customary interests between China and Japan as well as ethnic confrontations and the restraints of the Washington System were intertwined in a complex manner did not come undone, it had to be severed by a single cut of the blade. It was Ishiwara Kanji who was to lower his saber to the task.

As tradition has it, the Gordian knot was tied by King Gordius of Phrygia, and he who would cut it would become the king of all Asia. It was said that Alexander the Great stood before it unwaveringly, sword in hand, and severed it with a single blow. No doubt Ishiwara, too, concentrated his sword solely on the goal of Japan's taking control over the "crown of East Asia" based in Manchuria-Mongolia.

Launching the Plan for Control over Manchuria and Mongolia

In April 1919, the office of the Guandong governor-general was abolished within the Japanese military system, and the Guandong Army was launched as an independent military agency in Manchuria at the same time as the establishment of the Guandong Government (*Kantōchō*). The duty of the Guandong Army was to guard the Changchun-Lüshun Railway which had been transferred to Japan as a result of the Portsmouth Treaty concluding the Russo-Japanese War. This responsibility, though, was not limited to rail line supervision, as gradually the Guandong Army, as the military agency in Manchuria, assumed the role of guarding Japanese interests in the region by military action. All in all it acquired the qualities of a force intent on implementing military strategies vis-à-vis the Soviet Union.

Prime Minister Tanaka Giichi (1863–1929) presented his "Summary of a Policy toward China" at the Tōhō kaigi (Eastern Regions Conference) in 1927 to respond to the advances of the Northern Expedition being pursued by the Revolutionary Army of the Nationalist government. In it he argued that, in the worst case scenario that the disturbances in China spread to Manchuria and Mongolia, "irrespective of which direction they come from, we shall seize the opportunity and take appropriate action to protect it [the region] and maintain it as an area in which all peoples may continue to live in peace" (point eight). What he was proclaiming here was that the Japanese Army—namely, the Guandong Army—had assumed the all-important duty of guarding Manchuria and Mongolia, even if that meant ignoring China's territorial sovereignty. Of course, Manchuria and Mongolia were not at this time Japanese territory, and it should have been impossible for the Guandong Army, originally military guards over the S.M.R. rail lines, to devise this "self-defensive measure" covering all of Manchuria-Mongolia, well beyond the Guandong Leased Territory and the lands attached to the S.M.R. In spite of this, the Guandong Army did take the military initiative, seizing political hegemony in the Manchurian-Mongolian area, and in so doing announced that this "was terrain in which natives and foreigners would continue to live in peace." A thoroughly grounded conception (via Ishiwara Kanji) for the establishment of the state of Manzhouguo can be found within the logic whereby armed actions are aimed at offering all the peoples land on which they may live in peace.

Prior to the "Summary of a Policy toward China" of 1927, the Guandong Army had put together its "Views on Policy toward Manchuria and Mongolia" (dated June 1, 1927). However, with "Sino-Japanese coexistence and coprosperity as its goal" and with a suitable partner in Zhang Zuolin, whom Japan recognized as the leader of the Three Eastern Provinces, this was aimed at expanding the interests of Japan. Should Zhang not accept these conditions, the military had decided to replace him with another suitable partner. The Guandong Army was thoroughly imbued with this conscious-ness, and in June 1928 the decisive step was taken by Colonel Kōmoto Daisaku (1882–1955), a high-level staff officer in the Guandong Army, to murder Zhang by means of an explosion, and a military operation to solve the Manchuria-Mongolia issue would thus be executed in one fell swoop. The plan backfired, however, because of the strong reaction to such an ef-fort to turn the region into an area of special interest for Japan. The inci-dent involving the assassination of Zhang Zuolin decisively frustrated not only Tanaka Giichi's cabinet but the entire Japanese policy with respect to Manchuria-Mongolia. Japan and the Guandong Army were now thrown face-to-face with a deep crisis requiring the search for a new policy.

When Itagaki Seishirō (1885–1948), Kōmoto's successor, took up his post in May 1929, he began looking for a countermeasure. A Guandong Army intelligence meeting was held, and it was decided that, inasmuch as Manchuria sat on the brink of an explosive situation, the army would pre-pare for overall military action and begin to set policy in a more detailed manner. Behind this decision was the complete failure of the diplomatic initiatives of Foreign Minister Shidehara Kijūrō (1872–1951) who, faced with resolving the complex Manchuria-Mongolia issue, had been in negoti-ations with the Nationalist government in Nanjing, a regime which simply lacked the capacity to control Manchuria and Mongolia in any substantive way. Diplomacy having not resolved the problem, the Guandong Army reached the judgment that only armed force remained as a viable means of resolution. Be that is it may, with this decision the Guandong Army moved one step closer to the military occupation of the region, and in later years Ishiwara Kanji would claim: "May 1, 1929 is the anniversary of the Manchurian Incident."[4]

Having come to this conclusion, in July a staff officers' trip to northern Manchuria was carried out in the name of a strategic plan vis-à-vis the So-viet Union. En route, however, Ishiwara put forward a plan for the Guan-dong Army to occupy Manchuria and Mongolia. With the perception that the "resolution of the Manchuria-Mongolia issue was the sole road open to Japan," Ishiwara came to the conclusion that "resolution of the Manchuria-Mongolia issue can be completely achieved only once Japan took control over this region." And he expressed the wishful observation that by so do-ing Japan would "simultaneously bring an end to the anti-Japanese move-ment in China proper."[5]

Already in December 1927, a full half-year before Kōmoto Daisaku had Zhang Zuolin murdered, Ishiwara had reached the conclusion that the Japanese "absolutely had to take possession of Manchuria and Mongolia."[6]

He further emphasized the necessity of preparatory research concerning the possession of China proper. To be sure, if the Japanese army were to take direct control over Manchuria and Mongolia, they would not have to bother with the two-level diplomacy of a Northeast regime (under Zhang) and a regime in Chinese proper (under Jiang Jieshi). There would also be no need to take the detour of putting a pro-Japanese regime in place and using it to expand Japanese interests, and they would no longer be undermined by alienation and betrayal.

The plan for direct control over Manchuria and Mongolia was certainly a radical one, at least insofar as concerned the level of efficiency in controlling the region. Because it was to be a military occupation, however, obstructions and resistance to it were immense, and a more meticulous plan was needed to ensure efficiency. Thus, the Guandong Army entrusted to Captain Sakuma Ryōzō study of a detailed plan for controlling the area scheduled for occupation. Ishiwara himself moved ahead with investigative research after gaining the cooperation of Sata Kōjirō, head of research, Miyazaki Masayoshi (1893–1954) of the Russia desk, and Matsuki Tamotsu (1898–1962) of the legal affairs desk, all from agencies within the Research Department of the S.M.R. Sakuma spent over a year and completed his "Man-Mō ni okeru senryōchi tōchi ni kansuru kenkyū" (Study concerning control over occupied terrain in Manchuria-Mongolia) in September 1930. With this plan as its basis, a council was convened every Saturday from January 1931 by the entire Guandong Army staff and activists within the Research Department of the S.M.R to look into implementing an occupation of Manchuria and Mongolia. Only a portion of the written Sakuma plan now remains extant, but the subsequent draft budget for the first year of Manzhouguo was said to have been based upon it.

In any event, the plan to seize possession of Manchuria and Mongolia centered around Ishiwara was refined by the Guandong Army staff and others, and by June 1931 it had taken general shape. Toward what end was such a plan conceptualized?

Needless to say, he raised the issue of the "protection of Japan's legitimate vested interests."[7] As the crisis over Manchuria-Mongolia escalated due to the anti-Japanese movement, this had now become the central issue. However, once possession was achieved, interests could have been freely identified. Having rejected the framework of defensive conflict resolution for protecting vested interests, they had now boldly set out on a policy of outright possession, a point on which Ishiwara and his colleagues had heretofore laid scarcely any emphasis. In fact, the significance of a policy of seizing control had been perceived in order to acquire the resources available in Manchuria and Mongolia. This point was made clear: "Our national state of affairs has reached an impasse. The critical problems of population and foodstuffs seem all without solution. The only avenue that public opinion recognizes is boldly to open up Manchuria and Manchuria."[8]

Seizing control over this vast area was thus seen as necessary to break through the domestic difficulties Japan was facing by developing the region and strengthening Japan's basis for future economic growth. "Japanese prosperity will naturally revive through the rational development of Manchuria and Mongolia," Ishiwara argued, "and learned professional men will also be relieved."[9] In addition, he claimed, insofar as the worldwide economic depression had hit Japan with a profound blow, "the natural resources of Manchuria and Mongolia . . . are sufficient to stave off the immediate crisis and build the foundations for a great leap forward."[10] Thus, the possession of Manchuria-Mongolia was seen as the first step in the exploitation of natural resources in the region, and the wealth of those resources alone was seen as the key to overcoming Japan's general crisis. Of course, Ishiwara did not think that the resources of Manchuria and Mongolia were inexhaustible, nor that all problems would be resolved simply by taking control over the region. He fully recognized that "Manchuria and Mongolia are not sufficient terrain to resolve Japan's demographic problem, nor are the resources there sufficient for all of greater Japan."[11] However, even if they were insufficient, inasmuch as no other policy suggestion to break through the impasses Japan was then facing had been put forth, it was the only decision they could bet on.

For military men like Ishiwara and his colleagues, staff officers in the Guandong Army and officers at Army Central, though, resolution of these economic and social problems did not exhaust their concerns. Had that been the case, as Ishibashi Tanzan (1884–1973) argued after the Manchurian Incident: "Our political might did not extend to Manchuria and Mongolia. Through peaceful economic and trade relations, we were able amply to reach our [political] objectives. In fact, we were able to do a much better job of it that way, too."[12] This manner of dealing with the problems was clearly more reasonable.

The urgent question for Ishiwara and his colleagues was undoubtedly that of conceiving the possession of Manchuria-Mongolia as indispensable to Japan in the sense that it could resolve its national crises, and the judgment that this resolution would certainly hold sway over the national destiny was also probably at work. What then were the problems that would decide Japan's national fate? First was the issue of the establishment of a sphere of self-sufficiency to enable the pursuit of total war, and this was certainly linked to the reconstruction of the Japanese state. Second were the issues of national defense and the security for a strategic base, and these tasks were further entangled in the ideological problem of controlling Korea and fighting Communism. Of course, these two issues were connected and can be seen as two sides of the same coin, and thus they might be resolved together by gaining control over Manchuria and Mongolia. Hence, decisively at play here was the idea that "in order to prevent domestic unrest we need to advance overseas."[13]

The Formation of a Sphere of Self-Sufficiency and the Reconstruction of the State

World War I erupted in 1914 and fundamentally transformed the way war had been fought until then with the introduction of new weapons—poison gas, tanks, submarines, and aircraft—and the dramatic increase in the quantity of shells and ordnance expended. Because it was a protracted war over four years in length, a renovation in equipment, industrial might to support this materiel, and national mobilization were all essential to the successful pursuit of such a great war of attrition. It entailed as well a qualitative transformation toward the notion of "Total War" (*der totale Krieg*) in which all elements of the nation were directly linked to pursuance of war. As General Erich von Ludendorff of the German general staff emphasized, the success or failure of the mobilization structure for material and human resources of a state in time of peace would itself decide the difference between victory and defeat. The Western Powers were compelled to respond to this new state of affairs, and in Japan as well it was sharply highlighted as it became entwined with the setting of national goals from the years of World War I forward.

In an article published in 1917, entitled "Nihon no Ōshū senran ni taisuru chii" (Japan's position toward the European war), Chiga Tsurutarō (1857–1929) argued as follows:

The greatest lesson to be learned in the present war is that with population and wealth alone attainment of ultimate victory in war remains in doubt. A nation must be independent not only in machinery but in materials as well and must be able to acquire such goods on its own terrain before it can be said to have gained self-sufficiency in war supplies. Japan will not avoid being completely inept in a future war if it continues as it presently is. First, Japan lacks steel and its coal is not plentiful. Without steel, it cannot sustain a future war. Japan's pressing needs are thus to acquire the necessary steel and coal and to create institutions and economic organizations to make it independent in military supplies.[14]

With this in mind, Chiga proposed as a concrete policy that Japan and China "merge from the perspective of international law, forming a federated body." He went on to argue that "enabling us to make use of Chinese terrain, railways, and resources in time of war just as we would those of Japan proper" was an essential requisite for Japan's continued existence. This arrangement, of course, did not imply a federation based on equality. However, "it is necessary for self-defense that we must merge even if we have to compel China to accept it by sheer force."[15] A sense of crisis had emerged regarding what little remained of resource-poor Japan to the extent that Chiga was willing to publish such an insistent political argument in a popular magazine.

Furthermore, the shock felt by the army when it organized a large-scale committee to carry out a provisional military investigation and analysis of the conditions surrounding World War I was unmatched among the civilian population, for as a result of this analysis it was shown that Japanese military hardware had declined to a mere relic from the previous century. In spite of a great expansion in the power and accuracy of its weaponry, the Japanese army's basic materiel remained infantry rifles from circa 1905, the kind used in the Russo-Japanese War.

The expansion of industrial capacity and a stable supply of iron and coal to support it were the most important factors determining the military's fighting strength. Furthermore, should the war become protracted or turn into a war of attrition, it would become necessary to insure a continual supply of resources without relying on the warring parties, and this concern was linked to Japan's own task of forming a sphere of self-sufficiency. Looked at from this perspective, Japanese came to see China as the only arena in which to pursue this goal. Koiso Kuniaki (1880–1950), squad commander of the military geography desk in the China section of the general staff, wrote in 1917: "To neglect Chinese resources is, in fact, to be unconscious of the ruin of divine Japan."[16] Ugaki Kazushige (1868–1956), chief of the operations section of the general staff, noted in his diary early in 1918 that a "self-sufficient economic sphere" for Japan "necessarily extended to the mainland and particularly to China. It is essential that China and Japan forge a single economic unit."[17] Both men posited the pressing need for a unified body with China if Japan were to create a sphere of self-sufficiency. Thus, an "Industrial Munitions Mobilization Law" premised on the importation of Chinese-produced resources for national defense was promulgated in 1918. Inasmuch as China in its entirety could not be incorporated in one fell swoop into the Japanese sphere of self-sufficiency, however, a rank order was concocted whereby Manchuria-Mongolia had first to be taken possession of before turning to China proper.

Ishiwara Kanji's conception of Japan's taking territorial control over Manchuria-Mongolia was thus structured within this line of thinking. After taking control, he argued, "we are resigned to East Asia's being blockaded and at the appropriate hour will place under our control as well important parts of China proper. . . . We shall have achieved our goal when the road to self-sufficiency in East Asia has been established and we can profitably pursue a protracted war."[18] In short, Ishiwara's conception of total war was to take possession of Manchuria and Mongolia, make them part of Japan's sphere of self-sufficiency, and then, if this should incite another foreign war, Japan would be able to pursue it successfully by taking further control over China proper. "Our basic viewpoint," stated Ishwara, "is to support war with war, and if necessary a portion or even the majority of military expenses necessary for the navy shall go to the [Asian] mainland."[19] Thus, for Ishiwara, as long as Manchuria and Mongolia remained outside of Japanese possession there could be no growth and Japan had no means of survival. More than anything else, with the raw materials available in this

region, "we shall have nearly all the resources necessary for national defense, and they are absolutely necessary for the self-sufficiency of the empire."[20] This position was effectively self-evident to the Guandong Army
general staff.

To successfully pursue a total war, not only was it necessary to secure a
supply center for resources, but Japan also needed to firmly establish a
structure of general mobilization in order to directly link all the essential
constituents of the nation, such as a reorganization of the structure of domestic industry and the formation of a national mobilization system. To establish a general mobilization structure, a government with strong leaders
was demanded. However, among the military men of the generation that
had witnessed direct action in World War I, a sense of discontent and suspicion was gradually on the rise with respect to the ruling capacity of civilian
party politicians, men who had demonstrated a penchant for political
decadence, in the eyes of the military, while pushing policies of international
conciliation and arms reductions. The call went out to overthrow the party
cabinets and reorganize the state based on a military regime. Seizure of
Manchuria-Mongolia and the reorganization of the state were understood
then as tasks unifying the inner and outer aspects of the structure supporting pursuit of total war; their resolution was perceived as a pressing issue.

At a meeting of the Thursday Society (a national policy research group)
founded in November 1927, research and debate pressed forward on reno-
vations needed to achieve military preparedness and on the issue of
Manchuria-Mongolia. At one such meeting Ishiwara proposed, in preparation for the decisive war with the United States, an invasion of China and
the establishment of a base of operations there. In March 1928 a plan entitled "The Need for the Firm Establishment of a Full Political Authority in
Manchuria-Mongolia to Make the Empire Self-Sufficient" was decided
upon. The "Firm Establishment of a Full Political Authority" meant seizing
control over Manchuria-Mongolia. Furthermore, at the One Evening Society, formed in May 1929 after the Thursday Society and the Sprout Society
merged, the members resolved to reform the military and "place emphasis
on resolution of the Manchurian-Mongolian question," and a military resolution of the latter by a group at various levels with its nucleus of officers
was placed on the order of the day. It was even said that personnel posted
to the Guandong Army under Ishiwara and Itagaki were people linked to
the Sprout Society, the Thursday Society, and the One Evening Society.

In September 1930 the Cherry Blossom Society was formed around Lieutenant Colonel Hashimoto Kingorō (1890–1957) among others, and in its
plans for national reorganization seizure of Manchuria-Mongolia was
deemed essential: "With this meager piece of terrain [namely, Japan], our
great expectations for domestic reform leading to the betterment of our
people cannot be achieved." Yet, Hashimoto and his colleagues did adopt a
policy of dealing first with domestic issues and later with foreign matters,

for if they did not first carry out a national renovation in order to take possession of Manchuria and Mongolia, they believed it impossible to resolve the Manchuria-Mongolia issue itself. By contrast, Ishiwara assumed the primacy of seizing Manchuria and Mongolia: "first foreign affairs, then domestic matters"; as he put it, "it is advantageous to make resolution of the Manchuria-Mongolia issue primary rather than domestic reform."[21] Thus, when the plan for a coup d'état carried out by the radical wing of the Cherry Blossom Society failed in March 1931, the "first foreign affairs, then domestic matters" approach gained influence. In May 1931 Ishiwara came to the conclusion that "by creating an opportunity with a plot, it would not necessarily be difficult to force the nation to accept military leadership."[22] In August, Honjō Shigeru (1876–1945), commanding officer of the Guandong Army, issued an instruction to the effect that "I have profound expectations for this"; in September, he declared that "the time for final resolution [of this issue] approaches," and the countdown began toward military action.

In this manner, plans for the seizure of Manchuria and Mongolia were invested with importance for the formation of a sphere of Japanese self-sufficiency and for the acquisition of a base of operations for "renovation" which would precede domestic reform. However, for Ishiwara and the other army officers, the significance of taking Manchuria-Mongolia did not come to an end simply with a supply base to help form a sphere of self-sufficiency and a base of operations to work for national reformation. For them, whether right or wrong, the reason they had to first secure possession of Manchuria and Mongolia lay elsewhere.

Controlling Korea and Isolating Communism

The principal reason that Manchuria and Mongolia were considered Japan's lifeline was that Manchuria shared a border with colonial Korea, and it was thus seen as the front line in defenses against the Soviet Union and China. In other words, if the Soviet Union or China were to gain overwhelming force in the Manchuria-Mongolia area and expel Japan from the region, then Japanese control over Korea would itself be put seriously in jeopardy. This anxiety became an obsession that Japan had always to retain authority in the region.

The "General Policy on China" drafted as an agreement among the four ministries of foreign affairs, finance, army, and navy in May 1924 stipulated: "The maintenance of order in Manchuria-Mongolia is of great importance due both to the magnitude of the interest of said region to the empire and particularly to the control over Korea. To that end, we shall always give it our utmost attention." Itagaki also stressed the Soviet threat: "Were Russia just once to cross its frontier, [loss of] our continued control over Korea would become just a matter of time."[23] He thus was arguing strongly that seizure of Manchuria and Mongolia was essential to the defense of Korea, too.

Ishiwara and other staff officers of the Guandong Army, however, saw that "control over Korea would only be secure when our authority prevails in Manchuria-Mongolia."[24] Thus, emphasis on the close connection between seizing Manchuria and Mongolia and controlling Korea was never based simply on a military perspective. The ideological issue which arose in conjunction with this—the question of Koreans who were resident in Manchuria—was seen as far more urgent. The conflicts of interest, political rivalries, ideological strife, and ethnic hostilities between Japanese and Koreans, Koreans and Chinese, and Chinese and Japanese were all complex factors interwoven one with the next. They formed the central core of the Manchuria-Mongolia issue.

The flow of Koreans into Manchuria reached flood proportions following the Japanese annexation of 1910. In 1930 their numbers were said to reach 800,000 in the Jiandao and Dongbiandao regions. Most of them had lost their land by virtue of the land survey schemes and the plans to increase rice production implemented when Japan took control over Korea. These people had lost their sustenance and been forced into exile and migration. Many were also activists in the anti-Japanese movement opposing Japan's control over their country and fighting for independence. However, while the Korean governor-general's office strictly controlled surplus population pressure on the Japanese homeland, migration to Manchuria was ignored as a natural flow. The very existence of Koreans in Manchuria presented the opportunity for Japanese police powers to extend beyond their leased terrain on the pretext of protecting Korean farmers who were "the best Japanese subjects" while controlling the anti-Japanese movement of "recalcitrant Koreans" (*futei Senjin*).

By contrast, this heightened the Chinese sense of alarm, for "behind the Koreans were the Japanese, and on the pretext of protecting the Koreans, the Japanese made inroads with their police officials into the hinterland of Manchuria."[25] These Korean residents in Manchuria were seen by the Chinese as the advance guard of the Japanese invasion of Manchuria, and the Chinese further tightened agreements concerning restrictions on tenancy and residency for Koreans in Manchuria. More directly, at a Guomindang plenum in February 1931, a resolution was passed restricting the immigration of Koreans into Manchuria and Mongolia, and with the promulgation of the Korean Expulsion Order, the Guomindang proceeded with an effort to drive the Koreans out of Manchuria.

The Chinese also attempted to resolve the situation by encouraging the Koreans to become naturalized Chinese. Inasmuch as the Japanese nationality law, including the clause on the acceptance of the right of naturalization, was not enforced in Korea, Koreans (whom China formally recognized as naturalized) as persons with dual citizenship were subject to Japanese police powers, and this actually exacerbated the struggle surrounding the exercise of police authority between China and Japan.

The Korean exclusion movement in Manchuria as one link to the Chinese anti-Japanese movement gave birth to a chain of rivalries and resentments among the Chinese, Japanese, and Koreans as noted below:

To be sure, the political blow delivered by Japan to China will emerge as Chinese pressure on the Koreans from above. As a result, there will be an increase in Korean anti-Japanese thought and animosity which will promote their movement. If an order is issued to the Chinese to bring this under control, it will surely prove counterproductive and only fan the flames.[26]

The pivotal role that would set off this chain of rivalries would, of course, be played by Japan. In actuality, many disputes and troubles between Chinese and Manchurian Koreans engaged in agriculture had already arisen, and the number of incidents in which these disputes came to the surface and flared up between 1928 and 1930 reached one hundred. This surge reached its acme with the Wanbaoshan Incident (near the city of Changchun) of May–July 1931. More than the actual clash between Chinese peasants and Manchurian Koreans at Wanbaoshan, the subsequent false reports led to a tragedy for Chinese in various places throughout Korea with Korean retaliation and attacks. According to the Lytton Commission's Report, prepared on the basis of Chinese documents, 127 Chinese died and 393 were wounded. This incident together with the 1931 case involving the murder of Captain Nakamura Shintarō stirred up public opinion in Japan for a hardline resolution of the Manchuria-Mongolia issue. These events were seized as suitable opportunities to provoke the Manchurian Incident.

The issues surrounding Koreans in Manchuria were not merely those of ethnicity. The resistance movement against Japan and the Communist movement in which Chinese and Koreans cooperated posed ideological and public order questions as well.

From the March 1 (1919) Movement forward, Korean nationalists such as Hong Pŏm-do (1868–1943) in the Jiandao area had organized an army of independence and launched an anti-Japanese struggle. Then, in October 1920 the Japanese consulate in Hunchun was attacked, and Japan used this pretext to send troops into Jiandao "to root out the evils of recalcitrant Koreans and marauding bandits and thus eradicate the threat to contiguous terrain."[27] Many Koreans were murdered, and throughout the 1920s the anti-Japanese struggle and the effort to suppress it proportionately increased their levels of violence.

Meanwhile, parallel to these events, Communist movements were spreading both in Korea and in the Manchuria-Mongolia region. Founded in 1925, the Korean Communist Party had emigré activists in Manchuria, and it set up a Manchurian headquarters the following year in Jiandao which helped to increase their influence among Koreans in Manchuria. Even after the dissolution of the Korean Communist Party in 1928, the Manchurian headquarters continued its own activities. Following a Comintern directive around 1930, however, the Manchurian headquarters was disbanded, and its followers came under the direction of a Manchurian executive committee of the Chinese Communist Party. In this way, the joint struggle of Chinese and Korean Communists was forged on the Manchurian stage and found action in accord with the Chinese Communist Party under the leadership of Li Lisan (1899–1967).

On May 30, 1930 a large-scale armed uprising of Korean peasants organized by Korean Communists erupted under the slogans: "Down with all landlords! Down with Japanese imperialism!" This became known as the May 30 Jiandao Uprising. Although it was put down, risings continued at various places, and the maintenance of public order not only in Manchuria but in Korea as well became a serious problem. At the time of the Manchurian Incident the next year, Japan's Korea Army arbitrarily crossed the border, sending troops into Manchuria without waiting for official orders, because it was understood that the anti-Japanese Communist movement in Manchuria would undermine the foundation of Japanese control over Korea. As Toyoshima Fusatarō, staff officer of the Korea Army, recounted it: "There were many who were trying to destabilize public order in Korea from a base across the border where Japanese police powers did not extend. . . . As anti-Japanese feelings intensified in Manchuria, comparable words and deeds within Korea grew more severe with each passing day."[28] As he went on to note, there was an immediate need to send troops across the border into Manchuria:

From this standpoint, we might expect that a speedy resolution of the Manchuria issue would in this way enhance Japan's prestige, promote a sense of trust in us among the Korean people, and benefit our rule there. . . . Therefore, the Korea Army did not do this out of a sense of obligation to others' affairs, but sparks fell on our own heads at the same time.[29]

Thus, in order to retain stability in control over Korea, it was felt, resolute action in the seizure of Manchuria and Mongolia was called for. And, as noted earlier, it was clear that there were two aspects to stabilizing control over Korea through possession of Manchuria-Mongolia: revival of Japanese prestige and "prevention of the spread of Communism."

As Itagaki pointed out, were Japan to ignore the issue of Manchuria-Mongolia, then the Koreans' "ethnic mentality (*minzoku shinri*) will deteriorate, and they will come to the conclusion that they not rely upon Japan. This will exercise an immeasurable impact on [our] control over Korea and leave us in an anxiety-ridden condition. Ultimately, we can expect no true control over Korea until the Manchuria-Mongolia situation is resolved."[30]

His argument laid emphasis on the revival of Japanese prestige which the military had squandered. Furthermore, "the spread of Communism to Manchuria-Mongolia would send public order in Korea into immediate disarray. A chaotic situation affecting the peace of Korea would exert an acute influence on public order in Japan itself."[31] This argument developed the aim of using the seizure of Manchuria and Mongolia to preventing the penetration and spread of Communism into Korea and, perhaps, Japan as well. The Guandong Army, which had taken upon itself the task of preserving public order in Manchuria-Mongolia, saw the "spread of Communism to Manchuria-Mongolia" as a grave situation, a hotbed nurturing the anti-Japanese movement.

One of the objectives raised for the seizure of this area was, through the "purification of Manchuria and Mongolia," to suppress the "penetration of deleterious, alien thought" into Korea and Japan. For the Guandong Army, Manchuria-Mongolia represented the front line in the battle against Chinese Communism and the headquarters of revolution, the Soviet Union. In particular, the Soviet Union was seen as the ringleader of calamity which would "take advantage of our misfortune not only to spread Communism in Manchuria-Mongolia, but to aim at the destruction of the empire itself."[32] The seizure of Manchuria and Mongolia was thus essential as an ideological breakwater against the Soviet Union and as the area in which to intercept the spread of Communism. Indeed, it was a matter of course that anti-Communism would become one of the principles in the founding of the state of Manzhouguo.

A Strategic Base Against the Soviets

For the Guandong Army as a military unit in Manchuria, however, far more menacing than Communist thought was actual military force. In the eyes of the Guandong Army, who were in effect soldiers facing north, Manchuria-Mongolia was more than anything else a strategic base against the Soviet Union, and thus the seizure of Manchuria and Mongolia held great significance for them.

Although, as a result of the Russian Revolution of 1917 and the war of intervention following it, the Russian army in the Far East had collapsed, the Soviet Union had established its abiding influence in northern Manchuria by means of the Chinese Eastern Railway. Also, in the Sino-Soviet struggle surrounding the Chinese Eastern Railway in 1929, Russia's Special Far Eastern Army, founded just that year, had demonstrated its military capacity to suppress the forces of Zhang Xueliang who had been pursuing a modernization of materiel. "If Japan failed to possess some sort of influence in the Manchuria-Mongolia region," claimed Itagaki, "then the Russian army would probably without hesitation have pursued a military occupation of southern Manchuria, to say nothing of the northern Manchurian area."[33]

Such an observation was not some absurd anxiety. With the First Five-Year Plan beginning in 1928, the Soviet Union had been pouring its energies into western Siberia, its Achilles heel in the past, and the Special Far Eastern Army, whose garrison area covered eastern Siberia, was gradually being strengthened. Plain for all to see was a heightening disparity in military strength between a Japan engulfed in the world panic and reeling in the face of the depression and a Soviet Union advancing steadily with its Five-Year Plan.

In a judgment on the international situation made at a meeting of divisional commanders in April 1931, Tatekawa Yoshitsugu (1880–1945), head of the second division of the General Staff Headquarters, took the perspective that, although the current state of affairs in the Soviet Union did not as yet present an obstacle to the pursuance of Japanese state policy, "when the Five-Year Plan is completed, the increase in their national strength together with the freedom to implement policy through dictatorial government will present a grave threat to the empire together with a loss of time." Hence, he concluded: "When we take an overall view of the international situation, an active advance of the empire into Manchuria and Mongolia will be beneficial to us in our rapid pursuance of goals, while procrastination will only add to the accumulation of disadvantages." The true motive of this "active advance . . . into Manchuria and Mongolia" was the "possession of terrain overseas," and its range was taken to be "Manchuria and eastern Inner Mongolia, and perhaps lands of the Soviet Far East." The seizure of Soviet terrain was thus also contemplated.

This ominous sense of precaution toward the Soviet army, of course, put an even greater strain on the Guandong Army, the military force in the field. It was estimated that there was a "possibility of carrying out a plan of action on the Far Eastern front even while" the Soviet Union "was replenishing its national strength"; in other words, there was a possibility of carrying out an operation to seize Manchuria and Mongolia.[34] It was urged that "resolution of the Manchuria-Mongolia issue be taken at the earliest possible time for the reasons discussed above." As for the situation in the Three Eastern Provinces, it was decided that it was more advantageous to seize the moment and take control of Manchuria and Mongolia before the forces of Zhang Xueliang recouped their strength from attacks they had sustained during the Sino-Soviet battles of 1929. In any event, the objective in taking Manchuria and Mongolia from the perspective of anti-Soviet strategy went beyond eastern Inner Mongolia and southern Manchuria where Japan claimed special interests, but continued to pursue the Soviets into northern Manchuria. Once indicating that Japan's defense lines were drawn with a front line running from Heilongjiang across the Great Xing'an Mountain Range to Khölön Buir, then the next line would extend to the Maritime Province. Hence, as Itagaki conceived it, "we can not only check the Russian move toward the east and simplify our strategy with respect to Russia, but we can as well control the fate of China whose military preparations are incomplete."[35]

Ishiwara argued further that "in order to stabilize our national defense as the protector of East Asia vis-à-vis Russia, it is essential that a deep impression be made that absolutely no policy for the resolution of the Manchuria-Mongolia issue was possible other than our seizure of Manchuria-Mongolia."[36] He stressed that decisive action in taking control over this terrain, including northern Manchuria, need be taken before the Soviet Union succeeded in reviving itself. As far as Ishiwara was concerned, the Great Xing'an Mountain Range and the Khölön Buir region "had especially vital strategic value, and by getting the entire northern Manchuria area within our sphere of influence, Russia's advance to the east will become extremely difficult. It will not be difficult to arrest this movement with the strength of Manchuria-Mongolia alone." This point of holding back the Soviet Union's policy of advancement into the east toward Korea and even Japan by taking control over Manchuria-Mongolia was clearly meant to indicate that the Manchuria-Mongolia area was an exceedingly important strategic base.

Ishiwara, however, was not taking the position in favor of an advance to the north, such as we have seen in the views of Tatekawa and Itagaki, that for control and stability in Manchuria and Mongolia, Japan needed to take possession of not only Manchuria and Mongolia but Soviet terrain as well. Rather, by accomplishing the seizure of Manchuria and Mongolia, Japan would then be able to "avoid the burdens to the north and plan to advance heroically, as national policy dictated, either into China proper or into the South Seas area." In this sense, "Manchuria-Mongolia" was conceived of as the "most important strategic base without a doubt for the development of national prosperity." For Ishiwara the possession of Manchuria-Mongolia, insofar as it concerned anti-Soviet strategy, was aimed at preventing Soviet penetration into the east, and for the time being he believed they were succeeding in this objective. Ishiwara's basic stance on strategy with respect to the Soviet Union ran as follows: "We should work to the utmost to continue amicable relations with Russia."[37] For, even if the commencement of hostilities were unavoidable, that did not mean that Japan should advance troops beyond the borders of Manchuria and Mongolia, but should limit itself to promoting the collapse of the Soviet Union through anti-Soviet propaganda within Soviet territory. Yet, he did emphasize that the Mongolian People's Republic had been founded in 1924, and as regarded the necessity of an operation toward Outer Mongolia, "after Manchuria and Mongolia have come into our possession, we need to continue pouring our energies into appeasement of the people of Outer Mongolia, revival of their industry, and reorganization of their military. We shall then have made our influence fully felt should a war with Russia erupt."

It would seem that behind Ishiwara's taking this strategy vis-à-vis Russia lay the Imperial Defense Plan revised in February 1923. At the time of this revision, vocabulary used until that point such as "assumed enemy" (*kasō tekikoku*) and "hypothetical enemy" (*sōtei tekikoku*) were replaced by "objective" (*mokuhyō*). The Soviet Union was thus removed from the position of number one "hypothetical enemy," and a switch was being planned in the direction of "taking advantage of the principle of good will while all the time preparing an overpowering force." This change of plans was decided upon when "maintenance of mutually peaceful and friendly ties" was laid down in the Russo-Japanese pact signed in January 1925, and no room was allowed for military action against the Soviet Union. To be sure, at the time of the Manchurian Incident, Army Central in opposition to the Guandong Army's planned advance into northern Manchuria foresaw the danger of causing a Soviet military intervention or even a joint Sino-Soviet strategy. The Soviets, though, ultimately did not intervene even with the Japanese occupation of Chichihar and Harbin. Insofar as this situation was concerned, the notion of a Soviet menace was a needless worry. Despite the arbitrary dispatch of troops into northern Manchuria, this action enhanced the influence of the Guandong Army, and it became a cause for perceiving the mode of resolution on the spot as an amortization.

Although the Soviets did not militarily intervene at the time of the Manchurian Incident, soon thereafter, from about November 1931, they began increasing the strength of the Special Far Eastern Army. In April 1932, shortly after the founding of the state of Manzhouguo, the Far Eastern Navy was formed (in 1935 it was reorganized into the Pacific Squadron), and in December of the same year Sino-Soviet diplomatic relations were revived (a mutual non-aggression pact was signed in 1937). By virtue of such developments, the Soviet structure for military preparedness vis-à-vis Manzhouguo was steadily being strengthened. In this sense, that Manzhouguo was established without a major military confrontation was only possible at a time when the Soviet Union was perforce devoting its attention to domestic economic recovery. Indeed, Ishiwara was aware of this situation, and he reached the position that "Russia's current state of affairs offers us the best possible opportunity."[38] In September 1931 the Guandong Army took the step of military action for the seizure of Manchuria-Mongolia. However, the very fact that they succeeded in establishing the state of Manzhouguo without a Soviet military incursion caused the Guandong Army to miscalculate the Soviets' military strength and their will to fight. This contempt for the Soviets was linked to the crushing defeats suffered and heavy casualties sustained by Japan in the Zhanggufeng Incident (1938) as well as the incident at Nomonhan and the Halha River (1939).

The aim of securing Manchuria-Mongolia as a strategic base of operations was achieved by virtue of the fact that the Guandong Army, following the founding of Manzhouguo, took on actual responsibility for the defense of the entire terrain of Manzhouguo in the name of the "joint defense of Japan and Manzhouguo." This, however, spanned an immense border line which went precisely contrary to Ishiwara's intent to "avoid the burdens to the north," placed Japan in direct confrontation with the Soviet Union, became willy-nilly engulfed in the border dispute between the Soviets and the Mongolian People's Republic, and led irrevocably to a situation necessitating further strengthening of the military.

Why then did Ishiwara soon adopt a particularly optimistic view in the face of an increase in expected Russian military strength and rising Russo-Japanese tensions, and stress Manchuria-Mongolia as a strategic base to move in the direction of China proper and further south? In fact, for Ishiwara, far more important than the Soviet Union as a "hypothetical enemy" was the "objective" which needed rapidly to be pursued in preparation for war. The seizure of Manchuria-Mongolia was planned directly with waging war against this adversary as its most important goal. For Ishiwara the "objective" was the United States.

The Japan-U.S. War and the Final World War

Ishiwara's firm belief in the inevitability of war with the United States dated to 1927, and with the attack on Pearl Harbor on December 7, 1941 that war began. Fourteen years before the commencement of hostilities between Japan and the United States, he envisioned its inevitability, and while he wrote that it was inextricably linked to the aim of seizing possession of Manchuria-Mongolia, we may now take a rather dubious view of this line of reasoning. At the time, however, it was by no means odd.

We noted earlier that, together with the revision to the Imperial Defense Plan of 1923, the Soviet Union was removed from its position as Japan's number-one "hypothetical enemy." This change clearly indicated that some country had emerged which posed a threat to Japan greater than that of the Soviet Union (and, earlier, Russia), a country which had been seen as a defense menace to Japan ever since the Russo-Japanese War and which held the potential for waging war against Japan. At this time, it was the United States which supplanted the Soviet Union to become the number-one "objective" of the Japanese army and navy. However, in the earlier Defense Plan of Imperial Japan approved in April 1907, the United States was ranked just after Russia as a hypothetical enemy: "Although we should preserve [the United States] as an ally . . . we cannot guarantee that violent hostilities will not arise at some future date." In the area of naval preparations, it was decided that Japan prepare for war with the United

States: "As a rule we shall be on the offensive against the United States navy in East Asia." Already from 1919 forward the navy had begun making preparations for submarine warfare it assumed was coming with the United States.

By the same token, the United States too had, in the aftermath of the Russo-Japanese War, drawn up its Orange Plans in which Japan was seen as a hypothetical enemy. America foresaw the coming hostilies spanning the Pacific Ocean and was making preparations for them. Furthermore, the movement against Japanese immigrants in the United States, which had been on the rise since the decade of the 1890s, penetrated down to the individual states when in 1920 California passed its second law prohibiting Japanese ownership of land. Japanese exclusion continued in 1924 when the United States Congress passed an immigration law that contained anti-Japanese sections. This action led to anti-American protest rallies at various sites in Japan, calling for war with the United States. That anti-American feelings were brewing can be seen in the publication of such works as Satō Kōjirō's *Nichi-Bei moshi tatakawaba* (If Japan and the United States should go to war) (1920), Ishimaru Tōta's *Nichi-Bei sensō, Nihon wa yaburezu* (War between Japan and the United States, Japan will not be defeated) (1924), and Kawashima Seijirō's *Nichi-Bei issen ron* (On war between Japan and the United States) (1925).

As the level of animosity rose in the 1920s, the focus of the problem for both Japan and the United States was the question of China, in particular Manchuria and Mongolia. From the time that railway king Edward H. Harriman (1848–1909) purchased plans for the South Manchurian Railway in 1905, the United States had become deeply concerned with penetrating Chinese markets, including Manchuria and Mongolia. This concern manifested itself with such actions as the 1909 proposition for a neutrality plan on all rail lines in Manchuria put forward by U. S. Secretary of State Philander Knox (1853–1921) and America's taking the leadership in forging an international loan consortium for China in 1910 and 1920. In particular, based on the Washington system after World War I, the presence of the United States stood in the way of Japan's China and Manchuria-Mongolia strategy, restricting Japanese expansionist policy by compelling recognition of territorial integrity and the open door policy in China, supporting the unification of China by the Nationalist government, and investing in the construction of S.M.R. rail lines.

U.S. historian Charles Beard (1874–1948) had pointed out that the essential point of contention between Japan and the United States in the 1920s was the question of China, and for his part Itagaki Seishirō offered the following perspective.

In recent times the issue of the Pacific has attracted international attention. Yet, above all the focus is on the Manchuria-Mongolia issue. . . . At present, the United

States possesses great economic strength, and China proper is, of course, working steadily to extend commercial rights into the Manchuria-Mongolia region. Should a time come when the Pacific waves begin to thunder, then they will surely come to China's shores. Also, should someone interfere in the [Japanese] empire's Manchuria-Mongolia concern, it seems that it will be none other than the United States.[39]

Thus, the focus of the rivalry between the United States and Japan lay in the China issue and particularly the issue of Manchuria and Mongolia, and in the midst of this entanglement the idea of a possible war between the two countries arose. As Ishiwara noted: "The China issue and the Manchuria-Mongolia issue are not issues [for Japan] vis-à-vis China but vis-à-vis the United States. If we try to resolve them without a readiness to go to war with this enemy, it would be like looking for fish in a tree."[40] Ishiwara held to this view with great tenacity; indeed, it was an impregnable belief. He saw the military occupation of Manchuria-Mongolia as the only way to resolve the issue and that necessarily meant touching off a war with the United States. Thus, resignation to the coming of such a war was essential for the resolution of the Manchuria-Mongolia issue in his eyes. He even went so far as to argue: "If we are unable to truly oppose the United States, then Japan should completely disarm with alacrity."[41]

Would a Japanese seizure of Manchuria and Mongolia after all directly trigger war with the United States? On this point, most of the officers who held similar views on taking Manchuria-Mongolia and who met at the One Evening Society and other such groups were of a rather different opinion. Most of them believed that Manchuria and Mongolia were not terrain essential to the existence of the United States, and thus the Americans would surely not cross the line and commence hostilities with Japan; war with the United States should, at all cost, be avoided in their view. However, in Ishiwara's thinking, the facts that war between Japan and the United States was an unavoidable necessity, given the evolution to date of world history, and that all of Japanese policy including the Manchuria-Mongolia issue needed to be constructed with a view toward preparing for that war formed an iron principle with no room for doubt whatsoever. In other words, in the long run the Manchuria-Mongolia problem would be resolved by means of the supreme issue of a Japanese-American war. If there was no intention of launching such a war, then Manchuria and Mongolia were unnecessary and military preparations could be dispensed with. This option would be much better for Japan, he argued, than cleverly trifling with measures to avoid war.

According to Ishiwara, though, Japan could not at present escape its destiny of fighting a war with the United States. The reason for this was that such a war was not simply a struggle over political hegemony in the Pacific, but a war in which Eastern and Western civilizations, both of which had advanced across several millenia of human history, would confront each other in a final decisive battle, championed respectively by Japan and the

United States. For, "the final battle for both Eastern and Western civilizations presses closer with each passing moment."[42] This conceptualization itself can be seen already in embyonic form in the writings of Okakura Tenshin (1862–1913) as a historical perspective in which East and West are in confrontation or a showdown between Eastern and Western civilizations is imminent. In addition to being advocated by such figures as Naitō Konan (1866–1934), Mitsukawa Kametarō (1888–1936), and Nagano Akira (1888–1975), in particular Ōkawa Shūmei (1886–1957) forcefully offered a similar argument that, because Japan was engaged in a struggle against international Anglo-Saxon domination and aimed at building a new world order, the conflict between Japan and the United States was Japan's unavoidable destiny.

Ishiwara's case was unique, however, in at least one regard. He had come to his position both as a result of his research into the history of war and his belief in Nichiren Buddhism, as well as his distinct policy ideas on the resolution of the Manchuria-Mongolia issue. By tracing the international history of warfare, Ishiwara argued that wars of attrition and wars of annihilation had repeatedly alternated over time, and the future war following World War I, a war of attrition, would be a war of annihilation. Furthermore, with the emergence of weapons of mass destruction which could destroy an entire city at a stroke and the aircraft to transport them, he sensed that the coming war of annihilation would probably be the final world war. This final war would thus be that unprecedented, cataclysmic war of which Nichiren (1222–82) himself had declared centuries ago: "The great, hitherto unseen battle that would arise in the human realm" in order for a unified world to be realized. As Ishiwara saw it, this was none other than the war between Japan and the United States.

Having passed through this final war, Ishiwara believed, world civilization would become united and reach the stage at which "all within the four seas will return to the laws of the Buddha." He had acquired this conception of the war between Japan and the United States as the ultimate world war from his religious teacher, Tanaka Chigaku (1861–1939) of the National Pillar Society. However, conditions were not yet ripe for Japan to be able successfully to pursue this final world war; first, it was essential that China and East Asia as a whole be turned into a supply base for Japan "so as to become the champions of East Asia."[43] To that end, he argued, the most important thing for Japan was to begin by seizing control over Manchuria and Mongolia. Seizure of this terrain would invite war with the United States, but this war would not itself be a war of annihilation, only a war of attrition. He went on to describe his conception as follows: "Through a war of attrition with the United States which would be carried out close at hand, Japan would first unite itself domestically and fortify the foundations of its national fate. With the war of annihilation which would follow, Japan would succeed in the great task of world unification."[44]

Thus, there was to be a war of annihilation between Japan and the United States which would last a long time and be a final war, and there was to be a war of attrition between Japan and the United States of moderate length in preparation for the later war. The plan to seize control over Manchuria-Mongolia constituted one link in the war of attrition, as well as a task to be carried out as a great precedent to the war of annihilation. In this manner, the seizure of Manchuria and Mongolia was placed in a three-stage chain of events over a long stretch of time, and herein lay the distinctiveness of Ishiwara's plan for the resolution of the Manchuria-Mongolia issue.

Inasmuch as this chain of events was extremely tight and not something that could be easily skipped over, if Japan failed to take military action in Manchuria-Mongolia or the United States failed to declare war on Japan immediately after the Japanese seizure of the region—which is, in fact, what happened—then the war of annihilation between Japan and the United States would not take place. To that extent, Ishiwara's logic clearly disintegrated. This outcome was a dilemma born of an inversion of the cause-effect relationship, for he had come up with the thesis of a final world war first and then thrown the notion of seizing Manchuria-Mongolia into it. Nonetheless, inasmuch as Japan's military actions against China were a subterranean stream flowing into the great river of the commencement of war between Japan and the United States, Ishiwara's hypothesis actually did become manifest over a fourteen-year period of time. From the vantage point of 1930, though, Ishiwara himself saw the eruption of the war of annihilation with the United States as "several decades off." In December 1945 after Japan's defeat in the war, he announced: "With the appearance of the atomic bomb, humanity is about to rush into an era of the final war which we have advanced."[45] The time for the explosion of this final world war was not established, but Ishiwara did not see the Pacific War as it.

Thus, Ishiwara's plan for the seizure of Manchuria and Mongolia was not necessarily linked directly to the final world war. However, his idea of taking this terrain placed within the scope of war with the United States brought about a switch in the Manchuria-Mongolia issue which had until then been seen as a locally isolated situation. In other words, by connecting the United States as a "hypothetical enemy" with the national defense plan, Ishiwara had incorporated the seizure of Manchuria-Mongolia into the road that Japan should take, offering both a long-term perspective and world-historical significance. Anticipating a military resolution of the Manchuria-Mongolia issue from its defensive posture of guarding vested interests, the Guandong Army now acquired a clear plan of action which dramatically turned the tables. There is no denying as well that this offered great momentum to the movement to seize control over Manchuria and Mongolia.

While this approach of Ishwara's may have resolved matters internally by presenting a certain objective and perspective, still he could not wipe away the guilty conscience and sense of immorality that accompanied the naked violence of a military occupation. A logic was needed in order to have the seizure of Manchuria-Mongolia understood as an action taken with legitimate force as well as a plan for cohesion and efficiency of group strength at home—even if the other side never understood or accepted such a logic.

A Basis for Legitimizing the Seizure of Manchuria and Mongolia

A unique element in Ishiwara's conception of taking possession of Manchuria and Mongolia can be found in his reversal of the common-sense understanding of the domestic and the foreign and his reconceptualization of the straightforward military occupation of terrain under the sovereignty of another country as a justified action. The seizure of Manchuria-Mongolia by Japan was justified in Ishiwara's thinking by the following reasoning: "Not only was it necessary for Japan, but it would be most welcome for the majority of the Chinese people as well. That is to say, Japan should march forward and take this resolute action as a righteous cause."[46] To be sure, concealing the actual control over Manchuria and Mongolia by Japan, while claiming the autonomy of the people of the Three Eastern Provinces and recognizing China's sovereignty there, was patently unjustified. Yet, whether Japan was justified in gaining control over the region through direct military force belonged to another dimension.

As a diplomat who took international cooperation as his byword, Shidehara Kijūrō was said to have had as the ultimate objective of diplomacy the maxim: "Où règne la justice, les armes sont inutiles."[47] However, for Ishiwara the military man and scholar of the history of war, the contrary phrase, "justice is born where arms rule," was probably something he learned from his own military realism. Perhaps for Ishiwara it was as the Roman historian Livy had noted: "war is justice for those who see it as a necessity."[48]

In any event, the fact that the Guandong Army under Ishiwara and Itagaki advocated that the seizure of Manchuria-Mongolia was justified was not merely a nihilistic recognition that "might makes right," but was even more the product of their distinctive perceptions of China and the Chinese. For example, as Ishiwara put it, "I am extremely doubtful that the Chinese people will ultimately be able to construct a modern nation. Rather, I firmly believe that we can look forward to the natural development of the Han people and their future prosperity under the Japanese maintenance of public order."[49] This belief supported his conceptualization of the seizure of Manchuria-Mongolia as justified.

As Ishiwara recollected in later years, it had been his wish from his student days to see a rebirth of China and Sino-Japanese cooperation, and he earnestly held out hope for the Chinese revolution. When he learned of the success of the 1911 Revolution, he noted: "I had long prayed for a new life for China and was filled with hope for the future of China after the revolution. Together with the [Korea garrison] troops under my instruction at the time, we climbed to the top of a nearby mountain and shouted 'Banzai' indicating out heartfelt happiness at the prospects before the new China."[50] This happiness, however, lasted for only a brief period of time. Sun Zhongshan's compromise with Yuan Shikai, the trampling underfoot of the ideals of the revolution by Yuan, and the subsequent fighting among the warlords with their respective regional spheres of influence led him to opine:

Looking at this situation, I could not help but harbor doubts about the political capacity of the Chinese people. The Han people had a great culture, but I sensed that it might be impossible for them to build a modern nation. These doubts continued until before the Manchurian Incident, and because of the feelings I harbored I advocated an occupation of Manchuria-Mongolia as the only means by which we might resolve that issue at the time. Because the Han people lacked their own political capacity, the Japanese seizure of Manchuria-Mongolia was, I forcefully advocated, not only necessary for the existence of Japan, but it would be beneficial for the Chinese people themselves.

By the same token, Itagaki Seishirō was known as the "China hand in the military" for having been intially stationed in August 1917 in Kunming, Yunnan, and then having served in Hankou (Ishiwara was also stationed there at the time), Beijing (at the time he served as aide to Honjō Shigeru), Fengtian, and elsewhere. He came to the following opinion about the situation in China: "In the twenty or more years since the 1911 Revolution, civil war has followed civil war, and resolution of the problem of domestic unity lies way off in the distant future. . . . This is an age in which militarists are struggling for power as in the past, and none of the fruits of the democratic revolution can be seen as blessings to the people."[51] Accordingly, Itagaki came to the conclusion: "In planning for the well-being of the Chinese people . . . other than [the possibility] of a hero appearing who would thoroughly wipe out the professional militarists and politicians by force of arms, there is no better route to take than seeking the prosperity of the people in reliance on the appropriate foreign nation for the maintenance of public order." The Japanese military seizure of Manchuria-Mongolia, he continued to argue forcefully, would resolve that issue and guarantee the welfare of all the people presently residing there. Furthermore, at core "a peaceful life and enjoyable profession were ideals" for the Chinese people, whereas the consciousness of a nation was effectively non-existent. His view of the Chinese masses was thus that "it made no difference whatsoever to them who held political power or who held military power as long as [that party] took responsibility for maintaining order." It was Itagaki's firm belief drawn from many years observing China that no resistance or disorder would result from the seizure of Manchuria and Mongolia as long as the military action was successful.

Ishiwara had reached the unshakable determination that "overthrowing the militarists and bureaucrats who are the common enemy of the thirty million people in Manchuria is the mission that has been assigned to the Japanese people."[52] Thus, coexistence and coprosperity were promised for the peoples of Japan, Korea, China, Manchuria, and Mongolia on the basis of the Japanese seizure of Manchuria and Mongolia. Aside from Ishiwara, the legitimizing theory that the Japanese military would overthrow the feudal warlords and build a paradise for the peoples of the region was unanimously advocated by Japanese living in Manchuria. In his "research concerning control over the occupied terrain in Manchuria and Mongolia," Sakuma Ryōzō too offered as the direction for rule: "Install good government in the occupied area, protect public order, and plan to develop industrial transport. These will enhance the well-being of the Chinese, Koreans, Mongols, and all the other peoples who presently reside in Manchuria; they will make the region into a one of true comfort and will provide a plan for coexistence and coprosperity."[53]

In addition, the results of a Japanese seizure of Manchuria and Mongolia would then, it was argued, not be limited to the Manchuria-Mongolia region. With the emergence of a model of Japanese rule over this area, China proper would itself necessarily recognize the direction needed to pursue to get at the root cause of its disease. "In this manner," argued Ishiwara, "our control over China would be welcomed by the Chinese in their heart of hearts, and we would be able to lodge the intrinsic value of our military might for a long time in history."[54] The argument was now extended to legitimize Japanese control over China proper, and indeed it would not stop there. Japanese military resolution of the Manchuria-Mongolia issue by taking possession of that terrain would, according to Ishiwara, "advance unity and stability" throughout China and "protect the peace in East Asia."[55] The basis of this "peace in East Asia," Ishiwara went so far as to argue, was the Guandong Army's military seizure of Manchuria and Mongolia.

Why in the first place was it that only Japan's seizure of a part of the Chinese mainland—Manchuria and Mongolia—could be legitimized? As the basis for this legitimization, Ishiwara advanced the thesis based on a theory of race that Manchuria and Mongolia were not inherently Chinese terrain.

Manchuria and Mongolia do not belong to the territory of the Han people, but rather are closely linked to our country. Those who speak of ethnic [or racial, *minzoku*] self-determination must recognize that Manchuria and Mongolia are [territory of] the Manchurian and Mongolian peoples, and the Manchurian and Mongolian peoples are closer to the Yamato people than they are to the Han Chinese.

Although the present inhabitants [of the region] regard the Han race (*Kan jinshu*) as superior, they are much closer economically too to our country than they are to China proper.[56]

Even if Manchuria and Mongolia were not intrinsically terrain belonging to the Han people, there was a jump of logic in directly tying them to Japanese control, and by this logic there was no refutation for the reverse argument, the occupation of Japan by Manchus and Mongols. However, in Ishiwara's conception, of course, Japan would be doing the occupying by virtue of its capacities in economic development and maintaining public order. Should Japanese efforts fail, then it certainly seemed that Manchuria and Mongolia would fall into a state of chaos no different from China proper.

This position was taken by many Japanese, including scholars of East Asian history, such as Inaba Iwakichi (1876–1940, who was an instructor during Ishiwara's years in the army college), Yano Jin'ichi (1872–1970), and Wada Sei (Kiyoshi, 1890–1963). Furthermore, because they were frequently repeated following the Manchurian Incident, Fu Sinian (1896–1950) and others penned a rebuttal from the Chinese side, entitled *Dongbei shigang* (Outline history of the Northeast), in which they argued that China and the Northeast (Manchuria) were "inseparable."[57] Also, the Chinese representative to the Council of the League of Nations, Yan Huiqing (1877–1950), developed this rebuttal further when he claimed: "It is completely specious to argue that Manchuria is the land of the Manchus. Today, the majority of Manchus do not reside in Manchuria. . . . Thus, Manchuria is China, pure and simple."[58] Ishiwara must have known these facts, for in his position developing the notion of a final world war he asserted: "The Japanese national polity synthesizes all civilizations in the world, and it is the imperial task of our great Japan to offer absolute peace to those who aspire to it."[59] Declaring that "it is this great imperial task with which we shall rescue the world's humanity,"[60] he used this concept of Japan's task as a basis for legitimization.

As described above, despite the fact that the basis for legitimization was argued from a variety of positions, only four days after the eruption of the Manchurian Incident the plan for the seizure of Manchuria-Mongolia had to "retreat" to a plan for an independent country. What this meant was that, solely with the logic of legitimization prepared by Ishiwara and the other staff officers of the Guandong Army, they could not convince even Army Central, let alone foreign countries, that taking the path of a military resolution of the Manchuria-Mongolia issue was the next closest position. Furthermore, it was a completely powerless argument vis-à-vis China, which was burning with the flames of an anti-Japanese movement, and the United States, which was leading the Washington system. No matter how intricately fashioned their legitimization was logically, this was not a situation in which a military occupation would be internationally accepted.

The several points laid out here functioned in various way when addressed to the issue of Manzhouguo, despite the difference between seizure of terrain and an independent country. For example, the point that the Chinese people lacked a national or political counsciousness became the argument that, by just once denying this, the people of the Three Eastern Provinces did possess the capacity to form a nation and that Manzhouguo, separated and independent from China proper, was the manifestation of the voluntary will of these people. This became a basis for legitimizing an independent Manzhouguo. However, after the establishment of the state of Manzhouguo, there was a switchover, and now the people of the Three Eastern Provinces were said to lack a national consciousness. This was used as logic to argue that it was inappropriate to give them the franchise and appropriate to deny them the opening of a parliament. Further, it became Japan's mission to overthrow warlord Zhang Zuolin and plan for the maintenance of order in Manchuria-Mongolia. Here for the first time the position that the thirty million residents of the region could realize an ideal order of coexistence and coprosperity was articulated with respect to Manzhouguo in which all national defense was to be put into the hands of the Japanese military. It was promoted in the form of the paradise of Manzhouguo with good government and harmony among the five peoples.

In short, the basis of what Ishiwara and his colleagues used to legitimize the Japanese seizure of Manchuria and Mongolia was the view that only under Japanese guidance could the prosperity of the people living in that region be guaranteed and advanced. This eudamonism was linked most essentially to what the Japanese saw as the ideals of Manzhouguo—namely, "ethnic harmony" (*minzoku kyōwa*), in which the Japanese were the guiding ethnic group, and "paradise of the kingly way" (*ōdō rakudo*), which would result from this. Yet in Manzhouguo, which was foregrounded to take the form of independence based on the voluntary will of the people of the Three Eastern Provinces, there was apprehension about directly advocating the teleology which the seizure of Manchuria-Mongolia clearly and necessarily indicated, while the justification for it came gushing out transformed into the ideals of state-building. This did not, however, mean that the Guandong Army's objectives in seizing control over Manchuria and Mongolia had changed in the least. As long as Manzhouguo remained under the leadership of the Guandong Army, there was no reason to do away with the objectives of taking possession of Manchuria-Mongolia. Such was to become the basis and guidepost for managing Manzhouguo.

Chapter Two
Transforming Manchuria-Mongolia into a Paradise for Its Inhabitants
Building a New State and Searching for State-Building Ideals

The argument for seizing control over Manchuria-Mongolia put forward by Ishiwara Kanji and others ignored the Nine-Power Treaty concerning China which regulated the contemporary international order in the East Asian sphere, the Four-Power Treaty concerning the Pacific region, the Kellogg-Briand Pact, and the Covenant of the League of Nations. It also completely ignored the eventuality of a dispute actually taking place between China and Japan. The demands Ishiwara, the Guandong Army, and members of the "Reform" wing of the Japanese army put forward regarding Manchuria-Mongolia and what they expected to take out of that area were expressed in a straightforward manner, without cleaving too closely to past circumstances.

To that extent, however, should a plan for a military occupation and the imposition of a military regime by the Guandong Army be realized, international conditions—to say nothing of military supplies, the drafting of talented men for the administration, a fiscal basis, and the like—were all well beyond the ken of the Guandong Army alone. Faced with the ardent opposition of Army Central[1] to the seizure plan, the Guandong Army, despite their initial military victory, had to move to a plan for the establishment of an independent state. This was the first step on the road to the creation of the state of Manzhouguo.

Needless to say, the Guandong Army, having assumed a military occupation alone would ensue, was unprepared for an independent state. Thus, while maintaining as a basis a plan to retain control over Manchuria-Mongolia, they were also groping to get the cooperation of Chinese and Japanese residents in the region and to come up with a state structure and national ideals for the new independent state. It was only natural that the disposition of the Chinese living there, the geographical and historical

background of the Chinese Northeast, and international conditions necessarily be reflected in this, and these forces would come to exert a powerful
influence on the nature of the state in Manzhouguo.

In the short path to state formation—less than six months—Japanese for
the first time in their history faced the task of forming a complex, multiethnic state. All manner of dreams of multiethnic coexistence were incorporated, and numerous hopes were discussed. Naturally, many peoples in
Manchuria, foremost among them the Chinese, Japanese, and Koreans, who
were weary of ethnic competition, would welcome a peaceful state free of
fighting. Of course, these dreams, wishes, and peace were suspended under
the sword of Damocles—the Guandong Army. In any event, in the crucible
of dreams and ethnicity the fetal movement of Manzhouguo commenced.

Toward the Building of an Independent State

On September 18, 1931 the Guandong Army blew up the rail line of the
South Manchurian Railway (S.M.R.) at Liutiaohu. With this they were going to implement their long-standing plan for the seizure of Manchuria-
Mongolia, and, claiming that this action was the work of "violent Chinese
soldiers," the Guandong Army commenced military operations at once.
This event was the eruption of the Manchurian Incident, known in China
as the September 18 Incident. Thereafter, the Guandong Army with some
14,000 troops occupied the cities of Fengtian (present-day Shenyang),
Yingkou, Andong, Liaoyang, Changchun, and elsewhere. Despite having
acquired some 4,000 reinforcements from the Korea Army, which unilaterally crossed the border into Manchuria, and the proclamations from Army
Central and the Japanese government not to allow repercussions from the
incident to grow, the troops nonetheless spread the fighting by advancing
beyond their jurisdiction into northern Manchuria. They gained supremacy over the three provinces of the Chinese northeast with the occupation of Harbin in February 1932.

The military actions undertaken by the Guandong Army proceeded
comparatively smoothly. While this transpired, the United States and Great
Britain still had not recovered from the Great Depression; the Soviet
Union was absorbed in achieving the goals of the First Five-Year Plan and
announced a noninterventionist neutrality; the Nationalist Party led by
Jiang Jieshi had adopted a policy of nonresistance, intent first on unifying
China proper before confronting the foreign threat, and had concentrated
all of its energies in the encirclement and extermination of the Chinese
Communists. Roughly 110,000 troops, the main force of the Northeast
Army which boasted a total military strength of some 250,000 men, had
massed with Zhang Xueliang south of the Great Wall, while the remaining
troops were split up at a host of different sites. In a sense, the Guandong
Army caught them off guard by plan. The decisive reason for this was that,

in order that the fighting not spread, Zhang Xueliang, who was recuperating from an illness in Beiping (as Beijing was renamed after Nanjing became the capital in 1927), ordered the Northeast Army not to resist but to withdraw.

In spite of an initial, overwhelming victory under such remarkably fortuitous conditions, however, on September 22—just four days later—as a result of a staff conference which included Chief of Staff Miyake Mitsuharu (1881–1945), Itagaki, Ishiwara, Colonel Doihara Kenji (1883–1948), and Captain Katakura Tadashi, among others, the Guandong Army abandoned plans for retention of control over Manchuria-Mongolia and switched to a strategy for the construction of an independent state there.

With the support of our country, they can establish a Chinese regime with the Xuantong Emperor [Puyi] as leader and in which the four provinces of the northeast and Mongolia are the terrain. Thus will it be turned into a paradise for the peoples of Manchuria and Mongolia.[2]

This was the Plan for the Resolution of the Manchuria-Mongolia Issue that was implemented at the time. On the surface, it called for the establishment of an independent regime, but it was not in fact a plan for an independent state. According to entries in Katakura's *Manshū jihen kimitsu seiryaku nisshi* (Secret Political Diary of the Manchurian Incident), the Guandong Army was not consistent but "prevaricatory" concerning an independent state, and its true aim was visible in the state founded.[3] At the time Ishiwara still persisted in his plan to take possession of the terrain in question, while Doihara prepared a plan for a republic of five peoples in Manchuria-Mongolia. Ultimately, though, it appears that the conclusion was reached that military funds, troops, and the replenishment of weaponry would be forthcoming from the Minister of War and the Chief of the General Staff, who adopted a policy not to allow the incident to spread, in their substantive support for an independent regime. In particular, even Chief of Operations Tatekawa Yoshitsugu, who had been sent as a "peacemaker" by Army Central to observe the Guandong Army's military operations and who had originally advocated a military resolution to the Manchuria-Mongolia issue, in the end tacitly approved of the Guandong Army's actions. His fierce opposition to the plan to seize Manchuria and Mongolia was linked to the judgment that they had no choice but "to be demonstrably conciliatory rather than accept the military's long-desired plan for occupation."[4]

As concerned the plan of September 22, Ishiwara noted:

Army Central paid no heed to [our] position supporting occupation of Manchuria-Mongolia on September 19, and I could see that it was not going to come to pass with even Major General Tatekawa being completely opposed to it. Swallowing copious tears, we retreated to a plan for an independent Manchurian-Mongolian state. Although this was our final stance, we hoped that a future opportunity would arise and in the end there would be a day when our position on the land of Manchuria-Mongolia would come to pass.

The plan to set up an independent state in Manchuria-Mongolia was for Ishiwara tantamount to fighting back ten thousand tears, retreating, and then holding a final military position with the aim of awaiting an opportunity to effectuate the long-cherished plan of seizing the region. The Guandong Army group surrounding Ishiwara Kanji had been training for this goal ever since 1928, and just at the threshold of its implementation they were pitifully forced to retreat for lack of consent from Army Central. Furthermore, even this plan for an independent country, which was to be their fallback, final position, could not be openly declared, but had to be put forward in the form of the establishment of a pro-Japanese regime. To this extent there was an immense gap between Army Central and the Guandong Army in their respective plans for dealing with the Manchuria-Mongolia issue and in their judgments on the domestic and international situation.

In April 1931 General Staff Headquarters issued its Decision on Prevailing Conditions for 1931, and as a policy for resolving the Manchurian-Mongolian issue it posited a three-level structure: establishing a pro-Japanese regime under Nationalist government sovereignty (stage one), founding an independent state (stage two), and occupying Manchuria-Mongolia (stage three). There was a strong feeling of opposition among the military leaders, including the Army minister and the chief of the General Staff, even to the resolution of the first stage. Concerned about the intentions of Army Central, Tatekawa fervently advocated before Ishiwara: "The best plan is to establish a regime with the Xuantong Emperor as its leader and with Japanese support."[5] With the aim first of expanding the area of the occupation and building an independent state and then effectively offering results comparable to the occupation of Manchuria-Mongolia, Ishiwara and his colleagues on October 2 decided on a Policy for the Resolution of the Manchuria-Mongolia Issue, which further concretized the plan of September 22. There, Manchuria-Mongolia would become an independent state under Japanese guarantorship with Japan authorized to care for national defense and entrusted with supervision of railways and communications. Were the government not to accept such a plan, it was resolved that "military men of will in Manchuria would temporarily relinquish their Japanese nationality and rush headlong toward the achievement of the objectives."[6] It was further resolved to "replace the old slogan of 'protecting vested interests' with 'construction of the new Manchuria-Mongolia,'" and by propagandizing this widely at home and abroad they would foment the spirit needed to build a new state.

The creation of an independent Manchurian-Mongolian state covering the four provinces of the Northeast—Liaoning, Jilin, Heilongjiang, and

Rehe—and Inner Mongolia was pushed forward on the surface as an independent regime whose influence would thus be brought to bear on China. In order to plan for the maintenance of public order in various localities, already in the Plan for the Resolution of the Manchuria-Mongolia Issue of September 22, the following appointments had been made: Xi Xia (1884–1945) in Jilin, Zhang Haipeng (1867–1949) in Taonan, Tang Yulin (1871–1937) in Rehe, Yu Zhishan (b. 1882) in Dongbian (at the Yalu River in Fengtian Province, present-day Liaoning), and Zhang Jinghui (1872–c. 1962) in Harbin. These men, who were seen as "having been members of the Xuantong Emperor's clique and possessing contacts with the local military," were to create independent regimes in their locales; then, according to the plan of the Guandong Army, these regimes would "spontaneously" link up, secede from China proper, and build an independent state.

As early as September 24, a Fengtian Local Self-Governing Committee (renamed the Liaoning Regional Maintenance Committee on September 26) was organized with Yuan Jinkai (1870–1945) as chairman and Kan Chaoxi and Yu Zhonghan (1871–1932) as vice-chairmen. On September 26, Xi Xia set up a Jilin Provincial Governor's Office and dispatched a circular telegram announcing its independence from the Nationalist government in Nanjing. In Harbin on September 27, Zhang Jinghui continued this trend by establishing a Northeast Special Peace Preservation Committee. In addition, bribery and conciliatory efforts were made by furnishing war expenditures, arms, ammunition, and clothing to local militarists whose course of action had still not been determined—including such figures as Zhang Haipeng, Yu Zhishan, Tang Yulin, and Ma Zhanshan (1885/87–1950). Not only could the forces of men such as Xi Xia and Zhang Jinghui, with the support of the Guandong Army, boast overwhelming military superiority, but they engulfed many of the opposition forces affiliated with Zhang Xueliang in their provinces. This bred an exceedingly unstable situation for resistance.

Even with pacifying efforts, known as "internal maneuvers," the Guandong Army could not extricate itself from the fact that "the very nature of the incident was a struggle between China and Japan which made it extremely difficult to use Chinese."[7] To that extent the Guandong Army had no choice but to carry out measures aimed at forcible submission through the dispatching of troops and threats. However, capital provided to Yu Zhishan of 100,000 *yuan* and to Zhang Haipeng of 200,000 *yuan* may have succeeded, for one can see in a survey article—bearing the headline "Will an Independent State Be Built to Support the Xuantong Emperor? Alliance Emerges among Provinces of Northeast"—published in the *Manshū nippō* of October 16: "The rulers of the four provinces of the northeast ultimately will support the Xuantong Emperor who will become president. The establishment of the Yuan Jinkai Cabinet should settle things down with the building of a large, independent state and a federated republic."[8]

At the same time, Foreign Minister Shidehara Kijūrō in the cabinet of Wakatsuki Reijirō (1866–1949) announced internationally a policy not to allow the Manchurian Incident to expand and an early withdrawal of Guandong Army troops contrary to the plan to build a state impetuously underway by the Guandong Army at the scene. To that end, he strongly opposed the building of an independent state which was closely linked to the Guandong Army and advocated diplomatic negotiations with the Nationalist government in Nanjing toward resolving the whole incident. In response, Army Central, which was sympathetic to the cabinet's policy of not allowing the incident to spread, decided on September 30 on a plan to create a regime independent of China proper, and to begin a course of action contrary to Shidehara's diplomacy inasmuch as the Japanese "empire will lead and manipulate this regime from within and make it ever more reliant on the empire." On October 8 the Guandong Army, in an effort to check the actions of the League of Nations, bombed Jinzhou where the Zhang Xueliang regime had moved. In so doing they made Shidehara's objectives of an early troop withdrawal and negotiations with the Nanjing government untenable. Furthermore, an attempted coup d'état known as the October Incident in which the Guandong Army was involved was uncovered, and the situation continued to deteriorate as information about the independent actions of the Guandong Army spread. Army Central was dragged along with the Guandong Army. On October 23, it was reported that Imamura Hitoshi (1886–1968), operations section chief of the Army General Staff, was "losing no time in promoting" before the Guandong Army staff the creation of "a political center which would move in accord with Japanese wishes in Manchuria."

On October 24, the Council of the League of Nations adopted by a 13–1 vote a recommendation that Japan withdraw its troops from Manchuria by November 16. As if challenging this call, the very same day the Guandong Army decided on a "basic plan for the resolution of the Manchuria-Mongolia issue" and approved a proposal to "offer even stronger support internally to promote the movement to establish a new state which had hitherto superficially relied on Chinese." In concrete terms, this meant following a procedure of "working swiftly relying on internal support" and "proclaiming the foundation of a new state which will carry out an integration of the federated provinces" of Jilin, Heilongjiang, and Liaoning "and approve our demands in this regard."[9]

During this period, Tachibana Shiraki (1881–1945) observed in Japan that "it seems as though the government was being dragged along by the military during the Manchurian Incident. This was for the simple reason that genuine public opinion supported the military more than the government. It was not so much that the military pulled the government along, but that public opinion was spurring the government on."[10] Such was the extent to which public support of the Guandong Army's actions had been voiced. One reason for this phenomenon was that, due to the world panic beginning in the fall of 1929, "capitalism had produced an impasse for the Japanese national economy," and perhaps with this economic background the nation sought a resolution in Manchuria-Mongolia.[11] Another reason was that the military, upon reflection that it had been unable to resolve the Manchuria-Mongolia issue all at once in the explosion killing Zhang Zuolin, "thereafter looked to the need for support of public opinion, studied how best to arouse it, and hoped to achieve well planned objectives in this manner," thus manipulating public opinion with great vigor.[12] Through the rise of public opinion, in November the Shakai Minshū Party, a labor party associated with the right wing, decided to support the Manchurian Incident, and on December 11, with the collapse of the Wakatsuki Cabinet, Shidehara's diplomacy met its end. This change in events meant that the Guandong Army had taken over leadership as far as dealing with Manchuria and Mongolia was concerned.

On December 23, Army Central decided that, on the basis of the "an agreement reached between the Army Ministry and the Army's General Staff Headquarters," Manchuria-Mongolia "would for the time being become a region under the control of a government separate and independent from the government of China proper, and we shall eventually encourage it to become a protectorate of the empire." This switch marked a change from an "independent regime," a stage to which they had only just come, to the recognition of an independent state in the form of a Japanese protectorate. To that end, a plan for the building of an independent state was finally drafted, and it was concluded that "subsequent construction would be adjusted to fit a pace in which center and localities were in unison."[13] Thereafter, in 1932 when the Japanese government called for Itagaki to return to Tokyo, it announced a General Plan for Dealing with the China Issue on January 6 as a draft plan for the army, navy, and foreign ministries. The work to create an independent state based on a regime of federated provinces advanced by the Guandong Army was confirmed, and in addition a policy was adopted to "postpone as long as possible direct negotiations" with the Nationalist government in Nanjing. The plan recognized that, by creating an independent state as a fait accompli, this would "become the goal as all views on Manchuria-Mongolia would naturally be abandoned."

The planning for the seizure of Manchuria and Mongolia unilaterally begun by the Guandong Army had transmogrified into a plan for an independent state and finally was recognized as state policy. However, if we turn our attention to the international scene, from the Manchurian Incident forward the boycott movement against Japanese goods and the anti-Japanese struggle at various sites in China had become ever more violent. Secretary of State Henry Lewis Stimson repeatedly criticized the Japanese actions as an invasion. The aim of making "all views on Manchuria-Mongolia naturally be abandoned," as Japan intended internationally, was facing serious difficulties. Thus, Itagaki called upon Major Tanaka Ryūkichi (1893–1972), military attaché to the Japanese legation in Shanghai, to foment the Shanghai Incident of January 1932 and hence divert the concerns of China and the Powers away from Manchuria. In this incident some 40,000 were killed or injured and some 160,000 homes were fully or partially destroyed, the "sacrifice" paid to divert attention from the state-creating maneuver. The Guandong Army staff convened a state-planning conference which met ten times beginning on February 5, and piled details upon details for the schedule of state formation and state institutions. Then, on February 16 a meeting was held in Fengtian which brought together leaders from Manchuria and Mongolia—including Zhang Jinghui, Zang Shiyi, Xi Xia, Ma Zhanshan, Tang Yulin, Chimedsempil, and Lingsheng. They organized themselves into the Northeast Administrative Committee, and on the eighteenth this same committee issued a manifesto that stated: "Henceforth we renounce all connections to the Nationalist government, and the northeastern provinces are completely independent. . . . We seek prosperity for our many races living in East Asia." On March 1 at the residence of Zhang Jinghui, head of the Northeast Administrative Committee, the step was taken to announce the formation of Manzhouguo.

In this manner, local self-governing committees and local regimes were formed in many regions of the northeast separate from the central government. Proclaiming autonomy and independence, they merged to create a new government. During this time, they put off direct negotiations with the central authority as much as possible, and then having created a *fait accompli* they saw to it that all views on the issue would be effectively meaningless. In this way Manzhouguo was founded.

This method of separation and reintegration succeeded by all accounts in the formation of Manzhouguo. It set a pattern that became standard from 1935 in the control over occupied terrain in north and central China with the establishment of the following regimes: the Jitong Anti-Communist Autonomous Committee (Hebei province) in November 1935, the Inner Mongolian Military Government (Chahar province) in May 1936, the Mongolian Federated Autonomous Government in October 1937 (from September 1939, renamed the Mongolian Unified Autonomous Government), the Provisional Government of the Republic of China in December 1937 (Beijing), and the Reform Government of the Republic of China in March 1938 (Nanjing). Ultimately, the government of the Republic of China was formed in Nanjing in March 1940 as a central regime bringing unity to all of these. In this sense the work that went into founding the state of Manzhouguo set the pattern of rule exercised by Japan over occupied areas in China, what the Chinese called "areas lost to enemy hands."

This does not, however, mean that the founding of Manzhouguo met no resistance and that the Guandong Army's plans went into effect exactly as conceived. Contrary to such a superficially smooth transition, rather, there were all manner of quarrels that erupted between the Guandong Army and the local political authorities arising out of mutual distrust and differing political expectations. The absurdity that this actually spurred them on to build an independent state remained dormant.

The Provincial Government Independence Operation and Ishiwara's Switch

The success of a state-building operation of having local regimes secede and become independent of the central government and then reintegrate somehow needless to say necessitated the existence of a pool of human talent and political authority to respond to the demands on the spot. In the process of founding the state of Manzhouguo, names of such people had been mentioned in the Plan for the Resolution of the Manchuria-Mongolia Issue, dated September 22. Autonomous groups to preserve public order were formed in rapid succession by such figures as Yuan Jinkai in Liaoning Province, Xi Xia in Jilin Province, and Zhang Jinghui in the zone of Harbin and the Chinese Eastern Railway. These units functioned as cohesive nuclei for the state-formation operation by means of a united provincial autonomy.

Of course, the details by which these local regimes would come into existence and the ideas of the men connected to them were by no means identical. Although various orientations and interest relations were intertwined, we can still identify certain common threads. For example, because local officials appointed by Zhang Xueliang had taken refuge elsewhere or simply absconded, the functions of local administration and public order were paralyzed. Thus, it was claimed, an autonomous group was needed to fulfill these tasks. It had frequently been the Chinese manner of coping with exposure to a war situation to form autonomous groups in every locality while there was a political vacuum because of the fighting and to devise self-defense policies to revive the populace's livelihood. At the time of the Manchurian Incident as well, public-order maintenance committees sprang up in various localities. Tachibana Shiraki dubbed this *jiryō kōi* (self-curing actions). However, these groups went well beyond forming autonomous units, and in concert with the Guandong Army they issued proclamations of independence from the Zhang Xueliang regime. We cannot overlook the fact, though, that together with coercion from the Guandong Army, considerations of the inherent geographical conditions of China's northeast, the foreign and historical background, and the political forces at the time were all at work.

Why would Zhang Jinghui and the others align themselves with the Guandong Army? Although entirely from a Japanese perspective, Ōhashi

Chūichi (b. 1893), consul-general in Harbin, offered the following three points in a telegram to Foreign Minister Shidehara, dated October 4, 1931: (1) Zhang Jinghui and his fellows have a thorough knowledge of Japan's real power since the Russo-Japanese War of 1904–5, and historically they have seen that there have been fewer ill effects from planning for economic coexistence and coprosperity with Japan than aligning with Great Britian or the United States, as had Zhang Xueliang; (2) it was easy to join the Guandong Army's plan for the severance of the northeast, because these fellows "harbor a kind of ethnic provincialism" in which the Chinese northeast belongs to northeasterners, "lean toward a principle of securing peace within the borders and nourishing the local populace, and they are strongly opposed to [Zhang] Xueliang's inclination to consider Manchuria as one pure part of China proper"; and (3) "they feel extreme fear and animosity both for the Soviet Union's advancement eastward and China's Bolshevization, and to forge a resistance they must look for aid from Japan."[14] Thus, forces negotiating with the Japanese were hostile to the policies of the Zhang Xueliang regime; many had been pro-Japanese since the days of Zhang Zuolin and were thus naturally averse to Zhang Xueliang's anti-Japanese policy. Ōhashi's point of view was hence not completely off the mark.

Such conditions, however, by no means promised fealty to the Guandong Army. The intention of working together and the forms it took were many and varied, and there was no reason to expect that, Guandong Army propoganda notwithstanding, the four provinces of the northeast were uniformly intent on seeking independence from China proper. Take the case of Xi Xia of Jilin: he was a Manchu bannerman who looked forward to the revival of the Qing dynasty and was actively using the Guandong Army with that aim in mind. In Jilin Province, there was a strong orientation toward regional independence, the so-called "Jilin Monroe Doctrine," which made it easy to respond to the Guandong Army's operation pushing separation and independence both from the Zhang regime and the Nationalist government. Even in the case of the provisional government of Jilin, however, one diplomatic report noted: "Governor Xi is building a provisional government which must defer to our military. . . . He lacks the readiness to carry this through to the end." Not only that, but "what is being lost, of course, is that the people's hearts in general are rapidly becoming estranged from the new government."[15] In Heilongjiang, Zhang Jinghui found himself in a numerically inferior position to militarists Ma Zhanshan, Zhang Zuoxiang (1881–1949), and Wan Fulin (1880–1951) who opposed the leading supporters of Manchuria-Mongolia independence and this afforded him an extremely weak political base.

In Liaoning Province, to which the Guandong Army attached the utmost importance as the core of a provincial federation, a local self-governing committee was organized shortly after the eruption of the Manchurian Incident with Yuan Jinkai as its chair. The fact that this province was a stronghold for the Zhang Xueliang regime saw to it that the situation did not proceed precisely in line with the Guandong's Army's plans. Chairman Yuan Jinkai, who was the leader of the Wenzhi militarist clique of Fengtian, worked also as a member of the Northeast Political Committee and of the Inspectorate of the Nationalist government. After the Manchurian Incident, though, civil officials were deceived by a Guandong Army statement not to arrest them and were taken into custody, and Zhang took over the position of chairman. With respect to the Guandong Army's demand for a call for independence, one consul took a position of passive cooperation, as he related: "If by any chance we find ourselves under pressure, we can simply run away. If the local self-governing committee is but a transitional expedient to stabilize the present anarchic situation temporarily, then in this sense we are concerned."[16] As a member of the Wenzhi faction, Yuan Jinkai put his hope in the principle of securing peace within the local area and protecting the people: "In order to avoid being drawn into the civil strife in China, the northeast has seceded from the Nationalist government and will implement a civil administration."[17] However, the consul was thoroughly opposed to any conception of an independent regime: "No government in Jinzhou can in fact be independent. In any event, scoundrels cannot conceive of independence the way a class of intellectuals would."[18] Among the members of the local self-governing committee, from Yuan Jinkai on down, the spirit of opposition to the will of the Guandong Army and to avoid any notion of an independent regime remained strong, not only because it was fully expected that Zhang Xueliang's armed forces with their superiority in military strength would recover their lost terrain and return to Fengtian, but also because with the rising tide of the anti-Japanese movement radio broadcasts and leaflets from within China proper calling for the deaths of the members of this self-governing committee as traitors served as psychological restraints. Furthermore, not only Yuan Jinkai but many others as well believed that only Zhang Xueliang, Jilin Governor Zhang Zuoxiang, or Zang Shiyi, who was then under Guandong Army house arrest, could get the situation in the northeast under control. On this point, too, the Guandong Army, which had been trying to dispel the authority of Zhang Xueliang, Zhang Zuoxiang, and others was far out of touch.

The Proclamation of the Guandong Army Headquarters of October 4 disavowed recognition of Zhang Xueliang: "At present a movement for the establishment of a regime has emerged in many places. All together the people are singing the praises of the dignity of the Imperial Army, and there is not the least inclination to install their old party leaders. This is clearly the result of indignation against the oppression of many years of warlord self-interest." It stressed that they would root out the old regime and with an administrative power at various sites "quickly implement a paradise of coexistence and coprosperity for the thirty million inhabitants of Manchuria-Mongolia." This was not only for the local self-governing committee of Liaoning Province, but to bury the idea still strong within the Japanese government of their eagerly awaiting a revival of Zhang Xueliang and firmly promoting construction of an independent state. In order to clarify its intentions, the Guandong Army bombed Jinzhou on October 8, acting to destroy all possibility of Zhang Xueliang's regime returning to power. By so doing, the legitimacy of self-defensive action which Japan had been advocating lost all basis, and the United States, Great Britain, France, and other powers turned to an unbending anti-Japanese stance.

The Guandong Army had thus reversed itself and crossed over an impossible line. Vicariously having the local self-governing committee of Liaoning Province effect a provincial government, it had no choice but to declare severance of relations with the Zhang Xueliang regime and the Nationalist government. There was, however, a strong disposition that the call to break ties with the Nationalist government reject "the argument frequently made that they could not avoid criticism from the populace as traitors."[19] Thus, "as a result of pressure brought to bear on Yuan Jinkai by the Guandong Army" which had concocted this whole undertaking, "we have decided to add wording to the point of abrogating ties with the former regime of Zhang Xueliang and with the Nationalist government in a proclamation of the proxy implementation of a regime as demanded by the military."[20] On November 7, they issued a formal declaration. Katakura Tadashi noted in his diary at the time: "When Yuan Jinkai was summoned to military headquarters, he was extremely nervous sensing a danger to his life. He could not easily write a manifesto of independence for the local self-governing committee, and he made the necessary arrangements while being held against his will by the military."[21] Even in the *Manshū jihen shi, Manshū jihen ni okeru gun no tōsui (an)* (History of the Manchurian Incident, the Military General Command in the Manchurian Incident, Draft), edited by the General Staff Office, we read: "One could not help but shed a tear upon seeing his [Yuan's] true feelings, but gradually he came around."[22] These give us an insight to the situation at the time.

In this manner Liaoning Province became independent, changing its name to Fengtian Province on November 20. "It took the form of a vicarious provincial regime," as Yuan Jinkai "remained as indecisive as before, not formally wishing to become governor."[23] Around this time, the American journalist Edgar Snow interviewed Yuan, who had the following to say about his own mental state:

I have no desire to be governor of Manchuria, or even of this province. The position means nothing but embarrassment to me. I hope with all my heart that Manchuria may never be separated from China.

As for the proclamation to the contrary, which bears my name, that is bogus. It was prepared by the Japanese military. My signature to it was secured under military coercion.[24]

Because this interview was telegraphed to the United States and published there, "there are indications that Yuan Jinkai has recently vented his dissatisfaction in this manner to foreigners; he needs to be more closely watched by the military" and treated in such a way as to "prevent vile propaganda."[25] Yuan Jinkai was, however, establishing furtive contact with Zhang Xueliang and assuming a stance in opposition to the formal establishment of a provincial government in anticipation of the time when Zhang would retake control over Fengtian. Thus, it became necessary "by all means to appoint Zang and reject Yuan for the founding of the new government."[26] And, the Fengtian provincial government was thus organized with Zang Shiyi as governor. A 1911 graduate of the Japanese army cadet school, Zang had served as commander of the Manchurian arsenal and chairman of the Liaodong provincial government. Three months after the Manchurian Incident, he was imprisoned. Upon his release, he later stated, Itagaki compelled him to take an active part in the organization of a Manchurian regime, to entrust national defense to the Japanese military stationed in the Three Eastern Provinces, and to assume the military costs. In the face of personal danger, he had no choice but to affix his name to prepared documents.[27] Soon thereafter the Japanese forces stationed in the region became formally recognized under the "Japan-Manzhouguo Protocol." It has been claimed that Zang's mother eluded the vigilant eyes of the authorities and sent her imprisoned son opium glued to the bottom of his rice bowl, a suggestion that he give his life for the nation; when Zang surrendered and was released, she allegedly committed suicide.[28]

Following this tortuous path, finally on December 16 the Guandong Army dissolved the local self-governing committee, and with Zang Shiyi serving as provincial governor the ground was prepared for the independence of a Fengtian provincial government. On the same day, a Proclamation of the Guandong Army Command was issued. It loudly proclaimed: "The two provinces of Fengtian and Jilin are both fully prepared to declare their independence and cut off ties with the old regime. Heilongjiang Province is transforming its battle array, while Rehe Province and Inner Mongolia fortunately seem to be responding to this change. The thirty million residents of Manchuria-Mongolia are all equally admiring of good government and continue to hope for someone who will bring this to an end. . . . We can see that the trend toward the establishment" of independent states "is pulsating animatedly everywhere."[29] It would in fact, though, take another two months for the Guandong Army to gain complete control over Heilongjiang and nearly a year before Rehe fell to them.

While these state-building maneuvers moved forward, the plan for the occupation of Manchuria-Mongolia had not vanished from Ishiwara's mind, despite his having been forced unhappily to retreat to the stance of an independent state. In the Plan for Control over Manchuria and Mongolia, drafted on October 1, he proposed the following: "The unity and stability of the four provinces of the northeast shall be secured with Japanese might, and a simple form of government appropriate to the Chinese people will be secured with their [Japanese] protection." At the provincial and city levels, the Japanese allowed self-government based on a "system fitting the distinctive needs of the Han people," but at the center they implemented effective military control with the establishment of a Manchuria-Mongolia governor-generalship.[30] As late as December 2, when the structure of an independent state with former Emperor Puyi as leader had essentially taken shape, it was boldly asserted: "Ultimately, in the construction of the new Manchuria-Mongolia, it will be impossible to entrust the highest control to the Chinese, for clearly what will transpire is that they will soon fall into the same abuses from which they have always suffered. Thus, we shall go one step further and entrust the central government completely to Japan."[31] Indeed, there was a reluctance even to allow the establishment of an independent state.

Despite Ishiwara's strong attachment to the idea of seizing control over Manchuria and Mongolia, though, Fengtian Province became independent, and by late December the building of an independent state based on the autonomy of federated provinces was placed on the concrete agenda by Xi Xia and Zhang Jinghui via Zang Shiyi. At that point, Ishiwara, who was never able to dispense with his plans for taking control over Manchuria-Mongolia, made a turnabout and embraced a plan for an independent Manchurian state.

Ishiwara himself later explained his reasons for this transformation: "I saw with my own eyes the active cooperation with the Japanese military of influential Manchurians in the midst of the Manchurian Incident, their fervent anti-warlord sentiment, and from it their demonstrations of devoted effort as well as their political capabilities." Swept away were all his doubts about the political capacities of the Chinese. In his judgment, "it would have been one thing if this people lacked political ability, but because we could see that they had it and we could place our trust in this, there was no need to occupy and control."[32] As we saw earlier, Ishiwara had pointed to the absence of a Chinese capacity to form a state and their general lack of political ability as bases legitimizing a Japanese takeover of Manchuria-Mongolia. He had now come around to a new perception of these points, making his switch to support for an independent state unsurprising. It does not in the end, however, appear that this new stance represented Ishiwara's real feelings, in the light of the responses of the important Chinese players we have seen to this point. In his Instructions to Staff Officer Itagaki on His Trip to Tokyo of January 1932, an important document for Ishiwara after his conversion to the independent-state line, he expressed his misgivings that, once independent, the regime might return to the Chinese central government as a reason for the necessitating independence:

In the aforementioned eventuality [namely, reversion to the central government], the members of the new regimes in the various provinces at present would be seen as traitors which would lead to instability. They would be positively incapable of cooperating with Japan and discharging their duties as members of these governments. Thus, we need to form an independent state in name and reality so as to separate it clearly from China proper.[33]

The view expressed here in fact flatly contradicts the reasons Ishiwara gave for his change to support for an independent state. That he had come to actively back a plan for an independent state was not the result of his acknowledgement of Chinese political capability on the scene, but was a critical judgment he made while contemplating the possibility of a reversion of allegiances to the Chinese central government, deriving from his suspicions that the Chinese would comprise the various unstable provincial governments. In the movement toward independent statehood, to eliminate the suspicions and mistrust between the members of the new regimes in the various provinces and the staff officers of the Guandong Army, Ishiwara realized that the form of an independent state was necessary. In effect, blocked on his path of retreat, he crossed over to join in the plan for an independent state, because he found himself, like it or not, in a community of those bound by a common fate. The plan for an independent state had, of course, been decided upon all the way back to Army Central, and thus Ishiwara could not by himself continue to be a stickler for a policy of occupying Manchuria-Mongolia. Furthermore, calls for the state-building principles of ethnic harmony and the paradise of the kingly way which emerged at this time became important reasons as well prompting this change of views. "In form," he noted of his change of mind, "abandoning the occupation thesis was like switching in reverse to a negative direction, but in actual fact it proved on the contrary to be a great advance, and marked an active leap in a positive direction."[34] Ishiwara was the sort of man who, after having clung tightly to his thesis on the seizure of Manchuria-Mongolia, promptly switched to the pro-independence stance and dashed off in that direction, prepared to take it as far as it would go.

In a roundtable discussion between Chinese and Japanese organized by the *Asahi* newspaper on January 11, 1932, Ishiwara participated because he "wanted to convey to kindred spirits the change of views that he had undergone, for I would not earlier have wished to take part in such a meeting,"[35] and for the first time spoke in a public capacity on behalf of independence for the Manchurian state. Concerning the establishment of the new state, he made a heretofore unthinkable statement: "There is no need to distinguish between Japanese and Chinese. When the Guandong

Leased Territory is fully restored, the Commander-in-Chief of the Guan-dong Army will be unemployed. . . . The Japanese agency will be reduced to the smallest size," and those among the Japanese resident in Manchuria who "wish to be active on behalf of the new state will change their citizen-ship."[36] In addition, he claimed, when the newspaper published his state-ment, it changed his actual wording to a more roundabout phrasing. The gap between the image of Manzhouguo that Ishiwara hypothesized and that of other Guandong Army staff officers soon began to emerge. From a mili-tary perspective, Ishiwara saw Manchuria-Mongolia in a level-headed man-ner, and he dramatically changed his views as he was drawn to the various and sundry ideals of state formation that were being developed at the scene.

This change on his part from a conception of seizing Manchuria-Mongolia to the building of an independent state, not unexpectedly, de-scribed a development from a situation in which the Guandong Army was the sole driving force to one in which the views of various different forces on the scene, at the center of which remained the Guandong Army, com-bined to shoulder the work of state-building. In his confrontations with various currents, Ishiwara swayed widely between the two poles of military realism, with the creation of a state for strategic and supply-base reasons to assure victory in the final world war, and the idealism inherent in the cre-ation of ethnic harmony and the paradise of the kingly way.

Yu Chonghan: Peace Within Borders, Security for the Populace, No Military

One of the reasons for Ishiwara's change of heart was the existence of an ineradicable distrust for the leaders of the new provincial regimes in China. Ishiwara was of course not suspicious of all Chinese, for had this been the case, he would surely have held firmly to his support for an occu-pation of Manchuria and Mongolia. In a speech commemorating the eighth anniversary of the establishment of the state of Manzhouguo, Ishi-wara recounted the deep impression made on him by the words of one Chinese at the time of the aforementioned roundtable discussion between Chinese and Japanese:

Early on the moderator asked: "Is an independent state in Manchuria a good thing? Is an independent regime desirable? Do you really know?" Eight years ago the idea of an independent Manchuria was seen as absurd among the Japanese troops there. The view was popular at the time that an area such as Inner Mongolia, being under Chinese sovereignty, would appropriately become an independent regime. At that time the moderator of the *Asahi* roundtable asked: "Mr. Yu Chonghan, is it good for Manchuria to be an independent state. Is an independent regime a good idea?" Yu Chonghan replied clearly: "It must be an independent state." This was a Chinese man speaking! I believe that his courageousness surpassed that of the pres-ent Wang Jingwei. At the roundtable convened by the newspaper, this important figure in Manchuria had affirmed that it had to be an independent state. . . . There were not many high officials in Manchuria who, while occupying a pivotal position, would defer to no one and themselves aver that Manchuria had to be an independent state. While I have no close, personal connection to independence day in Manzhouguo, I am delighted to be able to state before everyone here today the great achievements of Mr. Yu Chonghan, the man who has done more than anyone else for the establishment of the state.[37]

Ishiwara thus praised Yu Chonghan as "the man who has done more than anyone else for the establishment of the state." Of course, as Ishiwara noted, there were not many high officials in Manchuria who had called for an independent state, and among the facts that Ishiwara divulged this was his way of pointing to Yu Chonghan as a prominent figure. However, putting aside the issue of numbers, mention of Yu Chonghan among the Chinese as a man who joined the great tide of Manchurian state-building in its ideals and in the activities that saw them to fruition was certainly not unreasonable for Ishiwara or anyone else. Evaluating Yu in this way does not immediately mean that Yu was a lackey of the Guandong Army who flattered them and served as their running dog. Yu Chonghan was probably just expressing his own views at this time on the issue of peace within local borders and security for the people, a position he had himself long held. For the Guandong Army, however, whose firm ideals were still unsteady, having the basis of legitimation to create an independent state in northeast China separated from China proper articulated by Yu Chonghan, a Chinese, was obviously something of great importance.

While his name was listed as a member of the Fengtian Local Self-Governing Committee founded on September 24, Yu Chonghan was recuperating from illness in the city of Liaoyang. In response to a request from Morita Fukumatsu (1875–1932), chairman of the Japan Residents' Council of Fengtian, he appeared in Fengtian on November 3. Due to indecision on the part of Committee Chairman Yuan Jinkai, the severing of ties with both the Zhang Xueliang regime and the Guomindang government and the formal inauguration of a provincial government were not making progress. Hence, the Guandong Army, engrossed in the stalled operation of state-building based on the autonomy of a federation of the four northeast provinces, was trying to break through the deadlock and, with Morita as an intermediary, forced Yu Chonghan to come out of retirement.

The *History of the Manchurian Incident, the Military General Command in the Manchurian Incident, Draft*, put together by the General Staff Office of the Guandong Army, has the following to say about the significance of Yu Chonghan's appearance:

Since he stepped forward to serve, Yu Chonghan has met with the members of the regional self-governing committee at his temporary residence in the city of Fengtian. As the guiding plan for the four provinces of the northeast, he advocates a policy of absolute peace within borders and security for the populace. On October 6, he decided to proclaim a severance of ties with the Zhang Xueliang regime and the central government in Nanjing, which Yuan Jinkai in his vacillation and indecision had been unable to decide upon.[38]

Although one of the tasks entrusted to Yu Chonghan by the Guandong Army had seen fruition, as far as they were concerned, more important than Yu's emergence from retirement were the political views he brought to the construction of a new Manchuria and Mongolia. On this point, the above-cited text noted: "[Yu Chonghan] paid a visit to military headquarters and expressed his views pertaining to construction in Manchuria and Mongolia. The commanding officer, of course, expressed his utmost approval. The army's plans for building Manchuria-Mongolia thereafter frequently relied on his views." Although on October 2 they changed slogans from "protection of vested interests" to "construction of the new Manchuria-Mongolia,"[39] for the Guandong Army, which was searching for something concrete to incorporate into their plans, Yu Chonghan's views were like rainfall in the midst of a drought.

Yu had worked as a Chinese language instructor at the Tokyo School of Foreign Languages, and at the time of the Russo-Japanese War joined the Japanese army and was awarded the Sixth Order of Merit for his actions. His ties to Japan ran deep. He subsequently held such prominent positions as councilor to the security command of the Three Eastern Provinces under Zhang Zuolin, administrative head of the special northeastern district, and chairman of the board of the Chinese Eastern Railway. He also made the acquaintance of Honjō Shigeru, who was working as an advisor to Zhang Zuolin at the time. Retiring from public office in 1927, he returned to serve as councilor to the security command of the Three Eastern Provinces after the death of Zhang Zuolin; however, soon thereafter, he again retired and gained an important place in the financial world. At first, he had been politically opposed, as a member of Zhang Zuolin's brain trust, to Zhang's invading south of the Great Wall into China proper, and following the death of Wang Yongjiang (1871/73–1927/28), he and Yuan Jinkai were known as the two pillars of the Wenzhi militarist clique of Fengtian. With the principle of "peace within borders and security for the populace," he advocated political and economic self-sufficiency and popular livelihood in the northeast. He had become estranged from the regime and lost all influence under Zhang Xueliang who had launched an effort to realign with China proper. His political stance was seen as useful by the Guandong Army, however, which was trying to get rid of Zhang and was intent on creating an independent state.

What, then, were Yu Chonghan's political views? In summary, he believed in the following points: (1) bringing an end to warlord politics, abolishing unreasonable taxes, and cultivating the strength of the people; (2) improving wages and quality of officials; (3) establishing a budget inspection bureau; (4) reforming the police system; (5) developing transportation and industry; and (6) gradually perfecting self-governing institutions by taking into consideration such concerns as local history, people's feelings, and customs. Through policies such as these, he hoped to make the northeast region into an area of quiet, comfortable living. Most timely and important for the Guandong Army, which was then conceptualizing an independent state in Manchuria, were two points: his absolute belief in the principle of peace within borders and security for the local populace; and non-support for a military by abolishing the local military forces and relying for defense on Japan.

The first of these, the principle of local peace and security, meant advocating self-protection and closing off contacts south of the Great Wall by severing the Three Eastern Provinces from China proper and effecting a government of the "kingly way" there. To bring such an ideal paradise into existence, it was essential to build an independent state which cut its ties to warlord Zhang's regime and the Nanjing government with their hegemonic politics. This was in effect a realization of the Monroe Doctrine for the provinces of the northeast, and this stance coincided, of course, with the plans of the Guandong Army, which was looking to gain control over Manchuria and Mongolia by cutting it off from China proper. At the time, Matsuki Tamotsu, having on orders from the Guandong Army drafted a blueprint of governmental and legal institutions for the new state, claimed that he leapt for joy when he got wind of Yu's views. In his opening statement of a plan for the creation of a new state, Tachibana Shiraki later offered a thoroughgoing policy of peace and security, in conformity with Yu Chonghan's views and because the building of an independent state was absolutely essential.

The second principle of non-support for a military was rooted in the defense posture that "there is no need for troops in a sacred government based on the kingly way, . . . for if we do not invade others, others will not attack us." He emphasized that "Switzerland provided an example in Europe of the principle of non-support for a military, and this was not necessarily impossible to implement."[40] Perhaps he acquired this information from his eldest son, Yu Jingyuan, who had graduated from a Swiss school of artillery. In any case, "if there is no fighting" in the northeast, "there will be no discrimination, and with no distinctions all will be equal to break new ground together in happiness." In order to "create a paradise here unsurpassed throughout the world," the first thing necessary to do was to abolish the military. Yu Chonghan's conclusion, more like a gamble, was that in so doing they would not again revert to the old style of warlord politics. This principle of non-support for a military was dubbed "the most brilliant of Mr. Yu Chonghan's views on the new regime and a great, logical plan." Yu argued that the independent state would have no armaments whatsoever, and that it would rely on Japan for its national defense should there be an attack from the Soviet Union or China proper. For the Guandong Army, whose first principle as a condition for the creation of an independent state was "management of national defense and foreign policy" by Japan, this was a proposition for which they had not even asked.

One thing we need to note is that support in China for a reduction in armaments, as opposed to warlord domination and increases in military expenditures, had begun with Sun Zhongshan and been debated long since. Also, Yu Chonghan was certainly not alone in arguing that one important link in government by the kingly way was not to have a military. Yuan Jinkai also offered as a political program: "Perfect the police system to maintain public order and absolutely do not train a military."[41] Zheng Xiaoxu (1860–1938), an early prime minister of Manzhouguo, also often called for abolition of the military as the essence of the principle of the kingly way. Furthermore, on the international scene, the antiwar Pact of Paris (Kellogg-Briand Pact) was signed in 1928, and Article I "condemn[ed] recourse to war for the solution of international controversies, and renounce[d] it, as an instrument of national policy in their relations with one another." The renunciation of war itself was thus not at all an extravagant notion put forward by Yu Chonghan. That said, though, effecting a principle of non-support for a military in a thorough manner, Yu must have seen the contradiction and irony to this principle which would entrust national defenses completely to the Guandong Army, a military force whose most important task was the pursuance of war. On further reflection, though, the plan of supporting a pacificism inherent in the principle of non-support for a military while entrusting defense to another nation and offering one's own land as a strategic base certainly resembles in some way the direction taken by Japan since the end of World War II. The great irony was not that of Yu Chonghan alone, and we most assuredly cannot laugh this off as some relic from the past.

Without a doubt, Yu Chonghan's political views brought home to the Guandong Army and Ishiwara Kanji certain pivotal points about the establishment of the state of Manzhouguo: the independence of Manzhouguo, the realization of a paradise of a government based on the kingly way and equality without discrimination of any sort, abolition of the military, and a reliance on the Guandong Army for its state defense. In this sense, when Ishiwara said that Yu was "the man who had done more than anyone else for the establishment of the state," he was not necessarily wide of the mark. Of course, Yu Chonghan's and others' alignment with the Guandong Army was not merely to realize his position on the principle of peace within borders and security for the populace. We must not overlook the fact that this shared goal was a product of the dynamics of the political and bureaucratic spheres in Manchuria, the economic base, and personal interests. On this point, Tachibana Shiraki observed that the great landlords in Zhang Xueliang's circle were warlords who behaved like capitalists; by contrast, Yu Chonghan, Yuan Jinkai, and their ilk were simply landlords and thus they were threatened as political and economic losers in the modernization policies of Zhang Xueliang. Also, there were many ordinary landlords in Manchuria who privately despised the Fengtian warlords for economic reasons, just as there were a fair number of local gentry who felt inclined toward the camp of Yu and Yuan. "Given the fact that this group," noted Tachibana, "may become our allies, [the Guandong Army] is trying to gain control over them. They are doing this quite consciously."[42]

According to Tachibana, the principles of peace within borders, a secure livelihood, and non-support for a military would not only perpetually eliminate warlord influence and its opposition to the landlord class for which pacificism and decentralized institutions were class advantages; together they comprised an ideology born of the earlier effort to reject capitalist and proletarian influence which had flooded into Manchuria together with the Guomindang from China proper.[43] From this perspective, it was now fully possible, perhaps necessary, to understand the political views of men such as Yu Chonghan and Yuan Jinkai. In other words, they were pursuing policies for their own advantages, and one cannot simply say that they were ingratiating themselves with the Guandong Army. Yet, as a result, one cannot deny that the very existence and activities of Yu Chonghan and others like him gave added momentum to the state-building schemes of the Guandong Army. Through his encounter with the actions and views of Yu Chonghan, Ishiwara too was inspired to switch positions from the occupation of Manchuria and Mongolia to support for an independent state. For Yu Chonghan, by contrast, might not an independent state in Manchuria have been the realization of a long-cherished desire?

After the establishment of the state of Manzhouguo, Ishiwara called for the abolition of extraterritoriality and the return to Manzhouguo of administrative authority over attached terrain. He went on one occasion to visit Yu Chonghan, who had fallen ill, and described the situation at the time in the following manner.

Mr. Yu Chonghan was extremely happy and arose from bed in the infirmary. He shook my hand and said: "Mr. Ishiwara, you are very good at business. From the perspective of the Manchuria railways, the 'attached terrain' is so small you can barely see it in with a microscope. However, in giving us this additional tiny piece of land, we will have gotten Manchuria in its entirety." Yu Chonghan held my hand tightly and sobbed huge teardrops. I cannot forget this scene even now.[44]

What thought came to Yu Chonghan as he seized Ishiwara's hand with own thin and weak hand and wept profusely? What expectations for Manzhouguo surfaced for Yu Chonghan, the man who had been most active and influential in the establishment of the state of Manzhouguo?

Whatever they may have been, the importance for Manzhouguo of Yu Chonghan's return to politics was the operation on the part of the Fengtian provincial government to break off relations with the Zhang Xueliang regime and the Guomindang government and the offering up of the ideal of creating an independent state—in a word, this was by no means a state-building effort completely from above. The principal motive behind the Guandong Army's regarding Yu as essential was to rally forces antagonistic to Zhang Xueliang and to provide support from the local Chinese residents for the new regime. The Self-Government Guidance Board was convened after Yu's emergence from retirement as an agency to advance the state-building project from below.

By adopting Yu Chonghan's proposal on November 10, 1931, the Guandong Army launched the Self-Government Guidance Board with Yu as its chairman. Yu himself particularly laid stress on the significance of local self-government in China, articulating his position to the Guandong Army: "Institutions of local self-government are most appropriate to the national character of the Chinese people."[45] The Guandong Army studied this, and "immediately agreed to set up the Self-Government Guidance Board with Yu Chonghan in charge of it."[46] Yu took a position emphasizing respect for older customs and practices: "A system of self-government requires reference to the history, practices, feelings, and customs of each local area" and acknowledging that "the realization of such lofty ideals in a single leap will be difficult." His position in support of guiding and reforming self-government was actually a call for a different direction. For the Guandong Army, which was pushing ahead with its state-building plans while engaged in warfare, "the construction of the new Manchuria-Mongolia" was an urgent task "planning for the eradication of the warlord politics above and the completion of local self-government institutions and the stability and welfare of the people below."[47] More than anything else, "instilling enlightenment in the masses of the various counties as well as forging a unity of spirit while preventing rebellious actions"[48]—namely, wiping out hostility for the Japanese and anti-Japanese consciousness among the residents of the occupied areas and the need to win over the people's minds and provide support and cooperation in the building of the new state—were acutely recognized.

Following the Manchurian Incident, numerous local self-government councils and public order maintenance councils were set up in Fengtian, Fushun, Andong, Muqihu, Sipingjie, Kaidong, Liaoyang, Gongzhuling, and elsewhere in the northeast. Most of them had Japanese advisors, and there were instances of conflict that broke out with the local residents due to graft and illegal acts. Further trouble resulted from the actions taken by the group surrounding Noda Ranzō, which seized the Tieling county government, organized a self-government council and a volunteer corps, and forced rapid self-government reforms. Even the Guandong Army found itself in a situation in which "these actions proved disadvantageous, for they threw the system into chaos and the people fell into a stupor. We keenly felt the need for regulation and liaison."[49]

Thus, already on October 24 prior to Yu Chonghan's return to politics, the Guandong Army decided upon the basic points in the founding of the Self-Government Guidance Board as the agency to oversee the local self-government councils and public order maintenance councils in the various counties. The army sought cooperation from Japanese living in Manchuria for the implementation of these endeavors. Those responding to this call were the Manchurian Youth League, the Majestic Peak Society (Daiyūhōkai), and the people assembled at the journal *Manshū hyōron* (edited by Tachibana Shiraki). Their active participation provided a great propelling force to the state-building movement, and all manner of dreams including the ideal of just government, ethnic harmony, the construction of the paradise of the kingly way, the revival of Asia, and human liberation were spun and offered as founding principles for Manzhouguo.

The Manchurian Youth League and Ethnic Harmony

The Manchurian Youth League was formed in November 1928. That year Japan had taken the measure of sending troops a second time to Shandong to protect its citizens resident there in the face of the Northern Expedition of the Guomindang's National Revolutionary Army. There followed the eruption of the Jinan Incident, and slowly but surely oil was being poured on the flames of the anti-Japanese movement in China.

That same year, Japan held its first general elections, and however imperfect they may have been, the views of adult men were reflected in government domestically. Japanese living in China, however, felt a sense of being left behind. Thus, to overcome the sad state of Japanese in Manchuria and give voice to their views on issues, the newspaper association of Dalian (Dairen) planned a Manchurian youth parliament as a a kind of moot diet; at its second session, the members resolved to found the Manchurian Youth League. In its founding manifesto, the League proclaimed: "Manchuria and Mongolia are terrain on which Japanese and Chinese coexist. By enhancing its cultural level and opening up its sources of wealth, we can help each other. It is the single great mission of our country to protect the limitless prosperity of our two peoples and the peace of East Asia for eternity."[50] This statement placed Manchuria-Mongolia in an area of Sino-Japanese coexistence and made cultural and industrial leadership there an ethnic obligation for the Japanese people. However, in spite of energetic propaganda for Sino-Japanese coexistence and coprosperity and the "limitless development of the Yamato people," amid the political turbulence from the expeditionary force sent to Shandong to the murder of Zhang Zuolin and the emergence of Zhang Xueliang, the Japanese in Manchuria confronted both rising Chinese nationalism and numerical inferiority. They were exposed to a situation in which "we may meet the fate of unfurling the white flag of surrender should we give in to this turmoil."[51] A palpable sense of crisis prevailed by the time of a meeting held three months before the Manchurian Incident at which speeches were delivered concerned with breaking the deadlock. On that occasion, a second manifesto was issued: "Our right to live in Manchuria is at present on the verge of a serious crisis, due to the systematic industrial pressure applied by the Chinese government and its illegal acts in violation of treaties. . . . If we just sit by and overlook the present situation, the interests of the empire will surely be destroyed, and the misfortune of national ruin will overtake our homeland."[52]

In order to surmount such a critical situation, the Manchurian Youth League set in motion from early 1931 a "movement for the establishment of a policy on the new Manchuria-Mongolia." It published and distributed pamphlets decrying the actual state of the anti-Japanese movement with titles such as *Man-Mō mondai to sono shinsō, zen Nihon kokumin ni uttau* (The truth about the Manchuria-Mongolia issue, an appeal to all the people of Japan).[53] It sent campaigning teams back to Japan and stirred up public opinion by investigating anti-Japanese actions at various sites in Manchuria and Mongolia and convening forums for speeches on the situation there. At its height the Manchurian Youth League had twenty-two branches in Manchuria and an announced overall membership figure of some 5000 (in fact, there were approximately 2300 members). The vigor of Japanese activities in Manchuria, though, actually fanned the flames of an anti-Japanese mood among the Chinese, such as in the National Diplomatic Council of Liaoning Province, and the Manchurian Youth League for its part saw the need for a defensive theory or slogan to use in competition with the anti-Japanese assault. This took shape in June 1931 when they - demanded "harmony among the various peoples presently resident in Manchuria-Mongolia."[54] This "harmony among the various peoples presently resident" had a defensive quality about it, calling both for the right to live in Manchuria-Mongolia and for equal treatment for the tiny ethnic group of Japanese who amounted to less than one percent of the thirty million residents of the region and were now exposed to attack. Although since its inauguration the League had been chanting such slogans as "Sino-Japanese unity," "Sino-Japanese youth harmony," and "Sino-Japanese coexistence and coprosperity,"[55] these all ultimately were premised on either Japan and China being on an equal footing or Japan being in a superior position. When they came forward with "harmony among the various peoples," however, the principal objective was a justification for the declining Japanese ethnic group to remain in Manchuria-Mongolia. Precisely as Itō Musojūrō has recounted it, "ethnic harmony" was a "slogan advocated by the Japanese living in Manchuria, especially those engaged in middle and small businesses, to cope with the nationalist anti-Japanese movement of the Chinese."[56]

Nonetheless, at the same time it is important to note that, like the meta-phor of a cornered mouse biting a cat, the call for "harmony among the various peoples" was adopted together with a call to "root out anti-Japanese education which ignored international faith." Also, the original text dis-guised a confrontational posture with respect to Zhang Xueliang in its call for "the eradication of the anti-Japanese regime." After the establishment of the state of Manzhouguo, it was explained that from the very start the call for "harmony among the various peoples" was an ideology aimed at "creating a nation of ethnic harmony." The extent to which this is true or false remains unclear, but according to Kanai Shōji (1886–1967) who served as director of the Manchurian Youth League, the thinking that was paramount within the League ran as follows: the principle of national self-determination that was dominant in the post–World War I period awoke and stirred up ethnic consciousness, but as a consequence the differences between peoples as opposed to the commonalities of all humanity were stressed; this tended to sharpen rivalries between ethnic groups and drew the world into chaos; there was hence a need to build a state based on eth-nic harmony guided by the principle of correcting these bad influences. Yet, to advocate these ideas under the Zhang Xueliang regime would be considered treasonous, and thus a call for "harmony among the various peoples" was transformed into an abstract expression. As the ideal state based on ethnic harmony, Kanai put forward the following explanation:

With the leadership of a strong state, the various peoples would come together and build a multi-ethnic nation. This will guarantee the state's independent identity. We must in this manner create a universe centering upon a guiding nation. . . . Bring-ing down the evil regime of Zhang Xueliang in this region and building a moral state in which the ethnic groups gather are truly the essential principles, and they provide the guiding thinking within the Youth League.[57]

It would be difficult to argue that before the Manchurian Incident this sort of thinking held sway. Rather, through cooperation with the Guandong Army and by participating in the post–World War I settlement, political maneuverings, and self-government leadership, thinking on ethnic har-mony changed from a demand of the ethnic Japanese for a guarantee of their right to live to a guiding principle of multi-ethnic state formation centered around Japan as the leader-nation.

Of course, the conception entertained by the Manchurian Youth League of an independent state in Manchuria-Mongolia based on ethnic coopera-tion was certainly an issue before the Manchurian Incident. For example, Yamaguchi Jūji (1892–1979) who was a leading member of the League, published an article entitled "Sanjūnengo no Man-Mō" (Manchuria and Mongolia in thirty years) in the June 1927 issue of *Kyōwa* (Harmony), the journal of the S.M.R.'s employees' association. He offered an argument in support of "abolishing the old provincial governments and amalgamating

Mongolia-Manchuria" to form "a single, self-governing state."[58] He anticipated that "the nationals in this new autonomous zone would be Han, Manchu, Mongol, Korean, and Japanese, who without distinction would participate in government as citizens of this autonomous zone and would shoulder the responsibilities of cooperation, as they planned for the realization of an ideal realm of mutual love, coexistence, and coprosperity." To be sure, the image conveyed here is of a self-governing Manchurian-Mongolian state, an ideal realm in which all ethnic groups cooperated from a position of equality. Yet, as the words of his title—"In Thirty Years"—indicated, Yamaguchi himself did not necessarily consider the materialization of a new state in 1927 to be possible. At the first congress of the Manchurian Youth League two years later, however, Nakao Suguru of the Yingkou branch raised the following as an agenda item: "To save the special zone of Manchuria-Mongolia from the whirlpool of chaos in China and to preserve peace perpetually, national assistance with the aim of establishing an autonomous Manchurian-Mongolian state can successfully be achieved."[59] This point was then debated at the second congress. The reason Nakao raised his proposal at this juncture was that, in spite of the fact that Manchuria-Mongolia was not inherently Chinese terrain and the Japanese had developed it at great personal sacrifice, he claimed, it was cursed by the ambitions of warlords, was falling into a wretched, decrepit state, and its people were suffering under a tyrannical, oppressive regime. On the basis of this understanding, "in order to break away from this panic-ridden era and bring on an eternal peace . . . the 30,000,000 people of Manchuria-Mongolia believe that to display the workings of an autonomous system here and then offer it as a model throughout China will enable everlasting peace in East Asia to be secured. With the sincerity of a good neighbor, we" trust that "giving national assistance, preserving the interests of the empire, and enabling the development of Manchuria-Mongolia are the essence of coexistence and coprosperity."[60]

The logic as propagated by the movement toward Manzhouguo statehood was to see Manchuria-Mongolia as a special zone. The structure of the argument was that the Japanese and the thirty million Chinese together were oppressed victims of warlord Zhang Xueliang and that to overthrow Zhang and create an autonomous state was both the expression of Japanese sincerity and the essence of ethnic harmony. Doubts were raised by members of the Manchurian Youth League regarding Nakao's views: was creating a new state in Manchuria-Mongolia not an intervention in domestic affairs and an obstacle to diplomacy; was it not inappropriate to renounce one's nationality once the new state came into existence? The item was tabled. At the fourth congress held on October 16–17 following the Manchurian Incident, however, things changed completely, and a number of resolutions—such as those "Concerning an Autonomous Manchurian-Mongolian Republic of Aligned Provinces," "On the Establishment of a

Concrete Plan for Ethnic Harmony," and "On Pressing Forward with the Movement for the Welfare of the Present Residents of Manchuria-Mongolia"—were approved.

With the passage of these resolutions, the Manchurian Youth League on October 23, using the name of its board chairman Kanai Shōji, proposed to Guandong Army Commander Honjō Shigeru a "General Plan for the Construction of a Free State of Manchuria-Mongolia." The plan stressed the following points: (1) a completely open door to the four provinces of the northeast; (2) on the basis of the principles of freedom and equality and with the goal of harmony among the various ethnic communities, making the presently resident populace into a free citizenry; and (3) the eradication of warlordism and through civilian rule forge a separation from wartorn China proper and anticipate a thoroughgoing economic development in the four northeastern provinces. In addition, the "freedom" of this free state would "mean something different from liberalism, as each ethnic group would be able to act freely in politics and the economy."[61] Together with a "completely open door," the Japanese residents of Manchuria sought a guarantee that they would be able to act freely without changing their citizenship. This demand clearly reflected the earnest prayer of the Manchurian Youth League, which felt trapped by the anti-Japanese movement and resigned to surrender and withdrawal, while at the same time "looking forward to the development of the Yamato people."

The Manchurian Youth League understood the Guandong Army's military actions as a golden opportunity in which all the accumulated abuses and misdeeds of the past could be resolved in one fell swoop. Maintaining on October 20 that the actions of the Guandong Army were motivated by the right to self-defense and abjuring the intervention of either the League of Nations or the Nationalist government in Nanjing, the Manchurian Youth League announced in a declaration that "Manchuria-Mongolia should enjoy self-governance for the upright people living there."[62] And, they resolved to cooperate with the Guandong Army: "It is the first step of the Yamato people onto the continent: step in sharply, jump in loudly."[63] The cooperation of the Manchurian Youth League with the Guandong Army was a timely offer for the latter which had until then been unable to gain the formal participation of Japanese agencies in Manchuria or the South Manchurian Railway in the government's expansion plan. The Manchurian Youth League was now put in charge of political strategies to restore industry, transportation, and communication as well as to gain control over commercial and agricultural associations. Principal among these, for example, were supervision and management of the Fengtian Electric Factory by Haraguchi Sumimasa, seizure and revival of the Shen-Hai Railroad by Yamaguchi Jūji, establishment of the Northeast Communications Committee by such men as Yamaguchi and Ozawa Kaisaku (1898–1970, father of the conductor Ozawa Seiji [b. 1935], whose given name was said to have been taken from Itagaki SEIshirō and Ishiwara KanJI), and revival of such government-run enterprises as mining, telephone offices, clothing depots, and arsenals with the creation of an industrial committee under Koreyasu Masatoshi. Furthermore, the Manchurian Youth League took part in planning the reorganization of the administrative agencies. Under Kanai Shōji, advisor to the Liaoning Regional Self-Governing Committee, a finance bureau was opened by Shikabe Mitsugu and others, a business bureau was opened by Hoshino Tatsuo among others, and a court commenced operations with Abiru Kanji. The reorganization of administrative agencies created jobs for Japanese advisors and consultants, and the Youth League adopted a plan of action "grounded in the principles of good government and Japanese control over real power."[64]

As soon as Kanai took up his position as an advisor, he immediately assigned Masutomo Kurakichi to carry out an investigation of the provincial government; in addition, he had Nakanishi Toshinori devise a plan for local administrative institutions and for the management of localities. Nakanishi had worked with Itagaki and Hanaya Tadashi (1894–1957) of the Guandong Army in formulating the Plan for the Institution of the Local Self-Government Guidance Board. On the basis of this plan, each county would receive instructions from the leaders of the Self-Government Guidance Board through Kanai on matters concerning self-government, and in this manner the Self-Government Guidance Board was put into place to accelerate the pace of the establishment of the new state.

Amid this string of events, the Manchurian Youth League created a façade of ethnic harmony. They were successful in mobilizing a number of Chinese, such as Ding Jianxiu (graduate of the Department of Political Economy, Waseda University) and Jin Bidong (graduate of the Japanese army's military academy) in reviving the Shen-Hai Railroad and reorganizing the Northeast Communications Committee, and Yu Jingyuan, Wang Ziheng (graduate of the Department of Political Economy, Waseda University), and Wang Bingduo (graduate of the Law Faculty, Kyoto Imperial University) in the Self-Government Guidance Board. Because work proceeded comparatively smoothly, it appeared, Ishiwara and others came to recognize the efficaciousness of the slogan of "ethnic harmony" in the work of state-building. Furthermore, after the explosion of the Manchurian Incident, the Manchurian Youth League on three occasions sent canvassers back to Japan in an effort to arouse public opinion and propagandize the building of a new ethnically harmonious state based on the founding ideal of the "Kingly Way." As this took effect, "ethnic harmony" as the slogan for the new state spread. Needless to say, the bulk of those Chinese who cooperated with the Manchurian Youth League had earlier been overseas students in Japan. In the Instructions for the Work of the Leaders of the Self-Government Guidance Board, it was also singled out that they "should employ as many as possible [former] overseas students in Japan and those conversant in Japanese as provincial officials." These two factors make it easy to assess the level of effectiveness of "ethnic harmony" and its efficacy as a slogan. In Manchuria, however, where resistance to the military actions of the Guandong Army remained extremely strong, there were people acquainted with the terrain by virtue of having lived there or who had personal contacts over the course of many years who joined hands throughout the locales in the work of maintaining public order and submission to the Guandong Army. In so doing, they without a doubt made the work of building a new state proceed more rapidly than even Ishiwara and his colleagues anticipated.

Together with the Manchurian Youth League, it was the members of the Majestic Peak Society, first and foremost among them being Kasagi Yoshiaki (1892–1955), who volunteered bravely to head off to the north with an even stronger sense of ideology and of mission in this work of state-building.

The Majestic Peak Society and the Great Wave of Asian Revival

In September 1928, Ōkawa Shūmei (1886–1957) of the East Asian Economic Investigation Bureau of the S.M.R. visited Zhang Xueliang and advised him, in opposition to the Three Principles of the People of the Guomindang, "to put a state based on the Kingly Way into effect in Manchuria and begin the writing of a new page in world history."[65] Ōkawa noted that Zhang approved of the construction of such a state, but in actual fact due to actions beyond his control things developed in a direction diametrically opposite to that urged by Ōkawa. Nonetheless, the idea of establishing the cornerstone of an Asian revival by constructing a state based on the Kingly Way in Manchuria-Mongolia and severed from China proper exerted a powerful influence principally on those connected to such societies as the Continued Existence Society (Yūzonsha) and the Society to Practice the Way of Heaven on Earth (Kōchisha), both founded by Ōkawa, and the Society of the Sun (Hinokai) at Tokyo Imperial University and the Revival Study Society (Yūkō gakkai) at Kyoto Imperial University, both organized under the umbrella of the former two. Young people inspired by the ideas of these groups dreamt of making them real and moved to Manchuria and Mongolia.

The Revival Study Society in Fengtian was comprised of such figures as Niwakawa Tatsuo and Etō Natsuo (1903–68) came together around a man by the name of Nakano Koitsu, who had come to Manchuria in 1927 and opened a legal practice. With a conception of building a state based on moral principles, they worked diligently to strengthen their ties to the Special Services Agency in Fengtian and the Guandong Army. Under the influence of Ōkawa Shūmei, Kasagi Yoshiaki, who was working at the East Asian

Economic Investigation Bureau, in 1929 joined the Continued Existence Society and took part in the establishment of the Society to Practice the Way of Heaven on Earth; transferred to the main headquarters of the S.M.R., he came to Manchuria and thereafter formed a similar group in Dalian. The Majestic Peak Society developed from a meeting at which these two groups came together. Aroung the fall of 1930, Zen master Haykujō Kaikai was living a peaceful existence at Baizhang Mountain, and this society was said formally to have taken its name in connection with the "majestic peak of solitary sitting," an expression of independence.

Altogether the Majestic Peak Society had some thirty or more members and, unlike the Manchurian Youth League, they did not proselytize their efforts to the outside world. Because they had no overall plan as a society per se, it remained unclear just what positions or objectives motivated them as a group. They did, however, gradually become more and more identified as a group cohering to the personality of Kasagi Yoshiaki and devoted to his ideas. Their foundations lay in Kasagi's notion of Asian revival and Buddhist belief.

In an article Kasagi contributed to the organ of the Society to Practice the Way which offered such principles as the "liberation of peoples of color" and the "moral unification of the world," he argued concerning the ideal form of a state that "the objectives and ideals of a state are embodied in its laws."[66] His use of such a term as "laws" already reveals how deeply immersed Kasagi was in Buddhism. He argued that the state that embodied these laws was "not the ancient state in which the objective was the ambition of a unified world for personal advantage, but a state built on the integrity of righteous power and the purveyors of justice to bring unity to the world, a state of the Kingly Way, a state which seeks to implement in this world of falsity the judgment of the gods."[67] Of course, the "state of the Kingly Way" conceived of by Kasagi at this time in 1925 was but one ideal type, a moral state which, with the enduring ideal of justice, could bring unity to the world. Such a state was still only an ideal at that time, and as a popular movement the effort to realize it entailed the revival of Asia and the liberation of oppressed peoples.

In 1926 Kasagi left the Society to Practice the Way and himself organized the League for the Revival of the East (*Tōkō renmei*). As its main program, he claimed: "The League for the Revival of the East shall endeavor to realize the just demands of the oppressed peoples of color spread throughout the world."[68] As is clear here, Kasagi's Asian revivalism was not limited simply to the revival of Asia but was directed at the liberation of oppressed peoples of color throughout the entire world. In this sense, he was denying any racial or ethnic prejudice or favoritism and had something in common with the mutual love of mankind advocated by Yamaguchi Jūji of the Manchurian Youth League. Nonetheless, as far as Kasagi was concerned, his heart pounded with a savior's sense of mission, for the peoples of color had suffered oppression around the globe because of Westerners; the Japanese people were in the camp of mankind's oppressed and, because they stood at the head of the oppressed peoples of color, would perforce lead them all to liberation. By contrast, he showed absolutely no consciousness of the fact that Japan stood on the side of the oppressor in Taiwan and Korea. Characteristic of the Japanese movement for an Asian revival was this extraordinary coexistence of a surplus consciousness of being oppressed and a lack of consciousness of oppressing. And, Kasagi was no exception. Yet, Kasagi's Asian revivalism after he came to Manchuria advocated as well a "spiritual revival of East Asia based in Buddhism" over which he would supervise a Society of Young East Asian Lay Buddhists. His powers of attraction over numerous young people seems to have been something based more in his personal qualities and conduct as a seeker of truth or founder of a religious sect rather than as political advocate. The Majestic Peak Society gradually evolved as a group of Kasagi's devotees based initially in the gatherings of members of the Continued Existence Society and Society to Practice the Way groups in Manchuria. After the Manchurian Incident, the number of members was said to surpass eighty.

The Majestic Peak Society convened a general meeting at the Miaoxin Temple in Fengtian on October 18, shortly after the Manchurian Incident. In response to the requests of staff officers of the Guandong Army, those present including Itagaki and Ishiwara who were resolved to cooperate in the state-building movement. In concrete terms, they deliberated over a plan drafted by members Nakano Koitsu and Niwakawa Tatsuo entitled Our Plan Concerning the Local Self-Government Guidance Board, and as a result participated in moving the Majestic Peak Society as a whole toward guidance in self-government. Guandong Army Headquarters adopted a draft plan drawn up by comparing this Plan with the direction and principles of self-government guidance drafted by Nakanishi Toshinori and others of the Manchurian Youth League; it was completed on October 24 as the Plan for the Institution of the Local Self-Government Guidance Board. Thus, the goals of the Local Self-Government Guidance Board were set as follows: "In accordance with the principles of good government and with the aims of bringing an end to irrational taxes, reforming the treatment of county officials, bringing together the various ethnic groups, and cutting off all ties to the old warlords, we take responsibility for the enlightenment of the local populace and their spiritual cohesion, and we shall work to prevent acts of rebelliousness."[69] Concretely, they had the local elite and other local bodies organize county-level self-government executive committees, and county-level self-government guidance committees sent by the Self-Government Guidance Board led and supervised them. The people who formed the county self-government guidance committees were men who, it was decided, would be "Japanese in the main." The aim of this system was to gain control over the local elites and local influential groups and to incorporate them into the structure of control, as the Guandong Army created circuits to extend its sway down to the lowest levels.

To sever local elites from the warlords and bring about cooperation with the military forces of a foreign nation by some sort of action, however, it was necessary to introduce the suggestion of such agenda items as bringing an end to irrational taxes, reforming the treatment of county officials, and bringing together the various ethnic groups. This was the reason that it was strongly advocated in the Bylaws of the Local Self-Government Guidance Board, by which it was enacted on November 10 that the Self-Government Guidance Board be based on the principles of good government by "conducting a clean sweep of the old elites with connections to the warlords and setting up a foundation in the principles of good government based in local self-government."[70] It was stressed that "good government" was synonymous with criticizing and eliminating the misgovernment, tyranny, and abusive political practices of warlord Zhang. Even if it might be used to convince others, profession of the principles of good government was a weak psychological spring to "mobilize the Self-Government Guidance Board to advance, disregarding all dangers, to an immediate readiness for sacrifice" on the very terrain where smoke from the fires of fighting was still rising.[71] Higher ideals and a sense of mission were essential to stir up the passions sufficient for one to risk one's life plunging into perils, to inspire oneself, and to support one's mind and body in even the most difficult of circumstances. More than simple logic, what was needed was a system of belief of a quality close to religious devotion, and the person who provided it with this quality was Kasagi Yoshiaki.

When the Self-Government Guidance Board was founded on November 10, it issued Declaration No. 1 of the Self-Government Guidance Board widely throughout Liaoning Province in the name of board head Yu Chonghan. It began with the words: "The true spirit of the Self-Government Guidance Board lies in the will to sweep away completely all past tyranny, misunderstanding, falsehood, and confusion under the sun and to establish a paradise on earth." It then continued in a similar vein:

Irrespective of the nationality of the residents, we must arouse the great mercy and compassion in their hearts and build their trust. With mutual respect and affection, we shall see this epochal heavenly task to completion. We must have the feelings and preparedness to take on our work with sincerity.

The so-called unease in Asia will ultimately become the radiance of Asia, the fortuitous omen that shall permeate the entire world and bring genuine great harmony to all mankind. We shall create an ideal realm never seen heretofore in history on terrain here suitable for the general good [literally, *daijō*, the Buddhist "Greater Vehicle"]. We shall devote all of our efforts to the great wave of Asian revival and to correcting racial bias. Our aim is the firm establishment of a universal justice for all. . . .

Before the many obstacles that the future has in store, the Self-Government Guidance Board will proceed down the path of selflessness as the enactor of the great ideal.[72]

This declaration was said to have been drafted by Kasagi and passed Yu Chonghan's approval; it was in substance a document of Kasagi's design, expressing the mixture of Asian revivalism and Buddhist belief which were hallmarks of his thought. He was arguing that there was a historically sacred mission at hand, a heavenly task of epochal proportions involving the building of this ideal realm, a paradise, unique in history, on terrain suitable for the general good—namely, Manchuria-Mongolia—and the construction of a base for the revival of Asia and universal justice without prejudice on the basis of race. They thus had to meet the task before them with mutual respect and affection, sincerity, and selflessness as well as great mercy and compassion. As Kasagi saw it, "the sacred work of building a state governed by the Kingly Way in Manchuria is one great intellectual movement. . . . One could as well call it from another perspective a spiritual, ethical, or religious movement."[73] With "the austerity of desirelessness" and "the devotion to the path toward bodhisattva-hood," the Self-Government Guidance Board charged itself with the "great duty for the millenium"; it was to spare neither life nor self as the "human pillar for the construction of a state based on the Kingly Way," and by ridding itself of all worldly evil passions it was to carry out this sacred task. This approach was known as the guiding spirit of the Self-Government Guidance Board, also called the Kasagi spirit or Kasagi-ism. Of course, this sort of superhuman, fanatical conduct gave rise to an atmosphere of self-importance, and for people who did not have equally strong beliefs, it was to become the object of bewilderment. Devotees of Kasagi-ism, supported as they were by a ferocious sense of mission, were regarded as driven by a mixture of their "heavenly duty" and a impression of fear and contempt. Gradually a gulf emerged between them and others associated with the Manchurian Youth League.

In any event, the members of the Self-Government Guidance Board, as the human pillars of state-building, headed for their "daring and indomitable" positions with a spiritual basis forged by Kasagi. Members were sent to fifty-eight counties covering Fengtian Province and part of Jilin Province by March of 1932 when the Self-Government Guidance Board dissolved. They were the bearers of a state-building movement from the bottom up. Following the establishment of the state of Manzhouguo, the members of the Self-Government Guidance Board were turned into county counselors as a result of the proclamation of the self-governing county administration and county bureaucracy in July 1932 and into assistant county magistrates as a result of the revision of the county bureaucracy in 1937. Divesting themselves of wealth and honor and acting in a selfless, pure fashion, "we shall demonstrate a spirit and moral energy truly suitable to a

state based on the principle of the Kingly Way and henceforth train the officialdom and the populace."[74] In so doing, they would carry on the orthodox position of the Self-Government Guidance Board. People who even
today idealize Manzhouguo often base their arguments on the lofty ideals,
hard-fought moral battles, and the Self-Government Guidance Board
which was passionately devoted to building a state, albeit in vain.

Simplicity, selflessness, uncompensated dedication, good government,
and the like had a certain utility as sectarian catchphrases to raise morale
for all those taking part. Yet, being compelled to behave in this way and to
be so "educated" whether one wished it or not was undoubtedly depressing
and disconcerting. It would not be difficult to imagine that the more hard-
ened the devotion of a true believer to the point of obstinacy, the more im-
passioned and single-minded one's devotion, and the added psychological
pressure for those people who wanted some self-control would surely weigh
heavily on their minds, hard to resist. By the same token, self-government
guidance is an expression fraught with contradictions. If being in control of
one's actions by one's own subjective will is the essence of self-government,
then by definition there is no space for guidance in essence to operate. If
self-government is only brought about and maintained by guidance from
above, then this really ought not to be called self-government. For many of
the people who assembled at the Self-Government Guidance Board, however, guiding and inculcating the Chinese with their assumed low level of
political abilities in self-governance was, without a doubt, seen as a perfectly
natural mission. Kasagi argued this point as follows:

If genuine self-government is developing in Manchuria, why has the populace continued its life resigned to the shackles of abusive politicians? Why are they restricted in their freedom by rampant local bandits, political bandits, commercial
bandits, and student bandits? They speak of the growth of self-government, but
aren't they really capable manipulators who hide in the clutches of malicious intentions and merely maintain their materialistic existence? Self-government without a
political, indeed a spiritual and moral, basis—the difference between the genuine
and the spurious is immense. There is more than enough room here for morally
courageous, albeit young, Japanese to set to work.[75]

In other words, without awaking the Chinese people who did not understand true self-governance to these facts, the establishment of a state
based on ethnic harmony and the Kingly Way would be impossible. For
this reason Kasagi considered self-governance and guidance as inseparable, and it was demanded of members of the Self-Government Guidance
Board that they "be ideological, emotional, and spiritual guides, teaching
what ought to be taught and rejecting what must be rejected."[76] Perhaps
we have here the paternalism similar to the members of SCAP (Supreme
Commander for the Allied Powers)—first and foremost, General Douglas

MacArthur—who saw the Japanese as little children who, because true democracy had never taken root in their country, went off to war without resisting militarism; and for their genuine liberation, these Japanese needed instruction in democracy. SCAP believed the Japanese had to be awakened to "the basic principles of local self-government" as the schools for democracy.

More recent times aside, not only did Kasagi, while advocating the cause of ethnic harmony, have no doubt whatsoever in his belief about the Japanese assuming the main leadership position as "the guide to the revival of Asia," but he understood the establishment of a state in Manchuria as the development of the Japanese imperial way carrying on the tasks of the Emperor Meiji. This point seems clear from the statement in the Rules of Service for the Members of the Local Self-Government Guidance Board, drafted by Kasagi without waiting for Yu Chonghan's revisions and enacted by Guandong Army Headquarters on November 4, before the actual establishment of the Self-Government Guidance Board, as a top secret document: "The ideals of the Self-Government Guidance Board are to serve and carry on the great plans of the Emperor Meiji and to attempt to confer on the land of Manchuria-Mongolia with its profound links to us the first step in the great mission which the true Japan has assumed in the world."[77] His firm belief was that "the imperial heart of the Emperor Meiji and the great compassion of bodhisattva of mercy will grow through Asia and extend to the world, and this shall be known as greater Asia."[78] These had become the precepts regulating all of Kasagi's words and deeds.

This view of Manzhouguo as an only child of the federation of the imperial way, as one stage in the growth of universal brotherhood—these emerged after the founding of the state, but they already existed in utero when the movement to establish a state began. Indeed, it was an extraordinary conception of a heavenly calling which afforded the Japanese the role of the guiding people, the saviors who assume the great mission of awakening the unconscious peoples of Asia, recapturing the Asia that had been stolen and leading them to liberation. By the same token, seeing the establishment of Manzhouguo as the cornerstone in the liberation of oppressed peoples and the prelude to the creation of a confederation based upon the Kingly Way, there were people as well concerned with the Self-Government Guidance Board who stressed that the construction of the state should be accomplished with the energies that arose from the autonomous organizations of the resident populace. These people include such figures as Tachibana Shiraki and Noda Ranzō, among others. Tachibana in particular noted that the establishment of a state in which the Chinese peasantry itself took hegemony would be the ideal of state-building by the Kingly Way, and that the politics and principles of the Kingly

Way based in self-governance should constitute the guiding ideals of Manzhouguo.

Tachibana Shiraki and the Kingly Way of Self-Governance

"He knows more about China than any of us." This evaluation was offered by the famed Lu Xun (1881–1936) who was second to none in mercilessly dissecting China, his homeland, of a Japanese, Tachibana Shiraki.[79]

Arriving in China in 1906, Tachibana worked for a number of newspapers—including *Ryōtō shinpō* (Liaodong News), *Sainan nippō* (Jinan Daily News), and *Kei-Shin nichinichi shinbun* (Beijing-Tianjin Daily News). As an individualist and a liberal, he used the notion of the "the freedom of self-growth" to wield a powerful brush, earning himself the reputation as the "[Hasegawa] Nyozekan [1875–1969] of Manchuria." He was not only a journalist, but pursued research into Chinese society which resulted in publications in the journals *Gekkan Shina kenkyū* and *Shina kenkyū shiryō*, and later in the volumes, *Shina shakai kenkyū* (Studies in Chinese Society) and *Shina shisō kenkyū* (Studies in Chinese Thought), both of 1936.[80] With each passing year, his renown as a scholar of China who lived on the scene rose. Tachibana himself once recalled of his activities: "I was often misunderstood to be a scholar of China, but my specialty has consistently been a commentator on Chinese society. My motivation for commenting on China was neither curiosity nor intellectual craving, but primarily aimed at a political objective. I was searching for theories and methods supporting honest and just relations between the Chinese and Japanese peoples."[81] Beginning just after the Russo-Japanese War and ending with the conclusion of the second Sino-Japanese War, Tachibana's publicist activities were supported by the exceedingly practical aim of trying to correct with anxiety and indignation the daily worsening Sino-Japanese relations. One might even say that he perforce lived his life in China as a great teacher of Japanese. Most Japanese journalists in China looked as Sino-Japanese relations only insofar they were gauged to Japan's national interests. Even the most conscientious and ardent sinophiles had a propensity, when China veered away from their image, to turn completely around and utter the harshest disdain for the backwardness of China. As such, Tachibana was truly a singular individual. What made this all possible was that, while making his life together with the Chinese people, living with Chinese society before his very eyes, he charged himself with fixedly observing his surroundings. Tachibana's dispassionate gaze rejected being simplistically drawn to ordinary opinions.

China seen through Tachibana's eyes was neither a stagnant country nor a disordered land, and neither was it consistent with the view espoused by such sinologists as Inaba Iwakichi and Yano Jin'ichi and later agreed with by the likes of Ishiwara Kanji and Itagaki Seishirō—namely, that the Chinese people lacked the capacity to form a nation. He merely stated that China "only had on hand a political organization unsuited to face armed struggle."[82] He saw Chinese society as a mass society that was undeveloped and concealing infinite energy. Thus, in his view, not only was it incorrect for Japanese "to flatter themselves unreflectively that they were more advanced than the Chinese" or "to think that the Chinese were a people completely lacking moral sentiments,"[83] but it was actually a biased view, extremely dangerous to Sino-Japanese relations.

While addressing this biased perspective, the problem with which Tachibana was most concerned and which continued to serve notice to Japan from across the sea was facing Chinese nationalism directly and not erring in coming to terms with it. The Japanese journalistic tone concerning the May 30 Movement which arose in 1925 with such slogans as "Recover the Concessions" and "Down with Imperialism" was strongly critical of China, a "second Boxer incident." Tachibana, though, boldly recognized the legitimacy of Chinese demands, and he urged Japanese to reflect historically: "The Japanese who in the past have committed far worse mistakes than the Chinese have an obligation now to demonstrate sincere shame for these errors and make a sharp change in their attitude toward China."[84] By "sharp change" Tachibana meant an end to the view of China based on self-interest and a transformation toward the principle of "egalitarianism" (taitōshugi, byōdōshugi) so that both peoples might develop equally. From this stance, "not always for China but in the interest of all the peoples of color in the world," Japan and the Japanese would struggle earnestly in an effort to "mitigate the arbitrariness and prejudice of the Western countries."[85] This principle of egalitarianism was, of course, applicable as well to Manchuria, and the following items were demanded: "First, the elimination from Japan's Manchuria policy of all political and military significance. . . . Second, in place of a foreign diplomacy linking the warlord [Zhang Zuolin] to us through personal ties, search out and find the loci of popular will and interest and act accordingly." Furthermore, "we must gallantly abandon treating Manchuria as the object of our population policy."[86] Needless to say, such demands not only meant the relinquishing of Japanese rights in Manchuria, but they were also sharply opposed to everything Ishiwara and his fellows sought for Manchuria-Mongolia. In spite of all this, why then did Tachibana later align himself with the military actions of the Guandong Army and pour all the learning and passion he possessed into the creation of the state of Manzhouguo?

Tachibana saw the actions of the Guandong Army and the Korea Army after the eruption of the Manchurian Incident as violations of military discipline and initially took a critical posture, but, in order to deepen his understanding of the incident, in late October he met and spoke with Itagaki, Ishiwara, and other Guandong Army staff officers at Guandong Army

Headquarters on top of the Tōtaku Building in Fengtian. As a result of this meeting, he claimed that he had come to an understanding that the actions of the Guandong Army would lead directly to

the construction of an independent state on the land of the four northeastern provinces as a foundation stone for Asian liberation. Not only would Japan place absolute trust in this and return all vested interests, but it would offer assistance to the extent that it was capable of so doing. . . . At the same time, it [the Guandong Army] anticipated indirectly reforms of the home country, liberating the working people from the despotism and exploitation of the capitalist political parties, and in this way aimed at encouraging momentum toward the building of an ideal state of the sort that would have the motive power to truly liberate Asia.

For Tachibana the actions taken by the Guandong Army were not blind militarism at one with the inclinations of the capitalist political parties, but rather they represented a completely new national and professional awakening oriented against the capitalists and against the political parties. In his view, they had advanced on the firm foundation of enthusiastic support from the masses of Japan's farming populace nationwide. As he put it, "touching the chord of this extraordinary national tension and of course feeling a certain amount of profound emotion . . . I looked to this new force as a trustworthy fellow traveler heading toward a specific point" together with Ishiwara and the officer corps; and he would work diligently to develop the guiding principles for the establishment of the state of Manzhouguo.

This was how Tachibana explained it himself about three years after this meeting in an article entitled "Watakushi no hōkō tenkan" (My change of direction).[87] Although an explanation for his change of views would probably include his catching up with the military, Tachibana had assumed the role of an egalitarian, harbored deep misgivings about the contradictions in capitalism as an economic system, and probably saw the Guandong Army—itself with a clear position of opposition to capitalism and the political parties and as intent on establishing a new state—as the driving force to break through the impasse reached by capitalism and to bring about a working man's democracy. Surely Tachibana, who had searched exhaustively for a remedy in an era of uniformly deteriorating Sino-Japanese relations, saw the actions of the Guandong Army as blazing a trail in the reform of China, for it had expelled for the time being certain warlord powers which prevented the Chinese people from developing. He saw the Manchurian Incident not as an invasion of the mainland but as the liberation of the Chinese people and Asia. By the same token, when he caught sight of an opportunity for the reform of Japan, Tachibana undeniably fell unconsciously into a non-egalitarian mode, addressing the China question from the perspective of Japan, an approach which he had criticized until that point. Insofar as he had consistently taken the stance of considering the Chinese position carefully before reaching a judgment, he had been able to see that the economic policies and the anti-Japanese postures of Zhang Xueliang were the manifestation of Chinese nationalism and were brimming with the possibility for development as a self-strengthening movement. Tachibana now found his attention drawn to the state-building movement for which the Guandong Army and Japanese resident in Manchuria "were risking their lives and rushing ahead before my very eyes." He gambled on this opportunity, but for Tachibana this gamble was more like a leap to his death.

Nonetheless, Tachibana "in particular sought peasant democracy for the state to be established in Manchuria and realized a most absorbing interest in fostering and encouraging it."[88] In his view it would indisputably be implemented based on discussion. The systematic realization of a peasant democracy that Tachibana understood to be the core principle for state-building in Manchuria was simply popular self-government. For Tachibana it would come to fruition through the practice of the Kingly Way. Becoming an advisor to the Self-Government Guidance Board, he together with Noda Ranzō authored The Fundamental Essentials of Popular Self-Government to Be Applied to Society in the Northeast (*Tōhoku shakai ni tekiyō seraru beki jinmin jichi no konpon yōgi*).[89] As they used the term, popular self-government "does not mean the literal application of autonomy with a written law as has been adopted in the local institutions of constitutional states of modern times, but it is to be a project to reform the realities and ways of life part and parcel of the cultural and economic conditions of Chinese society." As concerned self-government, then, compared to the West and China, Japan remained extremely immature, and the Japanese people could not lead the Chinese. If the organizations of families in Chinese villages, temple lands, guilds in the cities, urban commercial associations, and the like operated at full capacity, they would be linked to the realization of popular self-government. However, they had to be on the lookout for the emergence of hierarchical relations of control in the various organizations of self-government brought about by the development of capitalism. If these were not eliminated at the root, there could be no true self-government, and should the increasingly impoverished peasantry in particular fall into irredeemable poverty, the creation of the state of Manzhouguo as a peasant state might come to naught. Thus, for men like Tachibana the leadership objective of the Self-Government Guidance Board was "to help enhance the people's livelihood. . . . First, public order. Second, reform civil government; namely, abolish abusive taxes and alleviate burdens. Third, the reform of production and the structure of the - market and particularly cooperatives in the villages." These were set as the categories in which to emphasize leadership. Self-government as Tachibana used the term had the meaning of peasant self-government— namely, occupational self-government as well as ethnic self-government—for the peasantry was over ninety percent of the population, and the great majority was Han Chinese. In this sense, self-government was defined as "meaning that the people [*kokumin*] passively planned for their survival on the basis of group strength, and actively planned for the advancement of their welfare with the same methods."[90] The main content of this "self-government," then, was the protection of the survival of the citizenry and the enhancement of their welfare through group autonomy.

Tachibana proposed the establishment of the state of Manzhouguo as a "decentralized self-governing state" in which various sorts of self-governing associations formed strata to insure the overall autonomy for the populace. The construction of such a decentralized autonomous state, though, was itself linked to the realization of a state governed by the Kingly Way. Tachibana had published studies of government based on the Kingly Way from early on; already in 1925 he had expressed the view that "I do not see government by the Kingly Way to be a shimmering fact of high antiquity, but on the contrary I anticipate that it will be realized in the future, and together with bringing blessings to the political lives of the Chinese people, it will provide a great hint and stimulus to Western civilization which has now reached an impasse."[91] With study after study he raised the point of view that self-government would be the enactment of the Kingly Way in the state of Manzhouguo. In a speech given to the Self-Government Guidance Board, Tachibana spoke of the society that would be implemented under the Kingly Way and explained: "First, the lives of all the people would be protected; second, wealth would be developed and privately held; third, labor would be engaged in for society. The implementation of these three conditions is called the evolution of ritual [*liyun*, a concept from the ancient Chinese ritual text, *Liji*], the 'age of great harmony.'"[92] The Self-Government Guidance Board was conceived of as the nucleus of the society of the age of great harmony or the utopia to be realized under the Kingly Way. As the driving organ for the creation of the conditions of this distinctive state based on the Kingly Way, the Self-Government Guidance Board "was limited in the scope of its mission just to the fulfillment of county-level self-government units, although eventually by expanding this to national-level self-government, it" assumed the mission of "bearing the task of constructing the foundation toward the completion of the Kingly Way."[93]

In this manner Tachibana charged the Self-Government Guidance Board with the hope of building a a decentralized, self-governing state based on the Kingly Way. He himself in December 1931 formed the State-Founding Society (Kenkokusha) as the organ of an ideological movement to make up for the functional deficiencies of the Self-Government Guidance Board and to investigate, research, and propagate facts and theories connected to construction of a new state. The following February he published a manifesto of the new organization. Although Noda Ranzō was understood to have drafted this manifesto, it was completely consistent with Tachibana's approach. In this piece he defined the Kingly Way as "the great way of statecraft which views the realization of the Confucian idea of a society of 'great harmony' as necessary to protect the people's livelihood by making government more ethical and by socializing wealth."[94] He then went on to discuss the connection between the ideology of the Kingly Way and the establishment of the state of Manzhouguo: "The Manchurian Incident has brought about the collapse of the old northeastern warlord regime. However, a byproduct of the collapse of this regime has been the liberation of several million Manchurians and Mongolians as well as over 30,000,000 Chinese from the iron chains of semi-feudalism. Furthermore, this liberation had awakened the Asian essence of Manchurian society, and it will build anew a state based on the Kingly Way with the traditional ideology of livelihood and a self-governing structure." To that end, construction of a state based on the Kingly Way had, he argued, a historical and social necessity.

In other words, for the peoples of Asia, the ideology of the Kingly Way continued to live as a traditional theory of social life; when liberated from the shackles of the old warlords, despite being under semi-feudal social conditions, the prerequisites will have been met for the construction of a state rooted in the Kingly Way to emerge in the form of ethnic self-governance. The manifesto then went on to call for a federation based on the Kingly Way:

The establishment of a state based on the Kingly Way in Manchuria is not solely the paradise to be cherished for the Manchurian people alone, nor is it solely a lifeline for the Japanese empire, much less a theater for fascism. As we face a war for the existence of humanity in the world whirling about in the Pacific Ocean, [this state] must be something with a mission to serve as parent body for a federation based on the Kingly Way, the one and only force capable of protecting the existence of our Asian society rooted in the Kingly Way.[95]

In the expression, "a war for the existence of humanity in the world whirling about in the Pacific Ocean," we see the same thinking as Ishiwara Kanji, who conceived of a final world war between Japan and the United States and who saw Manchuria as the battleground of that war. Furthermore, the argument that the new state in Manchuria would provide the parent body for a federation of the Kingly Way in Asia resonated with the theory of an East Asian League advocated at a later date by Ishiwara and the Concordia Association (Kyōwakai) of Manzhouguo.

Tachibana added the concept of the Kingly Way as a basic principle for the establishment of Manzhouguo and, together with "ethnic harmony" advocated by the Manchurian Youth League, loudly called for it as the guiding ideal for the new state. Early on, in promoting the world historical significance of the Kingly Way, focused on the protection of popular livelihood and peasant self-governance, he claimed: "The mission of a state rooted in the Kingly Way in Manchuria is a tocsin for life resounding with the call 'Awaken!' to the peoples of the Kingly Way. In addition, it shall liberate all humanity from materialistic capitalist exploitation on the one hand and Communist destruction on the other, and must be the wellspring for a Kingly Way revolution which will inspire a life of great harmony."[96] As such, its emphasis had shifted to protecting the peoples of Asia from domination by capitalism and Communism and toward liberation of the peoples of the world. In this regard, it approached a view which made Manzhouguo the base for an Asian revivalism and the establishment of universal justice, a view espoused by Kasagi Yoshiaki and those affiliated with the Majestic Peak Society.

Thus, the Kingly Way—as expressed in such phrases as the "Kingly Way revolution"—was sublimated into a term symbolizing a revolutionary romantic passion concerned with the construction of paradise on the stage of Manchuria. The Self-Government Guidance Board and the Guandong Army then put this paradise of the Kingly Way to great practical use. By contrast, peasant self-governance and a decentralized, autonomous state as constitutory elements which Tachibana had stressed as inseparable from the Kingly Way were scraped off and cleanly dispensed with in the process of state institutionalization. Even before the inauguration of the Self-Government Guidance Board, in the Outline of a Plan for the Establishment of a Free State of Manchuria-Mongolia (*Man-Mō jiyūkoku kensetsu an taikō*) drafted by Matsuki Tamotsu under orders from the Guandong Army, we find a tendency toward the centralization of power; after the establishment of a central government, it read, "we shall gradually expand the powers of the central government and plan for the reduction of the power of the various local levels."[97] In the Self-Government Guidance Board, of course, the Guandong Army had decidedly negative views about the ruling and self-governing capabilities of the Chinese. Under such circumstances, there was scarcely any room for Tachibana's conception of peasant self-governance and a decentralized, self-governing state to find acceptance. Already a gap had developed between the organization of the Self-Government Guidance Board and the understanding of its function. Tachibana sought three characteristics in the Self-Government Guidance Board: 1) it not be something created by certain specified individuals or organs; 2) it not be something created on the basis of some sort of rational procedures; and 3) it be formed naturally and spontaneously based on the demands of the people who participated at the time in the movement to create the state.[98] This was clearly a factual misunderstanding. Perhaps Tachibana was unaware of the situation at hand, but he may have erred in where he sought to begin, going on to make common cause with people he should not have and reading completely different meanings and content into the same words. The opportunity in later years to crush the cooperative movement set in motion by men such as Satō Daishirō (1909–43), one of Tachibana's intellectual successors, as an anti-establishment movement had already sprouted by this time.

Be that as it may, even with this discordance, the principles of guidance in the establishment of the new state, with the Self-Government Guidance Board as one of its bases, were set into place, and an appeal went out for the participation of the Chinese masses in the state-building movement.

In January 1932 the Self-Government Guidance Board issued an Announcement to the Thirty Million People of the Four Provinces of the Northeast[99] which raised the slogans "Eradicate All the Agencies of Exploitation," "Down with Zhang Xueliang and His Running Dog Warlords," "Advance Industrial Communications by Reforming Production and Marketing Structures, in Particular a Cooperative Movement in the Villages," and "Impartiality, Correct Racial Prejudice." It appealed as follows:

Brethren of the Northeast!
The time has come for us all to be roused. . . . Brethren of the Northeast, shall we not rise as one and rush to complete the new state based on the spirit of self-government? Shall we not boldly push ahead toward a great harmony for mankind?
Elders and youngsters of the Northeast!
Before the many difficulties which await us in future, we shall complete our epochal heavenly task and advance along the sole path of selflessness, aimed at the establishment of universal justice.
Elders of the Northeast!
Working together in unity, let us rid ourselves of all the evil ways of the past and press on with the construction of an ideal realm.
Toward solidarity of all the people of the Northeast!
Toward the construction of a new state!
Toward the firm establishment of the spirit of self-governance! Make haste!

The Self-Government Guidance Board dispatched throughout Manchuria local offices for the movement to support state-building which incorporated self-government training sites and developed in each province a mass movement for the promotion of the establishment of Manzhouguo. On February 29, when the Lytton Commission arrived in Tokyo, an all-Manchuria congress for the promotion of state-building with some 700 delegates from all provinces and all ethnicities was convened in Fengtian. It issued a proclamation to establish a new state, "install a head of state, and advance the happiness of the populace based on the principles of good government and the Kingly Way."[100] It also unanimously approved an urgent motion to install Puyi as head of state.

The day for the founding of the state of Manzhouguo was close at hand.

Chapter Three
Toward a Model of Politics for the World:
The Banner of Moral State Creation and the Formation of Manzhouguo Politics

On March 1, 1932 the government of Manzhouguo, comprising primarily the four provinces of Fengtian, Jilin, Heilongjiang, and Rehe (actually, Rehe Province was not formally established until May 1933), issued a State-Founding Proclamation, named its reign period as Datong (great harmony), and announced that its flag would be a new five-colored design. On March 9, Puyi took up his post as chief executive—in the form of repeatedly accepting the offer of installation in that post by the thirty million people of the Northeast—and that very day laws were promulgated on the government's structure as well as on its bureaucracy and the protection of human rights. The leadership personnel of the government were also decided upon. On March 12 a diplomatic notice in the name of Xie Jieshi (b. 1878), minister of foreign affairs, seeking recognition for the new state was issued to seventeen countries around the world. On March 14 Changchun, which had been designated as the capital, was renamed Xinjing ("new capital," Japanese Shinkyō), and Manzhouguo made its debut for the first time.

Together with the founding of the state, large gatherings celebrating this event were held in all the cities. In cities like Xinjing and Fengtian, long celebratory processions mobilized by the Self-Government Guidance Board meandered through the streets, while streetcar floats and propaganda squads of automobiles sallied forth, and such slogans as "Paradise of the Kingly Way," "Coexistence and Coprosperity," and "Harmony of the Five Peoples" were in abundance. Contrary to the success of this parade and the profusion of slogans, however, by pushing through the founding of Manzhouguo and making it a fait accompli prior to the arrival of the Lytton Commission sent by the League of Nations, Japan only deepened its confrontation with China and drove itself down the narrow defile of isolation in the international community.

Founded under these international conditions, Manzhouguo was highly conscious of the fact that international eyes were upon it, while it proclaimed the goal of building a moral state and decided upon national institutions. The men in charge were looking for a form of rulership that would effectively protect the aims originally planned for by Japan. Because of its origins, though, Manzhouguo was saddled with limitations. It had taken form after separating from the Republic of China; on the one hand, it thus stressed a qualitatively different nature and discontinuity with the Republic of China, while on the other it accepted the political institutions and legal ideas of the Republic of China. In the end, it had to firm up an identity of its own in opposition to the Republic.

In addition to its relationship vis-à-vis the Republic of China, the political orientations, interests, and ulterior motives of a variety of men in Manzhouguo—local forces in the Chinese Northeast, the Qing revival clique, Mongol princes, and, of course, the Guandong Army and Japanese in Manchuria—were complexly entangled, and this cast a huge shadow over the ideals of state and forms of political structure and rulership.

The Motivation for Founding a State and Righteous Assistance

From days of old, Manchuria-Mongolia formed a separate country (*ikkoku*) of its own. Now, given the exigencies of the times, it must plan for its own establishment as such. It thus announces on this very day with the will of thirty million people that it severs contact with the Republic of China and inaugurates the state of Manzhouguo.[1]

With this State-Founding Proclamation, Manzhouguo set out on the road of independence as a nation. There are differences of opinion on whether Manchuria-Mongolia had originally constituted a separate country, or whether the times urgently necessitated its founding as a state; and whether Manzhouguo was founded with the will of thirty million people is certainly doubtful. However, on the basis of these assumptions, Manzhouguo seceded from the sovereignty of the Republic of China and appealed for recognition of its independence as a sovereign state. Yet, "severing contacts" and forming a state were not at all meant to imply that the two nations would continue to exist without relations between them. To convince its people that they were a "citizenry," Manzhouguo had perforce in its expression of state-building motives and ideals to emphasize its heterogeneity and fundamental difference from the Republic of China. In addition, because of the need to gain international recognition and to preserve Japan's vested interests, Manzhouguo could not deny state succession with the Republic of China. This contradictory stance of continuity and discontinuity with China was a characteristic of Manzhouguo from its birth, and these factors also surely contributed to the nature of the founding ideals and institutions of the state of Manzhouguo.

Needless to say, the business of founding a new state and doing so with the strength of ordinary men are extremely difficult. The reason for this may be that thinkers, ancient and modern, East and West, who have depicted the ideal government and society as a crystallization of their own political thought and have gambled their souls on the creation of an ideal state, have assumed that the state founders and lawmakers will combine knowledge and morality to an extent hitherto unknown among human beings in carrying out the task of founding the state.

Take, for example, the cases of Plato's *Laws*, Machiavelli's *Discourses*, Montesquieu's *Considérations sur les causes de la grandeur des Romains et de leur décadence*, or Rousseau's *Social Contract*. The state founders and lawmakers in these instances are imagined to possess characters similar to deities capable of carrying out a revolution among human beings.

Indeed, creating a new state can only ultimately be done, it would seem, by transforming the consciousness of the people living there, and to transform human consciousness requires ideals and an ideology with extraordinary magnetic attraction. The nuances of the composition of the state and its founding ideals are never actually drawn with a free hand. Even the founding fathers of the United States—Thomas Jefferson and James Madison, among others—who faced the difficult task of founding a state with sufficient courage to make the United States into an ideal republic, "the first new nation," had no choice but to advance state formation on a bundle of compromises amid their disputes surrounding antagonism for Great Britain, hostility among the states, and selection of a structure for the state.

Furthermore, there was certainly no reason to expect that the founding of Manzhouguo, which had been advanced through bloodshed, terror, and the self-interested actions of the Guandong Army's military occupation, might proceed by freely drawing up a conception of an ideal state on a pure white canvas. More than anything else, the image that this state was to assume was greatly restricted by the fact that it was to be a new independent state in northeast China which was then under the sovereignty of the Republic of China.

What necessitated Manzhouguo's birth? What could have been the raison d'être of Manzhouguo as a state? Insofar as a justification for it could not be asserted, if it were not certified as an independent state, then it would be impossible to supply the support of a "citizenry." And, without a basis for legitimacy, one would be hard-pressed to refute international criticism that it was a "puppet state" or a "bogus state." It was conceivable that Manzhouguo might scowl at the political trends in China and the world, while it could boast that its unprecedented state-founding ideals and governmental structure far outdid preexisting ones and had no equal. For example, at the very beginning of a text entitled *Senden no kenkyū* (A study of propaganda), published by the Public Relations Desk at the General Affairs Department of the State Council of Manzhouguo, the state is extolled for its superior qualities as a state in the following manner:

Our Manzhouguo is a newly arisen state rooted in the collective will of its thirty million people and born to implement a government of the Kingly Way based on the great principle of following the way of heaven and bringing peace to the people, to embody ethnic harmony, and to advance in perpetuity the welfare of humanity. The ideology and spirit of state-building in Manzhouguo are loftier than have ever before been seen in world history. . . . The emergence of Manzhouguo is a phenomenon which introduces a new model of morality, the freshest of political forms in the world, and the world's political scientists will have to develop a new political theory for Manzhouguo.[2]

Was the emergence of Manzhouguo in fact sufficiently unique to necessitate coming up with an original theory of politics? Did its political form offer a moral model, the freshest in the world? Also, at a symposium for both Chinese and Japanese held on the eve of the establishment of Manzhouguo, Etō Toshio (1883–1953), head of the Fengtian Library, made reference to the founding of the United States of America and noted that these founders, too, had had to express an "earnest dream" and a "sincere idealism" that were indispensable to state-formation. In any event, with a variety of these statements expressed at the time of state-founding, it was argued that the present establishment of the state of Manzhouguo embodied the pursuit of an ideal, a moral state. It was this state-founding ideal that indicated in a straightforward way how Manzhouguo envisioned itself and its own internal logic. Following that logic is crucial to an analysis of Manzhouguo.

Three documents expressed in microcosm the founding ideals of Manzhouguo: the State-Founding Proclamation of March 1, 1932; the Administrative Proclamation of March 9, and the Announcement to Foreign Nations on the Founding of the State of March 12. Taken as a whole these three documents may be read as forming a structure. The first one raises the necessity of state-formation through a critique of the warlords in the Northeast and the Nationalist government—namely, why Manzhouguo had to be founded; by contrast, the second one raises the legitimacy by which Manzhouguo was created as the ideal for state-founding; and thus the third one announces what position the state of Manzhouguo, now founded, had in the world.

In concrete terms, the Manzhouguo founders rejected the abusive rule of the warlords who as ringleaders over the twenty years following the 1911 Revolution had caused great misery for the thirty million people of the northeast. These militarists enjoyed fighting, lived in extraordinary luxury, were addicted to pleasure-seeking, and cared not a whit about ordinary people's lives, assiduously planning only to maximize their own personal gain. The monetary system was in thorough disarray, numerous industries has been closed down, public morality had gone to the dogs, and bandits ran rampant committing robbery and murder everywhere: the roads were strewn with corpses. Furthermore, their xenophobia had led them to lose trust on the foreign front. While the thirty million residents of Manchuria-Mongolia lived under the violent and unjust control of warlords, they had no alternative but to sit and await their deaths. They lived their lives with the sole wish of escaping these dire straits. Now, though, their time had come:

Now, what great good fortune! With help from neighboring forces [the Japanese military], all at once we shall force out the brutal, inhuman beasts, where for many years warlords arrogantly occupied the land and where misgovernment coalesced [i.e., land on which warlords had for many years remained fixed and perpetuated abusive rule]. Heaven has now given us thirty million people of Manchuria-Mongolia a prime opportunity for revival.[3]

In a word, with the righteous assistance of the Japanese military no longer able to sit by idly, they would drive out the warlords—namely, the Zhang Xueliang regime—and thus there would eventually be hope that people could live on the good earth in tranquillity and comfort. This, in sum, was to be the great opportunity provided by heaven.

In this manner legitimation for founding the state of Manzhouguo and for the Japanese military's participation in it were planned—by depicting the lives of the people under Zhang Xueliang's regime as utterly wretched, the populace yearning only for escape from the covetous and tyrannical evil hands of warlords, and the Japanese military—namely, the Guandong Army—unable to simply sit by and watch but, with the "friendship of a good neighbor," having no choice morally but to stretch out a helping hand and offer "righteous assistance." Contained in this construction was the idea that the warlords ruled in the way of despots or hegemons, and by contrast Manzhouguo was to be a government rooted in the Kingly Way. It reveals as well a kind of self-assurance that afforded the Guandong Army the role of an army of liberation, a savior. To be sure, under warlord rule expenditures on warfare had reached ninety percent of the local budget, and the overissue of currency had wrought havoc with finances and the currency system. However, one must not forget that it was Japan's Manchuria-Mongolia policy that had earnestly sought to use warlords such as Zhang Zuolin to expand its interests. Also, Japan was not alone in equating warlords with premodern mountain bandits and robbers, as the Lytton Commission and others shared this commonly-held notion. Undeniably as well the development of industry and the promotion of education were central goals of the Zhang Xueliang regime. As an ally of Jiang Jieshi, Zhang refused to hold on to his own territorial ground and sought to form a modern Chinese national state by integrating northeast regionalism with Chinese nationalism. Certainly, as pointed out by Yanaihara Tadao

(1893–1961), "even with the great expansion of military expenses under the northeast regime [of Zhang Xueliang], there was a prime opportunity to link up with the development of Chinese nationalism in Manchuria."[4]

Precisely because this connection was so clear, the brunt of the attack in the State-Founding Proclamation changed completely. Now, it was claimed that sweeping the Zhang Xueliang regime out and boldly seceding from the control of the Republic of China, which aimed at one-party rule under the Nationalist government and the Three Principles of the People—comprising people's livelihood, people's rights, and nationalism—were necessary to secure the good fortune of Manchuria-Mongolia's thirty million people.

One party despotically holds the government in its clutches. What does people's livelihood mean to it? In fact, it means death. What do people's rights mean? It means maximizing profits and nothing else. What does nationalism mean? It means just the party. It has been said that all under heaven belongs to the populace. It has also been said that the party rules the state. These are contradictory. They fool oneself and they fool others. No swindle can endure hard questioning.[5]

The Guomindang was indeed advocating the principle of people's rights and "all under heaven belongs to the populace," namely, that the source of political rights lay in the people. By the same token, this poition did contradict the one-party state structure run by a group of elites, what was called "political tutelage" (*xunzheng*)—namely, the idea that the citizenry were like small children politically and, with education and training by the Guomindang, they would mature and be able to enjoy the rights, such as the franchise, of a citizenry—and "ruling the state with the party" (*yidang zhiguo*), namely, ruling the Chinese state with the Guomindang alone. However, when Manzhouguo, rejecting the parliamentary form of government and not allowing even the existence of political parties, tried to criticize the Chinese political system because "the people's anger was seething for they are sick at heart with the evil of the political form of their government,"[6] this backfired. Also, the attack on each of the Three Principles of the People was not necessarily a counterattack corresponding to the content of their original meaning. Should the Guomindang's rule become even more tyrannical, the Three Principles of the People further contradict the ideals on which they were originally based, and the people's hearts become even more alienated, then there would surely have been no particular need to rebuke them. In spite of this, the reason that the refutation of the Three Principles of the People became so inflamed was that they were perceived as a threat undermining the very existence of Manzhouguo.

The Three Principles of the People were not simply ideas of the distant past belonging to Sun Zhongshan, but they had gradually penetrated the various strata of the Chinese populace in the process of the Nationalist government's national unification and had come to be understood as a symbolic representation of the aspirations of the Chinese people's future existence. The expression "the Three Principles of the People are principles to save the nation" indicates the expectations they embraced. Three Principles of the People textbooks functioned as teaching guides in the anti-Japanese movement. For this reason, on several occasions after the founding of the state of Manzhouguo, the government ordered the complete abolition of texts concerned with the Three Principles of the People and became desperate to "eradicate" mention of them.

For Manzhouguo itself to gain recognition and legitimacy and for its continued existence as a state, it recognized an urgent need to offer political ideals that would have sufficient force to be rid of and outdo the Three Principles of the People and all the beliefs upon which the Guomindang based itself. The Manzhouguo government also saw that it had to possess a persuasive power to overcome lingering suspicions of its new state harbored by the people of China in their heart of hearts. Its state-founding ideals included following the way of heaven and bringing peace to the people, democracy (lit., the principle of people as the basis of the state; Chinese *minbenzhuyi*; Japanese *minponshugi*), ethnic harmony, and the principle of the Kingly Way.

The Paradise of the Kingly Way: Following the Way of Heaven, Bringing Peace to the People, and Harmony of the Five Peoples

As concerned the principles of following the way of heaven, bringing peace to the people, and democracy, the State-Founding Proclamation of Manzhouguo stipulated that "Government will be based on the Way, and the Way is rooted in heaven. The principle for the creation of the new state is uniformly to lay emphasis on following the way of heaven and bringing peace to the people. The administration of government must follow the true will of the people and not allow for the willful views of personal opinion."[7] This proclamation was set against the crushing taxes imposed by warlords and the Nationalist government's system of party rule both of which ignored popular will and harmed the tranquility of people's lives. In content, it seems clearly to have been aimed at balancing the idea of all under heaven belonging to the public with the principle of popular rights and people's livelihood from the Three Principles of the People. The Announcement to Foreign Nations described a pitiful situation in which the Northeastern warlords "care nothing for the welfare of the populace and plan only for their own personal gain . . . causing the populace to fall into an extremely sad state of affairs." It went on to depict the political conditions of the Republic of China as having "loosed butchery on their compatriots for many years with the ravages of war and not allowed a time for there to be peace for the people's livelihood to thrive." By contrast, the government of Manzhouguo "would exert all of its energies to perfect legal institutions and thereby guarantee popular tranquility and advance their welfare."[8]

On the principle of ethnic harmony, the State-Founding Proclamation stated:

As a whole, the people who now reside on the terrain of the new state make no distinctions among races or between superiors and inferiors. In addition to the Han, Manchu, and Mongolian peoples who were originally from this region and the Japanese and Koreans—that is, people from other lands—those who wish to reside here in perpetuity shall enjoy equal treatment. The rights they receive shall be protected and shall not be violated in the least.[9]

This is the basis for the principle of ethnic harmony or the harmony of the five peoples whereby the Han, Manchu, Mongol, Japanese, and Korean ethnic groups would plan for coexistence and coprosperity all together and equally. We have already touched on how this concept of ethnic harmony was incorporated into the ideals of Manzhouguo's original founding. The concept, though, had another side to it, in that it took shape in confrontation with the principles of nationalism from the Three Principles of the People and the doctrine of national self-determination which aimed at equality among the peoples living in China and independence from imperialist oppression. Thus, the design to quietly eradicate a distinct national or ethnic consciousness which had become the root of anti-Japanese feeling was, needless to say, involved in the Japanese plan for Manzhouguo. Furthermore, having accomplished the Revolution of 1911 as a racial, anti-Manchu revolution with the principle of Chinese nationalism, Sun Zhongshan put forward the slogan of a republic of the five peoples (ethnicities) in order to create a firm foundation for republican government with representatives of the Han, Manchu, Mongol, Muslim, and Tibetan ethnicities. The republic of five peoples was certainly conscious of this effort. The idea of racial or ethnic equality—"no distinctions among races or between superiors and inferiors"—and impartiality had appeared already in the text of article five of the provisional constitution of the Republic of China (dated March 1912): "The people of the Republic of China are all equal. There is no discrimination based on race, class, or religion." Thereafter, this was to become the basis for national integration in the multiethnic state of China.

Be that as it may, the principle of the Kingly Way, it was claimed, was a comprehensive concept based primarily on following the way of heaven and bringing peace to the people, democracy, and ethnic harmony; it was seen as a new approach as Manzhouguo emerged in the chaotic face of contemporary world politics. Following the way of heaven and bringing peace to the people, democracy, and ethnic harmony bore significance as each was to be the antithesis of one of the Three Principles of the People. Thus, one can easily see that the principle of the Kingly Way was used as a countermeasure against the Three Principles as well as against the Nationalist government and Republic of China which were dedicated to them.

As one critic argued: "The significance of the founding of Manzhouguo has many aspects, but the fact that it has given genuine substance to government based on the Kingly Way as an important objective for statefounding is something which this writer understands as a kind of *object lesson* or the setting of an example to the Republic of China. I believe it is most appropriate to attach ethical significance to the founding of Manzhouguo."[10] This was by no means a unique or idiosyncratic argument, for one can find many essays of the time that took similar lines of attack.

By the same token, though, the State-Founding Proclamation asserted: "In implementing the principle of the Kingly Way, we enable all the peoples within the borders to ascend the spring dais in great splendor [namely, rule will be peaceful and beneficent]. Protecting the eternal honor of East Asia, we are about to create a model for the governments of the world."[11] Thus, the text was energetically propagandizing the fact that not only did the significance of the founding of the state of Manzhouguo bring an ideal realm of peace and happiness to the thirty million inhabitants of Manchuria-Mongolia, but it broke through the impasse reached by Western governments with a spirit of East Asian political morality and offered a model state altogether new in human history. The Administrative Proclamation claimed, in a similar vein: "Humanity must lay emphasis on benevolence, but in the event of international struggle one inflicts loss on others and gain for oneself. Benevolence, however, is weak. We have now founded a state and based it principally on morality and benevolence, and we shall eliminate racial and international struggle. The paradise of the Kingly Way should be seen as set on implementing these goals."[12] Hence, by creating a moral state based on benevolence, the Manzhouguo founders aspired to contribute toward effecting a world in which there would be no wars between peoples or states. Ikeda Hideo (1880–1954) wrote of this Administrative Proclamation: "It declares the materialization of the Kingly Way of the past 4,000 years. What is this if not the glad tidings emitting a magnificent brilliance to a world deadlocked by the hegemonic policies of the Western imperialists?"[13] He was certainly not sparing in his praise for Manzhouguo as the entity that would break through this impasse with high ideals replacing the domination of Western imperialism.

In addition to advocating the world-historical significance of this event, the Administrative Proclamation pledged that rooted in the principles of founding a moral state was esteem for international good faith, an open door policy, equality of opportunity, extraterritoriality, and the assumption of debts from the Republic of China. "Looking forward to friendship in diplomacy and wishing to contribute to world peace," the founders of Manzhouguo sought recognition from the countries of the world.

In this way, the founding principles of Manzhouguo concealed all manner of intentions and was depicted with all manner of expressions, such as implementing the principles of the Kingly Way and realizing a paradise of the Kingly Way. These were appealed to as reformist political principles which Manzhouguo established. However, rather than forging a new departure through a probing of the parameters of international politics, these principles were offered as a countermeasure in opposition to Chinese political forces and their political positions. The shadow of the Republic of China was profoundly cast over these ideals of Manzhouguo's founding. Also, by denigrating the Zhang Xueliang regime and the Guomindang far more than was warranted and by lauding themselves, these principles were clearly no more than political propaganda, ideology to legitimize the establishment of the state of Manzhouguo.

Nonetheless, whatever designs these state-founding principles may have been rooted in at the time, many people did understand the founding of the state with its banner of morality raised high as the point of arrival reached. Indeed, there were many who took the initial state-founding ideals as a "sincere dream," and died for the cause, scattering to the wildernesses of the north. It is undeniable that for them, whatever backgrounds and reasons they may have had, these were ideals worth risking one's life for. If the founding documents of Manzhouguo had actually been carried out, then this might have led to the firm conviction, as Hirashima Toshio, one of the leaders of the Manchurian Youth League, put it concerning the establishment of the state of Manzhouguo: "In political science and political philosophy as well, it is tantamount to the third revolution—following the revolution for liberty and the revolution for equality [the communist revolution]—a moral revolution based upon fraternity which cannot be worked out with liberty and equality."[14] As Katakura Tadashi noted, "one can say of the founding of the state of Manzhouguo that it was a revolution based on the Kingly Way,"[15] and we should probably not reject this as specious reasoning.

What the actual reality of "fraternity" and the "Kingly Way" was and how it would be realized, however, remained extremely abstract and vague in the state-founding documents. Perhaps, to the extent that it was abstract and vague, each person could respond sympathetically by weaving his own dreams and ideals and imposing images onto it. Although the concept of the Kingly Way was closely tied to the founding of Manzhouguo and enthusiastically spoken of by commentators, it was effectively the case, as verbal symbols go, that they seemingly shared ideas although each really differed from the next: same bed, different dreams. By the same token, that many Japanese in Manzhouguo advocated a government based on the Kingly Way was not unrelated to the fact that Japanese understanding of Chinese political thought tended toward concepts and was was much less concerned with real developments and real historical processes. The Kingly Way as advanced by Kaneko Sessai (1908–82) and Matsuzaki Tsuruo

(1867–1949), who were political thinkers on the mainland with considerable influence over the Japanese population in Manchuria, and Kanesaki Ken, a reporter for the *Manshū nichinichi shinbun* (Manchuria Daily News), was ultimately just a political philosophy used as a conceptual device to oppose tyranny, taking Chinese realities into account not at all. Among specialists on China, by contrast, there were strong misgivings expressed about proffering the idea of the Kingly Way without concrete policy measures laid out for the founding of the state of Manzhouguo.

For example, as mentioned above, Tachibana called for the Kingly Way as a form of self-government. In his essay, "Tairiku seisaku jūnen no tantō" (An examination of ten years of mainland policies), he urged Ishiwara Kanji that, if he were to use the Kingly Way as an ideal for the founding of Manzhouguo, the Chinese would understand his efforts, which would be expedient.[16] Tachibana is accepted now as an advocate of establishing a state based on the Kingly Way. However, in an article introducing Manzhouguo which Tachibana wrote and directed at the Japanese people just after the founding of the state, he wrote of the Kingly Way: "If we treat this concept as a practical guiding direction for politics, scholars of history will become tormented by a confusion of different theories, and politicians will be forced to taste the bitter cup of defeat. What sort of prospects for success are there in the minds of politicians who casually take up such a vexing issue and daringly proclaim it to be the guiding direction for management of the new state."[17] He was expressing a fear that they would simply use this idea of the Kingly Way without any accompanying content.

The great authority in the field of China studies, Naitō Konan (1866–1934), also indicated suspicions about using the Kingly Way as an ideal for state-founding:

The "Kingly Way" has frequently been appealed to as an ideal for state-founding. There is no difference of opinion among people that on the surface the two Chinese characters of the "Kingly Way" (Chinese *wangdao*, Japanese *ōdō*) are perfectly fine. However, it is much more difficult to explain with any clarity what their actual content is. In fact, even in China itself where the two-character expression "Kingly Way" was born, there is scarcely a period throughout history when the term was actually used. Thus, from antiquity on, it has been no more than a moral precept conveying an ideal. Furthermore, this ideal itself is perfectly fine and there is no difference of opinion on this, but many times in history we have seen how results contrary to the ideals are produced based upon the vagaries of those who implement them.[18]

Did the politicians of Manzhouguo, as Tachibana feared they would, taste that bitter cup by proffering the "Kingly Way" in a casual manner? Or, was it as Naitō Konan worried that they brought about results contrary to the very ideals themselves? Furthermore, did it become a "model of politics for the world" as the State-Founding Proclamation expressly stated? Whatever eventuality, there was no small irony in the fact that the state born of the military might of the Guandong Army would take as its founding ideal not the way of the hegemon but that of the Kingly Way.

Nonetheless, Manzhouguo emerged calling for the realization of an ideal realm on earth and a paradise of the Kingly Way in which humanity would live in peace: on one level it relied on exaggerated ideals and wishes to which were attached the significance of the third revolution of world history; while on another level it was greeted with simple embellishments and hyperbolic delusions, while expectations for it were tied to the final glory bequeathed in the shadows of Guandong Army control, and on a third level it brought with it immense fears.

The man who put an end to his retirement to shoulder responsibility for this government based on the Kingly Way was none other than Puyi, the last emperor of the Qing dynasty. Puyi, though, did not receive the mandate of heaven and take up the position of emperor in the state of the Kingly Way so as to effect the principles of following the way of heaven and bringing peace to the people. Why would the deposed Emperor Puyi be welcomed as head of state of Manzhouguo? Crowing as they did about a state based on the Kingly Way and citing the phrase from the *Yijing* (Classic of Changes) that, "He who protects the people is called the King," why was the head of state not made "king" or emperor?

The shadow cast by the Republic of China was becoming darker and darker.

The Dragon Goes Home: A Dream of Restoration

Manchuria—namely, the northeastern part of present-day China—was known as the land of the rising dragon of the great Qing, because its founder Nurhaci (1559–1626) rose from being a local chieftain of the Jurchen people to conquer the entire terrain and solidify a basis for the Qing dynasty (1644–1911). At 3:00 p.m. on March 8, 1932, Puyi, the former Xuantong Emperor, tenth in line in the Qing dynasty following the Manchus' conquest of China proper, got off the train at the station in the Manzhouguo capital of Changchun as the chief executive of the new state of Manzhouguo. Six days later, on March 14, the city would be renamed Xinjing, meaning "new capital."

Even before the train had stopped, I could hear the sounds of military music and the cheers of people on the platform. In the procession there were people wearing the Chinese-style long gowns and military jackets as well as those in Western attire, while others wore Japanese-style dress, all with small flags in their hands. I was filled with a sense of deep emotion. . . . As I walked before the line-up, Xi Xia pointed out without warning some yellow dragon flags amid the Japanese ones: "They are all former bannermen. For twenty years they have anxiously awaited a chance to see your majesty." Hearing these words, I could not repress the warm tears that welled up in my eyes, and my feeling of hopelessness grew ever stronger.[19]

Puyi had ascended the throne in 1908 at the tender age of two (three by Chinese reckoning) and abdicated it several years later when the 1911 Revolution brought about the founding of the Republic of China in 1912. Under the Conditions for the Preferential Treatment of the Imperial Household he had received an emperor's honorary title and pension, and for a brief space of time he had enjoyed a comeback (the so-called Dingsi [1917] Restoration) during warlord Zhang Xun's (1858–1923) occupation of Beijing in 1917. In 1924 warlord Feng Yuxiang (1882–1948) had all of his special privileges removed, and Puyi thereafter spent his days despondently under Japanese protection. Born into the imperial family and later deposed, Puyi found it difficult to suppress thoughts of imperial restoration. He retained a burning desire to return to the throne of the Qing dynasty, and when he finally understood that this would be impossible, he entertained the idea of escaping overseas to live freely. But, when he realized that this, of course, was not to be allowed, he continued to harbor only one implacable wish: to revive the Qing by any means necessary. Because he lacked the might needed to do this openly, though, his desire for the throne burned within him. For Puyi all that mattered was "a restoration of the motherland" and "a return to glory," and all speculation derived from these ends and converged on them.

An imperial welcoming party of former Manchu officials raising yellow dragon banners, the flag of the Qing dynasty, and kneeling before him awaited Puyi as he returned to the land of his ancestors as the chief executive of the new state. One can easily imagine that this sight caused Puyi to stifle tears of gratitude and made his body quiver with an excitement he had heretofore not felt. However, were the ultimate means to realize Puyi's great wish engaged: to become emperor of Manzhouguo, to subjugate China south of the Great Wall with that authority, to reenter the Forbidden City in Beijing, and to be the emperor of a "Later Qing" dynasty? Was Manzhouguo presented to Puyi as a steppingstone to this end?

The decision to appoint Puyi chief executive of the new state on September 23, 1931 has the impression of abruptness about it, taking place as the Guandong Army moved from its position of occupying Manchuria-Mongolia to conceiving of an independent state. One direct reason prompting this decision was the proposal of Major General Tatekawa Yoshitsugu from Army Central who, contrary to the commanding officer and staff officers of the Guandong Army, suggested on September 20 that "it would be a good idea to destroy the present regime in the northeast and establish a government with the Xuantong Emperor as leader and with support from Japan."[20] Itagaki, Ishiwara, and the other staff officers of the Guandong Army, who had thought only of occupying Manchuria-Mongolia and were not prepared with concrete plans for an independent regime or an independent state, had to hastily throw together policy ideas in the form they were received and plan for a unity of purpose with Army Central. However, behind the decision which superficially appears to have been a compromise on the part of the Guandong Army, negotiations between it, the Xuantong Emperor's group, and the Japanese Army undeniably played a major role from early on.

It is well known today that on two earlier occasions, in 1912 and in 1914–15, schemes were advanced to forge ties with the royalist party aimed at a restoration of the Qing dynasty, separation and independence for Manchuria-Mongolia, and establishment of a Manchurian-Mongolian kingdom with strong Japanese influence brought to bear. Army soldiers acting in concert with nongovernment people such as the adventurer Kawashima Naniwa (1865–1949) were deeply involved in the movement for an independent Manchuria-Mongolia. Koiso Kuniaki, who as Guandong Army chief of staff would later push for an imperial form of government in Manzhouguo, was one of them, although the connection between the Japanese Army and the party of the Xuantong Emperor gradually became estranged as the Japanese government switched directions and offered aid to Zhang Zuolin and moved to hasten the secession of Manchuria-Mongolia. The influence of the Xuantong Emperor's group on the Japanese military, however, was never completely severed.

In August and September 1927, Zheng Xiaoxu, Puyi's attendant, visited Japan to engage in some maneuvering with the Japanese, and he met with such important political and military figures as Konoe Fumimaro (1891–1945), Ugaki Kazushige, Yonai Mitsumasa (1880–1948), Suzuki Kantarō (1867–1948), Minami Jirō (1874–1955), Hiranuma Kiichirō (1865–1952), and Kiyoura Keigo (1850–1942), among others, to discuss the restoration of Puyi to the throne. He had the feeling, he claimed, that should the opportunity present itself, they would offer active support. Again, in August 1929, a secret emissary from Puyi paid a visit to the office of Kōmoto Daisaku (1883–1953) and conveyed the former's desire to be restored to the throne in Manchuria. Kōmoto immediately called on Koiso Kuniaki, head of the military affairs bureau, to test the waters about the possibility of making Puyi sovereign of the Three Eastern Provinces. Koiso agreed: "For the Xuantong Emperor, Manchuria is the original terrain of the Qing dynasty. Because this land has been usurped by warlords, it is only natural that it revert to the Aisin Gioro. Should the Xuantong Emperor be returned to the throne in Manchuria, we can come up with the theoretical underpinnings not to allow bothersome international relations to interfere."[21] Having heard this, Kōmoto made arrangements with staff officers Itagaki and Ishiwara in Lüshun to meet with Luo Zhenyu (1866–1940), Zheng Xiaoxu, and others at a later date. He persuaded them to find an agreeable spot and await an opportune moment. When the general contours of this meetings were reported to Itagaki and Ishiwara, Ishiwara allegedly betrayed a smile of satisfaction, saying: "Perfect window-dressing."[22] There is certainly ample reason to suspect the veracity of these actions by

Kōmoto and these words of Koiso and Ishiwara, and from then until the Manchurian Incident the influence of the Xuantong Emperor on the Guandong Army became extraordinarily vigorous.

Luo Zhenyu, the former official of Puyi who had once plotted a restoration of the Qing dynasty by taking advantage of the bombing death of Zhang Zuolin, went to visit Xi Xia in Jilin in the spring of 1931. Xi Xia, a member of the Aisin Gioro clan, was a descendant of Murhaci (1561–1620), a younger brother of founding Emperor Taizu (Nurhaci) of the Qing. He had graduated from the Japanese army academy and taken up a post as chief of staff to Zhang Zuoxiang, assistant commander in chief for security in the northeast and chairman of Jilin Province. Without a doubt, Xi Xia was extremely useful early on in working in concert with the Guandong Army, which was pursuing the construction of a new state in the form of a federation of self-governing provinces. Xi Xia had his own personal ambitions for political ascent through a Qing restoration, and Luo Zhenyu shared his views about returning Puyi to the throne. On a number of occasions, Luo negotiated with the commanding officer of the Guandong Army, claiming that because of the close ties between the Three Eastern Provinces and Japan, an imperial restoration would be difficult without the understanding of the Guandong Army (which Luo dubbed the "armed forces of our ally"). He repeatedly offered the argument that, in planning for peace in East Asia, there had to be Sino-Japanese cooperation, that it should commence with stability in the Three Eastern Provinces, and the best route for there to be peace in the Three Eastern Provinces was for the Xuantong Emperor himself to acquire popularity. When the Manchurian Incident occurred, Luo and Xi Xia urged the Guandong Army to appoint Puyi, and in the final analysis, Luo claimed, the army agreed.[23]

Thus, on September 22, when the Guandong Army decided to make use of Puyi, Luo Zhenyu was summoned by wire to Fengtian at Itagaki's behest, and after a meeting he joined forces with Xi Xia, Zhang Haipeng in Zhaonan, and others of the Xuantong Emperor's party to plan for the construction of a state. In addition to Xi Xia and Zhang Haipeng, the Guandong Army put forward the names of Tang Yulin, Yu Zhishan, and Zhang Jinghui as leaders of the independence movement. Surmising that "these men had been associated in the past with the party of the Xuantong Emperor and had contacts with the [Guandong] Army,"[24] the latter saw the group around the former emperor as the core of an oppositional force to Zhang Xueliang and from early on had opened lines of communication to them. On September 30, Itagaki sent Kamikado Toshikazu together with Luo Zhenyu to Puyi's headquarters to convey to him the news that he would be installed as chief executive of the new regime.

There are a number of possible reasons why did the Guandong Army set off on this venture of appointing Puyi. First, it decided that Puyi was a distinguished figure among the Manchu people and his reputation as the former emperor would insure his continued popularity as chief executive in the Northeast. Second, inasmuch as the Chinese northeast was the ancestral home of the Manchus, there was a strong possibility that, should he become head of state, international criticism could be averted. Third, Puyi harbored a ferocious antipathy for the Nationalist government, and it was decided that there was no worry at all that he might forge an alliance either with Jiang Jieshi or with Zhang Xueliang. Fourth, while he had the support of men such as Xi Xia and Zhang Haipeng, they could offer Puyi no real political clout, forcing him to rely on the Guandong Army. Fifth, in a state which took the form of a federation of self-governing provinces, should a powerful person from one province take control of the regime and give rise to opposition, it would lead to a rupture, and thus it seemed like a safe bet to turn one person like Puyi who had no firm base to speak of into a symbol and appoint him to a position of chief executive.

This is not, however, to suggest that Puyi was the one and only candidate for the new position as head of state. A movement to created a "glorious empire" centered around the person of Prince Gong (Puwei) was underway as well, and another plan to make a descendant of Confucius in Shandong Province the head of state was under investigation by the Guandong Army. Furthermore, there were active and ongoing machinations—led by the likes of Zhang Zongchang (1881–1932), Tang Shaoyi (1860–1938), and Wu Peifu (1874–1939), among others—to support Jin Bidong, seventh son of Prince Su (1866–1922), and thus create a pro-Japanese regime. Maneuverings of this sort reflected a consciousness unwilling to acknowledge all the political changes China had undergone in the previous twenty years since the 1911 Revolution by returning Puyi to the throne.

Of course, the Guandong Army never assumed that it had to make Puyi the chief executive. What the Guandong Army actually thought of Puyi can be seen in the following story. When Puyi was to flee from Tianjin, if by any chance he were discovered by the Chinese military and prevented from making good his escape, a gasoline drum had been taken on board ship with the pre-arranged plan to set the gasoline on fire and sink the living witness together with the ship. In fact, though, someone had to be made chief executive of this newly created, independent state, and the use value, even if only relative, of Puyi to the Guandong Army was, to say the least, extremely high.

The Guandong Army was only too eager for something else to result from luring Puyi out. This was linked to a scheme of the Guandong Army to have Inner Mongolia included as part of the territory of Manzhouguo. That is, various Mongolian princes had had close ties to the Qing court and resisted Han Chinese control. If Puyi, as a Manchu, could be used, the army expected that acquiring the support of the Mongols would be easy. Just as the Guandong Army expected, with Manchus and Mongols accepting the same sovereign, Guifu and Lingsheng of Khölön Buir and Chimedsempil of the Jirim League, among others, responded to this call. Ganjuurjab (who was for a time married to the notorious Kawashima Yoshiko [1906–1948]) and Jéngjuurjab, the orphaned sons of General Babujab, once the driving force behind a Mongolian-Manchurian independence movement, led a Mongolian Youth Party and were active in developing an Inner Mongolian independence movement and establishing a new state.[25] Thus, at a conference of representatives of the Mongolian banners on February 21, 1932, they decided to take part in the new state, issuing a manifesto which read in part:

We of the Mongolian people have historically been endowed with immeasurable glory and have long and profoundly felt the cruel treatment of misgovernment. . . . We of the Mongolian people now take this opportunity to pray for unity with the people of the northeast. We shall build an ideal state on the vast terrain of Manchuria-Mongolia and plan for the welfare of the populace by implementing good government. Our Mongolia, we vow with complete sincerity, shall support the installation of the Xuantong Emperor, and long may he reign without interruption.[26]

The Mongols, having faced ethnic dissension over nomadic territory due to Han immigration to the region they inhabited, were now joining in the construction of a new state which offered an ideal of ethnic coexistence on the condition that Puyi be installed as leader.

How is it that the idea of restoring the emperor held by former officials of the Qing dynasty as well as a portion of the Manchu and Mongolian peoples and Puyi himself could be so intensely felt? The number of Manchus at the core of this movement amounted to less than ten percent of the Han Chinese living in Manchuria and Mongolia, and many of them had been assimilated into the Han. In the case of Xi Xia of Jilin, his political base was highly fragile and vulnerable to attack by opposition forces under Ding Chao (b. 1883) and Li Du (1880–1956); and Zhang Haipeng's army numbered only some 2,000 men, had no battlefield experience, and "were extremely weak as fighters."[27] The Guandong Army could not, of course, completely sponsor the restorationists, and from the start the appointment of Puyi was not planned with the imperial system as a precondition. However, Puyi, who was pursuing only the dream of an imperial restoration, had no choice but to gamble on the Guandong Army, which hinted at the possibility of an imperial system of government.

In October 1931, when Puyi had already made up his mind to return to his ancestral land, he was visited by his former tutor Reginald Johnston (1874–1938) who had called him Henry in the Forbidden City. Johnston was looking for someone to write a favorable preface to his memoir, *Twilight in the Forbidden City*, which concerned Puyi. Promptly told by Puyi why he had left Tianjin, Johnston was elated as he firmly believed that Puyi would become the emperor of a new state, and he added a postscript to his work entitled "The Dragon Goes Home." In the following manner, he fore-saw Puyi's future:

The Dragon had come back to his old home.

... [H]e fled from the dearly-loved land of his birth, where he had been spurned, insulted, robbed and denounced as an alien, and returned to the old Manchurian home of his ancestors. . . .

Long ago a Chinese sage taught his countrymen this saying: *Ta nan pu ssū bi yu hou fu* [*danan busi bi you houfu*]: "He who emerges with his life from great perils will have a happy and prosperous future."

That the emperor has come successfully through great perils, no one will deny. . . . If the Chinese sage's words are true, his [i.e., the emperor's] future should indeed be prosperous and happy.[28]

Puyi was truly returning home with mixed feelings of love and hate for China. The reality awaiting Puyi there, however, was not the prosperous and happy one foreseen by Johnston. The position prepared for Puyi was not that of emperor, but the vague official post of chief executive over which the shadow of the detested Republic of China clung. Despite ardent sentiments—such as "If I cannot become emperor, what meaning is there to my life?"[29]—Puyi was not installed as emperor of the new state of Manzhouguo. For the time being, the dream of a restoration had utterly collapsed. The thought lifelessly recurred in the mind of a despondent Puyi: "Why have I traveled such a lengthy road to come to this place?"[30]

Why then was it that Puyi assumed the post of chief executive and not emperor?

The Chief Executive Recommends This to the Entire Populace

The fact that the Guandong Army had decided early on to appoint Puyi amplified opposition to its arbitrary actions, and it induced a loathing for Puyi himself. Even Ugaki Kazushige, governor-general of Korea, who was on amicable terms with the Guandong Army, noted in his diary for October 10, 1931: "Xuantong is a man of the past. We should also avoid making a warlord the head of state. If it is at all possible, I look forward to the es-tablishment of a new [political] force,"[31] by which he was implying one that was pro-Japanese but neither aristocratic nor militarist in background. Fur-thermore, those concerned about international opinion opposed help be-ing given to Puyi as a thoroughly anachronistic effort because it appeared to support revival of the Qing dynasty, and calls for the Guandong Army to act more prudently grew stronger. The navy rejected Puyi's recall from Tianjin, and Banzai Rihachirō (1870–1950), who was known as a promi-nent China expert even by the army, sounded the tocsin that there was a problem between the Japanese and Chinese in their respective evaluations of Puyi, and that the appointment of Puyi was based on superficial Japanese understanding of China.[32] In telegraphic instructions sent by Foreign Minister Shidehara to Consul-General Kuwajima Kazue (1884–1958) in Tianjin on November 1, 1931, he too indicated grave misgivings about the appointment of Puyi.

Considering the fact that at present the great majority of the residents of Manchuria are Han Chinese, assistance to the Xuantong Emperor will surely be unpopular even in Manchuria itself. All the more, the influence this will exert on China proper and the other countries of the world can amply be imagined under such catchphrases as counter-revolution and anti-democratic plot. As such, Sino-Japanese understanding will surely develop into an impossible state well into the distant future. In any event, our offering help to the Xuantong Emperor must be labeled a plan completely out of touch with the times. I believe that this may become the source of grave trouble for the empire's management of Manchuria-Mongolia in the future.[33]

These apprehensions on the part of Foreign Minister Shidehara were directly connected to the impending meeting of the Council of the League of Nations on November 16, and whatever motive lay behind Puyi's return from retirement, "we are planning an independent state in Manchuria . . . and once again we are" headed toward a scene of "indignation in world opinion."[34] Looking at the route that Manzhouguo would take thereafter, Shidehara's prescience hit the nail right on the head.

The anxiety elicited by the sudden enticement of Puyi was not limited to Shidehara, who had adopted a policy of not allowing the Manchurian Incident to spread, for it was rising as well at Army Central, which should have been apprised of the move to make Puyi chief executive. In spite of all this, the Guandong Army, out of necessity having created a *fait accompli* by the time the Council of the League of Nations convened on November 16, had Colonel Doihara Kenji of the Fengtian Special Services Unit concoct the "Tianjin Incident" and compel Puyi to escape from the city under martial law on November 10. On November 15, War Minister Minami Jirō cabled Guandong Army Commanding Officer Honjō Shigeru with instructions to the effect that, even if formal use of the notion of the will of the people of Manchuria-Mongolia were to be made, supporting Puyi "will cause the world to harbor suspicions concerning the intentions of the [Japanese] imperial army. . . . I fear that it will aggravate a seriously disadvantageous situation to the empire's policy with respect to the Powers. . . . Thus, for a time, whether Puyi is active or passive, we should like it that matters be guided in such a way that does in no way connect him to questions of the regime."[35] Self-control was being strongly urged.

Opposition arose not only in Japan, as we have seen, but also in Manchuria to the Guandong Army's implementation of a policy of assistance to Puyi. Zhang Jinghui, whom the Guandong Army had seen as aligned with the Xuantong Emperor, indicated his intention to resist aid to Puyi, and calls within the Fengtian militarist clique to support Zang Shiyi grew stronger. Furthermore, according to a report of a Japanese investigative group of the House of Peers to Manchuria and Korea, the situation was as follows: "The populace at large will not welcome the anachronism of the Xuantong Emperor. Even if an independent state is built with him as head of state, we believe that it will not be unified and will soon fall apart."[36] Among the Japanese in such groups as the Manchurian Youth League and the Majestic Peak Society, moreover, a fierce opposition arose. In their view, trotting out Puyi denied the hard fought achievements of the Chinese since the 1911 Revolution, was a foolish undertaking that rubbed people's nerves the wrong way, and wiped out the significance of the existence of the self-government guidance movement that they were promoting. To be sure, if they were to make the dubious argument that the establishment of a state in Manchuria was a spontaneous independence movement of the thirty million people living there in opposition to the Zhang Xueliang regime, then it made no sense to make Puyi, who was living in China, proper head of state. As Kanai Shōji and other argued, perhaps in opposing Zhang Xueliang it was appropriate to support someone like Yu Chonghan, who was an advocate of the principles of absolute protection of peace within the borders and security for the people.

Because of such clear as well as more tacit opposition to Puyi, there was another apprehension that the Guandong Army had to take into account. This was the fact that among the Chinese collaborators in Manchuria not only was support for Zhang Xueliang's return to Manchuria still strong, but China experts in the Japanese army, such as Major Shibayama Kaneshirō (1889–1956), recommended to the commander of the Guandong Army that no one other than Zhang could save the situation in the region. Although unknown at the time, the Shōwa Emperor (Hirohito) too is said to have thought Zhang's return appropriate.

The Japanese emperor recounted to Nara Takeji (1868–1962), chief aide-de-camp to the emperor, that contrary to the proclamation, issued by the Guandong Army on October 4, 1931, that it was about "to implement a paradise of co-existence and co-prosperity for the thirty million inhabitants of Manchuria-Mongolia . . . I fear that Commander Honjō's declaration marks an intervention in domestic affairs. Hereafter, there can be no further such actions . . . and the views of the army appear to be inappropriate."[37] This was an indication of the emperor's early displeasure with the establishment of the new regime. However, on January 8, 1932, he issued a so-called "gracious rescript" to the Guandong Army: "When the incident erupted earlier in Manchuria, the Guandong Army out of a need for self-defense took decisive action with alacrity, skillfully brought the masses under control, and speedily cut them down. . . . It fought bravely and hard, and plucked out the problem at its source. The Imperial Army's prestige was exalted at home and abroad. We profoundly applaud their unswerving loyalty."[38] The position taken here clearly lauded the military actions taken by the Guandong Army. Furthermore, on January 21 the emperor expressed the view to War Minister Araki Sadao (1872–1966) and Sub-Chief of the General Staff Mazaki Jinzaburō (1876–1956) that Zhang Xueliang's return to head a new regime "in Manchuria" was reasonable, and he hoped the Guandong Army would agree.[39] Of course, even if the views of the emperor were conveyed to the Guandong Army, there was absolutely no way that the Guandong Army could revive Zhang Xueliang after the proclamation of October 4: "At present a movement for the establishment of a regime has emerged in many places, all together the people are singing the praises of the dignity of the Imperial Army, and there is not the least inclination to install the old party leaders. This is clearly the result of indignation against the oppression of many years of warlord self-interest." The state-building movement had been advanced and the framework of the new state was taking form.

Having switched from its earlier position of seizing control over Manchuria-Mongolia, the Guandong Army had hurriedly decided to appoint Puyi, and it had no other candidates in reserve. The only avenue remaining to it was to take decisive action with Puyi. However, in order to mitigate the reaction against support for Puyi, it hoped to avoid using the form of an "imperial restoration." Despite strong demands from those supporting a restoration, the Guandong Army did not make Puyi emperor out of concern for the various ideological and political issues mentioned above. A more pressing reason, though, it would seem was that were it to try to boast of its superiority vis-à-vis the Republic of China, which had chosen a republican form of government, with the formation of an independent state separate from the Republic of China, it would have been impossible to strip it of a constitutional republican form of government.

In fact, all the conceptions of the new state concocted by Guandong Army men *on the surface* assumed a democratic polity and constitutional republicanism. In the *Man-Mō kyōwakoku tōchi taikō an* (Draft plan for rule in the Manchurian-Mongolian republic) drafted by Matsuki Tamotsu and submitted on October 21, 1931 as the first conception for founding the state of Manzhouguo, the polity, as the title indicates, was to be a constitutional republic, and the head of state was to be a president. The title of "president" had been used fairly consistently for the head of state of the Republic of China ever since it was initially adopted in the Temple of Heaven draft constitution of 1913, until June 1931 when a "chairman" of the national government appeared in the provisional political-tutelage constitution of the Republic of China. The president was selected by the parliament on the basis of nominations from delegates chosen by each of the provinces—grounded in the will of the people. Irrespective of what the head of state was called in the Outline of a Plan for the Establishment of a Free State of Manchuria-Mongolia—the second state-founding plan drafted by Matsuki Tamotsu on November 7—it noted: "Although there is no need to daringly persist in the form of a democratic polity, in fact it is essential that we adopt a system which can deliver government based in the will of the people. Thus, the head of state must represent the people's will."[40] This was, without a doubt, a conception devised with the polity and head of state of the Republic of China firmly in mind. Until it was later decided on February 24, 1932 to have "democratic government, with head of state—chief executive," a variety of plans were proposed for "president," "chairman," "state supervisor," and the like to be the name of the head of state. In all of these cases, there was the implicit assumption that the polity would be democratic and/or republican. Of course, the necessity of establishing this premise lay in the fact that, because the founding of the state of Manzhouguo outside the shadow of the Republic of China had called for the self-government of the thirty million residents of Manchuria and Mongolia and appealed to the harmony of the five peoples, a revival of the Manchu dynasty ran counter to popular self-government and could not but elicit discord and schisms among the various ethnic groups involved. Thus, the Guandong Army in its January 1932 deliberations with Army Central over the new Manchurian-Mongolian state made Puyi head of state and stipulated that "we append appropriate names for the head of state from president on down and do so to avoid a restorationist inclination."[41]

In the face of all this, together with Luo Zhenyu and Zheng Xiaoxu, Puyi, who had long yearned for nothing less than an imperial restoration, was unable to assess the true intentions of the Guandong Army. In addition to seeking assistance by sending envoys to Minami Jirō, Tōyama Mitsuru (1855–1944) of the Amur River Society, former Railway Minister Ogawa Heikichi (1870–1942), and others, the restorationists continued to request of Guandong Army Commander Honjō and Staff Officer Itagaki the realization of an imperial restoration. There was, however, a forceful opposition among those with political clout based in the Chinese northeast.

Beginning on February 16, 1932, a Chinese Supreme Council for Establishing a State completed an exhaustive examination of the complexities surrounding the issue of a state polity. At this meeting, Zhang Yanqing (as proxy for Xi Xia), Xie Jieshi, Wan Shengshi (d. before 1940, in Puyi's entourage), and Shao Lin (as proxy for Lingsheng of Khölön Buir), among others, spoke strongly on behalf of adopting the emperorship. In opposition, Zang Shiyi, Zhang Jinghui, Zhao Xinbo, and Zhao Zhongren (as proxy for Ma Zhanshan), among others, repudiated the imperial system of government as contrary to the times and unrelentingly called for adoption of a constitutional republic. With the February 18 declaration of independence of the new state in the name of the Northeast Administrative Council, the difference of opinion between the two groups remained unresolved. With no decision on governmental form, neither side was likely to budge on the subsequent distribution of powers. Thus, the increasingly impatient Guandong Army eventually reached the conclusion on February 24 with a plan that, modeled on democracy, the head of state would be a chief executive (*zhizheng*); and after several years of the chief executive's carrying out responsible government, if the people praised the morality of the chief executive and wished to install him as emperor, then they might move to the imperial system.

This title "chief executive" derived from the "provisional chief executive," a term which Duan Qirui (1865–1936) had dubbed himself in 1924. Because Duan was not legally selected to this leadership position by the parliament, following the stipulations of the constitution of the Republic of China, he stood clear of the title of president and opted for provisional chief executive. This origin for the title "chief executive" symbolized well Puyi's position, having become chief of state without a basis in the popular will. A variety of propitious explanations were then offered from various points of view about the position of chief executive, which was adopted as a compromise plan. As a condition for accepting the post of chief executive, Puyi and his associates believed that after one year temporarily serving in that position, he would ascend to the throne, and during that interval the form of government would be decided by a constitution. Those who wanted a constitutional republic saw that, without the support of the people, he would immediately lose his post.

The position of chief executive was decided upon in the Organizational Law of the Government, promulgated on March 9, and it was more or less comparable to a stipulation concerning the president in the Provisional Constitution (the new provisional constitution) of the Republic of China:

Organizational Law of the Government
Article 1. The chief executive rules Manzhouguo.
Article 2. The chief executive represents Manzhouguo.
Article 3. The chief executive bears responsibility for the entire populace.
Article 4. The chief executive recommends this to the entire populace.

Provisional Constitution of the Republic of China
Article 14. The president is head of state of the country and holds ruling power.
Article 15. The president represents the Republic of China.
Article 16. The president bears responsibility for the entire body of the populace.

The terminology in these documents clearly demonstrates that the position of chief executive conformed to that of the president. However, the stipulation corresponding to Article 4 was not to be found in the Provisional Constitution of the Republic of China. It was a unique item codifying a state-founding ideal which, based upon the collective will of the thirty million residents of Manchuria and Mongolia, attempted to implement a government based on the Kingly Way through the essence of living in accord with heaven and bringing peace to the people. This was not the chief executive receiving a recommendation from the entire populace, and legally it did not clearly indicate how he actually bore political responsibility. Tachibana Shiraki criticized it as no more than a fiction: "It ultimately will be a law solely on paper with no practical efficacy."[42]

The position of chief executive, then, emerged as a strangely jumbled product of three important items: the site for the restoration of the Qing dynasty, opposition to the Republic of China with its system of constitutional republicanism, and the fiction of the collective will of the thirty million residents of Manchuria and Mongolia. Komai Tokuzō (1885–1961), who became the first director-general for administrative affairs of Manzhouguo, explained the national policy in which the head of state was a chief executive in the following manner: "Although it is necessary in a republic to select a president on the basis of elections, because of difficulties in carrying out elections in the new state, the national polity will assume a semi-imperial scheme adhering neither to the imperial system nor to the republican."[43] It was as if one could speak of the sphinx-like appearance of a republican Manzhouguo. Furthermore, what Komai expressed as semi-imperial meant that the powers of the chief executive would be immense. According to the Organizational Law of the Government, it was stipulated that these powers would include

1. Enactment of legislative power by approval of the legislature (Article 5).
2. Governing the State Council and enactment of administrative power (Article 6).
3. Enabling the courts to exercise judicial powers (Article 7).
4. Promulgation of orders and emergency instructions (Articles 8 and 9).
5. Fixing the bureaucratic personnel system and making appointments (Article 10).
6. Declarations of war, making peace, and signing treaties (Article 11).
7. Command of the army, navy, and air force (Article 12).
8. Ordering of amnesties, special pardons, reductions of penalties, and rehabilitations (Article 12).

All of these bear favorable comparison with the powers of the Japanese emperor under the Imperial Constitution of Japan. "There is the possibility," Tachibana argued by way of critique, "that they have created the basis, in fact, for an autocratic nature to the [position of] chief executive," depending on how these articles worked.[44]

Puyi's inauguration ceremony on March 9 as chief executive with the aforementioned powers was said to "have been carried out with extraordinary splendor:"[45] "The new five-colored flag fluttered in the clear sky as the glory and hope for the future could be felt."[46] Consul-General Ishii Itarō (1887–1954) of Jilin, however, who was "compelled to participate in the ceremony," described it merely as follows: "The site of the ceremony was small and the decorations simple, a ceremony befitting the graduation from a professional school."[47] Concerning Puyi, whom he met for the first time on this occasion, Ishii recorded his impressions that "he was radiant with an indescribable refinement of nobility of a man who had once sat on the emperor's throne of China, but I was shocked by the look of ill fortune that was clearly revealed in his face. Being driven from the throne in his youth, the shadows of the past in which he had been continuously tossed about by a fanciful destiny and the apprehensions of a nebulous future which had now brought him to Manzhouguo may have brewed this unhappy physiognomy."[48]

Contrary to Ishii's observation, though, it was not an apprehension about the future that occupied Puyi's mind, but the fact that he saw the position of chief executive as a stage en route to "the jade throne of the emperor" and was wondering how best to use this stage to move quickly toward that jade throne. In accordance with the family precept of "working hard at government and loving the people," Puyi had made up his mind to be diligent in government and to express his powers as a moral sovereign. This diligence, though, did not continue for long. Puyi had no official business whatsoever that required his judgment, except performing ceremonial approvals. The "official powers of the chief executive," which were supposed to be extensive, "were simply written on paper, and I discovered that there was nothing for me to do."[49]

Puyi's discovery was correct. The reason the Guandong Army had appointed him was that its goal was the advent of precisely this situation. And, it was none other than Puyi himself who had invited this eventuality. He had traveled to Changchun from Fushun to take up his post as chief executive of Manzhouguo and en route had stopped at Tanggangzi, but his activities along the way were kept top secret and chronicling them was forbidden. According to Itagaki, Puyi had been compelled en route to affix his name to a letter. By signing this letter addressed to Guandong Army Commander Honjō, Puyi's and Manzhouguo's fates were set. The dragon had cut off his own horns and limbs.

In Puyi's autobiography, *Wo de qianbansheng*, Zheng Xiaoxu, who had been slated to become prime minister, is said to have signed this letter in Puyi's name, and the latter only learned of its content about six months later. After harshly rebuking Zheng for such excessively arbitrary actions, "I was so angry I couldn't do a thing except ratify a *fait accompli*."[50] His explanation of these "arbitrary actions" and "ratify[ing] a *fait accompli*" gives one a certain sense of black humor, a mysterious coincidence surrounding the relationship between the Guandong Army and the Japanese government following the eruption of the Manchurian Incident. But it was Puyi, of course, who signed the letter and his seal was affixed to it.

What then did this letter contain?

The Disjunction Between the Form of Government and the Reality of Rulership

Having proclaimed the principles of following the way of heaven, bringing peace to the people, and implementing a government based on the Kingly

Way, Manzhouguo was officially inaugurated on March 9, 1932. The Organizational Law of the Government and the personnel system for its various bureaus, at the pinnacle of which was the State Council, were announced, and the ruling structure of Manzhouguo as well as its national regulations were clearly laid out.

The preamble to the Organizational Law of the Government noted: "This is the basic law by which the government of Manzhouguo will be administered. This law will be abandoned, however, when in future the gist of the people's wisdom is extracted and a constitution for Manzhouguo is enacted."[51] As we see from this, this basic law established a temporary form of rule until such time as a formal constitution was to be written, and thus until such a consitution was formally adopted, this form of a simple basic law was comparable to the Provisional Constitution of the Republic of China. This did not mean that the constitution of the Republic of China was taken as a model; in fact, the political circumstances surrounding the constitution in the Republic of China were sharply criticized: "Those who possessed the genuine social authority to take responsibility for peace and unity merely appealed out of vanity to defense of the constitution or the safeguarding of it as a means of maintaining their moral station, while in fact they effectively avoiding the path of implementing the constitution."[52] Despite the fact that all manner of constitutional drafts were produced to a dizzying extent after the founding of the Republic of China, none of them successfully legitimized any of the various regimes in power. That fact, in other words, was seen as corroboration of China's continued incapacity to form a modern constitutional state, and it became a ground for arguing that Manzhouguo be kept separate from and independent of the Republic of China.

The enactment of a constitution in Manzhouguo was taken as an essential element to the formation of a modern state. In a commemorative message issued on the first anniversary in 1933 of the founding of the state, it was claimed: "Basic to the founding of a state in modern times is emphasis on the rule of law (Japanese *hōchi*, Chinese *fazhi*), and the basis of the rule of law is a constitution. . . . If no constitution is formed, then the foundation of the state will never be strong. Hence, by preparing and revising the items befitting a constitution and seeing it through to fruition with alacrity, we shall fortify the foundations of the state and bring it into accord with the popular will."[53] Clarifying the urgency attached to implementation of a constitution, the founders proceeded to inaugurate an investigative committee for a constitutional system.

Despite the subsequent activities of this committee, ultimately constitutional law in the form of a written constitution never materialized. Thus, the Organizational Law of the Government, initially conceived as a temporary measure, was revised together with the move toward an imperial system in March 1934, and it then functioned as a basic law code for ruling

Manzhouguo. In this regard, Manzhouguo's conceit that it was superior to the Republic of China as a constitutional state lacked any substance. Also, despite repeated and harsh criticisms leveled at the constitutional regime of the Republic of China, the Organizational Law of the Government and the bureaucratic personnel system were assiduously conscious of the legal system of the Republic of China and had been formed accordingly.

We have already noted that the articles concerning the chief executive of Manzhouguo conformed to the stipulations concerning the president in the Provisional Constitution of the Republic of China. As concerned the government's organization, in this case too it seems that the institutional forms adopted in Manzhouguo were based on those of the Republic of China, but with strikingly original differences and claims to superiority.

Premised on a system of centralized authority, the political organization of Manzhouguo adopted a system of four separate powers: legislative, executive or administrative, legal, and police. In concrete terms, there were bodies, or *yuan*, which gave structure to the central government: the parliament, which was a legislative body, the State Council, which was an administrative organ, the courts which were the machinery of the law, and the inspectorate, which carried out administrative examinations and budgetary inspections. All of the political organs of Manzhouguo, be they central or local bodies, fell under one or another of the four *yuan*, as depicted in Table 1. It was emphasized that while most constitutional states, including Japan, had adopted a system of the separation of three powers, the system of four separate powers displayed a distinctive and superior quality in the political structure of Manzhouguo. However, this system of four separate powers could, of course, scarcely be called unique to the political structure of Manzhouguo. Needless to say, it had been based on the five-power constitution—legislative, judicial, executive, inspectorate, and examination—advocated much earlier by Sun Zhongshan. It may be appropriate, then, to see Manzhouguo as consisting of this system minus the examination *yuan*, which among the five was a permanent organ for the selection of officials but did not, in fact, function as such and was regarded as useless.

While the state structure of Manzhouguo cannot be identified with the Republic of China, let alone the Nanjing government of the Guomindang, we should not ignore this issue. No matter how diligently these men appealed to its distinctiveness, the *Manshūkoku seiritsu no keii to sono kokka kikō ni tsuite* (On the circumstances surrounding the establishment of Manzhouguo and its state structure), published by the Research Section of the Army Ministry in 1932, stated the matter clearly:

We should note that the Nanjing government which was structured on the basis of the five-power constitution of Sun Wen [Sun Zhongshan] adopted a system of five *yuan*—legislative, judicial, executive, inspectorate, and examination—while the

TABLE 1. The Organization of Manzhouguo at the Time of Its Founding, March 1932

Chief Executive—Cabinet—Secretariat

A. Legal *Yuan* B. Inspectorate *Yuan* C. State Council D. Legislative *Yuan*

A. Supreme Court—High Court of Justice—Local Courts
Supreme Public Prosecutor's Office—High Public Prosecutor's Office—District Public Prosecutor's Office

B. Administrative Affairs Desk
Inspector's Department
Auditor's Department

C. Office of Administrative Affairs—Consumer's Desk, Paymaster's Desk, Personnel Desk, Secretarial Desk
Legal Bureau—Statistics Desk
Bureau of National Affairs—Training Desk, Research Desk, Public Relations Desk, Administrative Affairs Desk
Xing'an Bureau—Encouragement of Industry Desk, State Affairs Desk, Administrative Affairs Desk
Fengtian Province—Education Office, Industrial Office, Police Affairs Office, Civil Administration Office, Office of Administrative Affairs
Jilin Province—Education Office, Industrial Office, Police Affairs Office, Civil Administration Office, Office of Administrative Affairs
Heilongjiang Province—Education Office, Industrial Office, Police Affairs Office, Civil Administration Office, Office of Administrative Affairs
Special City of Xinjing
Eastern Provinces Special District
Ministry of Civil Affairs—Office of Hygiene, Office of Public Works, Office of Education, Office of Police Affairs, Office of Local Affairs, Office of Administrative Affairs
Ministry of Foreign Affairs—Office of Trade, Office of State Administration, Office of Administrative Affairs
Ministry of Military Administration—Office of Military Supplies, Office of General Staff
Ministry of Finance—Office of Finances, Office of Customs, Office of Administrative Affairs
Ministry of Industry—Office of Industry and Commerce, Office of Agriculture and Mining, Office of Administrative Affairs
Ministry of Communications—Office of Water Transportation, Office of the Postmaster, Office of Railroads, Office of Administrative Affairs
Ministry of Justice—Office of Punishments, Office of Legal Affairs, Office of Administrative Affairs

government of Manzhouguo is not establishing an inspectorate *yuan* or a judicial *yuan* and will handle legal matters in a special manner. It will also change the name of the administrative *yuan* to the State Council, and afford the inspection *yuan* an independent position vis-à-vis the State Council which is directly under the jurisdiction of the chief executive. It will also thus have extremely important powers to help prevent decay setting in in the new government.[54]

TABLE 2. The Principal Personnel of Manzhouguo, March 1932

Prime Minister	Zheng Xiaoxu
Minister of Civil Affairs	Zang Shiyi
Minister of Foreign Affair	Xie Jieshi
Minister of Military Administration	Ma Zhanshan
Minister of Finance	Xi Xia
Minister of Industry	Zhang Yanqing
Minister of Communications	Ding Jianxiu
Minister of Justice	Feng Hanqing
Director of the Legislative *Yuan*	Zhao Xinbo
Director of the Inspectorate *Yuan*	Yu Chonghan
Director of the Supreme Court	Lin Qi
Director of the Supreme Public Prosecutor's Office	Li Pan
Chairman of the Cabinet	Zhang Jinghui
Vice-Chairman of the Cabinet	Tang Yulin
Cabinet Members	Zhang Haipeng, Yuan Jinkai, Luo Zhenyu, Guifu
Director-General for Administrative Affairs in the State Council	Komai Tokuzō
Chief of the Xing'an Bureau	Chimedsempil
Governor of Fengtian	Zang Shiyi
Governor of Jilin	Xi Xia
Governor of Heilongjiang	Ma Zhanshan
Mayor of the Special City of Xinjing	Jin Bidong
Governor of the Eastern Provinces Special District	Zhang Jinghui

Despite this explanation, however, the Legal *Yuan* was set up like the Judicial *Yuan*, and the term "State Council" was not unique to Manzhouguo, being used generally in China outside the Nanjing government. The Inspectorate *Yuan* was distinctive from a department of administrative affairs insofar as it carried out investigations of the administrative bureaucracy and inspections of budgets, but precisely the same held as well in the Nanjing government and was thus not peculiar to Manzhouguo. Also, it would be easy to identify similarities between the names of the various administrative offices (comparable to those in a Japanese ministry) under the Ministry of Civil Affairs, their structures, and their organizations with those of the Nanjing government, the 1927 Beijing military government, and other regimes.

Of course, the facts that the names and forms of these institutions were the same or that they bore similarities did not necessarily mean that their functions and powers were identical or similar. For example, the Legislative *Yuan* of the Nationalist government in Nanjing had official authority to make decisions on such important matters as the law, the budget, amnesties, declarations of war, conclusions of peace, and signing of treaties.[55] However, the Legislative *Yuan* of Manzhouguo merely had an "approval" function; it could deliberate on draft laws and draft budgets as part of the legislative powers held by the chief executive and ratify them. Furthermore, even if the Legislative *Yuan* rejected a proposal, the chief executive could bring it up for reconsideration, and should the Legislative *Yuan* reject it again, it could nonetheless be approved and promulgated as law if, after consultation with the Cabinet which was the chief executive's advisory body, it was adopted. Thus, the Legislative *Yuan*'s powers were severely limited. The Guandong Army had decided that the Legislative *Yuan* would be merely nominal and saw to it that it would not convene.

Back in November 1931, when the constitutional form of government became an issue within the Guandong Army, it had already been stressed that constitutionalism for the new state was of legal, not political, significance. Legal significance meant that there would be in law independent bodies responsible for the three judicial, legislative, and executive powers; political significance referred to such things as the convening of a parliament or the implementation of a parliamentary cabinet system. One political reason offered for not adopting the constitutional form of government was that "the political consciousness of the people in Manchuria-Mongolia has still not developed in this sphere."[56] A reason put forward to legitimize the creation of a new state in Manchuria-Mongolia was the fact that national consciousness was lacking and political consciousness weak among the local residents, and thus Japan's leadership in the formation of such a state would be a blessing for the thirty million people living there. However, the same logic was used to reject convening a parliament after the state had been founded. Of course, the real reason for rejecting the adoption of the parliamentary system was that even the least limitations imposed by a deliberative body on control over Manzhouguo were seen as inexpedient.

The reason the Manzhouguo founders claimed the stipulation in the Organizational Law of the Government for a legislative *yuan* to convene in the future, for which from the beginning there had been no plans, was that it could not rebut the Nationalist government's attack on it as despotic, lacking a parliament and not a constitutional state. Nor clearly could they deny that it was a puppet state. More than anything else, though, one can certainly see at work here concerns that this new state would be exposed as a fraud: offering as an ideal for its foundation that its government would follow the true will of the people and then not even creating a parliament. By what possible route, then, was the Guandong Army going to attempt to use to control Manzhouguo at the level of political organization which was so amply divergent in law from reality, as we have seen?

In October 1931 Staff Officer Itagaki of the Guandong Army offered the following basic guidelines for Matsuki Tamotsu who, as advisor on international law to the Guandong Army, was responsible for drawing up drafts of various legal institutions for the new state: "If we can breathe life into these three conditions . . . —make Manchuria into a completely independent state, have it listen to what Japan says, and have it rely on Japan for national defense or even mutual defense—then it will work fine whether it is an empire, a kingdom, a republic, or any other polity."[57] At a glance, the condition that it be a "completely independent state" and the two stipulations that it "listen to what Japan says" and that it "rely on Japan for national defense" seem to be contradictory demands. However, this was no contradiction for Itagaki and his colleagues. What was meant here by a "completely independent state" was complete independence from the Republic of China and not at all to be independent of Japan. A "completely independent state" in this sense was an absolute condition to "move" Manchuria-Mongolia "in accordance with the will of the empire." This was also the reason that, from the perspective of international law, Matsuki rejected the thesis of an independent regime, which became firmly rooted in November 1931. In other words, according to Matsuki, "Manchuria-Mongolia forms one part of China and thus cannot sign treaties or conclude accords. . . . Because it cannot sign treaties with independent regimes, it is absolutely impossible for it to move in accordance with the will [of the empire]."[58]

In short, to get Manchuria-Mongolia to move in accordance with the will of the Japanese empire, it had to be a free state independent of the Republic of China with the agency to be able to conclude treaties. As treaties became the route by which Manchuria-Mongolia was brought to life, the next issue naturally became who actually controlled the capacity to sign treaties on the Manzhouguo side. This was one of the reasons that the Guandong Army was wedded to the idea of appointing Japanese as officials responsible for diplomatic negotiations and cabinet members whose job it was to ratify treaties. If Manzhouguo was to be recognized by Japan, then its foreign relations and treaty-making would perforce be the work of the Japanese living there. This was realized in the form of a letter sent to Guandong Army Commander Honjō Shigeru signed by Puyi on March 6, 1932.

This letter was appended to the Japan-Manzhouguo Protocol signed on September 15, 1932 but not publicly announced until after the war, dubbed the Puyi-Honjō secret accord. The main text of the Japan-Manzhouguo Protocol itself had only two items: 1. recognition of the vested interests of Japan and the Japanese in Manzhouguo; and 2. acceptance of Japanese troops being stationed in Manzhouguo for joint Japan-Manzhouguo defense in Manzhouguo. By contrast, Puyi's letter covered the following four items: 1. Manzhouguo will rely on Japan for national defense and the maintenance of order, and Manzhouguo will shoulder the costs; 2. Manzhouguo will rely on Japan and agencies designated by Japan for supervision over railways, harbors, waterways, and air routes, as well as the construction and opening of new roads, all of which the Japanese military deems necessary to national defense; 3. Manzhouguo will energetically assist with various installations that the Japanese military deems necessary; and 4. the recommendation and consent of the commanding officer of the Guandong Army shall be essential in appointing Japanese of great insight and renown to positions in the Manzhouguo Cabinet and the appointment and dismissal of Japanese to other central and local government offices.

These stipulations were to become the basis for the two nations' future signing of a treaty. Thus, on September 22, 1931 when the Guandong Army switched courses from the idea of seizing Manchuria-Mongolia, the direction it decided on saw fruition: "National defense and diplomacy will be managed in the Japanese empire *by entrusting them to* the new regime, while it will supervise important matters of transportation and communications."[59]

In one essential regard, this letter that sealed the fate of Manzhouguo had an artificiality about it that symbolized the nature of Manzhouguo itself. First, despite the fact that it was actually signed on March 6, it was dated March 10; also, despite the fact that Puyi did not issue this document on his own, it took the form of Puyi's unilateral reliance on Commander Honjō and his request for Japanese "assent" (Japanese *inka*, Chinese *yunke*); third, in response, the Guandong Army Commander on May 12 replied: "I have duly taken up your letter of March 10."[60] Perhaps the first item concerning the date may be explained in that, before Puyi was made chief executive, he had the Guandong Army accept this dating as a condition for his taking the post; and Puyi then signed it on the day following the investiture ceremony when Puyi had the power to sign treaties and accords, thus preserving legalities. In the second case, we can see that as of January 22 the ringleaders of the Guandong Army had decided to use the form of "reliance" (of Manzhouguo upon Japan): "The exchange of documents was to be a one-way affair, and in this form of reliance they would acquire national defense, the accompanying railway supervision rights, and the like. Herein lay the chief aim of pledging not to become involved in future entanglements."[61] In other words, in cases where such matters as national defense and the power to appoint or dismiss officials of the new state were decided by bilateral consultation, inevitably criticism would be leveled at Japan and Manzhouguo on the basis of violations of the Covenant of the League of Nations or the Nine-Power Treaty. To avoid such criticism, it was thus necessary to adopt the mode of one-way reliance. This arrangement was "accepted" on May 12 by the commander of the Guandong Army, which had no powers whatsoever to conclude treaties; by offering his assent to the chief of state of a foreign country on the most pressing issues between the two nations, he was surely in violation of the supreme authority of the Japanese emperor, who retained the power to sign such accords, and with the passage of time it was ratified by the Japanese government as a *fait accompli.* This mode of operations had been decided upon in February

1932, and the Japanese Foreign Ministry had sensed such a situation brewing. On February 13, Deputy Consul-General Morishima in Fengtian telegraphed Foreign Minister Yoshizawa Kenkichi (1874–1965) the following report:

As concerns such matters as national defense in relation to the new state, we take heed that concluding a secret treaty without authorization from the central government is the result of a violation of supreme authority. Reliance upon Japan for national defense, filling more than half of the posts in the [Manzhouguo] Cabinet with Japanese, appointing Japanese to bureaucratic posts . . . and in due time formally concluding treaties—these the new state unilaterally proposed to the [Guandong] Army commander, and as commander he decided just to accept them for the time being.[62]

Although he had said that he would "just accept them for the time being," he could leave it forever, because they would have to formally sign an official treaty sometime in the near future. On April 15, just before the Lytton Commission arrived in Manzhouguo, the cabinet of Prime Minister Inukai Tsuyoshi (1855–1932) approved a "Management Plan for the Railways, Harbors, and Waterways of Manzhouguo"[63] at a cabinet session. They nonchalantly added as an attached item Puyi's letter which contained the material outlined above, and the Japanese government as such ratified actions tantamount to violations of supreme power committed by the Guandong Army. With this cabinet decision, the Guandong Army commander unobtrusively responded that he acquiesced: "We have no objection to this."[64] Indeed, there was no reason to expect that he would have had objections to something whose content he had concocted himself.

Thus, by mounting any number of camouflage maneuvers and by legalizing the content of Puyi's letter, the Guandong Army, which until that time had been allowed only to station troops and carry out military exercises in the Guandong Leased Territory and on the land attached to the South Manchurian Railway, was now accorded the justifiable grounds to move at will throughout the entire terrain of Manzhouguo. It was understood that it might use any and every facility deemed necessary as it saw fit. Manzhouguo became the base of operations state for the Guandong Army.

Furthermore, in addition to the treaty route, by acquiring the power to appoint and dismiss Japanese cabinet members and officials, an access route to control the administration of Manzhouguo on a daily basis was created, and through this it became possible to make Manzhouguo "move in full accordance with the will of the empire." On January 22, 1932 the Guandong Army acknowledged that, in connection with the ruling structure of Manzhouguo, "the Legislative *Yuan* would be a formality and it would in fact be a centralized dictatorship."[65] To safeguard those responsible for this centralized dictatorship, though, the Guandong Army saw that it absolutely had to control the right of personnel management: "At the time of the founding of the new state, we needed to have a written document."[66]

Hence, so long as Manzhouguo existed, its ruling structure was in actuality decided by secret agreements which never rose to the surface, and this, of course, eviscerated the political form of the state established by the Organizational Law of the Government which had been publicly promulgated. On January 27, 1932, the Guandong Army put out the General Plan for Coping Successfully with the Manchuria-Mongolia Issue (*Man-Mō mondai zengo shori yōkō*). There the vision of the state was portrayed as follows: "Although the new state, avoiding all hint of being a restoration of the monarchy, shall on the surface be a constitutional republic with Puyi its leader, in fact it shall be a centralized autocracy which shall dovetail with the political authority of our empire."[67] Puyi's letter of March 6 to Guandong Army Commander Honjō was the instrument to insure that this vision would be realized in the new state.

While fiercely criticizing the one-party dictatorship of the Nationalist regime, Manzhouguo raised as its founding ideal a government that necessarily would follow the genuine will of its people. Yet, the government of this state, with a might that never considered the will of its inhabitants and was in no way restricted by legal institutions, in fact emerged with the aim of Japanese control through an autocratic executive organ. Not only was there an extraordinary disjunction in the nature of the polity between the Organizational Law of the Government and its reality, but there was as well a duality between the legal subjects and the actual rulers in the realm of control. These gave form to the distinctive nature of Manzhouguo's law and politics.

In the shadow of the Republic of China, the constitutional republic that Manzhouguo adopted at the time of its founding as a state was thus superficial in form. In reality, it was merely the facade of constitutionalism (*Scheinkonstitutionalismus*) which negated the principles of constitutionalism. And, thus, emerged doubts about its constitutional system, antipathy for its republican system, and disbelief concerning its realization of the will of people.

Four Key Concepts in Manzhouguo Politics

On March 12, when Manzhouguo issued its "Announcement to Foreign Nations on the Founding of the State," the government of Japan at a cabinet session decided upon the General Plan for Coping Successfully with the Manchuria-Mongolia Issue which recognized the importance which Manzhouguo possessed for Japan. According to this statement, "in relations of politics, the economy, national defense, transportation, communication, and the like, we expect that with assistance of the empire this place [Manzhouguo] shall manifest itself as an important element to the [future]

existence of the empire." Particularly in the military realm, it was emphasized that "the terrain of Manchuria-Mongolia constitutes the front line of
national defense for the empire vis-à-vis Russia and China."[68] We can see
from this declaration that the state-founding goal set by the Guandong
Army was subsumed within the national interests of Japan. Thus, the management of Manzhouguo was already perceived as a task linked not only to
the Guandong Army but to the larger Japanese government as well.

As concerned the actual implementation of management over Manzhouguo, "it should take shape, insofar as stipulated by the Nine-Power
Treaty, based in the autonomous designs of the new state." In order to
"guide" Manzhouguo in substantively preparing for statehood, it was firmly
required that Japanese "would form the leadership framework."[69] Political
decisions were formally to be based on the autonomous designs of these
Chinese, while it would be Japanese who held real ruling power under the
control of the Guandong Army. This distinctive character to rulership in
Manzhouguo—contrived in compliance to these requirements—may be understood on the basis of four key concepts. These concepts were: the allot-
ments of positions to "Japanese" and "Manchurians," a ratio of "Japanese"
to "Manchurians," concentrating business in the Office of Administrative
Affairs (Office of Administrative Affairs-centrism), and "internal guidance."

The first two notions were established as guides for the placement of
personnel within the political organization of Manzhouguo, and the Guandong Army retained sole control over such decisions. With every position
from the central government of Manzhouguo through the localities to the
department heads of government offices, there were stipulated "Japanese"
(*Nikkei*) posts and "Manchurian" (*Mankei*) posts. The term *Nikkei* legally
should have included Koreans, but in fact they were rarely added to the
category of "Japanese." The term *Mankei* was an inclusive expression covering Han, Manchus, and Mongols living in Manzhouguo, and it was used on
occasion as a generic for all non-*Nikkei*. In the central government
"Manchurians" were allotted the positions of prime minister, heads of the
ministries, director of the Legislative *Yuan*, director of the Inspectorate
Yuan, director of the Supreme Court, director of the Supreme Public Prosecutor's Office, chairman of the cabinet, minister of the imperial household, chairman of the secretariat, vice-ministers of civil affairs, military
administration, and finance; and in the local governments they were allotted the positions of provincial governors and county magistrates. To the
"Japanese" were initially allotted the posts of director-general for administrative affairs, assistant director-general for administrative affairs, all vice-
ministerships not allotted to Manchurians, heads of the offices of general
affairs, and department chiefs; locally, vice-governorships of the provinces,
assistant county magistrates, heads of the offices of administrative affairs, and
heads of the police affairs office. With each of the several structural administrative reforms, however, the *Mankei* vice-minister, under the pretext of

placing the right man in the right place, was allotted to a *Nikkei*; in the localities, as well, with each provincial administrative reform, governorships were handed over to "Japanese."

The aim of this allotment of positions to Manchurians and Japanese was to take a form wherein Chinese would basically be given the top administrative posts and Japanese the subsidiary ones, and the government's organization would operate on the basis of the autonomous initiative of the Chinese. The Japanese wanted to avoid all international criticism that Manzhouguo was a puppet state, and thus the same form was adopted in the chartered corporations and public companies within Manzhouguo. However, as pointed out by the Lytton Commission, "As regards the 'Government' and the public services, although the titular heads of the Departments are Chinese residents in Manchuria, the main political and administrative power rests in the hands of Japanese officials and advisers."[70] Ishiwara Kanji advocated the abandonment of this standard for allotting posts to Manchurians and Japanese: "It is not appropriate to fix a position which Japanese should occupy within the government of Manzhouguo. We should follow the just principle of the best man for the job without distinction as to Japanese or Manchurians."[71] Ishiwara's objective was the realization of equality for Manchurians and Japanese, and on this basis he sought to encourage the active participation of Chinese in the management of Manzhouguo, by advocating the abandonment of this system of allotting posts to Japanese and Manchurians and the employment of Manchurians on the basis of talent alone. Because appointments would be decided on the basis of administrative capacity in Manzhouguo which had patterned its administrative structure on that of Japan, Japanese were far more likely to gain bureaucratic posts in the end. Was this then a fairer system of personnel appointment?

Had Ishiwara's proposition been accepted, things would probably have moved in an entirely different direction from what he had envisioned. Once the provincial governorships originally allocated to the Manchurians were filled with Japanese, it was rationalized that: "Although they are 'Japanese,' this is justifiable in pivotal positions, and it actually indicates the true height reached by the harmony of the five peoples who are entirely fused."[72] To the apprehensions raised as "Manchurian" posts, one after the next, "were transferred to "Japanese," a counter-criticism was leveled: "This instance is, of course, not one in which Japanese officials are wishing for more than their due. Be they Manchurian or Japanese, important posts must go without hesitation to talented men."[73] On the premise that the Japanese language and Japanese-style administrative practices would be used, it was a certainty that Japanese would gain the highest positions if they adopted the so-called principles of "talent" and "merit." Yet, in an exceptional instance, to ameliorate the discontent of the Manchurians—as Japanese moved toward a monopoly over the most important posts—an arrangement was reached whereby one Manchurian would be allotted a post as assistant chief in the Office of Administrative Affairs in the State Council from July 1937 on. The Manchurians so appointed, though, were all men who had studied in Japan, and none of them had any real power— they were dubbed *peida* (ornamental supplements).

By the same token, the second concept of the ratio of Japanese to Manchurians established a fixed ratio of "Japanese" appointees to "Manchurian" appointees in all the bureaucratic offices of Manzhouguo. Because the bureaucratic posts which became the standard for this ratio were not necessarily clear, a precise numerical value for this ratio could not be prescribed, but according to Assistant Director of the Office of Administrative Affairs Furumi Tadayuki, the ratio of Japanese to Manchurians was five to five in the Ministry of Finance and the Ministry of Industry, four to six in the Ministry of Justice (each of these ratios would later change to six to four), three to seven in the Ministry of Civil Affairs, the Ministry of Education, the Ministry of Foreign Affairs, and the Ministry of Military Administration, and two to eight in the local offices, the provincial offices, and the taxation

TABLE 3. Number of Officials in Manzhouguo by Office and Percentage Occupied by Japanese

Central government office	Number of officials	Nationality: Chinese/Mongol/Japanese/Russian				Percentage Japanese
Secretariat	7	6		1		14.3
Imperial Household Department	108	96		12		11.1
Cabinet	18	9		9		50.0
Legislative *Yuan*	22	18		4		18.2
State Council	492	90		402		81.7
Ministry of Civil Affairs	1148	610		500	38	43.6
Ministry of Foreign Affairs	144	76		68		47.2
Ministry of Military Administration	222	124	11	87		39.2
Ministry of Finance	1406	773		633		45.0
Ministry of Industry	344	158		186		54.1
Ministry of Communications	583	344		239		41.0
Ministry of Justice	132	66		66		50.0
Ministry of Education	100	60		40		40.0
Ministry of Mongolian Affairs	72	7	30	35		48.6
Supreme Court	35	3		32		91.4
Supreme Public Prosecutor's Office	33	3		30		90.0
Inspectorate *Yuan*	73	31		42		57.5
Total	4939	2474	41	2386	38	48.3

(continued)

TABLE 3. *Continued*

Local government office	Number of officials	Nationality: Chinese/Mongol/Japanese/Russian				Percentage Japanese
Fengtian Provincial Office	244	134		110		45.1
Jilin Provincial Office	211	124		87		41.2
Heilongjiang Provincial Office	180	92		88		48.9
Rehe Provincial Office	123	70		53		43.1
Pingjiang Provincial Office	210	117		93		44.3
Jinzhou Provincial Office	130	77		53		40.8
Andong Provincial Office	133	78		55		41.4
Jiandao Provincial Office	75	51		24		32.0
Sanjiang Provincial Office	93	55		38		40.9
Heihe Provincial Office	61	29		31		52.5
Northern Manchuria City Office	42	31		9	2	21.4
Xinjing City Office	74	46		27	1	36.5
Harbin City Office	195	126		61	8	31.3
Xing'an East Provincial Office	103	1	67	35		34.0
Xing'an South Provincial Office	117		79	38		32.5
Xing'an West Provincial Office	75	3	39	33		44.0
Xing'an North Provincial Office	95	9	56	27	3	28.4
Total	2161	1043	241	863	14	39.3
Combined Totals	**7100**	**3517**	**282**	**3249**	**52**	**45.8**

Compiled from *Wei "Manzhouguo" guanli guoji tongji biao* (Statistical chart of the nationalities of officials in the bogus "Manzhouguo") (publication data unknown, dated December 1935, held in the library of Fudan University, Shanghai). In a report of the Manzhouguo government, the number of officials above those authorized as of March 31, 1936 was 4,652 central officials and 2,141 local officials.

inspection offices.[74] By contrast, the ratio calculated on the basis of figures made public in China in 1935, as Table 3 indicates, demonstrates that the number of Japanese was a high figure overall. (Because this table was published in China where "Manzhouguo" as a nationality and "Manchurian" as an expression did not exist, as one would expect, they were treated as Chinese.) As for the total number of "Japanese" officials, "using the principle of controlling the strategic posts with a small number," in the early years of the state the Guandong Army claimed that Japanese occupied 120 out of 600 central government positions, or 20 percent.[75] In May 1933 the overall number of Japanese officials reached 1,233, and according to the attached table in 1935 the number swelled dramatically in just a few years to 2,386, or 48 percent. The Japanese-Manchurian ratio was established as a rule so as not to have to confront the patent fact that in personnel terms Manzhouguo was being ruled by Japanese. However, despite the apprehensions of the Guandong Army, the trend toward increasing the percentage of Japanese could not be stopped. It was reported in May 1935 that, to the extent that the Guandong Army remained in control, "the ratio of Japanese and Manchurians has already surpassed one-to-one in central government offices, and the number of Japanese in the Office of National Roads is, in fact, 90 percent of the total number of officials."[76] Furthermore, it was true in every ministry of state that "we have employed several times more Japanese than the ratio in each ministry."[77]

Only the Office of Administrative Affairs in the State Council was treated differently with respect to the above two personnel rules. From the top position of director-general for administrative affairs on down, the assistant director, desk chiefs, division chiefs, and the like were all allocated to Japanese. Although the Japanese-Manchurian ratio of seven-to-three was taken as something of a standard, this changed to Japanese always occupying at least 80 percent of the positions. In particular, the Japanese effectively held a monopoly by controlling such pivotal functions as the paymasters desk, the personnel desk, and the planning desk. Thus, the Office of Administrative Affairs in the State Council was unlike other bureaucratic offices of state, for it was one agency in which a structure based on the presumption of predominant Japanese control actually saw fruition: "In fact it shall be a centralized autocracy which shall dovetail with the political authority of our empire."[78]

Once the Guandong Army had changed courses and began conceiving of a new state, it devoted greatest attention to how to make rule over Manzhouguo reliably reflect the aims of the Guandong Army and the Japanese government "in accordance with the will of the empire." This was first conceived in a plan put forth by Matsuki Tamotsu which, beginning with military and diplomatic advisors, would "appoint advisors of the empire in every political office, give them effective powers, and thus guide and supervise."[79] Matsuki proposed establishing a "Council of Advisors" composed of Japanese as an organ of political guidance.

Strong opposition, however, was raised to the idea of appointing such advisors or setting up such a "Council of Advisors," because it would disfigure the appearance of Manzhouguo as an independent state and injure the self-esteem of the Chinese participants in it. Furthermore, some Japanese in Manchuria, especially members of the Manchurian Youth League, argued that in view of the ideal of ethnic harmony, "for Japanese in the capacity of advisors or consultants to participate in politics was unacceptable, and it would be wiser to participate as direct constituent elements of the state."[80] For his part Ishiwara Kanji also strongly urged "not instituting advisors in the sense that they would supervise Chinese officials," and he advocated the need for Japanese to participate directly in politics as officials on a par with Chinese.[81]

In line with this trend, a plan to establish a Council of Advisors did emerge. According to instructions given by the Guandong Army to Itagaki Seishirō, who returned to Tokyo on January 4, 1932 because of a conflict with the central government, the proposed plan would constitute a Council of Advisors made up of one Manchu, one Mongol, three Chinese, and three Japanese, and "the aims and wishes of our empire would through the aforementioned Japanese advisors be conveyed to the central Manchurian-Mongolian government." Apprehensions remained strong, however, that while the three Japanese advisors on the Council of Advisors who would serve as an advisory organ for the head of state and would convey to the central government Japan's intent in rulership, it would in fact be far from thoroughly effective. On January 22, a plan was hammered out to "restrain the highest aims of the state with the powers of the Council of Advisors" and more directly "work to see that Japanese thrust themselves into the inner workings" of the new state. It was decided at this time "to expand the powers of the State Council, to take control over personnel and budget matters in the Secretarial Office, and place Japanese in the Industrial Office."[82] In the final analysis, Japanese control in Manzhouguo was planned around the two pillars of Japanese advisors and Japanese officials in the State Council. We have here the reason that in Puyi's letter he promised that the commander of the Guandong Army would have the power to appoint and dismiss Japanese advisors and Japanese officials. Using the power over personnel management, the Guandong Army acquired the means to have its aims reflected in rulership over Manzhouguo.

Also on January 22, it was confirmed that the "Legislative *Yuan* shall be a formality, for in fact it will be a centralized autocracy."[83] Power would be concentrated in the State Council over which Japanese officials would retain control, revealing clearly that this was to be a centralized autocracy. The duties that were assumed to belong to the Secretarial Office in the State Council were in fact undertaken by the Office of Administrative Affairs. They thus adopted the method of "controlling all aspects of the administration through the three essential elements of administration": personnel (people), revenues (money), and resources (things).[84] This was a form of rule by concentrating the most important work and powers in the Office of Administrative Affairs (dubbed Office of Administrative Affairs-centrism or State Council-centrism), and its extraordinary nature was extolled in the following manner:

In order to attain better administrative efficiency as a state, one which was rapidly founded, the centralization of powers is preferable to decentralization. Administrative items, once presented by the ministries to the Office of Administrative Affairs, will be reviewed by the each of the agencies under the Office of Administrative Affairs and then discharged for implementation to the various ministries through a meeting of the State Council. The administrative organization known as "Office of Administrative Affairs-centrism" is the most ideal method in the [present] transition period, and here we may identify a distinctive characteristic of the new state.[85]

Office of Administrative Affairs-centrism, however, was never intended as merely a stopgap measure for the period of transition. On the contrary, the chief aim of reforming the structure of rulership in Manzhouguo was to put in place an even more thorough strengthening of powers within the Office of Administrative Affairs. The fact that the enforcement of this principle was intensely sought meant that the powers of the Office of Administrative Affairs would expand over time. Just as the remarkable quality of Office of Administrative Affairs-centrism was praised to the stars, the Office itself was praised as "the most extraordinary within the political organization of Manzhouguo."[86] As concerned the functions of the Office of Administrative Affairs, it was explained that: "If we are to search in Japan for a comparable example, it would be something on the order of the Cabinet Planning Board, the Cabinet Legislative Bureau, or the Public Information Division of the Cabinet. However, its powers and the content of its work will be far greater than even all these three combined. In a word, it shall function as the central nervous system of Manzhouguo."[87] Some claimed that, in comparison to Japan, it corresponded to the Cabinet Secretariat. In any event, the Office of Administrative Affairs was seen as a new institution the likes of which had not been seen even in Japan, and it was hailed "in spirit as one manifestation of the reformist trend seeking to learn a lesson from the administrative abuses of past states and to adopt the latest institutions."[88]

From an organizational point of view, however, the Office of Administrative Affairs was no more than an advisory organ, a bureaucratic structure created to handle "items within the ministries concerning secret matters, personnel, accounting, and consumption needs" over which ultimately the prime minister held direct authority. The director-general for administrative affairs received his orders from the prime minister and handled the work of the Office of Administrative Affairs. The subsidiary regulations for the secretarial desk, the personnel desk, the paymasters desk, and the consumers desk were entrusted to the director-general for administrative affairs.[89] Thus, the director-general for administrative affairs held substantive control of state secrets, personnel matters, and finances, and important state business was decided upon and enacted by "Japanese" officials arrayed amid these various offices. For example, in compiling a budget, because the Legislative *Yuan* was not convened, the budget decided upon by the Japanese officials at the paymasters desk was regarded as the final budget, and the resolutions adopted at State Council meetings and inquiries of the cabinet were from start to finish purely formal procedures. This point remained true of Manzhouguo throughout its entire history and befit a centralized autocracy. It was accordingly claimed that priority apportionment of the budget in line with the objectives of Japanese management over Manzhouguo would be possible without concern for the will of the local populace.

What were the origins of such a plan for a system of centralized autocracy centered on the Office of Administrative Affairs in ruling Manzhouguo? Most likely, Tokyo Imperial University Professor Rōyama Masamichi (1895–1980) suggested the plan at an advisory meeting concerned with the legal system of the new state convened by the administrative division of the Guandong Army on January 15, 1932, and we can surmise that Matsuki Tamotsu drew up the concrete plan from this. Rōyama lectured at the employees club of the South Manchurian Railway on January 23, the day the meeting concluded, and he stressed that the northeast region of China simply could not escape its colonial nature, that the people had low political consciousness, and thus that a political organization suited to those circumstances had to be devised. As he put it: "The political organization created for this place must by all means be a political organization of some sort of oligarchic autocracy in which one ethnic group leads the other ethnic groups." He argued that they should adopt an oligarchic, autocratic political form led by Japanese. An oligarchic, autocratic form naturally contradicted a constitutional polity based on the civil rights of equality among the different ethnic groups, and he concluded that "to build an efficient, just government, a government without corruption, was more important that civil rights."[90]

Tachibana Shiraki quickly penned his opposition to Rōyama's position, arguing for equal civil rights for all ethnic groups, the opening of citizens' parliaments at the national, provincial, county, and village levels, and the establishment of a decentralized, autonomous state. "Autocracy," he claimed, "is inferior to democracy. The weaknesses of low efficiency and slow results in democracy may be inescapable, but they can help avoid the fearful, destructive effects which accompany autocracy."[91] He thus rejected a leadership role for the Japanese and again appealed for the adoption of a democratic political form. While Tachibana was pressed to choose between "democracy with low efficiency and high stability" and "autocracy with high efficiency and high danger," high efficiency was more important to the Guandong Army than certain riskiness, for its supreme task was to get the highest results from Manzhouguo with the least political cost. The "iron law of oligarchy" made famous by Roberto Michels (1876–1936) notwithstanding, to the extent that the Guandong Army sought functional rationalism organizationally, it had plans of this drafted at the highest reaches and the position of the central executive strengthened, which led to the tendency for effective power to be concentrated in the hands of a minority.

This all proved salutary for the Guandong Army, which had adopted "the principle of controlling the strategic posts with a small number" of people.

Thus, adoption of the guiding idea of concentrating important business in the Office of Administrative Affairs conformed to the quest for administrative efficiency, while at the same time indirectly enabled rule over all of Manzhouguo by controlling a few people who held real powers. The Guandong Army took this to be the best of all possible options. Hence, a concrete decision was reached to review measures introduced to State Council meetings at ordinary business meetings conducted by the director-general for administrative affairs and attended by the assistant director-general, and the Japanese chiefs, vice-chiefs, and desk chiefs in the Office of Administrative Affairs in each of the ministries. These meetings had no formal name and were variously called the Assistants' Meeting, the Wednesday Meeting, and from 1941 on the Tuesday Meeting. Hence, Manzhouguo policy was substantively set at meetings which had no basis whatsoever in the bureaucratic structure, and the principle of Office of Administrative Affairs-centrism was, in short, a system by which the "Japanese" officials controlled policy-making powers. Furumi Tadayuki, who served as chief of the Paymasters Desk in the Office of Administrative Affairs, and as assistant director-general of the same office, offered this evaluation: "When I think of the essential nature of Manzhouguo, especially in its relationship to Japan, I cannot help but feel that the principle of Office of Administrative Affairs-centrism is a well thought out system."[92] He continued:

If we make good use of the Office of Administrative Affairs which has been fortified by these "Japanese" officials, then we will be able to defend against anti-Japanese policies and actions without the Guandong Army's direct intervention into Manzhouguo. The reason for this is that the most important policies and measures of Manzhouguo are all decided upon by deliberative decision of the State Council and then by sanction of the government through review and a report on the views of the Cabinet; and although the Office of Administrative Affairs lacks any sort of power concerning national law or decisions concerning state policy, it can preview matters before implementation.[93]

Here was inadvertently expressed not only that the Japanese had no apprehensions concerning the fact that an agency which had no powers whatsoever in matters of state law would make substantive policy decisions, but even praising themselves for it, they effectively were asking just what the nature of modern Japanese rule of law was, something they raised proudly before the Chinese. While recognizing that the Office of Administrative Affairs had no real legal power, Office of Administrative Affairs-centrism was still lauded, and accordingly rule over Manzhouguo could be pursued in an efficient manner. Thus, the Office of Administrative Affairs was the core of power in Manzhouguo, and the Guandong Army controlled this core of power. Its means of control was called "internal guidance."

Although this internal guidance was also known as the "right of internal guidance," there was no basis in the laws of Manzhouguo for it to be called a right. Yet, the fact that the Guandong Army commander had the power to appoint and dismiss Japanese officials according to the agreement between Commander Honjō Shigeru and Puyi was understood to mean that a right of guidance in the execution of business while in office was collateral. There was no immediate issue of legality for this guidance to be "internal"; its essence was *de facto* legal force with control over personnel management. The Japanese government tolerated this planning for the realization of Japan's will to control by means of the internal guidance of the Guandong Army. In the Outline of a Plan for Guidance in Manzhouguo (*Manzhouguo shidō hōjin yōkō*) ratified by the Japanese Cabinet on August 8, 1933, it was determined that: "Leadership over Manzhouguo will fall primarily under the internal supervision of the Guandong Army commander and the imperial Japanese ambassador to Manzhouguo. It will effectively be carried out by the 'Japanese' officials." Furthermore, "the 'Japanese' officials shall become the nuclei for the management of Manzhouguo . . . and in order to streamline our control, we shall maintain the present system of Office of Administrative Affairs-centrism."[94] We can see the great emphasis placed here on these two sides of the same coin, internal guidance by the Guandong Army and Office of Administrative Affairs-centrism.

As the agency for internal guidance, the Third Section (later, the Fourth Section) of Operations of the Guandong Army responsible for political tactics and political affairs took over responsibility for matters involved in rule over Manzhouguo. On matters involving important political or administrative measures as well as decisions regarding the selection of "Japanese" officials, the Office of Administrative Affairs contacted the Third Section. After an investigation, reception of informal consent was requested in the form of a letter of approval—reading "On such-and-such a matter, [the Guandong Army] has approved, thus informing you of its decision"—in the name of the Guandong Army chief of staff to the director-general of the Office of Administrative Affairs. In addition, the Third Section controlled the right to personnel management of Japanese military men in Manchuria, including those in the General Headquarters of the Military Police of the Guandong Army and Office of Advisors in the Ministry of Military Administration. It used this power to carry out guidance over public order and disciplinary measures as well as military policy. It functioned precisely as a conning tower covering all aspects of Japanese management of Manzhouguo. Concerning the aim in executing Japanese state policy toward Manzhouguo: "This shall be primarily entrusted to the Guandong Army, and working to protect the integrity of the new state as an independent state, in the name of Manzhouguo we expect results through the 'Japanese' officials and especially the director-general of the Office of Administrative Affairs."[95]

Thus, the determination of politics in Manzhouguo required the following: how efficiently the aims of Japanese rule were being realized internally by Japanese officials under the guidance of the Guandong Army, while on the surface in order to avoid the criticism of international opinion that this was a puppet state or a protectorate adopting the guise of political decisions being made under the autonomous initiative of Chinese on the spot. Whether it was the allotment of positions to Japanese and Manchurians, the ratio of Japanese to Manchurians, the principle of Office of Adminstrative Affairs-centrism, or internal guidance, all symbolized the duality of the state's powers in law and de facto power, and were all temporizing measures, expedients to paint over this rift.

While continuing to be impregnated with contradictions based on this disjunction between surface and core, Manzhouguo was "made to adapt permanently to our national policies."[96] This became the underlying tone of Japanese-Manzhouguo relations.

Chapter Four
"The Long-Term Policy for National Management Will Always Be in Unison with the Japanese Empire"
The Paradise of the Kingly Way Stumbles and the Path Toward the Merging of Japan and Manzhouguo

In compensation for the blood and fear incurred, Manzhouguo nurtured in their infancy the many and varied dreams of a wide variety of people. However, self-calculation destroys dreams, and self-interest shatters hopes. The ideals of state-building simply patched over reality and functioned merely to suppress it. People perforce came to realize that the dreams they had invested in Manzhouguo were illusions, and they became firmly aware of the fact, right from the start, that this was not something easily manipulated.

With the founding of the state, Manzhouguo was already vehemently in the throes of the arena of stark realpolitik. How could this new state amid international criticism advocate legitimacy as an independent entity? How would it concretely operate as a state? In order to accomplish these tasks, what sort of relationship would be forged between Manzhouguo and Japan, and who would bear responsibility for it? The reality that this exposed is just what sort of state Manzhouguo would be. What sorts of ideas did the Japanese and Chinese tied to Manzhouguo entertain? What forms did their words and deeds take? How did they represent the distinctive character of the multiethnic state of Manzhouguo?

In this chapter, I shall describe characteristics of the political portrait of Manzhouguo by focusing on the relationship between the state and the individual there. In other words, my effort is tied to the nature of the modern Japanese state, how Japanese at the time understood it, and how the two were linked. For, as will become clear in this chapter, Manzhouguo existed as a mirror projecting a reflection of the state Japan should be; that is, when looking at a portrait of Manzhouguo, there was reflected an image of

Japan in one sense condensed and in another sense swollen. At the same time, this indicates how Japan, by the reflection from Manzhouguo, came to prescribe what its own state would look like.

With this in mind, let us follow the traces of Manzhouguo's transformations as a chimera and ascertain its coming to an end.

Evanescent Glory and Mounting Alienation

Once the first stage of the Manzhouguo problem has been completed, let's try our work elsewhere—so say the band of so-called entrepreneurs, speculators, and concession hunters. From now on they'll quickly be setting out en masse. Even in the city of Osaka with its special relationship to Manchuria and Mongolia, among the Chamber of Commerce and various business organizations they've formed a group, and in the name of an "investigation" they're testing the waters of graft.[1]

On January 22, 1932, the day that the founding of the state of Manzhouguo first appeared on the agenda of the press, the *Kyūshū nichinichi shinbun* (Kyūshū Daily News) reported in this story from Osaka that business opportunities were sprouting in Manchuria and Mongolia. The tone of this article gradually moved from the suggestion of the possibility of concessions and new business chances to one stressing reliability, a tone that was frequently iterated in the pages of this newspaper. This gave birth to the effect of rising public opinion in anticipation of the emergence of Manzhouguo; with its emergence this tone reached it acme, and the enthusiasm for it rose all the more.

On March 2, the day following the founding of the state, the *Ōsaka asahi shinbun* (Osaka Daily News) carried a special dispatch from Fengtian which reported that, in addition to such great business combines as Mitsui, Mitsubishi, Sumitomo, and Ōkura, "middle- and small-sized businessmen at the abyss of despair can seek a new realm to revive themselves. Thrusting themselves right into the midst of this Manchuria-Mongolia fever like a whirlwind, they come flocking to Manchuria-Mongolia, to Manchuria-Mongolia!" It went on: "For our country the founding of the state of Manzhouguo and the concomitant rise of new economic circumstances are literally the economic Messiah. . . . With the founding of the new state of Manzhouguo, a brilliant economic dawn sparkles on the land of Manchuria-Mongolia."[2] Every issue of the magazine *Ie no hikari* (Light of the Family), which was mainly concerned with agriculture and boasted a circulation of 170,000, was filled with articles bearing such titles as "The Fever of Emigration to Manchuria-Mongolia Pours over the Entire Nation."

Why was the establishment of Manzhouguo an "economic Messiah" for Japan? Why were Manchuria and Mongolia seen as a new world for economic resuscitation? Of course, these were not views based on firmly supported evidence, but merely wishful projections. Rather, that such excessive anticipation was expressed at all reflects the fact that the Japanese economy, about which there was a sense that, engulfed in the world depression and under attack by cold-weather damage and a poor harvest, had hit rock bottom, had of necessity to find in Manzhouguo its final escape hatch and break through the deadlock it faced. In distressed Japanese villages in 1931, numerous young women were sold into servitude, and a phenomenon known as *musume jigoku* or "hell for young women" emerged. The number of labor disputes reached a prewar high; the 26 percent employment rate for graduates from Tokyo Imperial University's Faculty of Law was at an all-time low, and the number of unemployed nationwide in January 1932, according to a publication of the Society Bureau of the Ministry of the Interior, reached 485,885. Numerous demonstrations for rice were held, and in July the Ministry of Education made public the fact that there were more than 200,000 pupils in Japan's rural and farming villages who were going to school without lunch. Furthermore, economic distress was causing cases of parent-child suicide one after the next, and the suicide rate was the highest that year, according to a statistical study of the causes of death since 1900. Turning the despair at the social and economic situation and sense of occlusion on its head, these all became the hopes invested in Manzhouguo. Such a process brought on the agitation for a Manchuria-Mongolia fever and a Manzhouguo boom: "To Manchuria-Mongolia, to Manchuria-Mongolia!"

In August 1932 when domestic Japanese anticipation for Manzhouguo reached its bizarre zenith, Yanaihara Tadao traveled to Manzhouguo "with the expectation that, since there had been such agitation in Japan over the Manchuria issue, some sort of frenzied mood must have been overflowing in Manchuria itself."[3] However, what awaited Yanaihara was not an extraordinary bubbling agitation, but, as he noted, a quiet far more peaceful than in Japan itself. Why was that the case? Yanaihara's judgment was that "in short, Japan still continued to stir with 'anticipation,' but Manchuria, it seems, has wakened to 'reality.'"[4] Yet, what "reality" had awakened in Manchuria? Concerning the excessively propagandized resources and rights in Manchuria-Mongolia, which may have provided a rationale, "whether it's a Japan-Manzhouguo economic bloc or the development of industry and the laying of new tracks for a train line or the issue of the migrant population, the spirit of leadership in these efforts is strongly tempered with a position on national defense and the military."[5] Despite the fact that an increased freedom of movement for Japanese was expected with the establishment of the state of Manzhouguo, because the Guandong Army intervened in any and everything, movement was actually restricted more than before the state appeared. This was, in fact, a natural result of the attempts of the Guandong Army to create Manzhouguo. The Japanese in Manzhouguo, though, in the half year or more following the establishment of the state, retreated into a strange silence. One reason for this taciturnity was that the image of the new state described in delirious terms and portrayed as a dream from the Manchurian Incident of September 18, 1931 onward gave rise to a "reality" with each passing day after the creation of the state, and accordingly the enthusiastic mood rapidly went cold.

At the time of the founding of the state, there was a movement among the Japanese bureaucracy to propose a state with something innovative, an ideal based in the principles of the Kingly Way. However, officials linked to the Majestic Peak Society who held these ideals were brought to their knees due to . . . [the incident] this past May [15]. The idealists are now no longer in the public eye. The process bespeaking the advent of the imperialist age has moved along according to all the rules. What I have seen satisfies my scholarly satisfaction as a scientific researcher in modern colonial policy.[6]

As Yanaihara Tadao, professor of colonial policy studies at Tokyo Imperial University, discerned, even in Manzhouguo, which should have been professing that it was providing a model as well as a new departure for international politics, the "process bespeaking the advent of the imperialist age has moved along according to all the rules." No matter how lofty the ideals proposed, a colony could only be treated as the object of exploitation according to the operative laws of a colony. This was the reality which his scientific research in the field of colonial policy taught, and Yanaihara perceived that Manzhouguo would be no exception to the laws. With this confirmed, was Yanaihara expressing "scholarly satisfaction" or not? As he saw it early on, the problem of Manchuria was a conflict between Japanese imperialism and Chinese nationalism, and Manzhouguo was a product emerging from that conflict.

He also firmly denied the position that Manzhouguo was the autonomous initiative of the people of the northeast. At the time of the founding of the state, he declared: "The basis of Japan's policy in China must be to aid in the unification of a modern state in China." And he noted the aphorism: "A calamity is the evil spirit that instills destructive intentions among the peoples of the world."[7] As far as Yanaihara was concerned, no matter how much beautiful, lofty propaganda was invested in ideals, the founding of a state in Manchuria could only bring about an intensification of Sino-Japanese enmity, furthering a rift between the two countries and not contributing to Chinese unity. No matter how lovely they may have sounded, the principles of state-building—such as "harmony of the five peoples" and "the paradise of the Kingly Way"—which attacked the northeastern warlords and the Nationalist government and emphasized the legitimacy of one's own state were spreading malicious ideas among the peoples of these states. Yanaihara probably saw the idealists themselves as calamitous spirits. Whatever illusions were strewn about, they would surely be wiped out by the grim realities of imperialism. Those who saw in Manzhouguo the realization of an ideal were purged, and as a result there ensued a fierce exploitation based precisely on the principles of imperialism. In short, Manzhouguo was never the ideal state that the idealizers called for, and as a "scientific researcher" Yanaihara was satisfied from a scholarly perspective when he made clear he had no ties to imperialist colonial control.

Whether or not this explanation is correct, in Yanaihara's eyes the movement to build a new state based on the principle of the Kingly Way and with a new point of departure had in just over 150 days from its establishment retrogressed severely, and a situation had emerged as he put it in which the "idealists are no longer in the public eye." If Yanaihara's observations were accurate, what then had recently been happening there?

The Self-Government Guidance Board, which commenced operations with two or three staff members at it main office in November 1931, went into each of the counties with principles for good government based on eradicating the warlords and establishing autonomy for the people of the county, worked hard in the state-building operation at the county level, and then finished its duties on March 15, 1932 following the founding of Manzhouguo and was abolished. At the time of its dissolution, the number of members on all local guidance boards had reached 234, and with such a large number they might have been seen as a major force of "Japanese" officials within the new government. However, the antagonism between the Majestic Peak Society and the Manchurian Youth League, which remained under wraps while they were engaged in a unified movement with the common goal of founding a state, came to the surface when state-founding was at hand and ironically the call went out: "Cooperate with hearts united, get rid of all evil ways of the past, and let us push ahead toward construction in the realm of ideals."[8] The rivalry between the two groups led to a decisive rift over the issue of the careful selection of personnel in the new government and how to pass along the duties of the Self-Government Guidance Board.

Most of the members of the Self-Government Guidance Board had thrust themselves into locales still smoldering from gunpowder and smoke, and devoted themselves without pay to the movement to build a state. They naturally anticipated that they would be appointed as "Japanese" officials in the new government. From the published personnel lists, however, while a large number of members of the Majestic Peak Society, many of whom were university graduates, were selected, members of the Manchurian Youth League—aside from Kanai Shōji, who received appointment into the Fengtian provincial government—were neglected with scarcely a single assignment in the central government. This selection of personnel was carried out by Wachi Yōji (1893–1978), staff officer of the Guandong Army, and Kasagi Yoshiaki of the Majestic Peak Society on the basis of the list drawn up by Matsuki Tamotsu, who drafted the organizational and bureaucratic system of the new government, while Nakano Koitsu of the Majestic Peak Society and Amakasu Masahiko (1890–1945) took part in personnel decisions as well. Kasagi had served as the head of the Personnel Desk in the S.M.R.'s main office in Dalian. When he negotiated to leave the S.M.R. and move to the new government, as the transition proceeded smoothly, he used his religious and political beliefs to screen potential appointees, using as a standard those experienced in the ideals of a rising Asia who walked the road of devotion to others. As a result, virtually all the Manchurian Youth League members fell through the sieve, causing discontent and a backlash. Nonetheless, the Manchurian Youth League, which had originally been composed of Manchurian residents from many different walks of life, was divided into those who became officials in the new government, those who remained in the Special Services Bureau of the Guandong Army, those who returned to their original professions, and those who were not appointed to posts and tried to continue the movement in the hinterland. They were unable to take unified, concerted action, and necessarily dispersed with the founding of the state of Manzhouguo (the dissolution ceremony was held on October 2, 1932).

Many of the members of the Manchurian Youth League who had rallied around the movement to found a Manchurian state with the slogan of "ethnic harmony" did not take part in the management of Manzhouguo at all but receded into the background, harboring great disillusion and resentment. By contrast, Kasagi and his associates in the Majestic Peak Society sustained a footing in the Bureau of National Affairs (in Manzhouguo's State Council) which was newly established by the government, and they came to exercise considerable influence within the Manzhouguo government. About four months after its birth, however, the Bureau of National Affairs suffered dissolution, and bearing grievous anger and malice even greater than members of the Manchurian Youth League, those affiliated with the Majestic Peak Society were driven from the government. Why then was the Bureau of National Affairs created only to undergo the fate of being abolished so soon thereafter?

With the dissolution of the Self-Government Guidance Board, dubbed the "womb for the birth of society by the Kingly Way" on the eve of the establishment of the state of Manzhouguo, a problem emerged: by what means and in what manner would such functions as the continued spread of the spirit of state-building, the growth of an ideology of autonomy, and the facilitation of administration be carried out, functions all performed to this point by the Self-Government Guidance Board? Kasagi had suggested the establishment of a National Council next to the State Council and directly under the Chief Executive within the government; it would serve as a guiding body for the realization of the ideology of state-building and the promotion of a moral politics. He also called for creation of a Public Relations Desk (originally, it was to be a Publicity Desk, and in effort to accord it the mission of spreading the law—namely, the truth—from Buddhist beliefs to a higher dimension, it became the Public Relations Desk), a Research Desk, and a Training Desk to handle personnel matters among the county-level self-government guidance people and to pursue the ideal of state-building. Matsuki Tamotsu and the others charged with drawing up plans for the Organizational Law of the Government were opposed to any plan for a National Council which would stand beside the State Council and would inevitably cause a bifurcation in the enforcement of state administration. They would not pass on this, arguing that the guidance and supervision of local administration should be the functions of the Ministry of Civil Affairs, which was the management office for domestic administration. Ultimately, they decided with the intervention of the Guandong Army to establish the Bureau of National Affairs as an agency directly under the control of the Minister of the State Council, and at the Public Relations Desk they supervised propaganda on the spirit of state-building, the fostering of national strength and proper guidance for the national will, and the spread of the ideology of self-government. In addition, they instituted a Research Desk and a Training Desk; the latter was a reorganization of the Training Desk in Self-Government placed under the direction of Kuchita Yasunobu (b. 1893). In actual fact, it inherited the principal tasks of the Self-Government Guidance Board. However, local administration and local personnel matters were to be handled by the Office of Local Affairs in the Ministry of Civil Affairs.

In this way a National Council did not materialize under the direct control of the Chief Executive, although the county-level self-government guidance people who were members of the Majestic Peak Society and had entered the Bureau of National Affairs had the self-assurance to claim that "self-government guidance is a divine entity to be enacted with the reception of the mandate of heaven, and it is most certainly not that which follows the dictates of a single Director-General of the Office of Administrative Affairs."[9] This indicated a posture of opposition around Kasagi to the State Council which took shape in the conflict between Director-General Komai Tokuzō of the Office of Administrative Affairs and Kasagi himself. According to Komai, such a move was understood in the following manner: "The Bureau of National Affairs will rally to Fengtian and Xinjing the former self-government guidance people in the various counties and organize them into county-level councils. The plan is to link them directly to the Chief Executive. . . . The issue then is a plan which shall attempt to organize two governments within one state. While it brandishes the superficial authority of the Chief Executive, it is a kind of treasonous act which seeks to direct a sword into the present government."[10]

Furthermore, with the idea that "the law codes are unnecessary for true men of will" and the principle of the Kingly Way—sublimely simple, like the legal concision effected by the founding emperor of the Han dynasty when he eliminated the excessively intricate, draconian codes of the Qin— Kasagi and his associates aimed at the realization of the ideal state. This aggravated the rivalry with the core of the government which was in a hurry to outfit a modern constitutional state and with Matsuki Tamotsu and his associates in the Legal Bureau. With the ideals of local self-governance and the decentralization of power into the localities, Kasagi and others were opposed to the consolidation of local institutions under centralized control toward which the Ministry of Civil Affairs was moving. Because so many of the county-level self-government guidance people ignored the Ministry of Civil Affairs which was the supervising bureaucratic office, an estrangement developed between Kasagi and Nakano Koitsu, head of the Office of Local Affairs in the Ministry of Civil Affairs and his staunch friend in the Majestic Peak Society. In addition, an incident was uncovered in which people associated with the Majestic Peak Society had protected Tachibana Kōzaburō (1893–1974) who had gone underground in Manzhouguo as a suspect in the May 15 Incident, and this was complicated by the fact that with the recruitment of students into the Training Desk of the Bureau of National Affairs carried out unannounced by Guandong Army Commander Honjō Shigeru and Director-General Komai Tokuzō of the Office of Administrative Affairs, among the examiners was Ōkawa Shūmei who was also tied to the May 15 Incident. Gaining control over this entanglement surrounding the Bureau of National Affairs became a major political task in Manzhouguo shortly after the state was founded.

The Guandong Army took secure control over the internal situation by focusing their concerns on the Office of Administrative Affairs. To that extent they deemed it appropriate to plan to unify the "Japanese" officialdom in Manzhouguo under the auspices of Director-General Komai and thus set the ball in motion for the abolition of the Bureau of National Affairs. In July the dismissal of Kasagi and thirty-one other bureaucrats in the Bureau of National Affairs and county-level self-government guidance personnel together with the dissolution of the the Bureau of National Affairs itself were announced; a new county-level bureaucratic administration was promulgated, and the county self-government guidance people were transformed into county-level councils. Thus, the Bureau of National Affairs, which was to carry on the orthodox line bequeathed by the Self-Government Guidance Board, disappeared in less than four months. Kasagi and others from the Majestic Peak Society who had brought together talented men with the awareness that they would work in obscurity across the vast terrain of Manchuria-Mongolia and who were enthusiastic about stirring up a great wave of a newly rising Asia from Manzhouguo were all driven from the government. To be sure, as Yanaihara Tadao had observed, a situation emerged in which "the idealists who sing in the key of the principle of the Kingly Way have been overthrown and now they're outcasts."

The issues surrounding the Bureau of National Affairs involved an opposition between basic directions to follow in state formation which the newly born Manzhouguo state faced: between the principles of bureaucratic control and self-government, between the principles of a constitutional state and those of the Kingly Way, between the principle of centralized rule and that of the local decentralization of power. As Kasagi and his associates argued, however, contrary to the control of Manzhouguo by means of Japanese imperialism and the pursuit of Japanese self-interest, was it not more appropriate to envision a struggle for the establishment of a paradise based on the principles of self-government, solidarity, and idealism on behalf of the welfare of the thirty million inhabitants of Manchuria-Mongolia? Perhaps one might disagree. When these men spoke of self-government, decentralization of power, and ideals, who—one might ask—would be doing the self-governing, on whose behalf was the decentralization of power aimed, and for whom were these ideals? The simple fact that as "governing officials" they relied upon themselves should enable to gain insight into this matter. When they spoke of the principle of self-governance or that of the Kingly Way, this was ultimately no more than propping up and promoting rule over Manzhouguo on another level by the Guandong Army and Japan. Tachibana Shiraki opposed Kasagi's movement and offered the following vitriolic critique: "The masses should have fixed in their memory the fact that, to the extent that they take an interest in a theory that mistakes the feudal spirit for the spirit of East Asia and a 'conceptual amusement' that confuses religious reform and ethnic harmony, this will be neither leisurely nor to their good fortune."[11] Tachibana's criticism hit the mark.

By the same token, precisely because there might be no good fortune, people might yearn for dreams and attempt to commit themselves to ideologies and "conceptual amusements." We have to recognize the fact that, in a world full of corruption, the establishment of Manzhouguo itself was a glorious deed intended to reveal the scope of the ideal society of the paradise of the Kingly Way, and this vision-like dream continued to have a power of attraction and continued to entice young Japanese to cross the sea to the continent.

With the dismemberment of the Bureau of National Affairs, the Training Desk was reorganized into the Daidō Academy, and now, it was claimed, this was the orthodox heir to the Self-Government Guidance Board. From the Daidō Academy, which became a hotbed of this "idealistic dream," nineteen classes or roughly 4,000 students graduated, until the breakup of Manzhouguo. Their beliefs—"be selfless and pure," and "volunteer for the difficult tasks"—were the mottos of the Daidō Academy. They had made their way into the remote terrain of intense cold in order to establish a "paradise of the Kingly Way" based on "harmony of the five ethnic groups," and on many occasions they had dyed the earth there with blood as they exchanged fire with anti-Manzhouguo, anti-Japanese forces.

Whether or not they knew of the existence of the Chinese people who had lost their home towns, lost their actual homes, or even lost their lives to these Japanese and the dreams to which they sacrificed themselves, within Japan proper the following sentences were incessantly brewing iniquities like beautiful dreams:

We are battered by the expression of this new, gentler world view in a form that allows for no political impurities at all. . . . What the facts are, I do not know, but Manzhouguo is manifestly moving forward. That is, "Manzhouguo" is now, for the first time since the French Republic and the Soviet Union, an unprecedented and bold new civilizational ideal and an expression of such a world view.[12]

This is highly seductive rhetoric: while saying "What the facts are, I do not know, but," the author asserts that Manzhouguo was "an unprecedented and bold new civilizational ideal and an expression of such a world view." He continued: "What is truly calamitous is the miraculous power of language which scatters dreams among young people."[13]

The Retreat of the Principle of the Kingly Way: A Frozen State-Building Ideal

Completely contrary to their initial desires, the men of the Self-Government Guidance Board who thus bore a heavy private burden on behalf of the state-building movement were successively kept away from the central government and driven away from Manzhouguo. As this situation ensued, the staff officers of the Guandong Army who were expected to be able to reach their anticipated objectives successfully were rejoicing at this turn of events.

To be sure, they were linked by a common goal that "military men and their sympathizers in Manchuria were for the time being divested themselves of Japanese citizenship and were dashing ahead toward the attainment of their objectives"[14] in the face of fierce opposition from the Japanese central government's Army Ministry, General Staff Headquarters, and the Ministry of Foreign Affairs. Yet, with the main strategy almost completed, how were these activities related to the new state, and what were they looking for in the new state? At this stage, one can now begin to see a rent in the unity binding the staff officers of the Guandong Army. From the differences in the way each took his stance, a cacophony emerged leading to mutual distrust. According to Katakura Tadashi, soon after the founding of Manzhouguo "its pros and cons were argued at every possible moment" among the staff officers.[15] In particular, "in opposition to the general affairs section which had responsibility for the administration of policy, other section staffers would be no party to this. Because the meaning of 'general affairs' was not precisely understood, section staffers were put in charge of trivial matters and grew increasingly discontented."[16] Thus, the fissure deepened between those staff officers who were enthusiastic about managing Manzhouguo and those staff officers who were too proud to be connected in any way to political stratagems. As this bifurcating trend developed, a distance grew within the "combination" that ranked the activist Itagaki with the resourceful Ishiwara as contemplation of Ishiwara's ideals for the establishment of the new state intensified. "Staff Officer Ishiwara took no part in personnel or any other policy matters; he was dissatisfied with the way they were being handled by Staff Officer Itagaki, and this caused a flare up of dissatisfaction."[17] Yet, Katakura offered the critical remark that "a lack of coherence in policy for the new state among the officialdom revealed that Staff Officer Ishiwara was a man who by nature was prone to change. Staff Officer Itagaki was the most tenacious of all."[18] From this statement one can see that deviating from the Guandong Army's aim of state construction, Ishiwara had given in completely to the construction of a "paradise of the Kingly Way" based on "harmony of the five ethnic groups," while the other staff officers were filled with distrust and discontent for this objective.

What in fact Ishiwara thought of Manzhouguo and how he believed it should be ruled underwent extremely wide fluctuations. On December 2, 1931 he argued that "the central government should rely completely on Japan."[19] However, on January 25, 1932, he shifted 180 degrees to a new position: "The Japanese and Chinese people should stand in complete equality."[20] Yet, from the perspective of administrative capacity at the time, he did acknowledge in the latter essay the leadership position of the Japanese: "It is only natural that for high-level officials we employ a considerable majority of Japanese, and for low-level posts we increase the number of Chinese officials."[21] Then, three months later, in a memorandum of April 22, he proposed to Obata Toshishirō (1885–1947), director of the general staff operations bureau: "The government of the new state should operate fairly on the basis of the just participation of the various peoples who live in Manchuria. . . . These peoples should implement a social and economic plan with complete equality."[22] He had thus changed to a stance of rulership based upon thorough ethnic equality. Needless to say, this direction flew directly in the face of the mutual understanding of the Guandong Army, which was that military headquarters would carry out the national policy of Japan in Manchuria and Mongolia through internal guidance over Japanese ministers and officials in Manzhougou. Furthermore, it contradicted the understanding that "although we shall advocate the principles of an open door and equality of opportunity, of utmost importance is the principle that we plan in the interests of Japan and the Japanese."[23] The Guandong Army had taken this as a natural assumption in founding the state of Manzhouguo.

It is difficult to imagine that this apostasy by Ishiwara was probably seen by other staff officers as an irrational argument pushed through forcibly against international opinion and domestic Japanese opposition and which completely contradicted the import of founding the state of Manzhouguo.

"Why in the world did we take such risks and make so many sacrifices?" they would have responded. Ishiwara's views escalated contemptuously in the face of such reactions and doubts among the staff officers. In June, he set out an innovative plan for ruling Manzhouguo, and he advocated in it for the first time an idea which abandoned policy leadership by the Guandong Army. This led to his becoming increasingly isolated by the other staff officers, and discord between the two sides became ever more severe. The conception Ishiwara laid out was for a Manzhouguo Kyōwakai or "Concordia Association" which would serve in place of the Guandong Army as an agency responsible for deciding the highest policy in Manzhouguo. In a letter to Isogai Rensuke (1883–1945), Chief of the Appointments Section of the War Ministry's Personnel Bureau, Ishiwara laid out his ideas on the present state and future for ruling Manzhouguo:

At present, the rulers are the commanding officers of the Guandong Army, and they decide highest policy. . . . The highest policy decided upon by these commanding officers is then executed by the government in Changchun. That is to say, the chairman of the State Council and chief of the Office of Administrative Affairs are political commissioners under the army's commanding officers. . . . However, the commanding officers of the Guandong Army cannot remain the rulers of Manzhouguo forever, and we must train their successors as quickly as possible. Yet, those successors ought not be like the despotic monarch Puyi, nor for that matter should they resemble the mass representative bodies and legislative councils based on the principles of liberty. We must conclude that there be a political body which is a representative entity based on the principles of control. The Concordia Association of Manzhouguo was in fact established with this goal in mind. With a sound and smooth development, it will gain the support of the 30,000,000 people [living in Manzhouguo]. Only then should sovereignty be passed from the commanding officers of the army to this body, and it should be seen as a government to implement the highest policy drafted and planned by the Concordia Association.[24]

Despite the fact that the Organizational Law of the Government stipulated that "the Chief Executive shall rule Manzhouguo," he pointed out in this piece that the real condition of rulership in Manzhouguo was self-evidently one in which the commanding officers of the army of another country held control as rulers. It required no treatise to note that the essence of a puppet state was exposed here in the discrepancy between this government organization and actual power. Ishiwara, though, had not the least doubt about this. In this sense, his realistic perceptions had no expectations from Puyi or the Legislative *Yuan*, as they were oriented toward a political system on the model of a single-party dictatorship.

What then was to be the political organization of the Concordia Association of Manzhouguo, envisioned as the nucleus of decision making in the future state of Manzhouguo?

The Concordia Association of Manzhouguo traced its origins to the Concordia Party formed by Yamaguchi Jūji (b. 1892) and Ozawa Kaisaku, both of the Manchurian Youth League which had been groping for a successor to the Self-Government Guidance Board after the formation of the state of Manzhouguo, together with Yu Jingyuan and Ruan Zhenduo. Ishiwara hated the fact that personnel decisions in the new state were monopolized by such men as staff officer Wachi Yōji and Kasagi. For his part, Kasagi criticized Ishiwara as a warlord for whom strategy was always most important. The rivalry between them was growing deeper and more profound. This competition naturally brought Ishwara closer to men such as Yamaguchi and Ozawa who had had nothing but disdain for Kasagi and those associated with the Majestic Peak Society, whom they saw as a group of office-seekers. By supporting the Manchurian Concordia Party of Yamaguchi and others which was trying to spread the ideals of state-building as a private movement, Ishiwara was attempting to realize reforms in the ruling structure of Manzhouguo into which there was no good reason for Guandong Army staffers to have any input.

Yamaguchi and his colleagues understood the essense of the Manzhouguo state as having been built to serve as a democratic revolution for the thirty million local inhabitants. This recognition was in itself, of course, problematic. In any event, however, while the Manzhouguo state may have been a democratic revolution, because it was an anomalous revolution based on leadership support from the Guandong Army, they understood that two essential elements to this revolution had been missing: "the principle of guidance and the unification of consciousness."[25] As the absent principle of guidance, he offered "ethnic harmony" (*minzoku kyōwa*), and on its basis he set as the goal of the Concordia Party of Manchuria to plan for the unification of consciousness among the thirty million residents of the region. In a declaration drafted in the middle of March 1932, it was stated: "We shall, of course, pay close attention to the maintenance of public order and plan for the increased well-being of the people's livelihood. We shall as well get rid of the ethnic biases of the past, plan for a great unity of the ethnic groups here now, and with our united cooperation we shall press on to see the realization of a popular government and reforms in the economic structure."[26] Thus, the movement raised as its objective the realization of a society not interfered with by "capitalist pressures" and "Communist agitation." In support of a conception of the Concordia Party of Manchuria, Ishiwara offered a one-party authoritarian model: "If we do not adopt the one-state, one-party principle, there will be the danger that a flood of parties will emerge, and we shall sink into ethnic strife in a Manzhouguo with a weak foundation."[27] One of Ishiwara's advisors, Miyazaki Masayoshi, offered the view that "both the Communist Party of the Soviet Union and the Chinese Communist Party pay party dues from the state coffers. This has become a general rule of modern political parties." With this view adopted, then a plan was drawn up to supply party fees from the state's treasury, and a decree was drafted which stipulated this as a special law. Denouncing, as they frequently had in the past, the one-party despotism of the Guomindang, the "invasion of Red bandits," and "Communist agitation," they now raised as an objective the elimination of the Guomindang and the Chinese Communists. We can see here the peculiar nature of law and politics in Manzhouguo, in that they took as a model the very thing which they actually opposed in structure and management.

Be that as it may, the draft decree concerning the Concordia Party of Manchuria was not approved by the Chief Executive once it had been agreed upon at a meeting of the State Council on April 15. Between this and the emergence of an idea of a "constitutional Kingly Way association" offered by Katakura Tadashi as "a party organization protected by state power,"[28] the two would exchange ideas and compromise on a unified approach, and the Concordia Party of Manchuria would change its name to the Concordia Association of Manzhouguo. Its opening ceremony took place at the State Council on July 25. For a time, the problem of the Concordia Party lay on the shelf and then suddenly it was pushed forward. Behind all this, the Bureau of National Affairs, which had a similar organizational objective and which had had a problematic relationship with it, was dissolved on July 5. The situation was such that a national "enlightenment" group to shoulder the spread of the state-building spirit had become necessary.

In its inaugural manifesto, the Concordia Association of Manzhouguo stressed that it rejected capitalism, Communism, and the Three Principles of the People. It stated clearly that "we shall follow the state-founding spirit, and with the Kingly Way as our principle and ethnic harmony as our concern, we shall strengthen the foundation of the state, carrying out our declaration on behalf of government by the Kingly Way."[29] Insofar as can be seen in this manifesto, as they initially planned it, Yamaguchi and his associates took ethnic harmony as their guiding principle and denied any role to capitalism or Communism, as they launched an "educative" organization that sought ideological integration in Manzhouguo. Among their members, however, were the following names: Puyi as honorary president, Guandong Army Commander Honjō Shigeru as honorary adviser, Prime Minister Zheng Xiaoxu as chairman, Chief of Staff Hashimoto Toranosuke, Komai Tokuzō (director-general of the Office of Administrative Affairs), and Staff Officer Itagaki Seishirō as honorary members of the board of directors. Without a doubt, from the very beginning this body was heavily tinged with a top-down bureaucratic structure, formed with the sanction of the Guandong Army and the Manzhouguo government, and whose operating expenses were subsidized by the state treasury. To that extent, beginning from the reflection that the founding of Manzhouguo was seen as an anomalous democratic revolution because of the guiding assistance rendered by the Guandong Army, the goal that brought together the Concordia Party of Manchuria which was to be one with the Guandong Army was now completely disavowed, and the original aim of a unified consciousness for the thirty million inhabitants of Manchuria was abandoned. In any event, the slogan of "ethnic harmony" proposed by the Manchurian Youth League was carried on among the activist ideals of the Concordia Association of Manzhouguo even after the dissolution of the Manchurian Youth League. As to the role of the Concordia Association and how it was to be mobilized in ruling Manzhouguo, there was no mutual consent among the Guandong Army, Ishiwara Kanji, and the Manzhouguo government, nor with private participants such as Yamaguchi and Ozawa. Thus, dissension eventually arose among the Guandong Army, the government, and Yamaguchi and his fellows over the movement associated with the Concordia Association.

Ishiwara set up the Concordia Association as the future rulers of Manzhouguo because it was a necessity to Japan's victory in the final world war, his long-cherished ambition. As he put it in a memorandum to Isogai Rensuke: "Taking hold of the thirty million inhabitants of Manchuria, we shall make Manzhouguo into an ideal paradise and celebrate genuine Japanese-Manchurian harmony as well as Sino-Japanese harmony. In so doing, our Japan should be able to attempt that final war against the white race as rulers of East Asia."[30] Thus, the Concordia Association was to turn Manzhouguo into an ideal paradise and aspire to Japanese-Manchurian and Sino-Japanese harmony, but it was certainly never to be a goal unto itself. One may entertain doubts about the evaluations of men such as Yamaguchi Jūji, who called Ishiwara an idealist set on realizing a paradise of the Kingly Way and ethnic harmony. To be sure, Ishiwara was not a shallow strategist, nor was he at this time naive to the extent of falling head first into a fiction of his own concoction, losing himself in his own aspirations. Related to the management of Manzhouguo in the same memorandum where he advocated "making Manzhouguo into an ideal paradise and celebrating genuine Japanese-Manchurian harmony as well as Sino-Japanese harmony," we can see this clearly from the following conditions he attached to it:

1. Irrespective of whether we can expect the support of the people [of Manchuria], should there be any interference by Chinese of importance, we shall decisively make this our terrain.
2. Should it be difficult to gain the support of the Chinese people, either we shall ourselves withdraw from Manchuria-Mongolia as a powerless entity or we shall squeeze them with pressure.[31]

In fact, the discourse inherent in Ishiwara's idealism was expressed as but one link in a coldly realistic technology for ruling Manzhouguo which concealed this final sanction. Of course, it was not the case that for Ishiwara, Honjō, Itagaki, or others that ruling Manzhouguo was their ultimate goal. Not one to express his personal views frivolously, even Honjō had stated: "I would like to usher in reforms of Japan from Manchuria."[32] As a base of operations for the reform of Japan, then, Manzhouguo had distinct existential significance. Although it was a fact that the Guandong Army led the Japanese ministries and the Japanese government as far as establishing the state of Manzhouguo, its role shifted sharply after the state's founding. Political party cabinets had collapsed already around the time of the May 15 Incident, and the military authorities, together with the establishment of a cabinet "supported by the entire nation," advanced to the forefront of Japanese politics as agents of rulership beside the bureaucracy and the political parties. For Army Central the popular spirit of "inferiors displacing superiors" that had been brewing in the process of the Manchurian Incident was renewed, and it became an emergency task to restore the controlling power over Manzhouguo to the Guandong Army, which crowed that "Army Central should instruct us only on points that its branches cannot decide."[33] By the same token, though, while excluding as much as possible the intentions of the Foreign Ministry, the Finance Ministry, the Ministry of Overseas Affairs, and the Ministry of Commerce and Industry, the army as a whole (including the Guandong Army) sought to gain possession of an absolutely superior position in control over Manzhouguo as a consequence of military actions taken by the Guandong Army.

The transfer in August of 1932 from the Guandong Army of staff officers—Honjō Shigeru, Ishiwara Kanji, Katakura Tadashi, Wachi Yōji, and Takeshita Yoshiharu, though excluding Itagaki Seishirō—who were the prime movers in the founding of Manzhouguo became a necessity in Army Central's restoration of control. This transformation of troop array "meant the extension of the center's controlling power and renovated Manchurian personnel in the founding era of rival chiefs."[34] At this time the commanding officer of the Guandong Army was also ambassador-extraordinaire and plenipotentiary to Manzhouguo as well as governor-general of Guandong, holding three positions simultaneously. Furthermore, the position of commanding officer of the Guandong Army moved from Lieutenant General Honjō to General Mutō Nobuyoshi (1868–1933), and chief of staff from Major General Hashimoto to Lieutenant General Koiso Kuniaki (former vice-minister of war), revealing an elevation of rank in each post. This change was aimed at strengthening the voice of the military in the organizational expansion into Manzhouguo and in the control over Manzhouguo within the Japanese government. To the extent that the Guandong Army was within the control of the state ministries, it enhanced its capacity to draft policy and its inspection function as an agency of control in Manzhouguo. This was linked to the raising of its position within the ministries of the Japanese government, and the ministries came to recognize an enlarged function for the Guandong Army. Together with the responsibilities of Mutō and Koiso, the Operations Bureau and the Special Service Bureau, which were charged with political leadership in Manzhouguo, expanded their staffing, and with the cooperation of the Economic Research

Association of the South Manchurian Railway Company (S.M.R.), the Guandong Army's controlling force in Manzhouguo grew significantly.

The transformation of military personnel meant as well a change in the direction of control over Manzhouguo. For Honjō and others, the basic direction in ruling Manzhouguo lay in the point that "we want absolutely to eliminate from Manchuria finance capital and the influence of the political parties."[35] However, Koiso and his associates moved toward an orientation which advised "a bold economic advance with perceptive attention to overview of policies profitable to the state without being misled by past demagoguery, namely by notice boards banning the entrance into Manchuria of the economic combines."[36] Upon leaving Manzhouguo, Ishiwara entrusted subsequent matters to Itagaki, the only one of his colleagues remaining there, and relied on him for a thoroughness of direction in the restoration of local administrative power in the SMR zone, the abrogation of extraterritoriality, the elimination of the military's political interference, nurturing the Concordia Association of Manzhouguo as the future rulers, and an end to special privileges for Japanese in the development of Manchuria. Once he was back home in Japan, though, when Ishiwara spoke directly with Nagata Tetsuzan (1884–1945), director of the second bureau of the general staff, he was informed that "the direction is that Manchuria shall gradually become our territory."[37] He was deeply stunned. In addition, Koiso, who refused to recognize the existence of the Concordia Association of Manzhouguo, brought pressure to bear until there emerged from among the "Japanese" officials in Manzhouguo in 1934 views calling for the dismemberment of the Concordia Association. With a reorganization in September, Yamaguchi Jūji, the assistant director-general, and others in the lineages of the Manchurian Youth League and the Concordia Party of Manchuria were expelled from the central secretariat. Sakatani Kiichi (1889–1957), assistant director of the Office of Administrative Affairs, and other Japanese officials replaced them, and bureaucratic control over the Concordia Association was gradually heightened. This transformation of the Concordia Association was not, as Ishiwara had envisioned it, a maturation of it as a political party that would come to have principal authority in Manchuria-Mongolia based on the support of the thirty million local residents. What it demonstrated was that the local "Japanese" officials who were receiving internal guidance from the Guandong Army were playing the main ruling role.

Already in July 1932, the *Tōkyō Asahi Shinbun* reported that it appeared as though Hoshino Naoki and other bureaucrats in the Ministry of Finance were being sent to Manzhouguo: "High young official to Manzhouguo. He goes extremely well-preparedness" (July 10); "Departure of a peace volunteer" (July 12). From that time forward, bureaucrats from the various offices of the Ministry of Communications, the Ministry of the Interior, the Ministry of Justice, and the Ministry of Commerce and Industry one after the next traveled to the mainland to become the "Japanese" officials within the Manzhouguo government. It was a situation in which "each of the government ministries opened shop in Manchuria."

As concerned this change, Yamaguchi Jūji argued that in the history of Manzhouguo a clear divide should be seen between events through August 1932 and thereafter, for the guiding direction of the Guandong Army was altogether different. In other words, while the guiding direction of the Honjō era "lay in protecting and nurturing Manzhouguo," thereafter "they turned Manzhouguo into a dependency and colony of Japan, based on capitalism."[38] This might also be diagrammed as a transformation "from assistance with independence to vassalage, from the principle of ethnic harmony to imperialism."[39] However, this transfer, more than a change in quality itself, might only have been a difference of depth in judgment as to which method was more efficient for attaining results. This was precisely in conformity with Ishiwara's conception of things. There was indeed no great difference between the Honjō era and that which succeeded it in the fact that the construction of "a national defense state linking Japan and Manzhouguo with the advance of a forceful reform policy through military leadership" in the control of Manzhouguo.[40] The principal difference was how to conscript capital and human talent toward this end.

There is no denying, though, that for those who were promoting the formation of a state in Manchuria, the Guandong Army's shift in personnel of August 1932 was profoundly felt to be the beginning of a sudden darkening of the stage which portended change. Tachibana Shiraki wrote in March 1934: "Since the summer of the previous year [1932], in truth I haven't met with even one piece of happy news concerning Manzhouguo, be it political, economic, or social."[41] Also, as concerned the construction of "a society governed by the Kingly Way rooted in the poor peasantry," he was seized by the dark premonition that "our future, objectively speaking, will of necessity turn that much gloomier."[42]

Having already been forced out of Manzhouguo, Kasagi Yoshiaki, Kuchita Yasunobu, and the other leaders of the Majestic Peak Society had been groping for a way to develop a pan-Asian movement in Japan. Having purged Kasagi and others and found a way to rule through "Japanese" officials, Director-General for Administrative Affairs Komai Tokuzō, who was opposed to having high-level "Manchurian" officials such as Prime Minister Zheng Xiaoxu, resigned his post as director-general in October, only three months after the purge. With the expansion of "Japanese" officials in Manzhouguo, he became alienated and left. Nakano Koitsu, who had parted company with Kasagi, also in October, like Komai, resigned his post as head of the Office of Local Affairs in the Ministry of Civil Affairs. Unable to realize his wish to become director of the Office of Administrative Affairs in Rehe province, Nakano abruptly left Manzhouguo and headed for Southeast Asia, where he passed away in an inn. The former Concordia

Party men such as Yamaguchi Jūji and Ozawa Kaisaku who had tried to use the Concordia Association to guide in the state-building principles of "ethnic harmony" and "a paradise of the Kingly Way" were estranged from the central figures in the Concordia Association. Thereafter, they split up, with Yamaguchi going to Mudanjiang Province and Ozawa leaving for Beijing. Ishiwara and Honjō, who had supported them, were no longer in Manzhouguo. About this time Tachibana Shiraki jotted down the line: "I am reminded of deep desolation." In a eulogy for Kishi Kishirō (1894–1933), who had worked hard for the emergence of a new intellectual approach concerning Manzhouguo, in the journal *Manshū hyōron*, edited by Tachibana, who had shifted from being a businessman to an adherent of the principle of the Kingly Way, and who died with his goal only half-fulfilled, the following sentences were offered as a tribute to him:

A theorist and a practitioner of the principle of the Kingly Way began his general retreat from the political front. . . . Instead of the principle of the Kingly Way being substantively experienced in the midst of the fields, this important and manifest event was a spectacle which had to have a propaganda function as antiseptic stuffed into a test tube, adornment on the show window of the Manchurian office of an international capitalist exposition. The principle of the Kingly Way did not commit suicide; it is about to be murdered.[43]

The "Manchurian fever" that arose in Japan with the founding of Manzhouguo and the temporary mania accompanying the revival of business conditions dropped off as the tide ebbed. A sad melody—entitled "Crying of a Shrike in a Withered Tree"—was at the time in Japan being hummed, as if muttered, with lyrics by Satō Hachirō and music composed by Tokutomi Shigeru.

Older brother's gone off to Manchuria,
Gunfire glistening in his tears.
The shrike's cold and crying out,
Older brother's even colder.

The Manchurian winter is said to reach as low as forty degrees below zero. In this intensely cold terrain of the north, state-building ideals rapidly froze. The shading was that much darker as an intense shaft of light.

A Thorny Path—Zheng Xiaoxu and Recognition for Manzhouguo

For Japan, which had created Manzhouguo amid the swirling eddies of international criticism, the next task was how to get recognition as an independent nation for what was seen as "a bogus state" and "a puppet state." Prudence was deeply rooted when it came to consideration of the position of the United States, a country which had taken a firm policy of non-recognition, as well as for the League of Nations. Before Japan had yet to recognize Manzhouguo, however, the view was voiced that this was a prime opportunity for Japan to annex Manchuria and make it "a second Korea," and if having it proved to be too much, then Japan could relinquish it. Still, the majority opinion was that Japan should with all alacrity recognize Manzhouguo so that it would not be isolated. Thus, at a session of the Lower House of the Diet on June 14, 1932, a resolution to recognize Manzhouguo was adopted without a single dissenting vote. Following this, the government laid out the Japan-Manzhouguo Protocol concerning recognition in a cabinet meeting on August 19, and in this connection Mutō Nobuyoshi, who had been appointed commanding officer of the Guandong Army as well as ambassador-extraordinaire and plenipotentiary, set off for Manchuria. He entered into negotiations with the Manzhouguo government over signing the Japan-Manzhouguo Protocol, and in rapid succession he concluded agreements with Prime Minister Zheng Xiaoxu over entrusting supervision of railways, harbors, waterways, air routes, and the like to the Guandong Army, establishing a joint Japanese-Manzhouguo airline company, and authorizing either Japan or a joint Japanese-Manzhouguo company with mining rights.

On August 25 Foreign Minister Uchida Yasuya (1865–1936) in a speech on foreign affairs at the 63rd extraordinary session of the Diet affirmed the implementation of recognition by stating that such recognition of Manzhouguo would "stabilize the current conditions in Manchuria-Mongolia and by extension was the only cure to bring about a long-lasting peace in the Far East."[44] Responding to questions after his speech, Uchida claimed that there was not the least doubt that Japan's recogition of Manzhouguo was a fair and appropriate approach. Thus, he claimed in defense of his position, "I have resolved that the nation is as one on this issue and will make no concessions in seeing this view to completion even if it means burning the nation to the ground."[45] This became known as Foreign Minister Uchida's "scorched earth diplomacy" (*shōdo gaikō*). Given this posture, on September 15 the Diet charged ahead with recognition of Manzhouguo, giving as a reason: "The Japanese nation recognizes the facts that Manzhouguo was created freely on the basis of the will of its inhabitants and that it is an independent state."[46] The Japanese mass media in unison welcomed the legal recognition of Manzhouguo which received it some six months after the establishment of the state, and the following sort of speech was carried in the press:

The day of recognition for Manzhouguo has arrived. The sincere aspirations of Manzhouguo and our fervent convictions have been united. So dawns a new era in world history. For Japan which has an interdependence and a coexistence-coprosperity relationship with this new life of an independent state as a bulwark to insure peace in East Asia, the day has come when we can publicly pronounce a blessing on this independence.[47]

The recognition, though, emerged from an effort to create a fait accompli out of the independent state of Manzhouguo before the report of the Lytton Commission, which was completed on September 4, was to be made public. As expected, the report stated clearly that "the present regime cannot be considered to have been called into existence by a genuine and spontaneous independence movement."[48] It flew directly in the face of the understanding of the Japan-Manzhouguo Protocol. On February 24, 1933, by a vote of 42 for, one against (Japan), and one abstention (Siam), the League of Nations voted not to recognize Manzhouguo. The Japanese representatives left the assembly, and on March 27 officially announced Japan's withdrawal from the League. This was a high price to pay for Manzhouguo's recognition, and in exchange for Japanese-Manzhouguo mutual defense, Japan was forced to travel the steep path of international isolation. This took shape as a focal point of opposition with the United States which had articulated the principles of non-recognition of Manzhouguo in the Stimson Doctrine on January 7, 1932, and it was linked as an undercurrent to the commencement of the Pacific War.

Hōchi Shinbun (September 16) reported on the spectacle of the signing ceremony of the Japan-Manzhouguo Protocol on September 15, the celebratory mood of Ambassador-Extraordinaire and Plenipotentiary Mutō signing, and the exchange of greetings: "Prime Minister Zheng wore a beaming countenance, returned salutations, exchanged a firm handshake, his facial features full of deep emotion, and then bowed lightly and took his seat."[49] However, according to the notes taken by First Secretary Yonezawa Kikuji and others who were present that day as attendants to Mutō, Zheng Xiaoxu's response to Mutō's greetings was altogether different:

Prime Minister Zheng was attempting to make his formal response rapidly, but he was unable to do so. He mumbled something in vain, the tension in his mien burning to an extraordinary extent, his face about to break out in tears—five seconds, ten seconds, thirty seconds. He wanted to finish his speech but couldn't. Like a storm, the rumblings in his heart were ample evidence of the complexity of strong emotions going through him.[50]

Zheng Xiaoxu had abruptly turned in his resignation six days before this signing and refused to attend meetings of the State Council. The reason given was discord between himself and Director-General Komai Tokuzō. This opposition had emerged just after the founding of the state of Manzhouguo, for we read in the *Hata Shunroku nisshi* (Diary of Hata Shunroku) for July 10, 1932: "Prime Minister Zheng seems to have become disgusted. He's been speaking about resigning, while the Japanese side has worked hard to restrain him from doing so. He has gradually been compelled to drop the idea."[51] This time, however, his intention to resign had become extremely firm. The Guandong Army, though, could not suspend the signing before its very eyes while shuffling prime ministers. To get him to change his mind, Komai would be transferred after the official ratification, and they managed to get through the signing eventually. The differences between Zheng and Komai were public knowledge within the Manzhouguo government, but Yonezawa was of the opinion that Zheng's intention to resign revealed more than just a will to attack Komai. Namely, he conjectured that "he would by signing [the Protocol] be designated with the disgrace of a traitor, and he feared that he would be seen by 400,000,000 Chinese forever after as the ringleader in the abandonment of Manchuria [to the Japanese]. Full of tension and anguished on the actual day of the signing, he may have tendered his resignation in order to avoid responsibility for this."[52] Thus, in the end the apprehension that Zheng Xiaoxu might refuse to sign did not go away, and seeing the extraordinary torment on Prime Minister Zheng's face, Yonezawa wrote that they had to bring the signing to a quick end; and postponing the entry of the date when they would carry it out, they first demanded his signature.

To be sure, it was clear that the real power in control of Manzhouguo, even in legal terms, was held by Japan by means of the Japan-Manzhouguo Protocol which included the Puyi-Honjō letter and the Mutō-Zheng pact. The Shōwa Emperor, Hirohito, personally appointed Mutō Nobuyoshi to his posts of commanding officer of the Guandong Army as well as ambassador-extraordinaire and plenipotentiary, and instructed him orally: "Work diligently to spread even better government than was the case in the era of Zhang Xueliang."[53] Together with recognizing the existence of Manzhouguo, the emperor had full knowledge of in whose hands real political power lay.

This was most keely felt by the man with the most responsibility for the implementation of state policy, the sole minister of state according to the Organizational Law of the Government, and it was this man, Zheng Xiaoxu, who had no choice but to put up with the humiliation of being under the complete control of the director-general for administrative affairs, a "Japanese" bureaucratic post. Soon after the founding of Manzhouguo, Zheng traveled to Xinjing (formerly Changchun) and, in reply to Yano Jin'ichi, who queried him about his aspirations for the future of Manzhouguo, Zheng smiled desolately and said in a bothered tone of voice: "I'm a hired traveling player, not the stage manager. Since the script was written by someone else, I've only been informed of the general plot line. So I can't answer your question."[54] In this exchange between Zheng and Yano, an authority on Manchurian history in Japan, who was advocating the legitimacy of the establishment of Manzhouguo and the significance of government on the basis of the Kingly War, one can see the sharp contrast between the reverie for and the reality of Manzhouguo. Zheng's claim that he was "a hired traveling player" carried with it the cynical self-deprecation that he was born in Fuzhou (Fujian Province) and had scarcely an acquaintance in this distant terrain to the far north where he held merely a nominal position. It was, however, an honest emotion.

Although prime minister in name, this position sat atop the balance of a tripod of the three cliques of Xi Xia and the Jilin clique, Zang Shiyi and the Fengtian clique, and Zhang Jinghui and the Heilongjiang clique. By one means or another, even within the State Council, Xi Xia had a base of power in the Ministry of Finance, Zang Shiyi in the Ministry of Civil Affairs, and Zhang Jinghui in the Ministry of Military Administration. By contrast, Zheng had no array of men supporting him, and the Office of Administrative Affairs in the State Council which should have been the foundation of the bureaucracy was a stronghold of "Japanese" officials which formed a huge enemy state to the "Manchurians." Of course, having no support among the people on the spot, he had no influence whatsoever among those people. The Qing restorationists who ought to have formed Zheng's political base had furthered their antipathy for him, because he had become prime minister and compelled Puyi to take the lesser post of Chief Executive. In particular, Luo Zhenyu, Chen Baochen (1848–1935), Bao Xi (b. 1871), Hu Siyuan (b. 1869), and others continued openly to reject Zheng's actions insofar as he had appointed himself prime minister. Furthermore, for Zheng, who had aspirations of a Qing revival, the fatal blow was the fact that there was a deep gulf separating him from from Puyi because of the slanderous attacks of Hu Siyuan and others on him. Puyi had actually intended to replace Zheng prior to the signing of the "Japan-Manzhouguo Protocol." Even if he had resigned, though, Zheng Xiaoxu would never have been allowed to cross the Great Wall and return to his hometown. The reason was that on March 5, 1932, the Manchurian Provincial Committee of the Chinese Communist Party and on March 12 the Nationalist government in Nanjing had issued declarations of nonrecognition of Manzhouguo. Also, the Nationalist government made it clear that Chinese who participated in Manzhouguo were engaging in traitorous activities and that they would be severely judged on the basis of the criminal code.

Zheng Xiaoxu's hope had merely been to place the northeast region of China under joint international supervision and set up an imperial government there. In order to realize this aspiration, it was necessary, paradoxically, to deny the independence of Manzhouguo by accepting the position of the Republic of China, namely the Lytton Commission's criticism of Manzhouguo as specious, issue a plan which would put China's northeast region under international supervision, and get Japan to accept it. The Lytton Commission's report thus paralleled Zheng's wishes well and hinged on what Japan would later do. However, in January 1933, the Japanese army occupied Shanhaiguan, and Guandong Army Commander Mutō claimed that "the final strategic point for military operations is drawing near." The military moved to seize Rehe Province, which had always been

conceived of as part of Manzhouguo territory, and then with Japan's withdrawal from the League of Nations, Zheng Xiaoxu's hope of shaking free
of Japan's yoke through joint international supervision was crushed. Zheng
was dejected and there smoldered within him a rising discontent for the
Guandong Army and "Japanese" officials who were steadily strengthening
their hold over the Office of Administrative Affairs in the State Council
and moving to take effective control over Manzhouguo himself. The only
resistance he was capable of, though, was to respond with silence to political decisions made by the Guandong Army and "Japanese" officials in
Manzhouguo. During the period of over three years that Zheng served as
prime minister, he is said to have preserved his silence at sessions of the
National Council, the highest decision-making body of government, and
uttered not a word. Yet, according to a Japanese secretary by the name of
Shirai Yasushi, he did not relinquish all government business, but worked
like a clock, rising from sleep at 3:00 a.m. (just as his residence was dubbed
the "Hut of Awakening in the Night"), going to work at 8:00 a.m., and returning home at 4:00 p.m. In addition to examining important documents
of state and signing the originals of all laws and government orders, he also
kept a daily record of his discharging of official duties.[55]

For a man like Zheng Xiaoxu, who had such an assiduous attitude about
carrying out his duties, the humiliation most difficult to bear was probably
the fact that the Japanese, having ensnared him in such a position and
compelled him to remain there still bore contempt for him as a traitor. Of
course, from the mouths of Japanese who had built Manzhouguo and supported it, no such words were articulated, as they would have had no meaning. This was definitely said by people who sought to stress international
faith even though they were opposed to Japanese national policy and domestic public opinion.

On his way to Europe and the United States, Ozaki Yukio (1859–1954)
observed the changing scene from the Manchurian Incident through the
founding of Manzhouguo. While in England, he learned of the assassination of his close friend Inukai Tsuyoshi and, aware that he himself might be
murdered, decided to issue an opinion paper on the direction in which
Japan was heading. To that end, he returned home and published an essay
entitled "Bohyō no kawari ni" (In place of a tombstone) in the January
1933 issue of the journal *Kaizō* to indicate that he was in fact risking his life.
In this piece was a section dealing with Manzhouguo that was not published. As concerned the state of affairs surrounding recognition of
Manzhouguo as an independent country and Japan's opposition to the
League of Nations, Ozaki averred:

If we were to allow the thirty million inhabitants of Manzhouguo to vote freely, the
great majority would probably vote against Manzhouguo. Furthermore, without
Japanese military and financial might, Manzhouguo would probably collapse in no

more than a few months. . . . If that were to happen, the whole world would see that Manzhouguo was a Japanese puppet and by no means an independent state. It is a waste of time and energy to think that by signing a treaty there will be some international value to all this. To take a position and oppose the powers of the world will surely end up all but vitiating our international faith which has already begun to dissipate.[56]

This was undoubtedly a sound argument. In a prophetic portion that followed, he wrote:

All the more, then, that the leading figures in Manzhouguo, with a few exceptions, are generally depraved individuals who have simply sold their country out for profit. For using these traitors to carry out these cheap tricks, the Japanese state will suffer greatly spiritually and materially. . . .
  Even in cases in which men have confronted the opposition of the entire world and died in battle, would not a fatalistic sense of comfort have been better than helping Manzhouguo, that collective nest of traitors, and committing double suicide?
  If one were to say that suicide were called for by virtue of the desires of the people,
  This would be no more than a pretense of being civilized.
  On the one hand, the imperial government thinks that it will lead public opinion, while on the other hand supporting and stirring up traitorous behavior.
  We'll help you sell your country out to build a country,
  How can they speak of the way of loyalty and justice?[57]

The contradiction embodied by the Japanese government, as pointed out by Ozaki, was that Manzhouguo was founded as a state for morality and justice; and after Manzhouguo's founding, order number two of March 25 of its State Council called for "the use and teaching of the Four Books and Classic of Filial Piety in school curricula and the honoring of Confucian morality," and this was to be an even more profound problem. For Zheng Xiaoxu, who was regarded as a deep personal believer as well as practitioner of Confucianism, who felt that Manzhouguo had to be a state run on the basis of the Kingly Way and establish a Department of Education because he esteemed moral education, and who also served as its head, this was clearly an absurdity which he keenly felt. Although he said nothing about it to anyone, he undoubtedly felt this contradiction personally. His long-time friend Masaki Naohiko (1862–1940) visited him and understood the situation as follows: "A composed and dignified gentleman such as the prime minister sits in his office and devotes all his energies to serving his lord as councilor so that Manzhouguo may remain at peace." After going on to describe Zheng's thirty years of diligent attendance, he claimed that he deplored the fact that Zheng had been placed in an isolated position, for "there is not a single person who can follow in his footsteps nor who has his influence." Despite his having fallen into a state of lonely contemplation, the reason Zheng persisted in holding his post as prime minister was that he still burned with the desire—not unlike a deep delusion—of reviving a dynasty: "The former court can be called the Former Qing and the Former Qing has now passed. Why can't we then call it [i.e., Manzhouguo] the Later Qing?"[58] A Manchurian empire controlled by the Japanese was of no use. The wish for which he lived was to revive a Later Qing dynasty and return to the Forbidden City in Beijing. And the only remaining means of getting there was to clear his foul name as a traitor.

This route, however, was closed off. Actually, it might be better to say that it was a route he had closed off to himself. Zheng had broken the taboo of criticizing Japan, a taboo about which it was most important for Zheng, given his position, to remain discrete. Nagao Uzan (1864–1942), who had been his friend since Zheng had served in the Chinese Mission in Tokyo in 1893, wrote of Zheng's character: "He always spoke his mind even when he disagreed with me. Indeed, it was never the case that once he had promised something, he would later go back on his word."[59] Thus, the reason Zheng remained submissive throughout was his ultimate desire to see Puyi returned to the throne and an independent Manzhouguo ruled by the imperial system. Concerning the transition to an imperial government, however, there developed a ferocious contestation between him and the Guandong Army which opposed a revival of the Qing, and this mutual antagonism became ever more conspicuous. In this atmosphere, anti-military ideas intent on opposing the Guandong Army, "antiwar" views, and views in which neutral Switzerland would be the model country for Manzhouguo began to appear. Zheng tacitly demanded that the Manchu emperor, precisely as stipulated in the Organizational Law, assume real political power together with the transition to the imperial system of government. As he put it on one occasion in reference to the Organizational Law: "It must be released to find its own fertile soil."[60] However, circumstances one year after the implementation of the imperial system of rule utterly devastated Zheng's aspirations, as Manzhouguo moved toward become subordinate to Japan in the name of creating a united Japan-Manzhouguo bloc. At the first anniversary commemoration of the founding of the state, Zheng, who had been stifled till then, finally gave vent to his dissatisfaction:

Manzhouguo is like a small child held in one's arms. We now want to set him loose so he can walk on his own. . . . Yet, if the person holding the child continues for no particular reason to hold onto him for a long time, the child will ultimately never become independent. . . . Under the circumstances with our Manzhouguo not yet having been allowed to stand alone, the Japanese government has not let it go so that it might stand up [on its own]. This is patently clear today.[61]

Having said this, Zheng went on to criticize himself in a pathetic tone for being "stupid and inept." As a critique of Japan, this speech was, of course, revoked, and the Guandong Army saw to it that Zheng was divested of his post. Puyi, who got wind of the anger brewing within the

Guandong Army, did not come to Zheng's defense, but conveyed his wish to have him removed from office as soon as possible: "For a prime minister to leak the discontent in one's heart is extremely indiscrete. . . . He lacks the ability and attitude to serve as prime minister."[62] After his visit to Japan in 1935, Zheng lost his loyalty to Puyi, who had himself begun to become absorbed in speaking of loyalty to the Japanese emperor.

Hoshino Naoki has left testimony of an episode at the time of his resignation: "[Zheng] seemed to be harboring considerable displeasure. He composed a poem which expressed his feelings and so levelled criticism at a certain group of men: 'Happiness is like flinging away one's jade wine cup.' The jade wine cup referred to an ancient story when Fan Zeng, advisor to Xiang Yu of Chu, disagreed with Xiang Yu and resigned. At that time he threw his jade wine cup on the floor and sought some joy as he dispelled his gloom. It was this historical event to which he was alluding."[63] We do not know what Zheng's true motive was, but Zheng's life after he left office was tightly restricted perhaps due to his words and deeds. This is substantiated by the following story:

He could not even withdraw money from his reward for meritorious service in establishing the state which he had put in a bank account, and he was not allowed to move and take up residence in Beijing. Under the severe scrutiny of the military police, he could not compose poetry, and with no other alternative he shut himself up at home and spent his time doing calligraphy. He died suddenly in Changchun in 1938. . . . However, he had had no illness, and his death was completely unexpected. Nobody knows the true cause of death.[64]

As for the cause of Zheng's death, Puyi wrote in his memoirs of a rumor that he had been murdered by Japanese. In fact, however, he had aggravated a cold which caused complications to an intestinal illness; he did not die from unnatural causes. In spite of the fact that he died in Changchun (then known as Xinjing) and the forms of a state funeral were adhered to, the very fact that Puyi and his circle did not even know the cause of death may suggest the nature of Zheng's last days. After his death, Zheng's one-time secretary, a Japanese by the name of Ōta Toyoo, established a group known as the Kogakusha to research the spirit of Taiyi (Zheng's sobriquet), build a Taiyi Shinto shrine in the yard beyond his own home, and enshrine a portrait there of Zheng Xiaoxu. He did this because, despite the fervent wishes of Zheng's descendants, the Guandong Army and the Manzhouguo government would not allow them to set up a grave stone for Zheng within China proper.

Zheng was a man about whom it was regretted that "there is not a single person who can follow in his footsteps nor who has his influence." Would Zheng have been pleased or displeased by the fact that there was not a single Chinese who followed in his footsteps but only Japanese after his death?

As Ozaki Yukio noted, in 1933 when he attacked the principal Chinese figures in Manzhouguo as traitors, Zheng sent him a piece of calligraphy addressed to the offices of *Kaizō*, the journal that had carried Ozaki's essay, "Bohyō no kawari ni." It reads: "Independent, one may face fierce thunder." By "fierce thunder" he meant indignation. In the final analysis, though, what was Zheng thinking when he composed this piece of calligraphy? How was he trying to respond to Ozaki's disdain? The day on which Zheng would remove the disgrace of being a "Chinese traitor, slave to foreigners" was gone forever.

The Chrysanthemum and the Orchid: The Imperial Manzhouguo Government and the Importation of the Japanese Emperor System

At 8:30 on the morning of March 1, 1934, Puyi ascended the Altar of Heaven built in Shuntian Square in the village of Xinghua on the outskirts of Xinjing, the capital of Manzhouguo, and carried out the enunciation to heaven (*gaotian*) ceremony by reporting to heaven that he had received its mandate and acceded to the throne. It was a clear day, although the temperature registered minus twelve degrees Celsius, and a strong southwesterly wind was blowing harshly. He was wearing the *longpao* or imperial gown with gold dragons embroidered on each shoulder front and back. On his head he wore a circular cap with a leather trim to which red tassels and pearl decorations had been affixed. Having completed the entire suburban ceremony, including the enunciation to heaven, attired in long deerskin boots, the ceremonial garb of the Qing court, he rushed back to his palace:

Everything was carried out with brevity and extreme quiet. The celebrants along the route dotted the way, forming a barrier. Many were local Japanese residents, while comparatively few were Manchurians. One could see nothing but police all the way from Datong Palace to the site of the ceremony. I saw not a single onlooker which tended to evoke a sense of desolation.[65]

In this manner, Ishimaru Shizuma, a military attendant to Puyi, recorded the day's events in his diary. Even Ishimaru, a man who was an ardent proponent of the imperial system, found he could not suppress a sense of "desolation." For foreigners who were not trying to conceal their doubts about the imperial system, the layout along the ceremonial route appeared as a spectacle arousing their rather different sensibilities. One of them, the journalist Edgar Snow, conveyed the bizarre quiet in Manzhouguo as it welcomed in the imperial system and hinted at the fact that Puyi was ascending to the throne: "Fifty thousand troops flank the route, two lines of soldiers facing each other across a pathway nearly half a mile wide, completely cleared of life. Japanese troops with fixed bayonets stand guard behind Manzhouguo troops, *sans* bayonets. And these are the Emperor's audience. No others, no roars of popular approval, no shouts of happy populace greet the imperial parade, but only the phalanx of uniforms. . . . Nothing stirs."[66]

In the afternoon of the same day, they celebrated the coronation ceremony at the Qinmin ("diligence on behalf of the people") Mansion with Puyi this time in the full dress uniform as Generalissimo of the Manzhouguo army, navy, and air force. After the ceremony, the Accessional Rescript was proclaimed, and together with the establishment of the imperial system, it was announced that the reign period would henceforth be designated as

Kangde, and the name of the country was to be the Empire of Manchuria (*Manzhou diguo*). The "Accessional Rescript" read in part: "We anticipate becoming a permanent fixture by always cooperating with and working together with the Japanese empire in all long-term plans for protecting the country and salutary tactics for governing the state." This was a declaration that complete cooperation with Japan in all aspects of national defense as well as statesmanship and state management were necessary conditions for the permanent future existence of Manzhouguo. Later, Puyi sat on the jade throne (made in Japan) of ebony, and accepted the sign of submission—the three kneelings and nine knockings or *ketou* (kowtow)— from the descendants of the Aisin Gioro clan who had come from Beijing. The enthronement ceremony then came to an end.

Puyi, who had been placed on the throne as the boy Xuantong Emperor and who had exited the stage of history after a brief restoration in 1917, now once again returned to the imperial seat, this time as the Kangde Emperor of the Empire of Manchuria. However, this was not encouraged by an enthusiastic encore. There was only the image of Japanese residents in Manchuria and a small number of Chinese turned out by the Concordia Association who stood continuously in silence as if frozen by the blustery, frigid wind. This scene vividly describes how the public rationale for the adoption of the imperial system was a fiction pure and simple: "The people who extol and praise the Kingly Way have with complete sincerity been following the chief executive's mandate of heaven and continually been petitioning for his enthronement as emperor."[67] Neither the Guandong Army nor the Japanese government, nor for that matter even Puyi or Zheng Xiaoxu, raised the issues of popular will or popular sentiments. To the contrary, they had exchanged the position of chief executive based on popular will for emperor based on the will of heaven and the mandate of heaven. This was openly elucidated as the objective of adopting the imperial system. For Japan, which had left the League of Nations two years after the founding of the state of Manzhouguo, there was no longer any need to remain fixed on the constitutional republican form of government of the Republic of China or to maintain a rival political form.

For the Guandong Army and the Japanese government, the task of implementing the imperial form of state lay in how to cleanse this new regime of any traits of Qing revivalism. By the same token, for Puyi, Zheng Xiaoxu, and their associates, the only and most important matter of concern was how to realize the adoption of an imperial system faithfully as a revival of the family line of the Qing dynasty. The focal point of this difference came to a head over the issue of the garments to be worn at the time of the coronation. Puyi and his followers stubbornly argued the case that he wear the *longpao*, as it was the formal attire for the imperial accession. The Guandong Army rendered the judgment that Puyi's imperial position was not a resuscitation of the Qing dynasty, but as an indication of the emergence of the Empire of Manchuria, he was acceding to the throne in the full dress uniform of the Generalissimo of the Manzhouguo army, navy, and air force. Puyi and his associates, however, demanded he wear the *long-pao* and they refused to give an inch. The result of bargaining and compromise between the two sides was to have two ceremonies: the ceremony held in the suburbs of the city in his *longpao* and the accession ceremony held in his military uniform. For the time being, the Japanese appeased Puyi's demands that his enthronement as the Kangde Emperor be understood as a revival of the Qing dynasty through the performance of the *ketou* by his fellow clansmen and former Qing officials. However, it was uniformly argued in public that Puyi's enthronement was *not* a revival of the Qing. Even Zheng Xiaoxu had to declare: "We were wrong and did not boldly adopt a government loyal to the principles and mission of state formation as would have been the case with a revival of the Qing dynasty."[68] It was emphasized as well in the *Kōtei sokui taigai seimeisho* (International manifesto on the imperial accession) that "our emperor of the Empire of Manchuria serves heaven. Having received his destiny, he established the Empire of Manchuria and became its first emperor. This, of course, is altogether different from the revival of the Qing state."[69] Stress was laid here on his place as the first emperor of this newly created "empire."

There was always the danger that the Empire of Manchuria might be confused with a Qing revival? While earnestly denying this eventuality, why was it that the Guandong Army and the Japanese government took the bold step forward at this time of adopting an imperial form of state?

The plan to implement in Manzhouguo an imperial form of government, the same polity as in Japan, was promoted by Koiso Kuniaki, chief of staff of the Guandong Army, who had earlier supported the movement surrounding Prince Su (with assistance from the Japanese military garnered by the mainland adventurer Kawashima Naniwa) for an independent Manchuria-Mongolia and who had been tied to efforts to revive the Qing dynasty. On February 23, 1933, more than half a year after assuming his duties, Koiso telegraphed an inquiry to Army Central which "anticipates the culmination of a temporary incident"[70] appropriate to making Puyi emperor. With the end of the Rehe battle, he sought to convey the message that a move toward an imperial form of government was called for as soon as possible. The reply of the vice-minister of war ran as follows: "As concerns the turning of Puyi into an emperor, insofar as the special conditions remain lacking, it is not as yet appropriate to discuss this issue."[71] This plan was then followed in the *Manshūkoku shidō hōjin yōkō* (Outline of a plan for leadership over Manzhouguo) which read in part: "While the state of Manzhouguo takes as its ultimate objective a constitutional monarchy, for the time being we shall continue to support the present system."[72] Despite this decision, though, on the basis of Koiso's request, Endō Ryūsaku (1886–1963), head of the Office of Administrative Affairs, put forward as the first task of the regime in Manzhouguo to implement an imperial system. In addition to Koiso, Endō planned together with the likes of Usami Katsuo (1869–1942), an advisor on matters of state, Ishimaru Shizuma, military advisor to Puyi, Irie Kan'ichi (1880–1955), assistant director of the Manzhouguo imperial household ministry, and Tsukushi Kumashichi (1863–1944) and Tanabe Harumichi (1878–1950), both Japanese councilors. They drew up a plan for the transition to an imperial polity and entered into negotiations with the Japanese government. In tandem with this development, the Guandong Army sent Harada Kumakichi (1888–1947), chief of the Third Section of Operations, to Tokyo to convey the atmosphere prevailing where an imperial system was supported and to relay the same views to Army Central. Finally, on December 22 the Japanese government decided to move ahead with the implentation of an imperial system.

The decision had been reached in a cabinet meeting that "at present finds [Manzhouguo] in a transitional chief executive system. Furthermore, because it has not been decided which polity will be adopted hereafter, many of the officials and ordinary people of Manzhouguo remain uneasy."[73] This situation was not a happy state of affairs, and it was decided that to effect an imperial form of state and bring to an end the issue of the polity "would be seen as exceedingly suited to our times."[74] In short, the cabinet saw the firm establishment of a polity as indispensible to the stabilization of people's minds. In spite of such language, though, it was extremely doubtful if the implementation of an imperial form of government would pay serious heed to people's concerns. This was addressed in the same document when it came to the issue of setting up an imperial state: "We shall eliminate all hindrance and constraint in the exclusion of the ideas of a sovereign local populace and in advancing the affairs of Manzhouguo and effecting a policy of an imperial state."[75] Strengthening the State Council so as to forward Japanese state policy, among other measures, was demanded. Far from emphasizing the people's frame of mind, stress was placed on excluding the will of Chinese living on the scene from rulership over Manzhouguo and on smoothly carrying out Japanese rule there.

The necessity of smoothly carrying out Japanese state policy by implementing the emperor system was stressed at this time as a response to the coming "crisis of 1936." As Tsukushi Kumashichi declared: "Japan, for which a national crisis is 100 percent predicted around 1936, must before then advance to an indisputable position the imperial task of Japanese-Manzhouguo creation."[76] The advocacy of a "1936 crisis" may be seen as a response to the mounting international threat posed toward Japan because of such things as the fact that Japanese naval construction would decline to an inferior position vis-à-vis the United States and Great Britain in 1936 due to the London accords on naval reduction and the fact that the second five-year plan in the Soviet Union, begun in 1932, would be nearing completion and Soviet military power would thus be strengthened. This was all military propaganda aimed at increasing armed Japanese strength and enlarging the military's political voice by fanning the flames of a sense of crisis. Yet, it was undeniable that the enhancement of Soviet state and military power was felt to be a threat in Manzhouguo, which stood right at the front line of a war with Soviet Russia. This sense of crisis became a driving force propelling the move toward an imperial system in Manzhouguo at an emergency pace, a position well conveyed in Tsukushi's argument:

In 1936 when the high tide of the emergency facing the empire shall arise, it shall be necessary to set the situation in Manchuria in a unified and stable sphere with respect to all changing circumstances. Thus, although the measures to be taken are, of course, many and varied, the establishment of the monarchical system in Manzhouguo is the most appropriate. . . . If the creation of a monarchy comes one day earlier, then it will benefit by one day the stability of the scene in Manzhouguo. It would be best to seek out an opportunity to do this soon while this present period is maturing.[77]

Why, though, was the promulgation of the imperial system said to be the best policy for coping with the stability of Manzhouguo and the international crisis? As concerned Japan's intentions in adopting a monarchical form of government, Edgar Snow inferred that, by making Puyi a puppet emperor, "to whose divine wisdom all Japanese manœuvres could be attributed, Manzhouguo affairs could be conducted with simplified dispatch. Whether it was to be Pu Yi's signature on a formal annexation agreement, or Manzhouguo's declaration of war on China, Russia, or some other Power (in support of her 'ally,' Japan), the move could be accomplished with a minimum of trouble and expense."[78] Of course, this would have never appeared on the surface in Japanese documents, however much an ulterior motive it may have been. For the most part, it was an ideological repulsion toward a democratic republic, expressed as a point of view in the following way: "Japan also has a monarchy, and it would be best if [Manzhouguo] had a similar form of government."[79] However, Japanese at the time would certainly not have forgotten that the very elucidation of the national polity was filled to overflowing with political meaning. Also, the monarchical system was deemed desirable from the perspective of balance and unified rule over the colonies of Taiwan and Korea. Yet, as Rōyama Masamichi pointed out, one substantive requirement was that "all long-term plans for protecting the country and salutory tactics for governing the state" involve "cooperation and working together with the Japanese empire." In this form control over Manzhouguo would advance, and thus a primary motivating force was that "it was impossible that the national structure and political form of Manzhouguo differ greatly from those of Japan."[80] This had already been a result of the transplantation of the Japanese legal system and administrative forms which were advocated by local "Japanese" officials. Furthermore, it was as well a premise for the advancement by force of a unified Japan-Manzhouguo.

With the implementation of the imperial system, the Organizational Law of the Government was revised into the Organizational Law of the Empire of Manchuria, and the stipulations concerning the chief executive which more often than not had conformed to the president of the Republic of China were transformed with reference to stipulations concerning the Japanese emperor in the Imperial Japanese Constitution. How was the position of the Manchu emperor to resemble that of the Japanese emperor in form? This can be seen in the following table (Table 4) comparing the principal revisions.

Thus, the position of the chief executive, who had held full administrative responsibility for the entire populace, was radically transformed into that of the emperor whose majesty was sacrosanct and about whom no question might be raised concerning responsibility for affairs of state or criminal law. Legal stipulations, however, under no circumstances, of course, guarantee any evidence of truth in the Empire of Manchuria.

For example, Article Eleven of the Organizational Law, which read that the emperor "controlled the army, navy, and air force," was virtually the same as Article Eleven of the Imperial Japanese Constitution, which read that "the emperor commanded the army and navy." However, according to the bylaws of the army and navy, the emperor's power of control in the Empire of Manchuria was entrusted to the Minister of Military Administration (in the transition to an imperial system, the heads of the various ministries

TABLE 4

Organizational Law of the Empire of Manchuria Constitution	Imperial Japanese Constitution
Article One **Section One** The empire of Manchuria is ruled over by the emperor.	**Article One** **Section One** The great empire of Japan is ruled over by the emperor from a single line going back 10,000 generations.
	Section Two
The imperial succession is separately determined.	On the basis of the Imperial House Act, the imperial throne is passed on through the male line of the emperor.
Section Two The sanctity of the emperor is inviolable.	**Section Three** The emperor is sacred and inviolable.
Section Three As the head of state, the emperor controls the ruling power and enacts it on the basis of this Law.	**Section Four** As the head of state, the emperor controls the ruling power and enacts it on the basis of the Constitution.

were renamed ministers). Unlike the Japanese emperor, the Manchu emperor did not have troops over whom he held personal control as trusted right-hand men. Furthermore, in response to the question of whether the Ministry of Military Administration held ruling power, such was not, in fact, recognized. This was because the army of Manzhouguo operated under a system which never emerged within the bureaucratic structure or the laws of the state of Manzhouguo. That system was the advisors' system whereby Japanese military men effectively controlled the armed forces of Manzhouguo. In terms of its status, this advisors' system was seen as an auxiliary of Guandong Army Headquarters; it comprised strictly Japanese military men and had no legal connection whatsoever to Manzhouguo. Yet, the advisors' system—and in particular the Supreme Advisor—held immense powers. According to the testimony of Sasaki Tōichi (1886–1955) who served in the capacity of Supreme Advisor: "This was not an open and public government organization. In fact, however, the Supreme Advisor was on an equal footing with the Minister of Military Administration. Without the consent of the Supreme Advisor (a Japanese), it was the practice that all orders and instructions would have no efficacy. There was not a single Manchurian who had the least doubt about any of this."[81] Saying that this was a position on a par with the Minister of Military Administration meant that no order would have the least effectiveness without the approval of the Supreme Advisor. Thus, the Supreme Advisor in fact came to have a superior position to that of the Minister of Military Administration. The Manzhouguo Army operated on the basis of such a system. On the day of the imperial Manchu coronation, Japanese soldiers bearing rifles with fixed bayonets stood in a row behind the backs of the Manzhouguo soldiers who were unarmed. This military array itself offered a frank indication of the nature of the two armies. In addition, the very fact that the Guandong Army had the ceremony of accession to the throne carried out with Puyi in the full dress uniform of generalissimo of the Manzhouguo army, navy, and air force seems to have gone beyond the intentions of the parties involved. The role played by the Kangde Emperor, Puyi, in the Empire of Manchuria and the function assigned it seem to have been filled with symbolism.

Thus, with the adoption of the imperial system, Manzhouguo entrusted to Japan "all long-term plans for protecting the country and salutory tactics for governing the state" and moved down the road toward slavery under the name of "cooperation and working together with" Japan. Also, in exchange for his sacrosanct and inviolable position, Puyi legally lost his effective political power. In other words, in place of the emperor, who had become politically without responsibilities, "the prime minister served and advised the emperor and, when issues arose, he took over responsibility" for the emperor (Organizational Law, Section Four). The prime minister thus became the man in charge administratively in the form of serving, advising, and assuming the responsibilities for the emperor. Yet, this concentration of powers in the hands of the prime minister was effectively a concentration of power in the hands of the "Japanese" officials through the principle of centralizing the authority of the Office of Administrative Affairs in the State Council. Furthermore, the relationship between the Guandong Army and Puyi operated, as Puyi noted in his autobiography, with "the Guandong Army like a high-pressure source of power and me like an accurate and prompt motor."[82]

In this manner, Puyi as emperor sought authority and power in the Empire of Manchuria which was ruled by the "Japanese" officials there and the Guandong Army. Puyi discovered this scheme at the time of his first trip to Japan in 1935. "The position of the emperor in Japan," he pointed out, "is the same as my position in Manzhouguo, and the Japanese should thus treat me just as they treat their own emperor."[83] On the basis of this logic, he would assimilate himself into the authority of the Japanese emperor and forge a united body together. On May 2, after returning home, Puyi issued his Admonitory Rescript to the People on the Occasion of the Emperor's Return in which he announced: "I am of one spirit with His Majesty the Emperor of Japan. All of you our subjects should be aware of this inclination. You should be united in virtue and heart with our friendly neighbor, so that we may lay a firm foundation for our two countries into the distant future together and promote the true meaning of Eastern morality."[84] This imperial edict was called a "great charter" (*daikenshō*) in the friendly relations between Japan and Manzhouguo, and the tone of it was redolent of "both empires as a single body inasmuch as the rescript appeared in the form of a unity with the spirit of His Majesty the Japanese Emperor and both Japan and Manzhouguo unified in virtue and heart." This stress on Japan-Manzhouguo unity of virtue and heart and the unity of spirit were more than just Japanese coercion but an initiative on Puyi's part himself. In the draft of his rescript, Puyi himself added the expression: "I am of one spirit with His Majesty the Emperor of Japan." Furthermore, on the day before the proclamation of the Admonitory Rescript to the People on the Occasion of the Emperor's Return, Puyi brought together all the more important "Japanese" and "Manchurian" officials at his palace and delivered a forty-minute speech to them. According to Puyi, "before this speech I did not consult with any Japanese at all and no draft was prepared, but a flood of oratory gushed forth."[85] In his autobiography, Puyi noted that he instructed the assembled to the effect that: "If there is anyone who is disloyal to the emperor of Manzhouguo then he is equally disloyal to the Japanese emperor, and if there is anyone disloyal to the Japanese emperor, he is just as disloyal to the emperor of Manzhouguo."[86] This marks Puyi's attempt to procure fidelity to himself by stressing his unified spirit with that of the Japanese emperor. Failing that, he planned to restrain the "Japanese" officials and the Guandong Army by stigmatizing such behavior as disloyal to the Japanese emperor. This was a form of counterattack to the devotion of the Japanese in Manzhouguo to their own emperor.

Puyi's strategy, however, was not destined to succeed, because for the "Japanese" officials and the military men of the Guandong Army there was no need whatsoever to treat him in a manner comparable to the Japanese emperor. In spite of this, to the extent that the Japanese and their allies formed an imperial system in Manzhouguo resembling the emperor system in Japan, the Japanese did express extraordinary enthusiasm for Puyi. An imperial household was formed to match the imperial household in Japan, and after the implementation of the imperial system, an orchid crest in a Japanese style was taken to match the Japanese chrysanthemum crest. In addition, an imperial court, imperial visits, imperial portraits, an imperial throne, and an empress were institutionally established in coordination with comparable fixtures in Japan. As such, the imperial system of Manzhouguo was created in imitation of the Japanese emperor system. However, the fact that precise terminology was employed to an exacting extent may indicate an orientation stressing differentiation rather than unity between the Manzhouguo and Japanese emperors. While they spoke of the unity of virtue and heart between Japan and Manzhouguo, clearly the Manzhouguo emperor—as a figurative "child emperor" (*erhuangdi*)—had been placed on a rung beneath the position of his counterpart in Japan. The Guandong Army, for its part, adopted the counterattack logic to Puyi's own counterattacking efforts to restrain "Japanese" officials and the Guandong Army: "The emperor of Manzhouguo has come to the throne on the basis of the will of heaven, and that is the will of the [Japanese] emperor. As a condition for reigning service to the [Japanese] emperor who is the core of our joint imperial way, his [i.e., the Manchu emperor's] heart is joined with the will of the [Japanese] emperor."[87] This statement frankly indicates that loyalty and subservience were preconditions for Puyi's reign in Manzhouguo. In addition, "the commander of the Guandong Army, as the [Japanese] emperor's proxy, should be seen as the teacher and guardian of the [Manzhouguo] emperor."[88] This indicated that the Guandong Army commander would instruct and tutor the Manzhouguo emperor in the spirit of the imperial will. Thus, the commanding officer of the Guandong Army was seen as a "supreme emperor" (*taishanghuang*) on a rung above the Manzhouguo emperor. In response, Puyi used fundamendal, transcendent elements which even the Guandong Army could not touch to unify himself with the Japanese emperor and restrain the Japanese officials and the Guandong Army. He strove to find the path to gain for himself the authority as emperor that would place him in a superior position to all.

Ultimately, Puyi ceased offering prayers for the ancestors of the Qing dynasty, which ought to have been his very reason for living. Instead, he opted for the route of taking Amaterasu Ōmikami (the Sun Goddess of Japanese mythology), the ancestral deity of the Japanese emperor, as the deity for the founding of the state of Manzhouguo and, by making Shinto his state religion, he acquired a divinity and authority comparable to the Japanese emperor, as a kind of living deity. Of course, this was not a plan Puyi himself devised, but something which surfaced in contacts with the Guandong Army. In order to drive home the unity of virtue and heart between Japan and Manzhouguo and the principle of ethnic harmony, in August 1937 the Guandong Army established a deity central to the beliefs of all the peoples of Manzhouguo and demanded of the Manzhouguo government that it build a National Foundation Shrine. Although this was discussed at the Planning Desk of the State Council and the central bureau of the Concordia Association, the government squabbled over various theories concerning the enshrined deity and remained deadlocked.

Before going to Japan for the second time in 1940 for the celebrations on the 2,600th year of the Japanese imperial reign, Puyi resolved, after having received a suggestion from Yoshioka Yasunao, attaché to the Manzhouguo imperial household, to establish a National Foundation Shrine and to enshrine Amaterasu Ōmikami there. When he returned home from Japan, Puyi promulgated a "Rescript on the Consolidation of the Basis of the Nation" on July 15, 1940. It was emphasized in this Rescript that the founding and prosperity of Manzhouguo were due to the "divine blessing of the Sun Goddess" and the "protection of His Majesty the Emperor of Japan." In addition, he proclaimed: "We have respectfully built the National Foundation Shrine to enshrine the Sun Goddess. We shall offer our deepest veneration and in our own person pray for the prosperity of the people, and we shall set an example for all posterity. . . . We thus hope that the basis of the nation may be consolidated by reverencing the way of the gods and the principle of the nation be established in the teachings of loyalty and filial piety."[89] After this rescript, Manzhouguo would continue to exist by virtue of the "divine blessing of the Sun Goddess and the protection of His Majesty the Emperor of Japan." The unification of Japan and Manzhouguo had proceeded to the point of having the identical state-founding deity. The National Foundation Shrine was built to be in tandem with the Ise Shrine, as was the Shrine to the Loyal Souls Who Founded the Nation built in tandem with the Yasukuni Shrine. As for these efforts at what might be called over-assimilation, there were voices of concern raised early on in the Japanese government, the Japanese imperial household, and the Japanese Shinto world, as well as in the Manzhouguo government and the Guandong Army. When Puyi expressed the hope that the Shōwa Emperor come and pray to the Sun Goddess in Manzhouguo, the Japanese emperor simply replied: "This being your majesty's wish, I must comply." However, his request to have the mirror of the object of worship be dedicated by the Japanese imperial court at the National Foundation Shrine was not granted. In his diary, Katakura Tadashi recorded his impressions: "Today, the Manchurian emperor made use of the National Foundation Shrine and Major General Yoshioka. He is planning for the stability of his throne."[90]

To be sure, the establishment of a National Foundation Shrine within the court and his offering of his own personal prayers to the Sun Goddess were probably connected with securing stability for Puyi's throne. However, this trampled underfoot Chinese customary practices which venerated one's ancestors first of all, and the plan to revere the deities of another country furtively substituted ancestors, as Puyi himself recognized, incurring "the ridicule and quiet denunciations of all the people of the northeast."[91] It was even worse than that, for he enforced upon people pain and suffering: "Everyone who walked past the [National Foundation] Shrine had to perform a 90-degree bow. Failure to do so would be punished for 'disrespect.' "[92] Furthermore, the authority and position equal to that of the Japanese emperor which Puyi tried to gain with the compensation of ridicule, denunciations, pain, and suffering of all the Chinese people ultimately did not come into his hands. In the first place, there were three things elemental to an empire that were missing from Puyi's empire, as noted by a German journalist. These three were: a constitution, a palace, and an imperial lineage. In Manzhouguo the imperial lineage was called the emperor's line, but there were no legal stipulations concerning it. Even the emperor's younger brother Pujie (1907–94) was not recognized in this imperial line, and for Puyi who had no sons the imperial line comprised one person only. This journalist saw the Empire of Manchuria as ruled by a state without a constitution, a court without a palace, and an emperor without an imperial lineage, and dubbed it the "three have-not nation."[93] The most important thing missing in this empire ruled over by an emperor who held a distinctive though isolated position was not a constitution, nor was it a palace or an imperial lineage. In fact, more than anything else, it lacked a people to acclaim the emperor heartily.

The palace that was never finished in the present-day city of Changchun in China was completed after the war by Chinese, and now offers a grand appearance as the Institute of Geology. However, when Puyi was in his court, the remodeled building which had formerly served as the Jilin-Heilongjiang Office of Salt and Tobacco Taxation, Guandong Army Headquarters and various ministries of the State Council had already seen to the construction over a wide area of numerous office buildings which remind one of such Japanese edifices as the Castle Tower, the Japanese Diet Building, the Kabuki Theater, the Kudan Hall, and the Tokyo National Museum, all boasting their own majestic appearances. Power was laid out in clear, regular array and took shape as the installation of political space. Compared to Guandong Army Headquarters which was called "the castle," the court was a destitute place. As he put it, Puyi spent his life "thrashing, shouting, fortunetelling, taking medicines, and being afraid."[94] This was the reality of the position of the Manzhouguo emperor to which Puyi had dreamed of ascending and the conclusion of his effort to reach parity with the Japanese emperor which had ended in failure. To Hegel's expression that "great historical events and great historical men appear twice in history," Marx noted in *The Eighteenth Brumaire of Louis Bonaparte* that he should have added "but the first time is as tragedy and the second time is farce." Perhaps Puyi's rule as the Kangde Emperor applies here as well.

The Xuantong Emperor, last of the emperors of the Qing dynasty, appeared now once again on the stage of history as the "Kangde Emperor," the first emperor of the Empire of Manchuria. Thereafter, no one would accede to the throne.

The Absurdity of a Unified Japan-Manzhouguo: Rivalries over Rule

"The various ethnic groups that comprise Manzhouguo, with scarcely an exception, are gradually but directly deflating the hopes about which we were enthusiastic shortly after the Manchurian Incident."[95] So noted Tachibana Shiraki of his impressions as he dragged along a disabled leg walking around various places in Manchuria following the Manchurian Incident. This was the same Tachibana who had earlier conveyed his dreams of bringing to fruition a society of great harmony in Manzhouguo. "The various ethnic groups who are the structural components of Manzhouguo are satisfied with the state they have built," and he saw as an indispensable precondition to the continued existence of Manzhouguo "support for this [state], namely implanting among these peoples a national consciousness."[96] Tachibana traveled around to many locales in the region to ascertain if this change had transpired. He was compelled to note that the attitude of the various ethnic groups toward Manzhouguo in the two and one-half years of its existence "pointed" both to his hoped for result and "its diametrical opposite."[97]

Apart from Tachibana's distress, it was in fact a serious question whether or not these various ethnic groups, aside from the Japanese living in the region, ever entertained the thought or harbored the desire for a state which they themselves built called Manzhouguo. This is, of course, true of ordinary people. It was rare even among people who had, in fact, participated in the efforts to build the state and who were lined up with the new government of Manzhouguo to find someone who truly believed that he had personally taken part in its construction and that it was his own. By contrast, resistance to Japan's controlling Manzhouguo had boiled up in many an innermost heart. Why then had they become Manzhouguo bureaucrats? A certain Chinese official, in response to a question put to him by Edgar Snow, claimed with disgust that the great majority of the Chinese serving as officials in Manzhouguo wanted to protect their own property and persons, fearing that if they ran away, their entire families would be murdered; they simply had no choice, and by no means was it the case that they were happily employed; most of the Chinese officials in Manzhouguo harbored anti-Japanese feelings, he continued, and many among the provincial and municipal officials secretly offered aid to the anti-Manzhouguo, anti-Japanese movement.[98] Furthermore, this resistance was not at all limited to people who had no choice but to serve as Manzhouguo bureaucrats. The same feelings were shared by people who actively participated in Manzhouguo.

You can't offend the fire brigade when there's a fire. No matter what, you have to welcome their arrival. After the fire is put out, though, which homes will be rebuilt is up to the individual homeowners, not something decided upon by this or that special request put by the firemen.[99]

For example, Kikuchi Teiji, the author of these sentences, noted of Ding Jianxiu, director of the Ministry of Communications, that: "One should remember that he remained from first to last pro-Japanese."[100] As Kikuchi points out, Ding, who graduated from the Faculty of Politics and Economics of Waseda University in 1910, was quick to cooperate with the Guandong Army soon after the Manchurian Incident. He had served as a member of the Fengtian Regional Maintenance Committee, chairman of the Shen-Hai Railway Protection and Maintenance Association, and chairman of the board of the Northeastern Communications Committee. He worked as an important pro-Japanese figure in Manzhouguo, supporting the establishment of the state and, after its founding, serving successively in such posts as Minister of Communications, Minister of Industry, and chairman of the Manchurian Electric Company. He must have expressed his displeasure with being called upon to do this and that by Japan and being made to work in the interests of Japan. One episode indicating that Ding Jianxiu was being compelled to work for Japanese interests is recounted by U.S. Ambassador to Japan Joseph Grew in his *Ten Years in Japan*. In July 1932, Ding visited Japan to seek diplomatic recognition for Manzhouguo, and he was interviewed by a group of domestic and foreign reporters.

To the great amusement of the [foreign correspondents], Ting [Ding], when he came into the room, was immediately surrounded by about seven Japanese officials. A correspondent said: "Do you favor the complete independence of Manzhouguo?" to which the Chinese replied in the affirmative, whereupon one of the Japanese officials whispered something in his ear, and he added: "In accordance with the self-determination of the Manchurian people." Another correspondent asked something about Japanese recognition, to which Ting replied. Again the Japanese official got up and whispered in his ear, and Ting added: "And we likewise hope for recognition by the United States." . . . [T]he correspondents could hardly keep from laughing out loud it was so ludicrous.[101]

This caricatured spectacle may have been an ordinary event in the rule of Manzhouguo, but one actually did not even see such spectacles in Manzhouguo because rulership was in the hands of the "Japanese" officials, under the internal guidance of the Guandong Army, a fact about which no one had the least doubt whatsoever. This produced the following situation, in the words of Edgar Snow: "Curiously, the Chinese most bitter against Japanese rule are those making money from it."[102] Forced into a humiliating position on a daily basis, the anger and ill feeling they harbored privately only mounted. With the intrusion of bureaucrats from Japan, "Japanese were taking positions from low-level officials right down to typists, as everything became Japanese in format and bureaucratized in the Japanese style."[103] Thus, the resentment of Chinese working in these government offices grew strong.

In November 1934 when Tachibana reported that the various peoples of Manzhouguo were finding their hopes deflated, Ōkura Kinmochi (1882–1968) made a report to the Shōwa Research Group on his investigation of conditions in Manchuria. In it he conveyed in the following manner the discontent vented by a certain high-level Chinese minister. It is a long document, but I shall cite the most pertinent testimony from it just as he wrote it.

There is not one good thing in the present state of affairs in Manzhouguo. For example, during the time of General Honjō, there were four "Japanese" officials for every six "Manchurians" in the central government. However, now it is a ratio of nine Japanese to one Manchurian (in actual fact, it is 7.2 Japanese to 2.8 Manchurians). These Manchurian officials they employ are all sycophants without any knowledge, and they are treated as incompetents. The production of documents and other business associated with office work are all done in the Japanese style. One can only imagine that they [i.e., the "Manchurians"] clandestinely are of a mind to seize control of the Manzhouguo government. Even in salaries, the general Manchurian official earns no more than 170 yen, and in fact only a few earn this much. Japanese get an eighty percent bonus. I really have no idea who the rulers of this state are. Although they claim that the army has withdrawn and relinquished Manzhouguo's governance, this merely means that they have relinquished it into the hands of Japanese officials in Manzhouguo. And, these Japanese officials have absolutely no fundamental plan. At the time that Manzhouguo was founded, we felt that Japanese and Manchurians would work together to build a magnificent new state, but one has no sense of this whatsoever from the present circumstances. Although one might say that the sole improvement implemented by Japan has been the unification of the currency [in Manzhouguo], everything else has worsened since the Zhang Xueliang era. If, under the present circumstances, a war between Japan and Russia were to break out, all of the Manchurians would probably rise up to oppose Japan.[104]

Having introduced his evidence, Ōkura stressed that this was by no means a unilateral Chinese view of things, and he went on to introduce it together with testimony from Japanese resident in Manchuria. Their reasons for being dissatisfied with the new state included such things as the highhandedness of opium-monopoly officials, the military police and local police, the tyranny of the "Japanese" officials, and the confiscation of small arms for self-protection. "It would be no exaggeration to say that, if the [Japanese] soldiers were now to withdraw," he added, "all Japanese would be summarily killed." And, he pointed out that the military leadership itself had said that, "if fighting between Japan and Russia were to commence, about ten divisions of the Japanese army will have to fight against the Manchurians."[105] This Japanese evidence clearly reflected the honest views of people who had daily interactions with other ethnic groups on the scene. However, even without this evidence, many of the items raised by high-level Chinese officials had been recognized as fact by both the Guandong Army and the local Japanese officialdom.

For example, right from the time of the founding of the state, the Japanese-Manchurian wage differential was both an issue in differing "Japanese" versus "Manchurian" rates of pay as well as the focal point for animosity between "Japanese" and "Manchurian" officials. Even in the salary law for civil officials of June 1934 which was to be enacted so as to correct this great pay differential, there remained a considerable difference in the standards and modes of living among the various ethnic groups. Insofar as there was a need to respond to real circumstances, they decided to offer a special bonus of 40 percent of base salary to officially-approved Japanese officials and 80 percent to junior Japanese officials. At this time, Xi Xia, Zhang Yanqing, Ding Jianxiu, and other Chinese officials were arguing that all ethnic groups should receive uniform and equal treatment and that if Japan was, indeed, a friendly neighbor, this should be demonstrated by ethnic salary equality. Furumi Tadayuki, salary department head at the Paymasters Desk of the Office of Administrative Affairs, the man responsible for drafting this measure concerning salaries, responded to them in generalities: "In order to talk about equality, we have to consider first of all whether ability is equal or not. The abilities of Japanese are higher, and their salaries must, of course, also be higher. Furthermore, their living standards are higher, for from the time of their birth they eat only Japanese rice and can not eat sorghum like the Manchurians. Also, when we speak of friendship, true friendship means asking for a bit more for the Japanese."[106]

In the face of this ethnic salary differential, students from the Datong Academy who had had the goal of implementing ethnic harmony arose in fierce resistance. Ishigaki Teiichi recalled an incident in which Korean students in opposition left the country: "This was a deeply felt scar for students of my year, and even now I remember the pain in my heart."[107] The ethnic differential in wages became a particularly big issue in the law on civil-official salaries enacted in September 1938, but the argument then arose that formal equalization of salaries was extremely kind treatment for good-for-nothing Manchurians and extremely poor treatment for the hard-working and talented Japanese. The ethnic salary differentials finally came to an end, without being eradicated, through a system of annual bonuses and salary supplements under the principle of "repaying talent." Shiina Etsusaburō (1898–1979), who in 1938 returned to the Ministry of Commerce and Industry from Manzhouguo, was angered that "a salaried man earning close to 1000 yen monthly suddenly fell to 200–300 yen."[108] However, one of the incentives for Japanese to make the trip to Manzhouguo were the exceedingly high salaries which, depending on individual cases, could amount to four or five times a normal Japanese salary.

Nonetheless, beyond the issue of wage disparities, what brought about the estrangement between "Japanese" and "Manchurian" officials was the fact that the Japanese controlled personnel management. According to Article Nine of the Organizational Law of the Empire of Manchuria, "the emperor determines the bureaucratic system, makes all appointments and dismissals, and sets official salaries." This function was to be carried out with the counsel of the prime minister. However, in whose hands did principal power for the bureaucratic system substantively lie? This point was realistically delineated at the time of Prime Minister Zheng Xiaoxu's resignation, when in spite of the fact that Emperor Puyi recommended Minister of Civil Affairs Zang Shiyi and Zheng recommended Jiandao Provincial Governor Cai Yunsheng, he was succeeded in office by Zhang Jinghui, head of the Manzhouguo Cabinet, on the orders of the Guandong Army. Concerning Zhang's appointment, Kamio Kazuharu (b. 1893), who was in charge of the Secretarial Desk of the State Council, conjectured: "The Guandong Army probably appreciated the fact that he understands no Japanese, cannot read Chinese texts, and seems to have no say in governmental matters."[109] Together with personnel matters, the two major forces within the Manzhouguo government, Zang Shiyi and Xi Xia, were transferred, respectively, to be head of the cabinet and minister of the imperial household. The political clout of Zang Shiyi, who was seen as the next prime minister, was thus suddenly recognized by all, and Puyi had also hoped to make use of Zang to strengthen his own political influence. Xi Xia had been a fierce critic of the Japanese-Manchurian ratios and wage differentials; by organizing the Man-Mō dōshi kyōshinkai (Manchurian-Mongolian Kindred Cooperative Society) and planning for a union of the Manchurian and Mongolian peoples, he was showing his hand as antagonistic to Han Chinese and to the Concordia Association. Considering these facts, the transfer of these two powerful men was certainly aimed at separating them from the political center and pigeon-holing them to the sidelines. These two men, who had already been relieved of joint duties as provincial governors at the time of the changeover from a four-province to a ten-province system for Manzhouguo in October 1934, a provincial reform measure aimed at strengthening the central power, had been cut off from their own power bases and were now uprooted even further. Now they were shut up in the cabinet and the imperial household, their political influence sharply curtailed.

By contrast, after losing his Harbin power base, Zhang Jinghui was said to "be forced to consider the setting sun of autumn" and the feeling at that time was that he had been far outflanked by Zang Shiyi and Xi Xia. Yet, because of the very fragility of his political power, Zhang was tapped to assume the position of prime minister. Together with Zhang Zuolin, Zhang Jinghui had at the time of the Russo-Japanese War joined forces and fought with the Japanese army. From that experience he had held the view that Manzhouguo should not be considered a state for the Chinese alone but should be considered a joint Japanese-Manchurian state. He is said to have publicly stated his view of Manzhouguo as follows: "Manchuria will flourish only on this basis. Young people don't know this history and are getting in the way of the Japanese. They are the source of trouble."[110] This was probably, of course, the very reason that Zhang Jinghui was selected. Known by the "Manchurian" officials as *Haohao xiansheng* (a yes-man), Zhang was seen as a yes-man who willingly followed the instructions of the Guandong Army and the director-general for administrative affairs. If this was an accurate evaluation, though, then perhaps one might say that Zhang never had any active desire to take part in ruling Manzhouguo. Matsumoto Masuo, who served as Zhang's secretary for ten years, wrote that Zhang Jinghui "would become engrossed, whenever he had a spare moment, in quiet sitting or copying out Buddhist sutras in his room [that is, the prime minister's chambers] all alone. . . . At times he made me think of a great priest who had reached some sort of enlightenment."[111] Matsumoto offers evidence to demonstrate that Zhang maintained an attitude of "saying virtually nothing at all about personnel matters and never betraying his feeling for or against a person." Even at meetings of the State Council, "at no time did he adhere to an opposing point of view" regarding proposals from the Office of Administrative Affairs.[112]

Under Zhang Jinghui, then, the centralization of political matters at the Office of Administrative Affairs moved ahead with even greater steam. As noted earlier, the exercise of great powers allocated to the emperor together with the implementation of the imperial system was legitimated only by the counsel offered by the prime minister. Thus, the prime minister came to possess the most extraordinary powers in Manzhouguo political affairs. A bureaucratic system in which political power was concentrated solely in the person of the prime minister was seen at the time as, "frankly speaking, a unique state past or present, the most bizarre of the bizarre."[113] This great power was then effectively exercised by the director-general for administrative affairs. For that reason all reforms of the administrative structure and all changes in positions held by "Manchurians" were decided upon by "Japanese" officials within the orbit of the director-general. When this state of affairs was presented to Zhang Jinghui, "he remained as un-moved as always. He then took a closer look and replied: 'It's fine. Let's move ahead with it.' "[114] And the matter came to an end.

As long as personnel matters were decided by such a system, it was neces-sary that the standards for appointments and dismissals depend upon on cooperativeness with the policies put forward by the Office of Administra-tive Affairs in the State Council. Han Yunjie, a graduate of Nagoya Higher Technical School who moved forward in the political world after the Manchurian Incident with an extraordinary ability in Japanese, a man who had served as minister of finance and minister of the economy, was fired al-legedly because he criticized the policies of forced buying-up of agricul-tural lands and the regulation of industry. Minister of Industry Ding Jianxiu was driven off to be head of the Manchurian Electric Company, and Minister of Public Welfare Sun Qichang to be a councilor in the Manzhouguo Cabinet, because they were said to have voiced discontent with economic policies. In his memoirs, Puyi noted: "The only measure of evaluation used by the Guandong Army in personnel matters was one's at-titude toward Japan."[115] "Japanese" officials in the Office of Administrative Affairs adopted the same evaluative measure for Manchurian officials.

Insofar as this became the standard of evaluation, it became all but in-evitable that men without strong ties to the Chinese political and economic worlds, men who had spent periods of study in Japan and who understood the political direction and administrative forms characteristic of contem-porary Japan, would be appointed to responsible posts. On the tenth an-niversary of the founding of the state in September 1942, a major reshuffling of personnel was carried out, and it was billed appropriately as a clean sweep of "all the various and sundry circumstances prevailing since the state-building operation." Men with experience as students in Japan were mobilized with the aim of establishing a wartime bureaucratic system. On the basis of this reshuffling, "the older ministers known as the 'found-ing fathers' retreated from the first line, and replacing them a generation of younger, up and coming, energetic men with considerable Japanese ed-ucations were selected en masse."[116] Men such as the following became the core of the Manchurian officialdom and formed its front facade: Gu Ci-heng (Minister of Communications, graduate of Tokyo Higher Normal School), Yan Chuanfu (Minister of Justice, graduate of the Faculty of Eco-nomics, Tokyo Imperial University), Xing Shilian (Minister of Public Secu-rity, graduate of the Cavalry Division, Japanese Army Academy), Ruan Zhenduo (Minister of the Economy, graduate of the South Manchurian Medical School, South Manchurian Railway), Lu Yuanshan (Vice-Director of the Office of Administrative Affairs, graduate of Miyagi Prefectural School of Agriculture), Wang Yunqing (Ambassador-Extraordinaire and Plenipotentiary, graduate of the Faculty of Law, Meiji University), Xu Shao-qing (Governor of Fengtian, graduate of the Faculty of Agriculture, Tokyo

Imperial University), Wang Xianwei (Mayor of Fengtian, graduate of the Faculty of Engineering, Tōhoku University), Wang Ziheng (Governor of Binjiang, graduate of the Faculty of Politics and Economics, Waseda University), Xu Jiahuan (head of the Statistics Desk, graduate of the Faculty of Law, Kyoto Imperial University), and Wang Qingzhang (Postmaster General, graduate of Tokyo University of Engineering), among others. With this personnel in place, however, still no transfer of power to these Manchurian officials was carried out. As the gossip of the time had it, they were "second-class imperial subjects," which meant that while they were fluent in Japanese and held posts reserved for "Manchurian" officials, they were seen merely as an expedient to be treated in a manner corresponding to the "Japanese" officials. This fact can be inferred from the following criticism concerning personnel: "Although they have tried to aggrandize themselves by selecting the up and coming, this has not necessarily been carried out in a thoroughgoing manner. . . . The notion that, because the great majority of the citizenry are Manchurians, ministerships must be occupied by Manchurians, is an overly optimistic ideal. Were we to be concerned about each and every matter of this sort, cooperation and national defense would be impossible."[117]

Zhang Jinghui offered no objection whatsoever to this personnel shift, and making cooperation with Japan first and foremost he never relaxed in the active delivery to Japan of resources and foodstuffs. He was thus dubbed the "Give-them-what-they-want" (*yaosha geisha*) prime minister. He compared Japanese-Manzhouguo relations to "two dragonflies tied to the same string." In the face of discontent for selling foodstuffs at extremely low prices to the Japanese, he reprimanded his critics by saying that famine "would be resolved by tightening their belts."[118] This kind of language was praised by Japanese and circulated among them as that which physically embodied Japanese-Manchurian friendship. In addition, he endorsed the Tripartite (Japanese-German-Italian) Alliance and early on expressed support for Japan when the Pacific War erupted. When he visited the government of Wang Jingwei (1883–1944), he appealed for "sharing joy and sorrow" with Japan, for "we are all in the same boat." In all these ways, Zhang Jinghui continued to stand consistently at the forefront of pro-Japanese cooperation. For this he was seen at the time as "a slave to the bone," yet still, according to the observations of Matsumoto Masuo, Zhang "seemed to harbor severe criticism in his breast"[119] toward Japanese rule in Manzhouguo and Japanese policy toward China. For example, he remained opposed to the forced sale of previously reclaimed land for colonial Japanese immigrants, and he frequently asked Hoshino Naoki to move with prudence on this issue. In addition, he sent Matsumoto to Minister of Overseas Affairs Koiso Kuniaki to press for radical reforms. Furthermore, seeing the eruption of the Sino-Japanese War as a particularly sad turn of events, he sought a quick resolution of it, declaring: "The Japanese military absolutely must not bring down the city of Nanjing. They must plan for peaceful means of some sort before doing so."[120] And, he is said to have conveyed to Hoshino his readiness to plunge into action wherever necessary toward that resolution.[121] However, what made Zhang angriest in his heart of hearts was the disdain with which Japanese people approached Chinese. Zhang did not understand the Japanese language, but he is said to have berated the Japanese for their "sense of superiority."

So deeply rooted were the words and deeds of Japanese imbued with a sense of superiority with respect to other peoples in Manzhouguo, where the appeal was for ethnic cooperation and Japan-Manzhouguo as a single entity, that they could not even be properly confronted. This situation was even recognized in a contemporaneous work entitled *Materials for the Education of Citizens as Seen in the Words and Deeds of Our Countrymen Overseas (Draft)* (*Kaigaichi hōjin no gendō yori mitaru kokumin kyōiku shiryō, an*) of May 1940, which was prepared by the Research Section, Army, Imperial General Headquarters with immediate corrections sought. It pointed to an antipathy within the officialdom as follows:

The majority of Japanese officials vociferously call for the pursuance of the policy of ethnic cooperation, but they have yet to divest themselves of the conventionalities of domestic [Japanese] officials, and this demands correction. Furthermore, because of the intensity of the harmful sense of superiority that colonial officials possess toward other ethnicities, they have made many mistakes consciously or unconsciously, and these have given rise to animosities with the general Manchurian populace from the Manchurian officialdom on down. Yet, the animosity of Japanese officials for Manchurian officials for the most part is rooted in the arbitrary behavior of Japanese officials and their excellent treatment in salaries as well as the antipathy of Manchurian officials for the tendency [of Japanese officials] to belittle them.[122]

As a root cause of this animosity, one might add the difference in bureaucratic management style of the Japanese and the Chinese. That is to say, "the 'Japanese' officials drafted a document to which they obtained agreement even from the lower functionaries and took it to their superiors, but it was the old ways of the 'Manchurian' officials that the superiors peruse a document, gave their necessary assent, and then it would be sent down to the lower functionaries. This gave rise to an unexpected incompatibility of points of view."[123] However, in cases in which the problem was such a divergence of administrative style, the Japanese form was always seen as that of a modern, civilized nation, while the Chinese was seen as feudal and therefore had to be "reformed" to the Japanese style. This sense of superiority exacerbated the animosities and served to deepen the gulf between the two parties. "Japanese" officials were, of course, aware of the harmful effects that this Japanification of the administration brought about. Looking back over their rule over Manzhouguo in the ten years from its founding, Assistant Director of the Office of Administrative Affairs Furumi Tadayuki, on the one hand, stressed the successes in state-building through ethnic harmony, but on the other he could not conceal the fact of what had come to pass:

Manzhouguo is a state with numerous ethnic groups. The great majority of its various structural components is comprised by the Manchurian ethnicity [i.e., Han and Manchu]. Naturally, these facts necessarily enhance the field of activities of Manchurians and the anticipation for the greatest service and contributions on their part to the establishment of Manzhouguo. In spite of this, however, many of Japan's legal institutions and structures have been transplanted there and have invited the result that the capacity for Manchurian activity has been narrowed. Furthermore, in the front line of actual politics which focuses on the Manchurian masses, the advancement of various policies and the heightened complication in administration have made it difficult for them to understand and cooperate. This has startlingly caused a decline in political and administrative efficiency.[124]

Having recognized this situation, how did they propose to deal with it? Furumi's solution ran as follows: "There is no need whatsoever for Japanese institutions and forms of administrative management to be reformed in the spirit of their objectives." Rather, in such areas as communications, hygiene, and mining and manufacturing, "it is necessary to introduce Japanese institutions and administration over a wide area." Yet, "we must change our thinking in such a way as to filtrate and absorb Japanese strengths into a Manchurian form. In particular, the first line of administration should be lowered to a simpler level." Nonetheless, Furumi saw lowering the first line of administration to a simpler level to be exceedingly difficult to realize in fact. The reason was that, in his view, "in the Japanese understanding of the matter, giving birth to Manchurian-style technology carried with it a difficulty comparable to seeking idiocy from sages." In the same piece, Furumi argued that "the 'measure' used by the Japanese people was weak as common tool for other ethnicities. . . . Accordingly, it would be difficult for other peoples to live in a home built on the basis of this 'measure,' and at times they would not want to enter it." He was thus arguing forcefully that the Japanese people had to seriously reflect on this matter, although he had audaciously affirmed that to produce techniques appropriate to Manchuria with a Japanese consciousness was "comparable to seeking idiocy from sages."[125] This deep-seated Japanese consciousness aroused the anger of even Zhang Jinghui, the man ridiculed as a "slave to the bone." "Manchurian" advisory officials (*sanjikan*), who were supposed to be the backbone of the Manzhouguo administration, were known by the homophone *sanjikan* (officials who do three things):[126] drink tea, read newspapers, and gossip. With each passing day, their anger toward the "Japanese" officials intensified.

"Manchuria is not a state in which Japanese and Manchurians cooperate, but a state in which they struggle with one another." This was the truth about Manzhouguo, and such a deep impression had been brought about by the staff officers of the Guandong Army, men who had been charged with bringing Manzhouguo and Japan together.

Metamorphosis: Chimera Transfigured

In September 1937 Ishiwara Kanji was dismissed as chief of the Operations Division of the General Staff of the army and transferred to serve as vice-chief of staff of the Guandong Army. Exalted as a man who had leapt to heroic status as the leading player in the founding of the state of Manzhouguo, he had then returned home like a returning victorious general. Nearly five years had now passed since he had worked with the Guandong Army. Unlike the era of his triumphant return which was full of great hopes for the future of Manzhouguo, however, Japan had now plunged into war with China, and deep in Ishiwara's heart the idea had sedimented that Japan "had now gotten itself into a terrible defeat, and the Japanese" had fallen into a "fate such that they will have no choice but to withdraw from China, from Taiwan, from Korea, and from the entire world to their narrow national terrain."[127] Ishiwara now painfully realized that it was none other than he and the staff officers of the Guandong Army who had led the way in the founding of Manzhouguo who were responsible for planting the seeds of this disastrous state of affairs.

Originally, if the commanding officer strictly applied the army's criminal code and "carried out executions for the arbitrary movement of troops," then Commander Honjō Shigeru and his staff officers in the Guandong Army who had brought about the Manchurian Incident should have been court-martialed. In spite of this, though, Honjō was promoted and received a baronage, and he was given the important post of chief aide-de-camp of the emperor. There was as well a granting of awards to Ishiwara Kanji and others who received promotions and decorations. Thus, a trend spread among the military bureaucrats that one would be honored even if one ignored discipline and the chain of command, as long as the results were positive. The ambition of outstationed troops rushed ahead uncontrolled in maneuvers into Inner Mongolia and political and military encroachments into north China. Ultimately, this led to the explosion of the Marco Polo Bridge Incident on July 7, 1937, and war with China. Although Ishiwara had adopted a policy of non-expansionism, he was unable to restrain the expansionists, such as Mutō Akira (1892–1948) and Tanaka Shin'ichi (1893–1976). In the end, in a scheme aimed at having him dismissed, he was transferred to the Guandong Army.

Five and one-half years after the founding of the state, Ishiwara appeared again in Manzhouguo. However, what he saw there was an image of

Manzhouguo at odds with what he had envisioned, with what he had dreamt of emerging. Unable to check the expansion of the Sino-Japanese War, he had been sent back to General Staff Headquarters, and feeling betrayed by the reality that Manzhouguo had become, Ishiwara developed a critique of this state ruled by the Guandong Army and "Japanese" officials in his inherently inflammatory tone. He demanded of Guandong Army Commander Ueda Kenkichi (1875–1962) a reduction in salaries and a personnel cut for "Japanese" officials and denounced Lieutenant General Hashimoto Toranosuke, president of the Concordia Association, in public speeches as "Nekonosuke"—that is, using the word for cat (*neko*) rather than for dragon (*tora*). While denouncing Chief of Staff Tōjō Hideki as no better than a sergeant or a private first-class, he also ridiculed Chief of Operations in the Guandong Army Katakura Tadashi as the king of Manzhouguo whose authority surpassed that of the Manchu emperor. Furthermore, he denounced the lavish official quarters in which the Guandong Army commander lived: "Look at the residence of the kingpin of the thieves. . . . Manchuria is supposed to be an independent state. They've stolen it. The residence of the Manzhouguo emperor has gone without repairs due to the present state of his citizenry, but the Japanese with their larcenous nature don't see this as the least bit odd."[128] And, not only did he offer Ueda Kenkichi a report on the need to transfer living quarters, but he stated plainly that he found Ueda unqualified for his position as Guandong Army commander. Such behavior could not help but set off a ferocious emotional battle with the Guandong Army brass and the local "Japanese" officialdom. In particular, the discord with Tōjō Hideki grew vehement like a personal hatred, while with Katakura Tadashi, with whom Ishiwara had for years carried on a teacher-student and friendly bond, he had opened a fissure that would be difficult to repair.

In August 1938, Ishiwara offered a position paper entitled *Kantōgun shireikan no Manshūkoku naimen shidōken tekkai ni tsuite* (On revoking the internal guidance authority of the Guandong Army Commander in Manzhouguo). In it he argued: "The sounds of military oppression fill the entire realm. . . . I believe that the time has come for the military to return to its original tasks. The Guandong Army has advanced troops before the time was ripe and must now soon lay down their arms. Thus, the army must revoke internal guidance over Manzhouguo and complete the independence of Manzhouguo quickly with a carefully worked out plan."[129] In this document, Ishiwara proposed the following ideas: abolish Section Four, which was the military's office of internal guidance, and give the Concordia Association the right to set state policy; create a structure in Manzhouguo which would itself support administrative officials to see to the furtherance of political independence; have the central Manzhouguo government be concerned solely with public order, the courts, tax collection, and running the economy, while relinquishing all other administrative matters to local control; abolish the assigned bureaucratic posts for Japanese wherein lies the "danger of turning such high officials as provincial vice-governors and assistant county magistrates into 'robots' "; and cede the South Manchurian Railway and the Guandong Leased Territory to Manzhouguo. It was not likely that any one of his proposals would have been accepted, and Ishiwara thus lost a place for himself even in Manzhouguo. Amakasu Masahiko (1881–1945) offered Ishiwara the coup de grâce: "Since Ishiwara's being in Manchuria was no longer good for Manzhouguo, I told him to go home."[130] Seven years earlier, Ishiwara had shed copious tears when he moved to an independent state, and now harboring untold grief and anger in Japan's having turned Manzhouguo into a subject state, he tendered his resignation. Crestfallen, he had no choice but to leave Manzhouguo in his Concordia Association uniform, and he never set foot there again. Thus, Manzhouguo was released from Ishiwara's hands in name and reality.

In fact, when Ishiwara went to Manzhouguo in 1937, it was far from the hands of the people who had taken part in its creation, having become a structure run by a iron pyramid of military men acting as bureaucrats, administrative technocrats, and managers of semi-governmental corporations. Symbolic of this structure were Hoshino Naoki (Director-General for Administrative Affairs), Tōjō Hideki (Commander of the Military Police of the Guandong Army and Chief of Staff of the Guandong Army), Kishi Nobusuke (Vice-Minister of Industry and Vice-Director of the Office of Administrative Affairs), Ayukawa Yoshisuke (1880–1967, President of Manchurian Heavy Industry), and Matsuoka Yōsuke (1880–1946, President of the South Manchurian Railway Company), known popularly as "the two *ki*'s and the three *suke*'s." Of course, with them all at the pinnacle, a large number of similar sorts of men milled around at the base of this pyramid. In addition, movement toward a Japan-Manzhouguo unification was advancing steadily and with extraordinary ingenuity, more than Ishiwara had imagined. In December 1937 the abrogation of extraterritoriality and the transfer of administrative rights to the S.M.R.'s attached terrain was finally accomplished; at the same time, Manzhouguo recognized no extraterritoriality for any other third countries. Thus, Manzhouguo regained its sovereignty and protected its independence. Concerning extraterritoriality, "through devotion to the duty of being united in virtue and heart, Japan seeks the healthy development of Manzhouguo, and bestows gifts from a broad-minded perspective. . . . Thus, there are no peoples among our citizenry who are clad in the armor of extraterritoriality. All ethnic groups shake hands in sobriety and openness and enjoy harmony together."[131]

It was then announced that Japan itself would relinquish special privileges in the interest of ethnic harmony. However, this should not necessarily be seen as a salutory arrangement. By abrogating extraterritoriality, Manzhouguo guaranteed that Japanese citizens would enjoy freedom of residence and movement throughout its terrain, the freedom to take up any occupation (public or private) in agriculture, industry, or commerce, and all manner of privileges such as landownership. Because of this understanding, Japanese rights and interests in Manchuria which had been an issue even before the Manchurian Incident were now all publicly recognized. Furthermore, it was stipulated by treaty that the Japanese government would carry out administrative tasks concerning Shinto shrines, education, and military affairs. In addition, it was specified that "Japanese nationals shall in no case ever be subject to treatment less advantageous than the people of Manzhouguo."[132] This was anything but sober and open insofar as it concerned Japanese. In short, then, for the Japanese the abrogation of extraterritoriality meant the exclusion of foreign nations and the transformation of Manzhouguo into identity with domestic Japan. In so doing, the further unification of the administrations of Japan and Manzhouguo was the objective.

By placing Manzhouguo in an identical legal situation with Japan and simply furthering the Japanese expansion into Manchuria, the wholesale Japanization of Manzhouguo was loudly touted as a necessary condition. From the time that Puyi touched on the theme of Japanese-Manzhouguo unity in virtue and heart in his Admonitory Rescript to the People on the Occasion of the Emperor's Return of May 1935, Tsukushi Kumashichi had been strenuously arguing: "In order to make Japanese-Manzhouguo relations like those of a parent and child, all of the issues confronting Manzhouguo—in politics, the economy, education, thought, and the like—must be reconfigured into a structure resembling those of the [Japanese] empire. Insofar as they cannot be, it will be impossible to make manifest a state of unity in virtue and heart."[133] The men responsible for transforming all things in Manzhouguo into something resembling things Japanese were the administrative technocrats—the "Japanese" officials—who had been ushered in there from Japan. The state bureaucracy fashioned from the outset by these Japanese officials in opposition to the Republic of China was "a reconfiguration of a structure resembling" the Japanese emperor-state. In 1937 the Japanization of law—criminal law, criminal litigation law, civil law, various commercial codes such as the universal law of merchants, civil litigation law, the law of forcible execution, and the like—was effectively completed. The great reform over the administrative structure, including such items as the discontinuation of the Inspectorate *Yuan* in July 1937 on the eve of the abrogation of extraterritoriality, demonstrated that Manzhouguo was being reconfigured into a bureaucratic structure resembling that of Japan, so much so that there was no need for it to conform at all to the state system or laws of the Republic of China.

One man who had personal experience with Japanese officials who were moving ahead on a daily basis forging a Manzhouguo in imitation of Japan was Morishima Morito (1896–1975). As he later testified:

I hoped that arbitrary military behavior would be restrained by them [i.e., the "Japanese" officials], but my expectations were completely betrayed. Ignorant of real conditions in Manchuria and of the customs, practices, and psychology of the Manchurians, they vainly degenerated into a standardized administration enmeshed in ideology and based on the omnipotence of laws and regulations. They transported to Manchuria the subordinate politics, the object of criticism even back in Japan, giving birth to the expression "legal bandits" (*hōhi*) which corresponded to "local bandits" (*dohi*).[134]

This evidence would lead one to believe that it was no exaggeration to see the distinctiveness of Manzhouguo's rule in its control by "Japanese" officials. Despite the ideals of the founding of Manzhouguo in such Asian expressions as following the way of heaven and bringing peace to the people, benevolence and love, the Kingly Way, and harmony, as well as opposition to and liberation from Western imperialist control, the basis for legitimacy in ruling Manzhouguo was ultimately sought in control based on laws produced in the modern West. This was a further indication that Manzhouguo was being "civilized" and becoming a modern state. In other words, *la mission civilisatrice* was the legitimizing basis for Japanese control, and in this point Japan was no different from the colonial control of Western European imperialist states of the time which Japan itself was criticizing. Insofar as Japanese were extremely stringent in the application of laws and regulations, this was probably even more calamitous for people on the scene.

In any event, beginning in July 1932 when the Ministry of Finance dispatched such men as Hoshino Naoki, Furumi Tadayuki, Matsuda Reisuke (1900–1984), Tamura Toshio (b. 1903), Yamanashi Takeo, Aoki Minoru (b. 1909), and Terasaki Hideo, the expansion into Manzhouguo with Japanese administrative technocrats, as Table 5 indicates, reached considerable numbers, even if we count only those who were high-level officials when they retired from various Japanese ministries. Of course, such officials were not sent in a random fashion, but their being dispatched directly reflected the political tasks—and the changes they were undergoing—to rule Manzhouguo. In other words, from the founding of the state through 1936, a period in which the enforcement of public order and the establishment of finance were considered urgent to the continued existence of the state, in addition to those, such as Hoshino, who were sent by the Ministry of Finance for the purpose of consolidating the basis of credit and finance and for the unification of the currency, those with a background in the Ministry of Finance, such as Sakatani Kiichi and Genda Shōzō, were employed. In addition, for the maintenance of public order and the consolidation of local institutions, the Ministry of Home Affairs in 1932 sent twenty-one management personnel—including Shimizu Ryōsaku, Governor of Wakayama Prefecture, and Shinagawa Kazue (b. 1887)—and the Guandong Government-General employed such men as Takeuchi Tokui (1888–1946), Hoshiko Toshio, and Shiohara Tokisaburō.

At this time, consolidation of the Manzhouguo postal and telecommunications systems was also an important policy task, and to deal with them the Ministry of Communications dispatched Fujiwara Yasuaki, Iino Takeo, and Okamoto Tadao, among others. The maintenance of public order was a consistently difficult task for Manzhouguo, and the Ministry of Home Affairs later sent such men as Takeuchi Tetsuo, Susukida Yoshitomo (1897–1963), Ōtsubo Yasuo, Ōtsu Toshio, and Kan Tarō. And, of the six directors-general for administrative affairs, four hailed from the Ministry of Home Affairs and had served as provincial governors: Endō Ryūsaku, Nagaoka Ryūichirō (1884–1963), Ōdachi Shigeo (1892–1955), and Takebe Rokuzō (1893–1958).

These personnel might lead one to believe that ruling Manzhouguo was being treated as an extension of domestic Japanese politics, as one of Japan's many prefectures. In any event, when the abrogation of extra-territoriality came to the fore in 1933, the number of those sent from the Ministry of Justice rose dramatically in order to draft legislation and consolidate legal institutions; among others, in rapid succession, Furuta Masatake, Maeno Shigeru (b. 1897), Oikawa Tokusuke (b. 1890), Shiba Kenbun, Aoki Sajihito, Sugawara Tatsurō, Mutō Tomio, and Ino Eiichi sailed across the sea to the continent. Inasmuch as the majority of those sent by the Ministry of Justice were judicial officials, a system was adopted whereby they were guaranteed reinstatement with the same treatment as those of their cohort after a three-year period, and as such their rotation was a quick one. However, among them in addition to Minakawa Toyoji who came to Manzhouguo around the time it was created and became the Director-General for General Administrative Matters in Manzhouguo's Ministry of Education, many judicial officials expanded the range of their activities into areas other than justice, such as Sugawara, who became General Manager of the Concordia Association and Mutō, who became head of the Public Relations Desk in the Bureau of National Affairs.

Having shored up its appearance as an independent state by 1937, with the injection of Japanese officials from the Ministries of Finance, Home Affairs, Communications, and Justice, Manzhouguo moved on to the development of industry as its next policy task. Of course, the development of natural resources in Manchuria and Mongolia and the increase in Japan's composite national defense strength were the primary reasons that the Guandong Army sought control over the region. The expansion of productive capacity was a goal pursued continuously throughout the period of Manzhouguo's existence. However, it was also driven by the need to crush the anti-Manzhouguo, anti-Japanese movement which at its peak occupied over 300,000 men and women from the founding of the state until roughly 1936. Eventually, in 1936 the development of Manchurian industry emerged as the central policy issue of the state. Thus, from 1937 through 1941 we enter an era of great emphasis on industrial growth. Symbolic of this move

Table 5. Manzhouguo Personnel

Government office or ministry	Number of retired officials	Number of reappointed officials after returning home to Japan
Imperial Household	8	1
Cabinet	4	
Foreign Office	31	7
Home Affairs	65	14
Finance	23	4
Army	14	
Navy		
Justice	114	16
Education	20	
Agriculture and Forestry	64	11
Commerce and Industry	35	11
Communications	18	6
Railways	3	
Overseas Affairs	4	2
Public Welfare	11	3
Board of Audit	3	
Total	**417**	**75**

"Manshūkoku kenri to naru itai kansha jin'in chō" (Personnel chart of retired bureaucrats who became officials in Manzhouguo), included in *Konoe Fumimaro kō kankei shiryō* (Materials concerning Prince Konoe Fumimaro), held in the Yōmei Bunko. The following proviso is attached as a note to the original source: "This does not include the Bureau of Local Affairs in the Ministry of Home Affairs and concerned foreign sites in the Ministry of Overseas Affairs, among others. These have not yet been tabulated by the office in the Guandong Government General."

was the five-year plan for industrial development. In order to secure natural resources, the Guandong Army transferred the Nissan Corporation under Ayukawa Yoshisuke to Manzhouguo and established the Manchurian Heavy Industry Company. Invited to share responsibility for the tasks of policy promotion were officials from such Japanese Ministries as Commerce and Industry, Agriculture and Forestry, and Overseas Affairs.

From the founding of Manzhouguo, the Ministry of Commerce and Industry in Japan sent such men as Takahashi Kōjun, Ono Gishichirō, and Minobe Yōji (1900–1953). Kishi Nobusuke, who was head of the Archives and Documents Section, claimed that their plan was to dispatch talented men with the following ideas in mind:

Section Four [the Operations Section] of the Guandong Army did as they pleased when it came to the administration of industry in Manchuria. In many instances, they miscalculated because they were military men. . . . It was impossible to go on this way. The finest men in the Ministry of Commerce and Industry went there to tackle the problems of industrial administration, and they should have taken over industrial administration from the military. In any event, I had no choice but to go.[135]

Seventeen men, including Shiina Etsusaburō, responded to this call. In 1933 Shiina took up his new position as the head of the Planning Department in the Manzhouguo Ministry of Industry, and, with the notion that investigation of resources was indispensible to industrial development, he established a Provisional Industrial Investigation Office. The data collected there were used in the drafting of regulations on control over important industries, for the selection of settlement sites, and for the construction of a dam. Following Shiina, the Ministry of Commerce and Industry sent, among others, Kanda Noboru and Inamura Toshizō.

In 1936 Kishi Nobusuke went to Manzhouguo, and under his auspices a controlled economy was pursued. At this time the policies of the five-year plan for industrial development and from 1939 the three-year plan for the advancement of the northern regions were pushed forward as development policies based on a twenty-year plan for resettling one million households (these three will be referred to below as the three great state policies of Manzhouguo). Over a twenty-year period, it was decided that the emigration of one million households or some five million people would be the goal. It was thus estimated that in twenty years the population of Manzhouguo would reach 50,000,000, one-tenth of whom would be Japanese. In order to carry out this colonial policy and the agricultural policy accompanying it, the Ministry of Agriculture and Forestry dispatched Noda Kiyotake, Inoue Shuntarō, Irako Kanzō, Ishizaka Hiroshi, and Kusumi Yoshio, among others, and the Ministry of Overseas Affairs sent such men as Inagaki Ikuo and Morishige Tateo. One further indication of the special nature of the times was the fact that Kodaira Gon'ichi (1884–1976), Vice-Minister of Agriculture and Forestry, was made Chairman of the Central Board of the Agricultural Development Cooperative Society, and Tsubogami Teiji (1884–1979), Vice-Minister of Overseas Affairs, was made President of the Manchurian Colonial Corporation. However, as the Sino-Japanese War expanded and Germany declared war in 1939, there was a dearth of labor power and supplies as well as delays in the distribution of supplies under the controlled economy. As a result, many of the policy goals connected with industrial development came to an end without achieving the results that had been aimed for within the time allotted.

After the eruption of the Pacific War in December 1941, all policy in Manzhouguo was concentrated in services or contributions that might be rendered in pursuit of Japan's war. Together with the increased production of iron, steel, and coal, the controlled collection of various foodstuffs— "Japan's food storehouse"—became the first priority. The requirement for the supply of food to Japan reached 3,000,000 tons in 1945. While the need for Japanese bureaucrats as necessary personnel in the military government in occupied territories rose during this period, it became necessary as well that they be thoroughly knowledgeable about the state of affairs in Manzhouguo as concerned the production and collection of food. Hence, the dispatching of new officials was sharply curtailed.

The actual selection of bureaucrats to be sent from Japan to Manzhouguo had followed a process of nomination and invitation by the Guandong Army. The latter retained the right to appoint and dismiss "Japanese" officials as it carried out this process for each of Manzhouguo's ministries. While the talent pool which the Guandong Army could itself commandeer was extremely limited, each ministry took the initiative in the management of Manzhouguo by "having each and every ministry send to the scene fine men with a future."[136] This was also an indication of an effort to train talent.

As noted earlier, in July 1932 three positions in the administrative structure for Manzhouguo were merged into one whereby the Commander of the Guandong Army also served as Provisional Ambassador-Extraordinaire and Plenipotentiary as well as Governor-General of Guandong. It had not, however, been the plan at any time to have one person acquire all this power and to have the administrative apparatus itself be so thoroughly integrated. Thus, Army Central and the Guandong Army did combine their administrative structures in Manzhouguo, and aiming at a structural reform that would make it easier to control, in December 1934 they established a Manzhouguo Office and abolished the Governor-Generalship of Guandong. In so doing a structure took form in which two positions were merged into one. With this administrative reform, the majority of administrative authority which had until that point been in the hands of the Ministries of Foreign Affairs and Overseas Affairs came under the control of the Guandong Army Commander. However, this development was immediately linked to the fact that Japanese control over Manzhouguo was the foundation stone of the Guandong Army's dictatorial structure. For, by the same token, "all police powers in industrial administration outside of the work of diplomatic consuls was returned to the Manzhouguo Office directly under the Cabinet."[137] In other words, concerning the effort by the Guandong Army to gain exclusive control over Manzhouguo, "on the civil side in the Cabinet, some argued that there had to be an organ with ties to the establishment of a state in Manchuria. . . . Aspirations in the form of what might be called extraordinary pressure from the civil side arose" and became the driving force for the creation of a Manzhouguo Office.[138]

The Manzhouguo Office was headed by the Army Minister. Also established therein was a Councilors' Conference made up of bureau directors of the various concerned ministries—such as finance, foreign affairs, home affairs, overseas affairs, commerce and industry, and the army—and the men who worked at the office were experts from the various ministries on Manchuria and Mongolia. Thus, with the "spirit of the combined efforts of the various ministries concerning the administration in Manzhouguo,"[139] the Japanese government took charge of policy coordination in planning for control over Manzhouguo as a whole. Concretely, in cases of policy tasks for which they sought implementation in Manzhouguo, "the Army Ministry would receive them from the Guandong Army and take them to the Manzhouguo Office. The latter would then contact the various ministries regarding matters of concern to them. When an understanding was reached, they would then return to the Army Ministry and on to the Guandong Army. Thus was created a mechanism for getting 'okays' concerning Manzhouguo. The requirements of the Japanese side followed a similar routing and were conveyed to the Office of Administrative Affairs in the State Council of Manzhouguo."[140]

Needless to say, in addition to this formal route, bureaucrats sent to Manzhouguo were aware of the inclinations of their original ministries or offices and sought to realize their policy aims. Furthermore, through groups such as the Japan-Manzhouguo Joint Committee and the Japan-Manzhouguo Food Committee, which were established as bilateral consultative bodies between Japan and Manzhouguo, the controlling aims of Japan's various ministries and offices were conveyed to the Manzhouguo government. In Manzhouguo's bureaucratic system, state law and policy were decided following a simple path from the various ministries to the Office of Administrative Affairs to meetings of the State Council to meetings of the Cabinet to the Emperor. In spite of this, the actual process of reaching policy decisions in Manzhouguo, as was clear to anyone and everyone there at the time, was exceedingly complex and far removed from the basic bureaucratic structure of the state. The essence of "independence" in Manzhouguo—as an independent state—can clearly be seen here for what it was.

In this way, control over Manzhouguo moved ahead through a system of "the combined efforts of the various ministries," and the dispatching of personnel to Manzhouguo became institutionalized as an organized response of all the Japanese ministries. Thus, guaranteeing status for bureaucrats who were sent in this manner naturally became an issue. In order to become an official of a foreign government, such as Manzhouguo was, even for a retired Japanese official, an investigation was begun in 1936 under a system of exchanging the number of years served in Manzhouguo as a Manzhouguo official for those in Japan and guaranteed reinstatement back home. The result was promulgated as imperial ordinance no. 881 in 1940. Of course, while the Manzhouguo government was a foreign government, even for Japanese bureaucrats, becoming an official in it was substantively the same thing as being transferred to another ministry or office within Japan.

Once the Pacific War began, Japan formed the Greater East Asia Coprosperity Sphere and established the Greater East Asian Ministry in November

1942 as its ruling mechanism. The Manzhouguo Office had jurisdiction over "foreign affairs matters concerned with Manzhouguo." Yet, Prime Minister Tōjō Hideki publicly declared that "there will be no diplomacy within the Great East Asia Coprosperity Sphere." Controlling Manzhouguo was not seen as diplomacy but as one piece of domestic politics. Concerning this arrangement, the Nationalists' broadcasting from Chongqing claimed (and not inappropriately): "Under the rule of the puppet governments which was rapidly put up in Manzhouguo and other [Japanese] conquered areas, they have formally become colonies of Japan and are areas ruled directly by the Japanese government."[141] Thus, the sending of officials to Manzhouguo, a foreign country, was treated in the same way as taking up a domestic assignment, and ruling Manzhouguo was handled in the same way as direct rule. Just as Carl Schmitt (1888–1985) had criticized the state of British and French colonial control, Manzhouguo was in the following position: while as a foreign country it was distinct with respect to Japan in its domestic law, in international law it excluded other nations in the same way as it would have domestically (*staatsrechtlich Ausland, völkerrechtlich Innland*).

Japanese-Manzhouguo relations were gradually transformed from equal ties as independent states to a position conforming to domestic Japanese affairs, and this change can clearly be seen even in official public documents from Manzhouguo. For example, in the Manifesto on the Founding of the State (March 1, 1932), it simply stated: "Lending a hand to our neighbor (*linshi*)." In the Japan-Manzhouguo Protocol (September 15, 1932), this became: "Good neighborly relations (*zenrin*) between the two countries of Japan and Manzhouguo." In Puyi's Admonitory Rescript to the People on the Occasion of the Emperor's Return (May 2, 1935), Japan became the "friendly country" (*youbang*) as in the expression, "united in virtue and heart with that friendly country." In the Rescript on Commemoration of the Fifth Anniversary of the Founding of the Concordia Association (July 25, 1936), it had changed to "ally" (*mengbang*) as in: "We shall never alter in our reliance upon our ally, the Empire of Japan." In his Rescript on the Tenth Anniversary of the Founding of the State (March 1, 1942), the term used was "parental country" (*qinbang*) as in: "We shall contribute to the great East Asian holy war and offer our support in the great task of our senior [parental] country." The term *qin* in *qinbang* can mean "close" or "intimate," but in this instance it bore its other meaning of "parental." Thus, with each change in terminology, Japanese-Manzhouguo relations moved from an equal footing to unequal, hierarchical ties. Japanese-Manzhouguo relations were patterned after a parent-child bond with "a parent who can see things clearly and a child who is respectful and loving." As Puyi put it in his Rescript on the Tenth Anniversary of the Founding of the State, this parent-child relationship "exhausts devotion in repaying our debt of gratitude," the key point being that, in order to repay this parental debt to Japan, Manzhouguo had to unilaterally exhaust its devotion and filiality. Evidence of this parental respect was the unremunerated compulsory labor and the foodstuffs which Manzhouguo farmers had to deliver while they themselves were starving. In his autobiography, Puyi noted that, in the six years following the founding of Manzhouguo, altogether 36,620,000 tons of grains were exported to Japan, and from 1938 the number of those drafted into unremunerated labor through compulsory requisitioning reached 2,500,000 each year.

This transformation in Japanese-Manzhouguo relations brought about, as one would expect, a deterioration in Manzhouguo's state-founding ideal itself. That is, it had been claimed that "the unification of the two countries in fact marked the confluence and union of the spirit of coexistence and coprosperity of brethren within the four seas which was rooted in Japan's own great state-founding ideal—namely, the great spirit of universal brotherhood (hakkō ichiu)—with the founding of the state of Manzhouguo whose essential principles, fully in line with this [great spirit], were following the way of heaven and bringing peace to the people and the harmony of the five ethnic groups."[142] The founding of Manzhouguo was taken here as a manifestation of the spirit of the imperial way of universal brotherhood. Kyoto Imperial University Professor Maki Kenji (1892–1989) had already in 1934 stressed the necessity of a change from the principle of the Kingly Way to that of the Imperial Way: "At present, Manzhouguo has formed a state based on the Kingly Way, and with Japan's principle of the Imperial Way as its referrent, must work for the eternal security of the royal family."[143] In 1938 in Manzhouguo, however, the following fear was expressed:

When the state was first founded, it was adorned from top to bottom with the Kingly Way. At some point recently it has changed to the Imperial Way, and the reason for this change has not been made clear. . . . There is, however, one thing to be uneasy about. This is the huge problem of Japan, as the leader of East Asia, conveying its holy policies abroad, and when it behaves in this completely unreflecting self-conceitedness, there is the danger that it might reflect [negatively] on the face of the Japanese emperor.[144]

Yet, while the reason for the change from the Kingly Way to the Imperial Way was not indicated, the view that "Manzhouguo is the initial manifestation of the creation of an ethical world based upon the immense will of the emperor"[145] was enunciated just as if it had been a self-evident ideal since the founding of the state. For Li Shaogeng, the Manzhouguo minister in Japan, "the basis of our nation's ideology is to mature, develop, and be unified with the Japanese way of the gods. As a manifestation of universal brotherhood, the Japanese spirit of state founding, our nation is the first child of the Greater East Asia Coprosperity Sphere."[146] Perhaps it was perfectly appropriate that this sort of transformation be seen less as a change in the content of the state of Manzhouguo and more as the gradual emergence of its own essence.

Hence, in Manzhouguo, now denied the state-building principle of the Kingly Way, a state "could emerge for the first time . . . permeated fully with the imperial policy of universal brotherhood . . . by virtue of the majesty of the Sun Goddess,"[147] and the other state-founding principle, that of ethnic harmony, was also compelled to undergo considerable change. Until then the significance of ethnic harmony was taken to be:

The various ethnic groups would simply come to the understanding that they would cease struggling among themselves and work together. Now, however "ethnic harmony" has become a necessary condition by which the various peoples wholeheartedly devote themselves toward the realization of a principle of state-building. These are not surface conciliatory relations, for they are based on the spirit of service to the realization of the Japanese principle of state founding, and the other ethnic groups shall work to follow their lead.[148]

Ethnic harmony then did not mean equal coexistence on the surface, but had been transformed into vertical, hierarchical leader-follower relations in which there was service to and following of the Japanese who were the leading ethnicity. Whatever this may have meant, one cannot call it ethnic harmony.

Thus, with the start of the Pacific War, the two state-founding ideals—the Kingly Way and ethnic harmony—found the clock turned back. This meant, needless to say, the conclusion of these ideals of state formation. Already, with the insertion of the Japanese emperor system into Manzhouguo through "Japanese" officials in the flesh, one part of the body of the chimera—the dragon portion (the Manchu emperor and China)—had changed with its own flesh and blood into a sheep (the Japanese emperor system) and lost its original form.

Now, the chimera had completed its metamorphosis into a monster with the head of a lion and the body of a sheep.

The Necessity of Cooperation in Both Life and Death: The Fate of "Japanchukuo"

Manzhouguo then was undergoing on a daily basis a transformation by which it was being assimilated into the Japanese state or emperor system. One French writer allegedly referred to it as "Mannequinchuria" (implying a kingdom of mannequins). The French word "mannequin," of course, means someone who does what he is told, a puppet. In the same way, in the impressions of an American businessman who traveled there, Manzhouguo would best, he claimed, have been called "Japanchukuo" (or "Japanzhouguo," in the spelling used in this volume). To be sure,

Manzhouguo was seen as part of domestic Japan and its rule was treated as an extension of domestic Japanese politics, and to that extent it may indeed have been appropriate to dub it "Mannequinchuria" or "Japanzhouguo." However, the problem for us is to understand the nature of the change that transpired while Japan and Manzhouguo were repeatedly exchanging projections and reflections. In other words, what impact did possession of Manzhouguo have on Japan itself, and what sort of disfigurement did it experience as a result? Without an understanding of these issues, it will be impossible to assess Manzhouguo's true historical significance.

First, focusing this mutuality on the Manzhouguo side, we have already pointed out that the culture of Japanese bureaucratic administration was enforced, and Chinese officials unfamiliar with it were regarded as useless. The citation which follows demonstrates this point fully.

The Manchurians are undoubtedly incapable. Yet, rather than importing Japanese administrative organization and the ways of administration which are translated versions of European political science and then applying them as is to Manzhouguo, maybe the way Manchurian officials do things would be far more appropriate in handling matters involving rule over the actual people of Manzhouguo. Furthermore, can Japanese, irrespective of whether they are more fitting to the tasks at hand, complete the work throughout all points in Manchuria with the number of persons available? This is the present situation in the newly risen Manzhouguo, a translated government unresponsive to the popular will. With this instrument, the Manchurian people will gradually lose their vitality. They lack anything remotely resembling national enthusiasm or national excitement. What in the world will happen to Manzhouguo? . . . The level of unity in virtue and heart is unknown, but a unity in virtue and heart based in making the Manchurians into robots is undesirable, and it will create institutions which will give the Japanese a sense of superiority. No matter how much one exclaims that they not display such a sense of superiority, it will be of no use whatsoever.[149]

After these sentences were written, the Japanization process only grew stronger and with no improvements at all. Thus, even though such a criticism did not appear openly thereafter, it was most certainly not the case that the Japanese legal and political forms had been received and taken root in Manchurian soil. This fact indicates the bottomless depth of the silent abyss of despair.

We cannot, however, see the policies, administration, and legislation implemented in Manzhouguo as direct transplantations or literal translations from those of Japan. The U.S. magazine *Fortune* ran a special issue on Japan in April 1944, and it aptly referred to the government of Manzhouguo as the "Army school for civilians in Manchuria."[150] As this phrase makes clear, Manzhouguo itself functioned as one laboratory or training center. Namely, in *Fortune*'s understanding, the Japanese army, which still did not have the political clout or knowledge to effect changes as it wished in Japan proper, therefore turned Manchuria into a training place for men and for organization methods. They were determined that Manchuria should be their private school-room, and they worked out effective and total controls of everything from major economic and political matters to the daily comings and goings of the inhabitants. . . . Actually the military owed a great deal to Manchuria. There they trained their political front men. . . . There they developed a backlog of power that considerably strengthened their position in politics back home.[151]

There are, of course, exaggerations here, but within the army Tōjō Hideki, Koiso Kuniaki, and others had been prime ministers, while among civil officials Endō Ryūsaku and Tanabe Harumichi had been chief cabinet secretaries, Hoshino Naoki had been head of the Cabinet Planning Board and chief cabinet secretary, and Ōdachi Shigeo had been vice-minister for home affairs. In addition, under Minister Kishi Nobusuke within the Ministry of Commerce and Industry in 1941 were Vice-Minister Shiina Etsusaburō, Head of the General Affairs Office Kanda Noboru, and Head of the General Affairs Section Mōri Hideoto, as well as other high-ranking personnel with considerable clout repatriated from Manzhouguo. Even among the staff officers of the Guandong Army, men such as Itagaki Seishirō, who had been army minister, Mutō Akira, who had served as head of the Bureau of Military Affairs, Akinaga Tsukizō (1893–1949) and Ikeda Sumihisa (1894–1968), who had been heads of the Overall Planning Office, and Iimura Yuzuru (1888–1976), who had served as head of the Total War Research Institute, among others, were all military men who played important roles in the implementation of total war.

Expanding our time frame through to the postwar period, the number of "Japanese" officials who became staff officers and members of parliament or regional public bodies is staggering. One can scarcely deny the function that Manzhouguo played as a personnel training center. In addition, they selected "men on whose shoulders the future Finance Ministry would rest"[152] and sent them to Manzhouguo; in this way the Finance Ministry—and it was not alone—took advantage of Manzhouguo for personnel training.

In policy, legislation, and administrative structure as well, one could cite numerous examples in which Manzhouguo provided for Japan an experiment or advance test. Ishiwara Kanji had noted, as one of the original principal objectives in occupying Manchuria, that "given our national conditions, we shall rapidly found a state, press forward with expansion outward, and resolutely push on with domestic reform on the basis of conditions we encounter along the way."[153] Thus, it was expected that Manzhouguo would function as a springboard or a testing bench for this resolute pursuit of domestic reform. In fact, there gathered in Manzhouguo people who "were driven by an enthusiasm to attempt to carry out here what was impossible to do in Japan proper."[154] Their administrative nucleus was the Office of Administrative Affairs in the State Council. Backed by the military might and secret funds of the Guandong Army, the Office of Administrative Affairs consistently pursued "consolidated strengthening of the planning and control functions," and on this basis aimed "at the firm establishment, simply put, of a powerful government."[155] To that end, such organs for national policy planning and policy drafting as the Planning Desk in the Office of Administrative Affairs and the Planning Committee were set up, and there thus emerged a politics of planning distinctive to the administration of Manzhouguo. The principles of control and planning which developed along with these strings of key concepts—namely, planning-guidance-management and planning-control-mobilization—were powerfully influenced by Taylorism in the United States, the Gosplan (State Planning Agency) in the Soviet Union, and the four-year plan in Nazi Germany. What made this "politics of planning" particularly possible in Manzhouguo was the system at work there, unchecked by the Japanese Diet and with an administration managed without any relationship to the will of the local populace.

One has the sense that, beginning with the three state policies of the Five-Year Industrial Development Plan, the Three-Year Northern Promotion Plan, and the Twenty-Year One Million Household Emigration Plan—and continuing with the General Industrial Location Plan, the Five-Year Plan to Establish Self-Sufficient Villages, and the Ten-Year Increased Agricultural Production Plan, among others—the Manzhouguo administration was inundated by plans. This profusion of plans did not, of course, all necessarily produce results, and the majority of them remained on paper only, ending up with, as it was noted at the time, "planning politics without so much as a whiff of the local terrain—thoroughly ineffective politics."[156]

That said, the General Industrial Location Plan, for example, did in fact precede Japan's own national land planning, actually becoming a model itself. Mōri Hideoto, Minobe Yōji, and others learned from the politics of planning in Manzhouguo and later led in the formulation of planning in the Planning Board and General Planning Office in Japan. Thus, we cannot ignore the fact that the politics of planning flowed back to Japan, where it exerted considerable influence. Manzhouguo's Planning Desk (established in November 1935) as an agency of state policy planning was the predecessor of the Planning Office in Japan and the Planning Board which replaced it (both founded in 1937). Furthermore, the State Council and the Office of Administrative Affairs in Manzhouguo were themselves highlighted as models in the founding conception of a forceful national policy integration and driving agencies aimed at forming a national defense state. For example, in the Plan for the Reform of the Political Administration (*Seiji gyōsei kikō kaikaku an*) of 1936, which Ishiwara Kanji drafted at the Japan-Manzhouguo Finance and Economic Research Association organized by Asahara Kenzō (1891–1967) and Miyazaki Masayoshi, among others, the plan called for scrapping the cabinet system, establishing a state council, placing an economic staff headquarters and an office of administrative affairs directly under the authority of the state council, and giving the latter personnel and budget control. And, even in the Draft Plan of a Policy Concerning the Implementation of a Five-Year Plan for Heavy Industry, compiled by the Army in 1937, the establishment of an office of administrative affairs was called for. Furthermore, in numerous instances, individual measures and policies were effected in Japan proper on the basis of experience gained in Manzhouguo. One such example would be the system for the supervision of grains. This grain supervision law in Manzhouguo was drawn up by men surrounding Kodaira Gon'ichi, who had been sent to Manzhouguo by the Japanese Ministry of Agriculture and Forestry. Why was it drafted in Manzhouguo? He explained as follows: "The intent of the grain supervision law was to implement experimentally in Manchuria first the national supervision over grain which has recently become such an issue in Japan."[157] In order to prevent in advance any disorder that might take place by direct implementation in Japan, Manzhouguo was used as a testing laboratory.

At the same time, however, what made a great sensation upon being introduced into Japan after experimental trial in Manzhouguo was the Concordia Association and its ideology, which rejected Diet politics and called for a one-party state system. In September 1936, Guandong Army Commander Ueda Kenkichi issued a statement castigating party politics and calling for the Concordia Association to become the organizational body of political practice: "Government by the Diet poses a grave danger for it can easily descend into democratic, materialistic, Western-style government, and we must by no means adopt such a model for Manzhouguo."[158] As a critique of Diet politics by the military which was suddenly beginning to intervene in domestic politics in the aftermath of the February 26 Incident, this document elicited a sense of crisis and called for a response by the party politicians. On January 21, 1937, Hamada Kunimatsu (1868–1939) of the Seiyūkai acknowledged at a plenary session of the Lower House of the Diet that the military was the driving political force and that it was advancing into the realms of politics and the economy, thus making the present situation an effective adoption of the Concordia Association's ideology:

This political ideology in Manchuria will naturally come to Japanese soil as well and seems to be the sort of thinking actually that wishes to come ashore. . . . By virtue of a new structure forged by a cooperative unity of the military and the populace, we may move forward with a mighty government and expel the idea of constitutional government as the norm. Will we not then be thoroughly ensconced in its spirit? This ideology has already crossed the sea and come on land in Japan proper.[159]

Through a critique of the Concordia Association, this pronouncement by Hamada rang a clarion call for the intrusion of the military into politics.

He did not indicate how either the Concordia Association or its ideology would concretely enter Japan, but the Concordia Association had come at that point to be seen as a model political movement in Japan after the organization of the Imperial Rule Assistance Association as a result of the movement for a new political structure under Prince Konoe Fumimaro (1891–1945). The view emerged that "we must not overlook the fact that the Concordia Association's movement in Manchuria has exerted a lethal influence among the existing political parties in Japan. The formation of the Imperial Rule Assistance Association and other cooperative groups have closely followed the Concordia Association's movement."[160] In fact, the organizational form of "mass rule" among the groups who cooperated with the Imperial Rule Assistance Association was used at the national conference of the Concordia Association. This "mass rule" form—"mass" in name only—was initially proposed by Sakuta Shōichi (1878–1973), Vice-President of Manzhouguo's Kenkoku University, as a replacement for the principle of unanimity. Something which would form the basis of a principle for leadership, it was a method of voting which, the chairman of the Concordia Association claimed, "took a farsighted view of the trend of opinions of the constituent members and brought unity to rule with a consciousness of the goal of state-building which thoroughly permeated the state and its citizenry."[161]

Beyond this example, the citizenry of a state which holds colonial land or something comparable to it were themselves being controlled by a principle which controlled that land. To the extent that Japan worked to unify itself with Manzhouguo as a close ally, what was projected from Japan to Manzhouguo had its rays of light intensified all the more and then was refracted back from Manzhouguo to Japan. To be sure, Manzhouguo was conceived as a laboratory or experimental state for Japan, and it functioned accordingly. However, with flows going in both directions so frequently, there were both feedback and adjustments made. This was as true of the regulatory law on heavy industries, the general mobilization law for the state, and the national land plan. When unification proceeded with the administrative organization of such things as concurrent posts held by the heads of the local chapters of the Imperial Rule Assistance Association, at the same time a secondary unity was being effected between the government and the Concordia Association in which the heads of administrative organs, such as provincial governors, concurrently served as the provincial heads of the Concordia Association. Koyama Sadatomo, who shouldered responsibility together with Tachibana Shiraki for the journal *Manshū hyōron* and functioned as a spokeman for the movement led by the Concordia Association, argued forcefully for the guiding character of Manzhouguo as an experimental state: "Because Manzhouguo is a rising state, when laying out a new state structure we may often return to the drawing board and easily try out the unexpected. In the wake of the

Manchurian Incident, all thinking people are conscious of the fact that we need to move forward with resolution of the Manchurian issue in order to plan for the renewal of all phases of the government of Japan."[162]He then went on to argue: "Test in Manchuria, apply in Japan—if Japan can step forward boldly based on the spirit of the founding of a nation, then Manchuria will of necessity receive [Japan's] guiding influence. This arrangement shall be repeated any number of times in future and for perpetuity."[163]

Indeed, it was a vicious circle for perpetuity. Just like the image of Japan and Manzhouguo as mirrors set against one another, Japan forced its image on Manzhouguo and Manzhouguo on Japan as the two piled up limitless images one of the other. It thus became increasingly difficult to discern which was the self and which the other. Even if Japan were to have its own image distorted by refraction from Manzhouguo, by smashing and destroying the surface of the Manzhouguo mirror, would Japan have been able to revert to its own original form?

Japan and Manzhouguo, however, had to continue working in close interaction not solely at the level of ideology, policy, or legislation. Deterioration of the war situation had developed to such a state that foodstuffs and iron and steel procured from Manzhouguo were drying up and the prosecution of the Asian-Pacific War was becoming extraordinarily difficult. According to *Riben diguozhuyi qin-Hua shilüe* (Brief history of the Japanese imperialist invasion of China), edited by Liu Huiwu and Liu Xuezhao, "from 1932 through 1944, Japan plundered over 223,000,000 tons of coal, over 1,100,000 tons of pig iron, and over 5,800,000 tons of steel from the Chinese Northeast."[164] For Japan, Manzhouguo had become an essential condition to its continued existence. And, of course, for Manzhouguo the existence of Japan was the primary condition for its own existence as a state. On the very day that Japan declared war on Great Britain and the United States, Puyi issued his Rescript on the Present Situation in which he pledged: "Life and death, existence and demise cannot be separated. . . . Together as a united people, we shall exhaust all fidelity to service and, with our national strength united, we shall come to the aid of our ally."[165] Precisely as he put it, both states—whose life and death bore an inseparable relationship of rising or falling together—came tumbling down toward the abyss of death.

And, so, the armies of the Soviet Union entered the war against Japan on August 9, 1945; on August 14, Japan accepted the Potsdam Declaration and the Guandong Army was thus disarmed; on August 17, at a meeting of its State Council, Manzhouguo was dissolved. Just after 1:00 A.M. on August 18, in Dalihua, Tonghua Province, Emperor Puyi read a proclamation on the dissolution of Manzhouguo and on his abdication of the throne, just before he fled. Here he brought the history of Manzhouguo to a close. As he later described it: "The words 'relying on the divine blessing of the Sun Goddess and the protection of His Majesty the Emperor of Japan'—words which had been absolutely essential from the start—remained in the draft of this proclamation. However, Hashimoto Toranosuke [President of the Bureau of Worship] forced a bitter smile and excised them."[166]

This was how Puyi recorded it in his autobiography. Perhaps anyone, not just Hashimoto, would have been unable to repress a bitter smile when Puyi referred to the dissolution of Manzhouguo and his own abdication as "relying on the divine blessing of the Sun Goddess and the protection of His Majesty the Emperor of Japan." Perhaps, though, there was no expression adequate to describe the conditions surrounding the existence and collapse of a state such as Manzhouguo.

Having left his throne, Puyi shook hands individually with each of his high officials one by one and bid them farewell. Premier Zhang Jinghui, unabashed by his advanced years, was deeply despondent at Japan's defeat, but a high-level "Chinese official" who witnessed this scene was said to have let out an audible sneer.[167] This high official was none other than Xi Xia, the man who had worked so hard to see that Puyi became Emperor of Manzhouguo, who at the time of the founding of the state had led the welcoming delegation of former Manchu officials bearing aloft yellow dragon banners at the Changchun railway station, and who had wished to become the premier of Manzhouguo only to end up cut off from all effective political power as head of the Imperial Household Agency. Why did Xi Xia act in such a virtually scandalous manner, letting out this sneer oblivious to whomever was around him? Was it due to his anger that even at that late point in time they were still tied to their "close ally," Japan? Or, was it derision aimed at men including himself who had gambled everything on Japan? Or, was it directed at this burlesque played out by the state known as Manzhouguo? We have no way of knowing from our present vantage point. However, it would certainly seem that more or less the same impression as that of Xi Xia was harbored among the high-level Chinese officials and their attendants. Whether or not the abdication ceremony was completed, the high Chinese officials—beginning with Xi Xia, who as head of the Imperial Household Agency should have been following the lead of his emperor—were now searching for a means to eke out their very existence and clamorously fled to the four winds. Soon thereafter, it was said, not a single Chinese official remained to bid Puyi farewell as he departed from Talizi.

At precisely the same time, words were being scribbled down in the handwriting of Amakasu Masahiko on the blackboard of the chairman of the board of directors' office at the Manchurian Film Corporation located in the former capital, which now returned to its name of Changchun. Amakasu was a captain in the military police and was best known for his role in the murder of Ōsugi Sakae (1881–1923), the anarchist murdered in 1923. After coming to Manchuria in 1929, he took part in special operations in conjunction with the Guandong Army and carried out plots in Harbin with the aim of setting up the state of Manzhouguo. In addition, he served as a guard for Puyi and was involved in secret maneuvers on many fronts. Following the establishment of the state of Manzhouguo, he served successively as chief of the police in the Ministry of Civil Affairs, consultant to the Imperial Household Agency, chairman of the Dadong Company, which handled coolie labor that entered Manchuria, head of general affairs for the central branch of the Concordia Association, and chairman of the Manchurian Film Society. He was a man with political clout who maintained authority with power to sustain it in ruling Manzhouguo. As it was said of him: "During the day, the headquarters of the Guandong Army controlled Manzhouguo; at night Amakasu did."[168] It was this Amakasu who wrote down the following the words on the blackboard:

Ō bakuchi, moto mo ko mo naku, suttenten
The great gamble, without antecedents or offspring, all lost.

We cannot say to what extent these words reflect Amakasu's feelings. However, it was a clear fact that Manzhouguo was a great gamble for the Guandong Army and for Japan as well. With no clear prospects for success beginning with the Manchurian Incident, an action was provoked irrespective of its chances for success, and continuing through a series of decisions such as the establishment of the state of Manzhouguo, recognition of that state, and withdrawal from the League of Nations.

On the morning of August 20, 1945, Amakasu took his own life by cyanide poison. With no place for him in Japan, he had been one of those who staked his life on the great gamble of Manzhouguo. When Manzhouguo, the land out of which men such as Amakasu spun dreams, disappeared from this world, perhaps all ties that had bound him to this world also ceased to exist. He had tied his life to Manzhouguo, a state he among others had created. He ended his life a martyr to Manzhouguo.

Yet, here was a man fully complicit with the dark side of modern Japan and bearing responsibility for the assassination of Ōsugi Sakae, a man who did not shift the blame for his role in the creation of the state of Manzhouguo. Perhaps this was the final way things played out for a man such as Amakasu. His remains were transported, accompanied by 3,000 Japanese and Chinese, in a firefighter's wheelbarrow to the Huxi Hall behind the main offices of the Manchurian Film Corporation. A cord to the right was drawn by Japanese and one to the left by Chinese, and the funeral procession was said to extend one kilometer.[169] With the extinction of Manzhouguo, what in the world would the Chinese who had joined the procession pulling Amakasu's corpse along have been thinking as they walked down the road that day? Were they repaying hatred with morality? Or, was it that the dead know no national boundaries? Or, perhaps they were sending Amakasu off to eternity together with Manzhouguo and saw this as the first step in the future creation of a new state.

On August 20, the very day that Amakasu was laid to rest, General Mikhail Prokof'evich Kovalev and his men of the Soviet Army took over the offices of the General Headquarters of the Guandong Army on Taiping Avenue. That day Puyi, who was already far off in Siberia, began his life of detention.

Chapter Five
Conclusion
Chimera, Reality and Illusion

The Two Sides of Manzhouguo: Ethnic Harmony and Ethnic Antagonism

In this way Manzhouguo was born and it was snuffed out.

From the perspective of 4,000 years of rise and fall of eras, of chaos and order, in Chinese history, the fifteen years and five months of Manzhouguo's history were no more than a flash in the pan, a blink of the eyes. However, the import of history cannot be weighed by length of time. Manzhouguo's significance in history can only be assessed as the sum total of loves and hatreds in the lives of the people who lived there. Whatever significance we assign to Manzhouguo as we look back on it now, we can only point to what should be carried on and what deserves heartfelt criticism on the basis of this level of fierce loves and hatreds which filled both its ideals and its realities. Even if it were to be described beautifully in words and praised lavishly as a concept, without examining what Manzhouguo really was, we cannot carelessly assess its historical importance.

In order to focus on a depiction of its appearance as a state, I would like to conclude this book with a glimpse at one aspect which must be addressed and which has been ignored to this point. How are we to think about the many and sundry images and theses concerning Manzhouguo that I raised in my introduction? I should like to offer my views on this issue by way of a conclusion.

We young Japanese at the time were burning with passion to establish an ideal state on Manchurian terrain in which there would be ethnic harmony, and thus we hurried off to Manzhouguo. We poured our hearts and souls into building such a state. . . . As history moved forward, the ideal of ethnic harmony would have gradually increased in radiance. Without this, I believe that perpetual peace in the world is impossible to attain. In this sense, then, the ideals of building that state of Manzhouguo will live on forever.[1]

Furumi Tadayiki thus summarized the historical significance of Manzhouguo. There were many who advocate ethnic harmony, the banner raised by Manzhouguo, as the basis for the future attainment of world peace. Throughout the world today, ethnic strife continues unabated, and with each new piece of news about such bloodletting, the need for different peoples to harmonize and to cooperate can be felt all the more strongly. Why does ethnic difference give rise to such fiercely antagonistic emotions? Why can we not honor our differences? Standing at the end of the twentieth century, this thought has become ever more trenchant. However, is this ultimately connected to the fact that the ideal of ethnic harmony to which Manzhouguo gave birth "gradually increased in radiance as history moved forward"?

The Japanese in Manzhouguo discriminated against the Chinese in numerous areas of daily life. At parties or banquets, they would be sitting around the same tables, eating the same food, and drinking the same wine, but the Japanese would be served white rice and the Chinese would get sorghum.[2]

Although "ordinary fare" (literally, "daily tea and rice") was a term used at the time, "ordinary" under ethnic harmony and Manzhouguo was the fact that there was patent discrimination in rice itself.[3] According to one source, "with the coming into being of Manzhouguo, there were differentiations made—Japanese ranked first, Koreans second, and Manchus and Chinese third. As for food distributed as well, the Japanese were allocated white rice, the Koreans half white rice and half sorghum, and the Chinese sorghum. There were also salary differentials."[4] As concerned the difference in quality of foodstuffs, one person who advanced this policy was Furumi Tadayuki himself: "I thought this manner of distribution was perfectly appropriate, though criticism of it was raised. Although it was said that rice was allocated only to the Japanese and that we did not give rice to the Manchurians, in fact they did not customarily eat rice. In any event, I believe that this was a proper mode of allocation."[5] Furumi was by no means alone in his insensibility to the ethnic discrimination revealed here and the apathy not to be able to infer that there was a problem even after it was pointed out to him. However, rather than dwell on whether this was right or wrong, it would be better to read the following testimony about the state of affairs in the army cadet school of Manzhouguo. This army cadet school was established alongside the Kenkoku University as the highest military and civil institutions of higher learning, respectively, in Manzhouguo. It was seen as an elite training institute which bore responsibility for the state for ethnic harmony. What was ordinary here?

Chinese and Japanese each occupied half of the positions as pupils at the cadet school. Their curricula and teaching materials were the same, but there was a wide difference in their treatment. Take uniforms, for example—the Japanese students of all classes all wore new ones, while the Chinese students, in addition to streetwear, were largely outfitted with old ones. Bedding and other life necessities were the same as uniforms, the Japanese had new things and the Chinese old.

There was even a distinction in food. Japanese pupils ate primarily white rice and other nutritional riches. Chinese pupils ate only sorghum, the red sorghum used as feed for the horses and oxen. The students who at the time contracted stomach disorders and stomach ulcers are even today, over forty years later, afflicted with chronic illnesses. Clearly, this was one manifestation of "ethnic repression."[6]

At Kenkoku University, by contrast, from the start all students were said to have eaten an equal mixture of rice and sorghum, at the insistence of the Japanese students.[7] There are numerous newspaper articles about the schools that adopted this system. Yet, the fact that such stories appeared in the form of newspaper articles, it has been argued, is counterevidence that discrimination in food was generally practiced, and that anyone other than a Japanese who ate white rice could be punished for an "economic crime." Furthermore, the differential in salaries may be seen in Table 6. Even on trains, the Japanese rode in a special class while Chinese rode in ordinary compartments, and Chinese were not allowed to ride on the special ones.[8]

There is also historical evidence, such as the following, which gives us insight into the reality of ethnic harmony. It was said that the commanding officer of the Guandong Army drew up and distributed notebooks known as Rules of Service especially for "Japanese" officials. The contents of these booklets have not as yet been made known in Japan. Furumi reports that Japanese-Manchurian ratios were recorded under the designation of *Kanri*

TABLE 6. Wage Differentials in Industries Run by Japanese[7]

	Factories		Mines	
	Real income (yen)	Percentage vis-à-vis Japanese of the same sex	Real income (yen)	Percentage vis-à-vis Japanese of the same sex
Males				
Japanese	3.78	100	3.33	100
Koreans	1.52	40.2	1.30	39.0
Chinese	1.09	28.8	0.98	29.4
Females				
Japanese	1.82	100	—	
Koreans	0.76	41.8	1.02	
Chinese	0.53	29.1	0.30	

Based on an August 1939 investigation by the Rōkōkyōkai, in *Manshū rōdō nenkan* (Manchuria labor year book) (Xinjing: Ganshōdō shoten, 1940), 26, 40.

kokoroe (Rules for officials),[9] but it remains unclear just what these were as a whole. Wang Ziheng, who served as secretary to the prime minister until the very end, saw his office mate Matsumoto Masuo's *Fuwu xuzhi* (Rules of service), and from a memo he transcribed he must have seen its content. Although this material is full of contradictions and full trust cannot be placed in it, we nonetheless find in it such passages as: "We need to sow dissension between the Korean and the Chinese peoples and not enable them to become too friendly. When these two peoples come into conflict, if right and wrong are in equal portions on both sides, then we shall support the Koreans and suppress the Chinese. If the Koreans are in the wrong, then we must treat them the same as the Chinese." In addition, the text has detailed notes on the ethnic character of various groups and on policies for dealing with them. For example, we are told that it noted with respect to "Manchurian" officials: "Be they pro-Japanese or anti-Japanese, be attentive to everything in their words, deeds, and public and private lives. Do not forget the words [from the ancient Chinese text, *Zuozhuan*]: 'If he is not of our race, then he will of necessity be of a different heart.'" Also: "Property belonging to all peoples other than the Japanese should be reduced. Do not allow it to increase."[10] I do not believe that all of this is accurate, but as corroboration we might mention that one of the tasks set by the military police of the Guandong Army in its Special Policy for Dealing with Manzhouguo in Wartime (*Tai-Man senji tokubetsu taisaku*) concerned "the policies of dissension and antagonism among the various ethnic groups—make use of them."[11] It is quite clear here that they saw mutual antagonism and discord among the various ethnicities—and least of all ethnic harmony—as a means of rulership.

The greatest issue confronting ethnic harmony in Manzhouguo, however, was the ethnocentrism of the Japanese who were advancing this very policy:

Indeed, our Yamato race harbors superior qualities and preeminent strength within, and we shall guide the other races [ethnicities] with magnanimity without. We shall shore up where they are insufficient and encourage where they do not exert themselves. By *making those who are not obedient obedient*, we shall move together to perfect a moral world. This is our heaven sent mission.[12]

We have here stereotypical exaggerations reflecting the *Zeitgeist* of Japan in the 1930s, and reading it now we need make some allowances. However, that said, there is no denying the fact that this also contains a self-important, excessively self-conscious sense of the Japanese people. For those unable to separate themselves from such a consciousness, harmony as a relationship untouched by and not touching all matters of politics, the economy, and culture was probably unattainable. In fact, in the "ethnic metling pot" of Manzhouguo, the Japanese had almost no contact whatsoever with other ethnic groups and lived apart from them.

To be sure, the historical experience of the complex ethnic state of

Manzhouguo was an attempt at the formation of a multiethnic society in which peoples of different races, languages, customs, and values coexisted and in which Japan was involved on a large scale for the first time in its history. What was in fact carried out, though, was not aimed at the coexistence of heterogenous elements, but a society in which harmony was attained by obedience to homogeneity. Thus, a monolithic integration through guidance and servility was the goal. It emerged in the form of expelling the heterogeneous elements, "making those who are not obedient obedient." Together with "bandit suppression" and "enforcement activities," "extermination" efforts aimed at opponents through the military police, the Special Services Agency of the Guandong Army, and the secret spying network (Hoankyoku), thought "reform" activities were enforced involving the housing of "thought delinquents" in Thought Reform Guidance Centers and Protective Supervisory Centers.

Genuine ethnic harmony would probably have entailed different peoples and cultures intermixing and giving rise to conflict and friction, and with the sparks which this conflict would arouse forming a vital source, a new social integration and culture would take shape. If this is true, then there is no reason to expect that this could have been attained by Japanese who constructed a Great Wall in their minds and placed great store in giving civilization and regulations to other ethnicities, for these Japanese who understood diversity as chaos.

But this would not have been limited to the Japanese. No matter how exalted and extraordinary a people may be, under conditions of invasion, ethnic harmony cannot be realized. And, if there were such a people who could do this, they would not from the start intrude upon other peoples and force their own dreams upon them. For the Japanese, "harmony" meant "assist the Japanese,"[13] and "ethnic harmony" thus meant "assisting the Yamato people in their invasion of China"—or so the people of northeast China were said at the time to banter.

Ethnic harmony is both a dream of humanity and an essential precondition. However, I would argue that, in whatever sense we use the expression "ethnic harmony," in the case of Manzhouguo we cannot speak of it as any sort of "ideal that would live on forever."

A Life of Ease and Comfort: Snow like a Knife . . .

As we plan to open up industry and communications, we advance the welfare of the different peoples living in China, Korea, Mongolia, and Manchuria. We are planning for a genuine realm of comfort, coexistence, and coprosperity.[14]

We honor the interests of the Chinese masses and work to realize the ideal of a life of ease and comfort. We thus shall contribute to the opening up of Manchuria and Mongolia.[15]

It was in this manner that the Guandong Army took control over Manchuria and planned for coexistence and coprosperity among the various ethnic groups living there, raising the ruling ideal that they would bring about "a realm of comfort" or "a life of ease and comfort." Later, in addition to such expressions as "a life of ease and comfort" and "coexistence and coprosperity," we find in the documents on the founding of the state of Manzhouguo an abundance of such terms as "following heaven and protecting the people," "economic development," "tranquility for the people," "advancing the welfare [of the people]," "bringing contentment to the people's livelihood," and the like. We find this even in the Manifesto on the Establishment of the State which promised for Manzhouguo: "All people living on the terrain shall ascend gloriously to great prosperity."

There is a historical document put together by the Supreme Public Prosecutor's Office of Manzhouguo entitled *Manshūkoku kaitakuchi hanzai gaiyō* (Outline of crimes on reclaimed land in Manzhouguo, 1941). The following testimony concerning the sale of reclaimed land is recorded therein:

Korean farmers in Huadian County, Jilin Province: They told us, people who have nowhere to go, to give them our homes in November or December. We thought we were going to be killed. It was truly sad.

Chinese landlord in Emu County, Jilin Province: No matter how poor the land, since we cannot sell it at the price that the Manchurian Colonization Company bought it, we shall not sell it. [When we responded as such,] I was beaten by a staff member of the provincial government. The next day, a staffer from the provincial office came and decided that he would forceably buy 300 *shang* [= 2,100 *mou* = 320 acres] for 40,000 yen. If that land were privately sold, it would go for over 100,000 yen, making this effectively a seizure by the authorities. These unfair puchases are making all families unhappy, and they contradict the essence of the true establishment of the kingly way and a paradise on earth.

Chinese farmer in Emu County, Jilin Province: Although bandits have stolen our golden objects, they have not seized our land. The Manchurian Colonization Company forcibly bought our land which is the basis for the farmers' livelihood. As farmers, the loss of the land has caused terrible suffering.[16]

Not only was the land—the farmers' very livelihood—confiscated, but they were turned out of their homes in the dead of winter onto frigid terrain with nowhere to go. It is only natural then that the Chinese called the colonial office (*kaituoju*) the "office of murders" (*kaidaoju*). Tsukui Shin'ya, who participated in these forcible purchases of land for development in Baoqing County, Sanjiang Province, in 1938, was drawn to Manzhouguo by the ideals of harmony among the five ethnicities and the principle of the kingly way. He graduated from the Daidō Academy and, in the spirit of contributing with "selflessness and purity," he entered a village, seeking a point of contact with Chinese. The following is what he recorded of his thoughts at the time of a forcible purchase of land:

We trampled underfoot the wishes of farmers who held fast to the land and, choking off their entreaties full of lamentations and kneeling, forced them to sell it. When we thrust on them a dirt-cheap selling price, even if the colonization group resettled the terrain, I was saddened that we would be leaving them to a future of calamity, and I felt that we had committed a crime by our actions.[17]

In this way, land which over the course of several decades had been opened up and farmed by Chinese and Korean farmers who were now filled with resentment for the people who were driving them off it was becoming the "great earth of wishes" and the "new realm" offered up to the likes of Japanese farmers, people who had changed professions due to overall consolidation of small- and middle-level businesses, and youth-volunteer brigades for the colonization of Manchuria-Mongolia. These Japanese colonial immigrants were made to bear the brunt of the economic contradiction within Japan; they were also made to shoulder a link in the national defense: "In time of need, they would be instrumental in shoring up supply lines on the scene and to the rear."[18] While there was certainly no reason to expect colonial immigration policy to resolve such contradictions, this practice merely exported the contradictions and increased the conflict between Chinese and Korean farmers, on the one hand, and between them both and Japanese colonial immigrants, on the other. Perhaps those Japanese who immigrated were themselves victims in the sense that they were saddled with a fate, due to national policy, of becoming the inflicters of pain.

This, then, is what emerged on the good earth that was supposed to produce a life of ease and comfort—the creation of bloc villages for the operation of "separating bandits from good people," severe seizures of farm produce, delivery of labor, forced savings, the movement to contribute metalic items, and the like. Let's listen once again to the testimony of Tsukui Shin'ya who stood at the forefront of this movement:

While exchanging gunfire with anti-Japanese volunteers at Boli and Baoqing Counties [Sanjiang Province], I witnessed the flames of private homes burned down for the purpose of building bloc villages. At the time I frequently queried young anti-Japanese fighters who had been taken prisoner, and I came to sense the great distance between the "state-building ideal" of "Manzhouguo" and the ethnic consciousness which these people possessed. As a means of short-circuiting this, I agonized with a guilty conscience over our operations and passed a sleepless night in a village on the front lines encircled by anti-Japanese troops. Within this environment, we learned of the eruption of the "Marco Polo Bridge Incident" and experienced a great sense of frustration about the future of "Manzhouguo."

The special training course of the Guandong Army. The year that the Pacific War broke out, I was in Tongyang County [Jilin Province], and from that year the demands of the military administration increased sharply. The forwarding of agricultural produce and the commandeering of laborers shot up proportionately to the expansion of the war itself. The situation in foodstuffs ultimately brought on starvation for a group of poor farmers within the county, and inhumane labor management in the military's construction and coal mines frequently increased the numbers of the dead. When I went to observe Mishan County [Dongan Province], I saw several dozen corpses of laborers in the county lined up in the rain. With the sense of a crime having been committed, I foresaw punishment.[19]

Tsuchiya Yoshio, a member of the Chichihar Military Police under the Guandong Army, visited Lindian County, Heilongjiang Province in mid-winter of 1944, and observing the scene he listened to the voices of old Chinese farmers: "The control economy has reached an extreme, and the lives of our farmers have declined to their lowest point. . . . There were homes in the areas without clothing and bedding. There were even children living there naked."[20] Tsuchiya himself wondered how they could possibly live without clothing in the dead of winter in the prominent grain region of northern Manchuria, and he was in fact appalled when he saw two naked children. He heard that their father had gone off to perform labor service two years earlier, and no one knew if he was now alive or dead. Because he knew full well that, if Chinese workers assembled in "labor hunts" were involved in construction efforts necessary to war strategy, such as the building of military encampments, they would be mercilessly shot or buried alive, and Tsuchiya realized what the fate of their father had been. On his way back, a Japanese policeman at the Kang'an Police Station casually recounted to him: "That sort of thing is not the least bit rare around here. In nearby villages, newborn babies are placed in 'straw baskets' filled with grass and raised that way."[21] Tsuchiya was again stunned upon hearing this story. But his atonishment was not over yet. "As a result of my investigation, there is still too little land here. In the area along the Great Wall in Rehe Province, half of the residents live without clothing in utter despair. Without any assistance, they will simply flicker out of existence."[22]

On this frozen soil where the temperatures reached −30° or −40° C, in what possible sense could living without a stitch of clothing be understood as "ascending gloriously to great prosperity?" In other words, how was this a region full of great fortune in which life was easy and comfortable under the warms rays of the spring sun? Tsuchiya, who was to be charged as a war criminal later, found a line from a poem by a Chinese poet which, he claimed, moved him: "Snow like a knife . . ." For all except the Japanese, Manzhouguo was a state in which the snow came pelting down, piercing people like a knife. This was life in Manzhouguo, especially from 1941, where people spent their time under the withering frost and scorching sun—far from spring breezes and calm.

In China they use the expression "*sanguang* policy" to summarize the policies adopted in Manzhouguo. In the military field, "*sanguang*" (three alls) referred to "kill all, loot all, burn all." In the economic field, "*sanguang*" referred to "search all, squeeze all, loot all." There may be people who regard this as an exaggeration for the sake of simple rhymes. However, if there was anything at all left without having had it all stolen, then who would have ignored and not dressed their own child in a single garment when the thermometer dropped to −30° or −40° C?

In his introduction to the novel *Bayue de xiangcun* (Village in August, 1935) by Xiao Jun (1907–1988), which describes the bitter struggles of the anti-Japanese forces in northeast China, Lu Xun (1881–1936) drew the reader's attention to the fact that the essence of the author's thinking can be summed up as follows: "People gasping before the disaster of lost sky and land, lost grass, lost sorghum, lost grasshoppers, lost mosquitoes."[23]

Not only was their land, grass, and sorghum stolen from them, but the sky and even the mosquitoes which usually cause harm. Lu Xun was offering sympathy to Xiao Jun's cry here and not only here, for there is a pathos and insatiable anger which make the body of one so dispossessed tremble. This was fury in restraint.

Before such words spitting up blood, Japanese boasts about the "development" or "legacy" of the accomplishments of Manzhouguo, such as the following, resound with emptiness and cruelty: "When Japan was defeated in the Pacific War in August 1945 and it reverted to China, it [Manzhouguo] had become terrain on which what was once wilderness now encompassed numerous modern cities and which embraced modern industry prominent throughout East Asia. . . . Whatever the impetus to this may have been, it is a historical fact that Japanese technology and effort led the way."[24]

Extraordinary development did not offer even a single garment of clothing to a naked child.

A State Based on the Kingly Way: A Military Garrison State Without a Citizenry

The face of a bandit, cornered and trapped, spewing blood,
His eyes reveal that he is still very young. (Suda Kōsai)

Smeared with fresh, wet blood,
He cannot dig his hands into the sand,
A dead Chinese soldier. (Horiuchi Kishun)

Troops fallen in the pacification campaign,
Thirty-four skeletons are no more. (Katō Tamaki)

A letter received about how fascinating bandit subjugation is,
And my heart goes out to my friend on the battlefield. (Akigawa Jūshio)

The fighting in Manchuria has abated of late,
Only five or six soldiers fighting and dying on each side. (Tani Kanae)[25]

These were all songs about "subjugating bandits" in Manzhouguo. Each from its own position expresses a look and a feeling with respect to

Manzhouguo. But, the thought that emerges running through them all is an inexpressible inconsolability for an absurdity: in Manzhouguo which was supposed to be ethnically harmonious and a paradise of the kingly way, "why did people have to kill one another and hate one another?"

Changing perspectives, from the position of those who were anti-Manzhouguo and anti-Japanese, the burning anger at the absurdity of "why must our land be taken away from us, must we be driven from our home villages, and must we spend our days in no settled abode?" led them to pick up guns. As for what a state based on the kingly way and Manzhouguo meant for the people opposed to Manzhouguo and the Japanese and how it stood in their way, we have a poster dated April 26, 1936 which was distributed in the region of Hulin County, Binjiang Province, by the People's Revolutionary Fourth Army of the Northeast:

Announcement to the Masses to Oppose Japan and Save the Nation
Comrade workers, peasants, merchants, and students!!
Under the gruesome rule of the Japanese bandits for the past five years, we do not even know who of our mothers, fathers, and brothers have been butchered. We do not know if our wives, sisters, or sisters-in-law have been raped or forced to become prostitutes, or if our homes have been burned down, or if the deeds to our land and our weapons have been seized. Our people's merchants and workers have all been driven into bankruptcy.

Everyday at numerous sites we Chinese are being murdered and thrown into the river. We cannot even count the dangers awaiting us: burned to death, buried alive, strangled, dying in jail, and the like. We have also experienced the phenomena of death from poverty, freezing to death, and starving to death. The Japanese bandits are not just happy calling up troops, but they make them slaughter Chinese. Bloc villages are engaging in wholesale massacres.[26]

There should be no need to describe in detail once again the deeds mentioned here. How are we, though, to understand the "wholesale massacres" by concentration in the bloc villages mentioned at the end of this announcement? By forcibly moving to a single site households spread throughout regions in which public order was not secure, these "bloc villages" were established in order to cut off the residents from offering food, weaponry and ammunition, and information to "bandits" and enabled those places to be used as bases for punitive expeditionary forces. This was further advanced by restricting uninhabited areas and by the operation of bringing residences together, while in the bloc villages they built a mud wall roughly three meters in height around an outer moat, set up watchtowers and batteries at the four corners, and opened access through four gates. By using fingerprints for all residents age twelve and older, possession of residence certificates, transit permits, and licenses for the purchase and transport of merchandise were enforced. Within the village, either a police branch office or a village office was established, and a minimum of ten armed policemen was charged with supervisory duties. In addition, self-defense corps were organized by young men and women, and aside from military training they engaged in such labors as reconstruction of roads and communications facilities. Rendering to the state secret information about "bandits"— namely, those supporting in one fashion or another the activities of men and women resisting Japan and the Manzhouguo regime—was encouraged, and a system of monetary rewards put into place. This was the reality of what the government called the "lesser society of the kingly way," and the bloc villages were its fortifications and garrisons themselves. These bloc villages were constructed in many provinces from Jiandao to Jilin, Longjiang, Andong, and Fengtian. Conditions of residence within them were altogether inferior, of a sort dubbed "human barns." In order to construct these bloc villages, they had to forcibly remove peasants from the homes and land where they were long resident and move them there. The extent of suffering to these peasants is attested to in a text found in the *Manshūkoku shi, sōron kakuron* (History of Manzhouguo, overview and essays) which stressed the legitimacy of building these bloc villages: "When, standing before a peasant house, we ordered the operations group to burn down the house, I watched the young and old women wailing ceaselessly and their belongings being carted away, and it broke my heart."[27]

Together with the construction of these bloc villages, the *baojia* system was implemented to secure public order. The *baojia* organization was officially defined as follows: "First they organized ten households into a *pai*, the smallest unit; a *jia* was constituted by the *pai* within the boundaries of a village or that which corresponded to it. The *bao*, the largest unit, was organized on the basis of the *jia* within one police jurisdiction unit."[28] In urban areas in general ten *pai* made up a *jia*. A mutual responsibility system was applied in the *pai*, as the basic unit of the *baojia* system. In instances in which someone emerged from a *pai* who wrought havoc with public order, the entire *pai* bore communal responsibility and paid a fine known as the "joint responsibility duty" (*lianzuojin*). However, in cases in which crimes within a *pai* were prevented before their occurrence and reported to the police, the "joint responsibility duty" was mitigated or exempted. Furthermore, self-defense corps were organized by men age 18 to 40 within the *baojia* structure as it became necessary for them to assume policing as well as self-defense functions. The *baojia* system was implemented nationwide, and it was reported at the end of 1935 that there were 1,458 *bao* and in excess of 440,000 *pai*.[29] The *baojia* system also made residents maintain surveillance on one another and aimed at maintaining the public order and suppressing the anti-Manzhouguo, anti-Japanese movement.

Thus, with the implementation of bloc villages and the *baojia* system (from 1937 known as the defense-village system), Manzhouguo, the state of the kingly way, was structured as an organization right down to the foundations of its very existence to fight against anti-Manzhouguo and anti-Japanese activities on a daily basis—the state as a whole was transformed into a military garrison. It thus became a garrison state. Because it was a state based on a sense of morality—namely, a state of the kingly way—there could be no opposition, and opponents of it had to be liquidated. Under requirements of this sort, everyone had perforce to keep on an eye on everyone else. This is perhaps what Georg W. F. Hegel had in mind when, in his *Philosophy of Right*, he described a genuine "galley ship state."

While constitutional government based in morality, benevolence, and civilization was being invoked, powers of "summary execution as in battle" were being invested in the soldiers and police officials. The power to "execute as in battle" was allegedly to suppress "banditry," and "it could be implemented based on discretion" in response to circumstances.[30] In short, if someone were deemed an enemy of Manzhouguo, he or she could be killed immediately. This power of "summary execution as in battle" was enacted in the Temporary Laws on Punishing Bandits which went into effect in September 1932, shortly after the creation of the state. This law was, however, abrogated in December 1941 and replaced by the newly enacted Law on the Maintenance of Public Order. From this point forward, the power to summarily execute was deemed "to be effective for the time being," and thus it in fact remained in effect until the state of Manzhouguo collapsed. We can clearly see another face of Manzhouguo in its profuse promulgation of laws against the detested "bandits" and in its ostentation of cultured rule with all the trappings of a legitimate legal system. This is further proof that resistance to a state run on the basis of the kingly way was deeply grounded and continued to exist to the extent that there was no adherence to the forms of rule by law.

The bloc villages, *baojia* system, and the like were merely the choices made to defensively fortify the transition to a garrison state in the face of the anti-Manzhouguo, anti-Japanese offensive. However, in response to the increasingly protracted nature of the Sino-Japanese War and the rise of border tensions with the Soviet Union and Mongolia as a result of a number of military confrontations—such as the Zhanggufeng Incident (1938) and the Nomonhan Incident (1939)—Manzhouguo felt compelled to reorganize its internal infrastructure into a wartime configuration with more active personnel mobilizations.

With the implementation of the five-year plan for industrial development in 1937, the Guandong Army decided: "We must work more assiduously than in peacetime for organizational maintenance and effect something similar to a wartime structure. We must rapidly lead so that all preparations, both material and spiritual, for war are in place."[31] From this year they began drafting troops based on a quota system. In April 1940 a National Troop Law was promulgated which plunged ahead with a system for drafting soldiers. On this basis it was their aim "to improve on the attainments of the soldiers who comprise the core of our national army and train the core elements of our people."[32] An important point made in speeches was that Chinese persons drafted as a result of this law would be used as a force to emphasize the ideals of the state and to preserve public order. The barracks became the site of education at which fidelity to Manzhouguo would be stenciled in.

Beside this measure, the government of Manzhouguo intoned its principle of general military service, and insofar as able-bodied males were not heeding the call to this service, a National Labor Service Law was promulgated in November 1942 which was intended to insure service to the state. This National Labor Service Law, said to be modeled on the Nazis' *Arbeitsdienst* system, took as its objective: "To make the youth of the empire volunteer for national construction projects for high-level defense . . . to enable the concept of service to the state to flourish, and thus to push forward with the attainment of the ideals of state-building."[33] On this basis, labor service to the state became compulsory for a total of twelve months over a three-year period from age nineteen. "If the barracks are the arena in which the people are trained, then it shall be necessary to house them in fine facilities and to train our youth who do not bear the duties of our troops."[34] Thus, conscription and labor service were the two wheels as the "training of the populace" proceeded, and the goal was the procurement of fidelity to the state.

For Chinese conscripted by the National Troop Law, however, far from feeling Manzhouguo to be a state that genuinely deserved protection, it was the "bandits" who were to be "suppressed" to whom they felt close. Needless to say, their martial spirit was low, and many of them deserted. Also, for people who had been compelled to sell their grains at prices less than 50 percent of the cost of production, there was certainly no reason to expect a generous attitude in following the National Labor Service Law which necessitated three months' service each year. Many ran off or otherwise evaded service, making mobilization extremely difficult. Facing such a situation, the Manzhouguo government set its sights on total control of the "populace" and decided to implement a system of population registers from January 1944 which provided rolls for the entire populace sealed with the fingerprints of all ten fingers of all males age fifteen and above who lived in the country. They thus hoped to "gain control over human resources necessary for heightening the total might of the state, supply identification documents for the people of the empire, and thus establish a structure for the harmonious operation of the state administration, especially in labor mobilization."[35]

In spite of the eager political guidance of the Manzhouguo government by virtue of the "overall service of the populace" with the National Troop Law and the National Labor Service Law, the identification documents for the "populace" with the "training of the populace" and the Populace Registers Law, and the national construction for high-level defense with the mobilization of the "populace" through these measures, in fact of the over 43 million residents of Manzhouguo, there was not so much as a single legal citizen of the state of Manzhouguo.

How can this have been so? For all the numerous plans and drafts that were drawn up, in the final analysis Manzhouguo never established a nationality law. We can thus examine in detail all these plans and drafts that have been left to us, but the fact that a nationality law was never enacted was not due to the difficulties of legislative techniques. The greatest impediment to promulgation of a nationality law was, I believe, the minds of the Japanese in Manzhouguo who, while dubbing it an ideal state based on ethnic harmony and the kingly way, continued to refuse to separate themselves from Japanese nationality and to take on Manzhouguo nationality. The paradise of Manzhouguo, state of the kingly way, had perforce to become a garrison state without a citizenry.

The Extinction of the Chimera

In this manner, Manzhouguo—hailed as a state of ethnic harmony, a place of ease and comfort, a paradise of the kingly way—found it hard to escape its character as one of ethnic discrimination, coercive exploitation, and a garrison state. Furthermore, the state was one of multiple ethnicities and no citizenry, a mosaic state. Perhaps it was no more than an apparatus formed solely from a control structure and a rulership organization.

In state formation as a control structure, Manzhouguo's level of success in the formation and integration of a citizenry was low. This fact alone did not mean that Manzhouguo was indifferent to the creation of a citizenry. Indeed, insofar as it was apparent that the "Manchurians" lacked the tendency toward the formation of a nation, the Japanese military became obsessed with forcibly assimilating them 120 percent, until they were effectively transformed into Japanese subjects. Emperor Puyi was never sought out as an object for national self-identification. Rather, Puyi himself had already converted to belief in the Sun Goddess and the Japanese emperor, and the state of Manzhouguo had set its foundations in the way of the Japanese deities. Thus, insofar as they offered the men and women who comprised this state an object of self-identification, it could lie here and nowhere else.

Thus, a self-identification was enforced toward a chimera which transformed its lion's head and lamb's body—that is, Japan itself.

In 1937 Manzhouguo announced an education system in which the basic direction of language education was: "Based upon the spirit of Japan and Manzhouguo unified in virtue and heart, Japanese will be stressed as one of the national languages." Hence, Japanese was fixed as a national language of Manzhouguo, beside "Manchurian"—it was forbidden in Manzhouguo to use the terms "Chinese language" (*Chūgokugo*) or "Chinese people" (*Chūgokujin*)—and Mongolian, and as the first national language which was assigned to be learned throughout all the territory of Manzhouguo. As it was put at the time, "training in Japanese is required in all schools, and it is promised that the common language in the future Manzhouguo shall be Japanese."[36] This in spite of the fact that Japanese numbered, at most, three percent of the overall population of Manzhouguo.

After language came religion. Shinto belief, which was sufficiently difficult for even Japanese to comprehend, was forced upon the other ethnic groups. By 1945, 295 Shinto shrines had been erected, and in addition to shrine visits for worship, the removal of hats and the most respectful salutations were enforced when walking in front of a shrine. Furthermore, state-founding shrines and state-founding memorials to the dead were built on the grounds of every school, and worship was carried out daily. At the same time, an ersatz Japanese emperor system emerged in which school ceremonies in imitation of the Japanese system were instituted and a picture of the Manzhouguo emperor and a copy of one of his edicts were installed in the Enshrinement Pavilion which had to be preserved, in the event of fire or other disaster, even if it meant sacrificing oneself. On December 8, 1942, the first anniversary of Japan's commencement of hostilities against the United States and Great Britain, Decree Number Seventeen of the State Council of Manzhouguo enacted Rules for the People, which carried the following items:

- The people are the fount of the state and shall think of developing the way of Shinto. They shall revere the Sun Goddess and work hard to be loyal to the Japanese emperor.
- The people shall take as fundamental loyalty, filiality, benevolence, and righteousness. They shall endeavor to perfect ethnic harmony and a state built on morality.
- The people shall honor diligence and expand the public good, look with intimacy upon their neighbors, and in their jobs assiduously contribute to the vitality of the national destiny.
- The people shall be firm in character, reverence constancy, honor integrity, and take coutesy as a basic principle. In so doing, they shall endeavor to extol the national way.
- The people shall with all their strength realize the ideals of state-building and press on to the attainment of the Greater East Asia Coprosperity Sphere.[37]

It seems clear that this document sought, in the same way as the Rescript on the Consolidation of the Basis of the Nation of 1940, in the way of Shinto the foundations for its statehood and, while accepting Japanese mythology, enforced belief in the Sun Goddess. It was the same in nature as the Japanese Rescript on Education and the Oath of Imperial Subjects enacted in Korea in 1937. The school observances which included recitation of these

Rules for the People took the following form. First, there was the raising of the flag (depending on the school, the Japanese flag might also be raised); then, all in attendance bowed in the distant direction of the State-Founding Shrine, the Japanese Imperial Palace, and the Manzhouguo Imperial Palace; a silent prayer then followed for everlasting good fortunes on the battlefield and the heroic spirits of those soldiers of the Imperial Army (namely, the Japanese army) who had perished there; then, there was a reading aloud of the "Rules for the People" and an admonitory lecture by the school principal. When in the midst of the last of these the Japanese or Manzhouguo emperor would be mentioned, all teachers and students were to come to attention. Finally, state-building physical exercises were carried out.

The same sorts of things were carried out in the Manzhouguo army, which received training and guidance from Japanese military advisors. First, all troops bowed in the distant direction of the State-Founding Shrine, the Japanese Imperial Palace, and the Manzhouguo Imperial Palace, and all stood silently in prayer for the Imperial Army. In addition, there was a compulsory recitation of the Rescript on the Military (issued by the Manzhouguo emperor, who was a generalissimo just as in Japan) and the "Rules for the People," followed by the reading aloud of Shinto prayers. These prayers are what most riled Pujie, younger bother of Puyi, who worked to the utmost to hold back his criticisms of the Guandong Army: "Even if we accepted the Guandong Army's guidance over the Manzhouguo army, I really wanted them to stop the long-distance prayers aimed in an easterly direction and intoning the name of the Sun Goddess. . . . Also, because [the troops] had a poor understanding of just what they were saying, they were beaten and kicked—it was terribly violent."[38] Even Pujie, who had been sent to the mainland from the Japanese army cadet school, found this painful. It is difficult to imagine how mortifying this experience was for common soldiers who knew no Japanese.

Furthermore, when ordinary people were interrogated by Japanese military police and other police officials at police stations, if asked "What are you?" and they did not reply "Manchurian" (*Manzhouguoren* or *Manren* in Chinese), they could be beaten to the point of death.[39] Could the injection of such a "national" consciousness pursued in terms that can only be called coercive be effective? On August 17, 1945, Korean and Chinese students paid a visit to the office of Professor Nishimoto Sōsuke (1909–1990) of Kenkoku University to bid him farewell. They spoke as follows:

A Korean student: You may not know this, Professor [Nishimoto], but aside from one or two of us who hailed from Cheju Island, most of us Korean students at Kenkoku University belong to an organization for the independence of the Korean people. However, as soon as Korea is liberated from Japanese domination and becomes independent, then for the first time genuine Korean-Japanese cooperation can take shape. I return now to Korea for the rebuilding and independence of the motherland.

A Chinese student: Every day at Kenkoku University, Professor [Nishimoto], we carried out long-distance prayers to the east. Perhaps you knew how we felt on these occasions. Every single time, we prayed that imperialist Japan would have to be defeated. Then came the order to engage in the silent prayer. That silent prayer! This we took to be the signal of shining swords, swords being polished to bring down Japanese imperialism. In Chinese the terms "silent prayer" (mo^{4}dao^3) and "shining sword" (mo^{2}dao^1), as well as "long-distance prayer" (yao^{2}bai^4) and "certain defeat" (yao^{4}bai^4), have practically the same pronunciations. We have felt the good intentions of you and your colleagues, and to that extent we must apologize. However, no matter what your good intentions may have been . . . the reality of Manzhouguo was nothing shy of a puppet regime of Japanese imperialism. Regrettably, this is an uncontrovertible fact.[40]

The chimera had already been destroyed and was just awaiting the August 18 declaration of the dissolution of Manzhouguo. Furthermore, as a result of necrosis in which one part of the body loses its life functions, it had been separated from its backbone.

Nishimoto later noted: "As I was listening to these words, I had the thought that I was hearing the deafening roar as our 'Kenkoku University' went pitifully and without resistance to its demise."[41] To be sure, it "prepared the raw material for the main pillars of support" to control Manzhouguo.[42] From this perspective, the fact that Kenkoku University looked on in vain as Manzhouguo collapsed and Japan was defeated, while it had trained students who were sharpening their intellectual swords, should probably be taken as a defeat for the education offered there as well. Yet, as the first principle of the law enabling Kenkoku University to come into existence stated, it was "to train human talent of pioneering leadership in the building of a moral world which, having mastered the mystery of the spirit of state creation and thoroughly investigated the abstruse doctrines of knowledge, would themselves put into practice [what they had learned]."[43] If they illuminated the spirit of Kenkoku University, then did not the Korean students in their own words master the mystery of the spirit of state creation as that of ethnic harmony and put it into practice? Paradoxically, Kenkoku University succeeded in educating these students, and by "going pitifully to its demise" one might say that it actually achieved its ends.

The valorous words of the Chinese students were words full of emotion: "No matter what your good intentions may have been . . . the reality of Manzhouguo was nothing shy of a puppet regime of Japanese imperialism. Regrettably, this is an uncontrovertible fact." To that extent, these seem not to be words indicating in a precise manner the actual nature of life in Manzhouguo as a chimera. These would not, then, be the kind of words appropriate to sending the chimera off to its death.

And, yet, in spite of all this, as I noted in the introduction to this volume, in the postwar period—even now—many people continue to align themselves and sympathize with the views of someone such as Hayashi Fusao, who argued that "Asian history will itself not allow us to disregard it by invoking the Western political science concept of a 'puppet state'."[44] This view—namely, that Manzhouguo was not a puppet state of the Japanese, and we cannot explain the Japanese-Manzhouguo relationship on the basis of a Western political science concept—was not something that first cropped up in the postwar era, but was, in fact, the language used some time ago to express the legitimacy of Manzhouguo as an independent state and the distinctive nature of Japanese-Manzhouguo relations. For example, Kanesaki Ken objected to the idea of Manzhouguo as a puppet state: "In China they say that Manzhouguo is a puppet of Japan, that it has no independence with respect to Japan."[45] He went on to describe the nature of Japanese-Manzhouguo relations:

The relationship between the two countries of Japan and Manzhouguo was originally a tie without parallel in the West. The government by the kingly way in Manzhouguo cannot be explained with Western political science. Thus, because cooperation between the state of the imperial way and the state of the kingly way cannot be gauged by Western international law, there is no need to do so. We shall help that state implement a government by the kingly way which cannot be understood with Western political science. Our relationship will also be of the kingly way, not necessarily of law. This is not a relationship which should be gauged on the basis of Western international law.[46]

To be sure, as Kanesaki argues, the claim that political science and jurisprudence which were born in Western society can explain all societies and all phenomena is intellectual arrogance, and to persistently claim that one can generalize in this way may be seen as a form of intellectual imperialism. If indeed, however, Japanese-Manzhouguo relations did produce a distinctive form of international relations under the influence of such new principles, then this would necessarily enhance the capacity of explanation to clarify with concepts and systems even Western political science and jurisprudence themselves. To take the position that "Asian history will itself not allow us to disregard [Manzhouguo] by invoking the concept of a 'puppet state',"which trips off the tongue in Western political science and jurisprudence, this is in itself intellectual arrogance, something manifestly different from intellectual imperialism.

What sort of history and where in the world would we find this "Asian history itself" which will not allow us to see Manzhouguo as a puppet state? From the very beginning of the state, the Republic of China and the anti-Manzhouguo, anti-Japanese fighters, who may have numbered as many as 300,000, continually rejected Manzhouguo as a puppet state. The Chinese students from Kenkoku University whom we touched upon earlier were apparently not included in this "Asian history itself." Whenever "Asia" is offered up for discussion, we Japanese past and present always use it as a pretext for deception. If we have no intention of slighting our own lives, then I strongly feel that in the twenty-first century we need absolutely to avoid deceiving ourselves and others with this discourse of "Asia."

Furthermore, the flip side of this argument is that Western political science and jurisprudence themselves, the latest in Western science and technology—"civilization"—are what comprised the grounding for Japanese encroachment upon Asia and legitimization of control over Manzhouguo. That this "civilization" itself gave birth to barbarism, plundered and was dispossessed, hated and was despised, caused injury and was injured, and murdered and was itself killed all gave form to a period of relations between ethnic groups—namely the era of the chimerical Manzhouguo.

Now that the reader has made his or her way through this book, perhaps the true image of the chimera is becoming clearer, and perhaps there is no longer any need to revisit the question of whether it was a puppet state or not. There is, though, just one more historical document I would like to refer to in this context. Commander Honjō Shigeru of the Guandong Army, who pressed Komai Tokuzō into taking up the position of first director-general for administrative affairs in Manzhouguo, encouraged Komai in the following manner: "Would it not be the height of cowardice, having created a 'puppet government,' to then run away from it?"[47] For these two men centrally involved in creating Manzhouguo, it was thoroughly self-evident that this was a puppet regime. *Dai Manshūkoku kensetsu roku* (Chronicle of the founding of the great state of Manzhouguo), which includes this sentence, was published in 1933 by the publishing house of Chūō kōronsha and was accepted as self-evident by Japanese at the time.

There is one further point in this connection which I must mention, and that is the question of the "good intentions" of the Japanese in their control over Manzhouguo. As noted on several occasions in this work, whether or not one sympathized with the ideals of Manzhouguo, I do not believe that the Japanese who worked to see that Manzhouguo's existence would continue were necessarily driven by evil intentions. This may be my bias as a Japanese, but it strikes me that all parties from their various positions and in their varied ways harbored "good intentions" for Manzhouguo. And, it was by no means the case that they were completely insensitive to the divergence between "good intentions" and "reality." Furumi Tadayuki, for example, who was Assistant Director of the Office of Administrative Affairs, offered the following recollections as he looked back over his own ten years of experience in governance from the founding of the state:

Clearly, among the Japanese who have taken a guiding position in the state and formed the core, there is the gnawing recognition that we have here a "misgovernment of good intentions." Namely, the results of efforts carried out in Japanese consciousness, Japanese character, and Japanese ways have failed.[48]

Thus, while aware that it was bad government and a failure, because of these "good intentions," in the final analysis, they never corrected it in the firm belief that the Japanese administration was superior to that of Manzhouguo. By tabulating their "good intentions" in this manner, the discourse that sought to legitimate their rule in Manzhouguo continued to remain strong even after the war. For example, as Takamiya Tahei (1897–1961) recalled from his experiences at the time: "For the local residents, the governance of Manzhouguo was not something evil."[49] Then, having recapitulated rulership over Manzhouguo, he raised the Japanization of administration as a point missing from consideration and resolves it as follows: "In particular, the reckless firing off of laws and regulations was never understood by the Manchurians who could not form a constitutional government. They excoriated the 'Japanese' officials [in Manzhouguo] as 'legal bandits.' As Japanese unfamiliar with colonial administration, this was an oversight of good intentions."[50]

"Misgovernment of good intentions," "oversight of good intentions"—if in fact this was a case of "good intentions," is everything to be forgiven? There is much that might be written on this point. I shall, however, refer here solely to a citation from the ancient Chinese text, the *Shujing* (Classic of documents), to which Puyi referred in his autobiography: "Natural disasters can be avoided, but man-made disasters are unavoidable." That is, disasters caused by people, no matter how much they express their good intentions, cannot be averted.[51]

Finally, then, in what historical topology may we consider the Manzhouguo which did exist and then did disappear?

Itō Takeo (1895–1985) once called Manzhouguo a "phantom country." Perhaps, though, we should not completely rule out the possibility of seeing this artificial country as a utopia produced by Japanese modernity, a utopia moreover which gave birth to the most severe and tragic of realities. At the same time, though, we must never forget that by raising the banners of the kingly realm and paradise on earth as well as ethnic harmony, Japan wrought havoc with the ethical sensibilities of the Japanese people themselves and paralyzed their sensitivity as individuals with respect to other ethnic groups. However, while including this aspects of things, Manzhouguo in the final analysis was probably as Takebe Rokuzō, the last Director-General for Administrative Affairs, put it. As he saw it, "Manzhouguo itself existed as a secret fund of the Japanese army."[52] Still, modern Japanese history has flowed from the first Sino-Japanese War of 1894–95 to the Russo-Japanese War of 1904–5, the second Sino-Japanese War (1937–45), and on to the Pacific War, and with that last defeat Japan was cut off from Manchuria for a time. The armed forces, emperor system, and bureaucracy to which modern Japan gave shape appeared as a focal point in condensed form, and by the same token the way in which it related to other countries, principally China and the Soviet Union, also formed another focal point. From an altogether different line of sight, perhaps we can see this as an era in which one war was preparing for the next world war, an era in which the call for a Communist revolution resonated widely, and this gave birth to and nurtured Manzhouguo. All these themes of our century, the twentieth century—world war, revolution, ethnicity, Asia, liberation from oppression, ideal state—became mixed together into an undulating heap. In this sense, an inquiry into Manzhouguo is directly linked to an assessment of the problem of modern Japan and the problems to which the twentieth century has given birth.

Thus, the chimera made its life of just over thirteen years and five months with "imperial Japan." Although its success or failure may not tell us anything about history, the idea that the seizure of Manchuria was, as Ishiwara Kanji conceived of it, "Japan's sole path to survival," remains highly suspect. Yet, there can be no doubt that the establishment of the state of Manzhouguo was the path leading to destruction for modern Japan.

Nonetheless, while the life of this chimerical Manzhouguo craved and gobbled up the unlimited riches of the terrain in China's northeast, it soon underwent a transformation and merged in life and death with its mother body. The chimera of Greek mythology spit fire from its mouth, ravaged terrain, and pillaged homes.

The ordinary manner in which the chimera is used in Western languages is, of course, in the sense of an illusion, a bizarre illusion. But, how many disasters were wrought and how many lives undermined because of this bizarre illusion. I believe it was Hagiwara Sakutarō (1886–1942) who wrote: "With the passage of time, everyone disappears like an illusion." Indeed, the past is like a vast dream. The great majority of the people who lived in Manzhouguo are now no longer alive, and they are thus not with us now. With the Soviet entrance into the war against Japan in 1945, the chimera of Manzhouguo was destroyed, and with the passage of time, forty-six years later the Soviet Union disappeared from the face of the earth together with the illusion known as Communism. And, the century moved toward its end.

However, even with the disappearance of states and the passage of peoples, the past lives on as solemn fact. Perhaps we believe it to be gone for good because our minds abandon lessons from the past as memories to be left behind and the tension thus completely dissipates.

Manzhouguo—which brought together people's dreams and hopes, crimes and rage, tragedies and privations, and sucked their blood and sweat and tears—disappeared. However, while taking its condensed history as food for thought, the great land of China's northeast is vast and limitless, sustaining people even today and spreading out to eternity.

Afterword (May 1993)

Over twenty years have now passed since that evening. An odd feeling, which I felt then, even now strong at times and weak at other times, is revived like waves crashing on the shore.

That evening, just as we completed seminar every time, we went to Professor Nagao Ryūichi's (b. 1938) home. It was probably the flow of the discussion on Pan-Asianism, the theme of that day's session. With his characteristic soft smile, Professor Nagao said: "So, what do you think?" And he took from his bookshelf and showed us a copy of *Kasagi Yoshiaki ihōroku* (Memories of Kasagi Yoshiaki).[1] There was certainly no reason to expect that someone like me, who shortly after entering college was still so thoroughly ignorant of the subject, would be able to comprehend its contents. However, what remains fresh in my memory to this day is the profound, overpowering shock I felt in the sentences, full of indignation, which shot out from between the lines. This impression was only amplified within me as time passed. At the time, I lost my bearings and trembled as I read these sentences, the likes of which I had never seen before. Yet, all manner of emotions are clearly expressed in *Kasagi Yoshiaki ihōroku*—pride and cherishing of the memory for an era burning with idealism, as well as anger, anxiety, and pain for the frustration and banishment. And, for those who did not share his idealism about Manzhouguo, and were not likely to ever be convinced of its validity, one senses a sharp feeling of exclusion.

Over the next few years, as is so often the case, I never again felt the initial deep impression I had had. From that evening, though, I found it difficult to approach Manzhouguo to which Kasagi and many others went. Once I stepped into that terrain, though, it was as if I was being dragged into a pitch-black, surrounding darkness. While I hesitated before the noxious sense that Manzhouguo elicits, I began to track down whatever had been written about it, and I continually had the feeling that something was not quite right. No matter how I attempted to grab hold of what was beyond the thin film, it eluded my grasp. And, it would not conform to what my first impressions had been.

James Joyce wrote in *Ulysses*: "History is the nightmare from which I am trying to awake." Perhaps, despite the different genres, Manzhouguo is for me the nightmare from which I would like to awake.

Notwithstanding, after a preparatory meeting in 1986, Professor Yamamoto Yūzō began a joint research group entitled "Studies of 'Manzhouguo'" at the Institute for Research in the Humanities of Kyoto University. In the pitch-black darkness, I now prepared to face Manzhouguo, my nightmare. I learned a great deal from the people involved in the research group, from the numerous disciplines with which they approached their work, and from their extensive accumulated knowledge—in addition to Professor Yamamoto, they included Furuya Tetsuo, Nishimura Shigeo, Soejima Shōichi, Imura Tetsurō, Okada Hideki, Mizuno Naoki, Matsuno Shūji, Matsumoto Toshirō, Murata Yūko, Okumura Hiroshi, Nishizawa Yasuhiko, and Yasutomi Ayumi. Through a string of animated discussions in the research group lasting until March 1992, I began to feel as thought the contours of Manzhouguo were finally beginning to surface, albeit dimly.

From the fall of 1987 I spent a year of desultory reading of historical materials at the Harvard-Yenching Institute of Harvard University, and the chimera as an image with which to grasp Manzhouguo gradually took form. After returning to Japan, I frequently met with Mr. Miya Kazuho of the magazine *Chūō kōron*, and we spoke of the idea of my writing a book about Manzhouguo. Mr. Miya proposed the idea to me and opened an avenue to pursue it which eventually gave shape to an image. I followed this path and for the first time put my image of Manzhouguo into words. The result was an essay, "Saigo no 'Manshūkoku' būmu o yomu" (Reading about the last "Manzhouguo" boom), which appeared in *Chūō kōron* in the June 1989 issue. Responses to that short piece were mixed, both at home and abroad, and I realized that I could not dismiss the subject solely as an image. But, how was I to respond? After a bit of hesitation, Mr. Miya said to me: "If you don't try and write the book, you'll never get started." With that I made up my mind, and my path was illuminated thereafter by Mr. Hayakawa Yukihiko, head of the editorial department of Chūō shinsho, a division of Chūō kōron publishers.

After contracting to write the book, I traveled to China shortly after the Tian'anmen Incident. I was responsible for instruction at the Beijing Center for Japanese Studies, which is a postgraduate school created to train Chinese scholars of Japanology. In addition, I collected historical documents and, together with my colleague Nomura Shin'ichi, a scholar of Korean ethnography, traveled to China's northeast region. Getting to know the massive expanse of the northeast and the great number of Koreans living there is a difficult experience to come by. In the early spring of 1990, I returned home and set to writing. My plan was to have the volume take shape by the sixtieth anniversary of the Manchurian Incident in 1991. However, I was unable to meet that deadline. One day my pen stopped and I was unable to write a word, as if possessed by something or other, and it turned into several days and then continue for several more days. Still, with Mr. Hayakawa's encouragement, in March of 1992 I was able to turn in a draft covering through chapter two of the present volume. I had thought that, once I set to work on the book, I would be able to write it, but I was still unable to comply fully. Each chapter, more than the writing of an article, was heavily laden with pain and weightiness.

I sensed a kind of dread in the act of writing. Much of the truth about Manzhouguo has concealed itself in original documents destroyed by fire or lost. A number of pages probably hundreds or even thousands of times larger that the historical documents that do remain to us now and in the depths of silence—that which has never been relegated to memoirs and has never been spoken of. Am I reaching out into empty space in an effort to grasp an illusion? As I resisted such feelings of uncertainty and irritation, several times I was ready to give up and abandon the project altogether, and then Mr. Hayakawa's encouraging letters and telephone calls revived my spirits. I thought that he must have been ready to abandon the project himself. However, whenever he would listen to my lame excuses for why I could not write, he would patiently but firmly find yet another way to break through to me, and I would ultimately find my way back onto track.

The aim itself of this book to attempt to understand Manzhouguo as a chimera is perhaps a product of an illusion that emerges as we come together with something of a altogether different nature. And, while I have called this a "portrait of Manzhouguo," I may not have depicted its real flesh and blood. In all honesty, this is a limitation. I have only tried to offer Manzhouguo in a form to the extent that I am now able to comprehend what it was for those people who created and lived in it. Of course, the true face of Manzhouguo cannot be understood solely from a Japanese perspective. Chinese and Korean points of view are also essential. However, what should be more than understandable is that for me as a Japanese, this has been most difficult to do. When this topic is approached from Chinese and Korean lines of vision, then they may find that my view is biased and my approach one-sided. If such critiques are forthcoming, I look forward to sharing this history in future.

No book is completely the work of a single person, as all rely on the past accomplishments and points of view of many others. This book owes a debt to a particularly large number of people who helped it to take shape. I cannot begin to gauge the help received from the members of the aforementioned research group on Manzhouguo. I do not even know how to express my gratitude. It is not that this book represents the views of the research group in some sense, nor that it should. To the contrary, on a variety of points there will be many who accept my views and many others who will adopt opposing positions. A glance through the works in the footnotes will make this point clear.

Again, as I have noted, this book would never have been conceived save for conversations with Mr. Miya Kazuho, and I would have abandoned it long ago without the indefatigable encouragement of Mr. Hayakawa's patience and timeliness. I shall never forget both men's kindnesses.

Since moving to my present position at Kyoto University in 1986, I could never have written a book of this sort had not certain scholars at Kyoto University been present—Hazama Naoki, Yoshikawa Tadao, Ono Kazuko, Mori Tokihiko, and Ishikawa Yoshihiro—who never begrudged me their guidance in willingly responding to my misguided questions about China. I offer them here my heartfelt thanks. I must also offer a simple, profound thanks to the staff of the library of the Institute for Research in the Humanities, who invariably dealt immediately and with a smile to my search for documents one after the next.

For assistance on a variety of ordinary matters, not just concerning documents, let me thank Minamoto Ryōen, Ishida Takeshi, Shimada Kenji, Matsumoto Sannosuke, Asukai Masamichi, Gavan McCormack, Kurihara Ken, Matsuo Takayoshi, Okada Tomoyoshi, Higuchi Yōichi, Satō Shin'ichi, Suzuki Tadashi, Tanaka Shin'ichi, Kaneko Fumio, Kaneko Masaru, Hirano Ken'ichirō, Hamaguchi Yūko, Shibutani Yūri, Tsuchiya Hideo, Iwasaki Ryūji, Hiraoka Moriho, Yanagisawa Asobu, Akabane Takayuki, Kumada Toshirō, Li Tingjiang, Zhang Qixiong, Feng Wei, and He Yuefu.

This book is the result of the kind assistance of all the people mentioned above.

Finally, my prayers go out to my parents, especially to my mother who, in October 1992, suddenly fell ill with bleeding from a subarachnoid hemorrhage and who since has been trying to return to her daily life.

Interview with the Journal *Kan: rekishi, kankyō, bunmei* (2002): How Shall We Understand Manchuria and Manzhouguo?

Japan's Geopolitical Conceptions

Kan: Let me begin by asking how, from the perspective of world history, are we best to understand this place, Manchuria? The Western powers began their advance into Asia from the middle of the nineteenth century. While Russia began to move south, the other Western powers took aim at invading China and Manchuria. In the midst of all this activity, Japan, too, moved into Manchuria. Within this context, how would it be best for us to see the actions taken by Japan?

Yamamuro: This is an immense question, and there are an assortment of different perspective from which to try to answer it. For example, at the first Japanese Diet session in 1890, Yamagata Aritomo (1838–1922) gave a speech on what he termed the "interest line" and the "sovereignty line." These ideas had basically been drawn up by Inoue Kowashi (1843–1895). The "sovereignty line" concerned national frontiers; it was a view of national defense based on a spatial recognition that, in order that the national borders be protected, one had to first protect one's "interest line." If Japan was to rule Korea, it would have to first establish an "interest line"— namely, before Korea, Manchuria and Mongolia would have to be brought under control. Hence, in this Japanese spatial perception, the idea was conceived to create an intermediate, demilitarized zone beyond the national border. Without this, there would be no security.

This position carries with it a certain danger, although, given the geopolitical conditions surrounding Japan, the Korean peninsula was thought of at the time as a dagger thrust into Japan's side. And, only Russia was approaching this dagger. To defend against it, Korea had to be taken. To defend Korea, Japan would have to proceed further into the contiguous terrain of Manchuria and Mongolia. Japanese geopolitical understanding at the time required such an apparent necessity, and this was closely linked to the argument for "Manchuria-Mongolia as Japan's lifeline."

By the same token, Japan's advance onto the Asian mainland became an issue only after the Boxer Uprising, when Russia refused to withdraw its troops after suppression of the Boxers and kept them remaining in place. This move on Russia's part gave rise to the formation of the Resist Russia Volunteers among Chinese students in Japan at the time, and the Qing government itself tried to restrain this response and made no seeming effort to rid itself of the Russian forces.

This turn of events was tied to the position taken by Sun Zhongshan (Sun Yat-sen, 1866–1925) who, in exchange for support for his revolutionary movement, offered to cede control over Manchuria to Japan. As far as China was concerned, Manchuria was land "beyond the pass"—namely, uncivilized territory. For the Qing dynasty, of course, this terrain was long sealed off as the ancestral homeland of the Manchu people, the land on which the Qing dynasty had arisen. Having lasted nearly 270 years, the Qing dynasty now no longer saw the value in defending their old haunts. In a sense, something like an air pocket developed in this region. And, Russia entered it.

At the same time, the United States, which supported Japan in its war against Russia in 1904–1905, did not, because of the Open Door policy, take colonial possessions, despite efforts by Edward H. Harriman (1848–1909) after the war to purchase railways in Manchuria. As Secretary of State Philander Knox (1853–1921) put it, the U.S. would "smoke Japan out" of Manchuria by extending its own economic grip there. In order to deal with this situation, Japan for its part refused to pull out of Manchuria.

The Significance of World War I

Yamamuro: However, the most important thing given the situation in world history at the time was the eruption of World War I. For the first time in this war, mankind engaged in a system of total war, and Japanese such as Ishiwara Kanji (1889–1949) were especially conscious of this fact. To win at war, then, a nation had to increase its economic and productive might. Above all else, coal and steel were deemed the most important resources in the production of weaponry at that time, but Japan lacked them. Manchuria would enable Japan to obtain these resources. In this form, the influence exerted by a system of total war was huge, and, I believe, from there it probably entered a different stage. Manchuria during the era of Gotō Shinpei (1857–1929) and Manchuria after World War I were spaces with decisively different significance. In the era of Gotō Shinpei and his colleagues, Manchuria was simply an agricultural region producing soybeans, among other things, and a granary, but after the Great War it became the greatest strategic material base for implementing a system of total war.

There are, of course, other ways of thinking about this topic. As Ishibashi Tanzan (1884–1973) argued, trade would better enable protection of the resources in the region in a stable manner than seizure and occupation. Did it, in the final analysis, pay to incur such an immense cost for Japan to take control over the region? Even if Japan did not occupy the area, if it developed it and engaged in trade, Japanese would probably be able to secure the resources it needed.

Yet, when we look at the subsequent history in which it was turned into an economic bloc, his understanding may not necessarily have been on the mark. In fact, when Japan later occupied French Indochina, the United States ceased exports of oil and steel and froze Japanese assets. Thus, given the circumstances at that time in the world, whether or not free trade by itself would have worked well remains dubious. Hence, as the Japanese army and Ishwara Kanji conceived it, if they failed to protect Manchuria as a colony, they would be unable to provide a stable supply of coal and steel to Japan—as a realistic perception of the world at that time, this was not necessarily wrong. By no means do I mean to imply that it was perfectly fine to administer colonial control, but the conception of the need to protect Manchuria does seem to have been one choice given the development of world history following World War I.

In any event, World War I had a decisive impact in human history. There is nothing, I would argue, that we can say about the history of the twentieth century if we remove World War I from the picture. Whether it is the issue of ethnic self-determination or the rise of the Nazis, if we exclude World War I, it cannot be understood. The origins of all subsequent human history can be found there.

What was initially thought would end in about forty days—"back by Christmas" in the saying of the time—ended up turning into a four-year quagmire of warfare and witnessed all manner of subsistence goods being poured into it. With World War I, war itself underwent a transformation for human history in every sense that it possessed for human existence itself. Human beings themselves were used as cogs. All human life became thoroughly enveloped in war on a daily basis. This change is of decisive importance in thinking about Manzhouguo, and the same is true for the modern history of Japan. In particular, in debates over the issue of Japanese colonial rule, such consideration had scarcely existed.

The Significance of Manzhouguo as Seen from the Form of Control

Kan: In an essay written in 1996 entitled "Shokumin teikoku Nihon no kōsei to Manshūkoku" (Manzhouguo and the structure of Japan as colonial empire),[1] you used the concepts of the "transference of ruling forms" and the "circulation of rulership talent" to analyze Japan's colonial rule. What were your objectives in doing so?

Yamamuro: Most important for me is the fact that Manzhouguo cannot be understood solely as a question of Manzhouguo. It makes no sense, as far as I am concerned, to consider the problem in a form of a self-delimiting "history of Manzhouguo." We need to situate Manzhouguo as one part within the Japanese imperial system.

Thus far, the whole topic of the Japanese empire has been addressed in the form of Korea, Taiwan, and eventually the Greater East Asia Co-prosperity Sphere with Manzhouguo not part of the picture. By contrast, once we understand the distinctive important of Manzhouguo, we have no choice but to adopt the view that the inflow and outflow of forms of rulership and ruling talent gave shape to the Japanese imperial system.

In addition, Manzhouguo needs to be properly placed not only within the world of East Asia but in the context of modern world history. Yet, the problem remains—and it is a difficult one, indeed—as to the framework one should employ to carry out such an overall study and what source materials should be used.

Kan: On the eve of the founding of Manzhouguo in 1932, were there not changes in the forms of rulership and in rulership talent?

Yamamuro: On the eve of the founding of the state of Manzhoguo, the form of control was very different. To be more precise, the position of the Guandong Army was decisively different. Let me offer a piece of illustrative, anecdotal data. Before Manzhouguo was founded, officers and commanders of the Guandong Army were given the lowest-priority seating at such events as banquets held by the president of the South Manchurian Railway Company. In other words, they enjoyed an extremely low status, a position solely as guards along the South Manchurian Railway (S.M.R.) lines. In the world following World War I, Manchuria came to be situated as the mainstay in the Japanese system for total war, and hence the status of the Guandong Army gradually rose.

World War I was important for another reason as well: the diffusion around the globe of the principle of ethnic self-determination. It was amid this trend that Chinese nationalism was heightened, giving rise to a movement for rights recovery in Manchuria and Mongolia. Insofar as the response to this movement was to crush it militarily, we entered a spiral of Chinese nationalism only growing stronger, the position of the Guandong Army rising, Japan demanding further extensions of its authority, and military force being reinforced. In 1915 during World War I, Japan thrust the Twenty-One Demands before the Chinese government, and this entailed an effort to gain control over Manchuria by, among other things, the placement of Japanese advisors within the Chinese government. In terms of relations between Japan and China, at this point in time the goals of a Japanese invasion were blatantly sought. In China even now the Twenty-One Demands are seen as emblematic of Japanese aggression.

Kan: When Gotō Shinpei assumed the presidency of the South Manchurian Railway Company in 1906, Manchuria was said to have slid into a state of "rule by three heads": the Guandong Governor-General's office, the Japanese consulate, and the South Manchurian Railway Company. He reportedly said that "three heads are no good." How did relations among the three develop from 1906 to 1932?

Yamamuro: It is difficult for me to say in just a word, inasmuch as circumstances differ depending on the time frame involved. If we look first at Manchuria, the consulate and the Korean Governor-General's office were exceedingly important. Take the issue of the Jiandao region. Japanese authority did not intrinsically extend to this area, but over a long period of time the Korean Governor-General's office did possess policing powers there. After Manzhouguo came into existence, the issue became whether the Korean Governor-General's office would retain policing powers over the Koreans in Jiandao, which was part of Manzhouguo, or if Manzhouguo would rule over them. In form Manzhouguo was an independent state, but it was the Korean Governor-General's office which had the long experience and the know-how with respect to Jiandao. Thus, the latter could not be completely ignored.

Similarly, the Guandong Governor-General's office was a military structure which in 1919 changed into a civilian-run Guandong Government and in 1929 changed again into the Department of Overseas Affairs. Fundamentally, though, it retained ruling powers over Guandong Province. Also, it merely policed the railway lines for several dozen meters on either side along the S.M.R. By the same token, the S.M.R. produced enormous profits; in form, it was under the supervision of the top official in the Guandong Governor-General's office, but it had administrative powers over the attached areas as well.

When the regime of Zhang Zuolin (1873–1928) came into existence, laid parallel tracks to the S.M.R., and began to siphon off all the S.M.R.'s profits, a military force to contend with Zhang—namely, the Guandong Army—began to amass power. Severely hit by the world economic crash, the S.M.R. fell into a business depression which had effected it deleteriously. What this meant for the mushrooming of power at the time of the founding of Manzhouguo was that the president of the S.M.R. remained as a post which the Japanese Diet appointed, but selection of Japanese plenipotentiaries resident in Manzhouguo and the governor-general of Guandong were left entirely in the hands of the commander of the Guandong Army. In other words, until Manzhouguo came into existence, it had been ruled entirely by civil officials, but afterward—form and appearance notwithstanding—it was essentially a military administrative system. The power of the commanding officer of the Guandong Army became absolute, combining three positions (or heads) into one.

Gotō Shinpei's Conception of Colonialism

Kan: Did things then veer away from the direction set by Gotō Shinpei?

Yamamuro: Gotō Shinpei served first as Japan's civil governor in Taiwan, and this experience had a major impact on him. As he conceived it, the policy for running a colony was extremely simple: "military preparedness in civil garb" (*bunsō teki bubi*). In a word, it was not domination through the undisguised use of force, but control based on source materials and surveys. He firmly held that this—not military force—was the most important point in colonial management. Already during his Taiwan years, he employed Okamatsu Santarō (1871–1920) to carry out an investigation of the old civil customs of Taiwan. This project led to the compilation of the famous *Shinkoku gyōsei hō* (Administrative law of the Qing state). Only ten years before Japanese control, Taiwan had officially become a province of the Qing dynasty, and it was not a region to which Qing administrative law basically extended. Accordingly, the work had no intrinsic meaning, but an enormous amount of money and personnel went into the production of *Shinkoku gyōsei hō*, and Gotō's conception of control was thus well expressed in the nature of the project itself.

Gotō himself later went to Manchuria, and he brought Okamatsu along with him in creating the largest think tank in the world: the Research Department of the South Manchurian Railway Company. Within Japan as well, in response to the call from Professor Shiratori Kurakichi (1865–1942) of Tokyo Imperial University, a Research Bureau for the Study of the Geography and History of Manchuria and Korea was established. This move would exert a profound influence on the subsequent development of Japanese sinology and Japanese scholarship on East Asia.

Were surveys of these sorts then carried out simply for the purpose of control? My sense is that it would be more accurate to see that in Gotō's own view ruling and knowing the actual state of affairs were identical. He likened his science of the state to that of medicine. Thus, to learn the root of a disease and cure it, one had to gain control over it, and this accorded with knowing the true state of affairs appertaining. Such a view is clearly altogether different from rulership by means of power in Manzhouguo.

For example, to establish policy on civil law in Manzhouguo, there was the issue of the law of inheritance, and thus a study of civil practices was carried out. As a result of this survey, two volumes were published, and the remainder appeared after the war. This immense research report is extremely valuable in learning about civil customs in Manchuria. Responsibility for it after the war fell to a man by the name of Chigusa Tatsuo

(1901–81), the presiding judge in the Tokyo district court. The survey was highly scrupulous and attentive to detail, but did not lead to legislation nor well resuscitate the subject at hand. The thirteen years it took to carry out the research was probably too short to lead to the creation of a form of rulership, which as Gotō believed was not based on military force, responsive to the local people's sensibilities. I am not suggesting that a longer period of rule would have been preferred, but the reasoning that only sees Japanese rule in Manzhouguo as control by "legal bandits" tracing over Japanese law is a reflection of the inability to breathe life into these surveys.

Meanwhile, the *baojia* system and measures for dealing with bandits remained in place unchanged in Taiwan. Thus, when Gotō moved from Taiwan to Manchuria, many from his Taiwan entourage made the trip as well and made the best of their experience in rulership from their years in Taiwan. Hence, I have called this the transference in the form of rulership. It was not simply Gotō who came up with it as president of the S.M.R., for we must recognize the links from his years as civil governor of Taiwan.

Kan: Itō Hirobumi's (1841–1909) conception of colonies stood in sharp contrast to that of Gotō, did it not?

Yamamuro: On the topic of the advance into Manchuria, Itō Hirobumi's views diverged from popular opinion. In fact, he had a point of view which rather calmly judged international conditions and Japan's own strengths.

When Manchuria was initially seized as territory, all manner of debate arose within the Japanese government, including the view that holding this terrain was beyond Japan's capacities. There were even plans to sell the S.M.R. because it was impossible for Japan to manage. Thus, there was clearly at the time no unified sense within the Japanese government to retain control over Manchuria. I think that politicians of the era understood how far Japanese limits went. Victory in the Russo-Japanese War was an accidental outcome. With the eruption of the Russian Revolution of May 1905, Foreign Minister Komura Jutarō (1855–1911) among others knew full well that Japan had barely won the war, and they did not lose their heads and believe, as the Guandong Army later would, that they could resolve all matters with their own military might alone. This sort of self-control with respect to one's own power was shared by Japanese political figures at the time, including Gotō; it was aimed at rule with as little cost and as little resistance as possible, without the use of brute force, and in line with real conditions. It was common knowledge that rule based on military force would incur a cost and would surely elicit a reaction. There was, I believe, a consciousness of the risk involved in colonial management. Once such a balanced sensibility disappeared, Manzhouguo could be founded by the Guandong Army at a later date.

Kan: As you know, there is a published discussion [from 1909] between Gotō Shinpei and Itō Hirobumi, entitled *Itsukushima yawa* (Evening chat at the Itsukushima Shrine [in Hiroshima]). Gotō argued that Japan had to join hands with China and Russia. Unfortunately, though, Itō traveled abroad to have this discussion and was assassinated in Harbin that same year. What do you think of Gotō's conception of things as outlined in this exchange?

Yamamuro: Gotō was given the nickname of "large wrapping cloth" which is an indication of his powers of conception. As it only appears in Gotō's biography, I remain somewhat dubious about the veracity of the "Itsukushima yawa" itself, but as you have just pointed out, assuming the possibility of such a dispute, he had the notion of a Eurasian confederation arising from the need to resist the threat of an American advance into the region. This idea is linked to the plan for Eurasian diplomacy that began to be articulated during the recent tenure of Prime Minister Hashimoto Ryūtarō (b. 1937). Should Japan move solely within Asia, or should Japan forge ties with Eurasia, including Central Asia and Russia? This issue was, in a significant way, presaged in the conception of diplomacy offered by Gotō. Later, Kuhara Fusanosuke (1869–1965) proposed the idea of making the northeast portion of the Asian continent into a demilitarized zone for Japan, China, and the Soviet Union. Had Gotō's ideas been advanced to a certain extent in a realistic direction, then perhaps there would have been no expedition against Russia, and the circumstances surrounding Manchuria might have developed in a different direction. But, his ideas were to remain fixed as conceptions, and thus how realistic they were or, more specifically, how Russia might have responded, remain unanswerable problems. Later, the Russo-Japanese neutrality treaty signed with the Soviet Union is an experience which actually did backfire. As a possibility, though, the importance of his conception remains, I believe, immense.

Relations Between the Guandong Army and the Japanese Central Govenment

Kan: Incidentally, tell us something about the relationship between the Japanese central government and its local agencies in Manchuria. I would imagine that they differed before and after the creation of the state of Manzhouguo.

Yamamuro: As for the governor-general of Guandong prior to the founding of Manzhouguo, the central government's control through the Ministry of Foreign Affairs and the Department of Overseas Affairs was effective. Indeed, as far as human talent was concerned, officials in the Ministry of Home Affairs were not temporarily transferred to special positions. By the same token, the S.M.R. was an agency producing immense quantities of profit, and particular when the era of political party rule emerged, ferocious squabbles over the position of the president ensued. Thus, the era of Gotō Shinpei, Nakamura Zekō (1867–1927) and other early S.M.R. presidents were altogether different from the subsequent years.

When Manzhouguo came into existence, what was known as the third section (Operations; later, the fourth section) of the Guandong Army was charged with guidance in political affairs, and it issued virtually all directives under the rubric of "internal guidance." The central government, thus, had effective control to this extent. Of course, this was extremely dangerous for the Japanese government, inasmuch as it was creating a Secretariat for Manzhouguo Affairs and various Japanese-Manzhouguo councils and trying to retain control over them. Initially, at least, the Operations Section of the Guandong Army, which used the S.M.R. as a brain trust, was in fact able to control Manzhouguo. The thirteen years of Manzhouguo's existence is a history of a struggle for hegemony in which the Japanese government sought to restore to its authority what had fallen into the hands of the Guandong Army. As an issue in Japanese domestic politics, this was a struggle between the army and the civil officialdom.

Installation of a Top Secret Fund by the Guandong Army

Yamamuro: Furumi Tadayuki (1900–83), who served as assistant director-general for administrative affairs in Manzhouguo, once said: "Manzhouguo is an immense installation created by a top secret fund of the Guandong Army." The Japanese army was able to engage in extensive activities, such as intelligence gathering, throughout Asia, because it had sufficient funds which Manzhouguo siphoned off. This practice cast a huge shadow over postwar Japanese politics, beginning right with Prime Minister Kishi Nobusuke (1896–1987). The basic source for the monetary fund was opium. This was the problem which Gotō Shinpei worked hardest on in Taiwan; by making the sale of opium a monopoly, Gotō tried gradually to reduce the quantity of it available. He took the same approach in Manzhouguo, and although it was said to have been well regulated in Manzhouguo, this was in fact not the case. Opium production provided the richest source for such a slush fund. It was not only produced in Manchuria, but steadily flowed into Manzhouguo via Turkey, India, and Shanghai. The opium produced colossal profits which became the financial source for Japan's military schemes. The very fact that Amakasu Masahiko (1890–1945) gained such power in Manchuria was due to this money. While Kishi was a mere bureaucrat, Amakasu had at his disposal a slush fund of some ten million yen—which would come to ninety billion yen (roughly $800 million) today—for his special operations. This is difficult to prove on the basis of documents, the only corroboration being oral testimony, but younger scholars are now examining materials in such places as the Public Record Office in Great Britain on the remittance of opium, and this issue will probably be cleared up in the not-too-distant future.

Was Manzhouguo a State?

Kan: Can we see Manzhouguo as you have described it as a state?

Yamamuro: One could argue in many different ways the extent to which it was unified as a state. Thus, your question cannot be answered simply. What I regard as most problematic is the fact that it never issued a nationality act. The minimum requirements of the modern sovereign state would be territory, sovereignty, and a populace, but Manzhouguo had no nationality (*kokumin*). One might argue that in this regard it lacked the appearance of a state. However, its ruling structure did take shape in virtually complete form over thirteen and one-half years. In 1937, in particular, it abrogated extraterritoriality, making Japanese rule over it vanish in form. Thus, it was fully outfitted with the appearance of an independent state.

At the same time, as we always must say when discussing Manzhouguo, there were numerous young Japanese bureaucrats focused on the "harmony among the five ethnicities" of Manzhouguo and the "paradise of the kingly way" as well as many students who moved to Manchuria with the same goals. In this sense, although the reality of life in Manzhouguo diverged sharply from appearances, we still need to take cognizance of the fact that these many young people were trying to pursue the ideals of Manzhouguo.

Chinese students who now come to study with me have read my work in the field of Asian studies, but they have not read anything I have written about Manchuria. Although I have not asked they why, I would surmise that probably my research on Manzhouguo does not sit well with them.

Japanese Views of Manchuria

Kan: How were Manchuria and Manzhouguo viewed by Japanese at the time we have been discussing?

Yamamuro: Views of Manchuria before Manzhouguo and Manchuria after the state was founded differ sharply. For example, Natsume Sōseki (1867–1916) has a character in his novel *Kōjin* (Wayfarer) who travels to Manchuria and then returns to Japan, and he depicts this character in ghastly terms, a man effectively in a state of ruin. In his travel narrative *Man-Kan tokorodokoro* (Here and there in Manchuria and Korea) as well, he writes about Chinese coolies as if they were ants, a point which is considerably problematic in assessing Sōseki's work. In short, then, while there were people burning with enthusiasm for the ideal of the place Manchuria, as the expressions "Manshū goro" (Manchurian ruffian, vagabond) and

"Manshū rōnin" (Manchurian adventurer) indicate, there was a pervasive image of a place where men who could not live in Japan or who had been compelled to leave had found refuge and were carrying on secret maneuvers. And, for those who survived until the time of the withdrawal in the immediate postwar period, there remained a certain discrimination toward men who returned home to Japan from Manchuria.

Modern Japan's Only Asylum

Yamamuro: By the same token, when we consider the political space of Japanese modernity, Manchuria seems to possess distinctive significance. It is important to remember when considering Japanese modernity that with the exception of only a very small number of people, such as the actress Okada Yoshiko (1903–92) who defected to the Soviet Union in 1938, and the translator and dramatist Sano Seki (1905–66), scarcely any Japanese took refuge abroad. The issue itself of why there were so few Japanese refugees is important, I believe, in understanding the history of Japanese modernity. In modern Japanese history, Manchuria appears to be something of a space for taking quasi-refuge.

The S.M.R., too, provided a site accepting of large numbers of leftist converts. In this sense, it was the only asylum in modern Japan. A moment ago, I mentioned a certain image of Manchuria that was invested with ideals and in which was sought that which could not be realized in Japan. I think Shiba Ryōtarō (1923–96), the famed historical novelist, was no different in this regard. He was drawn to Mongolia out of a yearning for the wilderness of Manchuria and Mongolia. It bore the sense for him of an asylum to which one might escape from the space Japan blockaded. This phenomenon was not limited to men, for looking at the memoirs of Japanese women as well we see some who went to Manchuria because they could not develop personally in Japan. For example, there were a certain number of women who had dreams of developing into teachers or who wanted to teach people of other ethnicities.

In this sense, we have two polar images of Manchuria in tandem: the extremely dark image of a Manchuria as a hellish abyss and that of Manchuria as a site for asylum. Whichever extreme would emerge would depend on the person, and the image of Manchuria, then, was inevitably rent asunder. Although this is a bit of personal experience, I became quite close to Professor Matsuda Michio (1908–98). When I was writing *Kimera: Manshūkoku no shōzō* (Chimera, a portrait of Manzhouguo, published in 1993 [the volume herein translated—JAF]), he once said to me: "It's strange that you're using your energy on such a thing as this. As far as we're concerned, it'd be just fine to forget Manzhouguo altogether. It's bizarre that such a thing ever existed." I have never forgotten these strong words of his to me. For people who lived through it, Manchuria remained an object to be rejected but which continued nonetheless. I think that this is one of the reasons that evaluations offered by postwar scholarship on Manzhouguo has been split in bipolar fashion.

The Consciousness of the People Who Moved to Manchuria

Kan: What sort of people moved to Manchuria? What sort of consciousness of it did they take with them at the time?

Yamamuro: There are numerous cases of Japanese emigrants to Manchuria and the different forms their settlement patterns took. For example, I was particularly interested a group of migrants from the town of Kutami in Kumamoto Prefecture, a group of people who had suffered discrimination in Japan. After the war only one person from Kutami remained alive, all the others having been massacred. In order to eradicate their despair in Japan, the people moved to Manchuria and experienced the same kind of failure there and were discriminated against. They were unable to set down roots and were driven to move to reclaimed land. They died off and left no memoirs or other records, but discrimination followed them, despite their having expected that they would be going to a new land full of hope, a place free of discrimination. In the end it may have been the structure of Japanese society, but that structure had been brought over to Manchuria.

Not only did numerous Japanese farmers sent out as part of Japanese agricultural enterprises make the trip to Manchuria, but there is the case as well of urban businessmen from the Musashi-Koyama shopping street in Shinagawa Ward, Tokyo, who closed down every store on their shopping street and moved en masse to Manchuria. Kishi Nobusuke took charge of the arrangements for middle- and small-sized enterprises, and amid such "arrangements" there were numerous men and women who had been unable to make a living in Japan, who moved to Manchuria. The motivations and experiences behind the reasons for these many and varied people to relocate to Manchuria are just as many and varied and cannot be summed up neatly at this stage of our research. Rather, I think at this point that we need to record as many of their stories through interviews as we can for posterity.

What is clear is that in many cases they moved onto already tilled land; that is, they evidently entered terrain that they knew others had already been tilling. One important point, then, is how we seek to understand this. I myself have taken down a number of such oral testimonies, and at one point in the process, a man came forward and said: "We moved onto those people's land, and thus when the war was lost, it was only natural that we would suffer." Yet, it remains unclear to me if he actually drew this from his own experience or not. He may actually have heard such an argument later and then reformulated his experiences in accordance with it. Thus, it is another question altogether if such a consciousness actually existed at the time. Even when you take down oral testimony, then, it remains unclear if what you hear reflects actual experiences of the time or not. It is true, however, that all of this together forms the entirety of a human life. In fact, on the basis of just such a consciousness we have seen cases of people who participated in a reforestation campaign, received much help from Chinese students, and accordingly took a fresh look at their own Manzhouguo experience.

Of course, the people recounting their past are describing events from roughly their own twenties, meaning that they did not usually make the move to Manchuria on the basis of their own autonomous decision. Nonetheless, the next ten years or so represent the last chance we will have to transcribe these people's testimony—in other words, time is short. I myself spoke with a number of men who attended either the Daidō Academy or the Kenkoku (National Founding) University, men who have died in the past two or three years. In this important sense, there is a distinct limitation to the furtherance of research on Manzhouguo itself. Research making use of Chinese materials began in the latter half of the 1980s. We need now to compare and contrast it with the testimony on the Japanese side. This has been possible only in the fifteen or so years from the later 1980s. Thus, there is still much that we don't understand. More Chinese-language material will probably be published in future. Hence, before I rush to conclusions, I think it would be better to consider the research possibilities that these materials will open up for us.

Manzhouguo as Viewed from China

Kan: How was Manchuria or Japanese-controlled Manzhouguo viewed from the perspective of China?

Yamamuro: The view from China has consistently been that Manzhouguo was a "bogus state" or a "puppet state." This perspective is closely tied to Chinese views of the Sino-Japanese War. Manzhouguo came into existence in 1932, and with the conclusion of the Tanggu Truce in 1933, Japan stopped there for a time. Thus, if the Japanese invasion did not expand further outward from Manzhouguo, the Chinese government had taken the stance that, while it would not recognize the state of Manzhouguo, if the Guandong Army withdrew as far as the Great Wall, there would be no further problem.

Japan, though, commenced invasions beyond Manchuria, into Inner Mongolia and North China, and China had no choice but to make an issue of Manzhouguo. For, the Japanese invasion continued to widen as a ripple effect outward from Manzhouguo. Thus, in the Sino-Japanese peace negotiations, China had no option but to continue calling for the non-recognition of Manzhouguo and for the abolition of Manzhouguo itself.

Had Japan stopped with the former three provinces of the northeast (beyond the Great Wall), the Nationalist government would surely have avoided a military conflict and adopted a method of planning for a favorable turn of events through diplomatic negotiations. Despite this, Japan created the Mengjiang regime under Prince De (Demchudongrub, 1902–66) in Mongolia, and then with the same means used to establish Manzhouguo, they set up a series of puppet regimes in North China. These naturally gave rise to opposition, and Manzhouguo, the point of origin, itself necessarily became an issue. As long as it continued to exist, it was said, Sino-Japanese negotiations could not take place. I am of the opinion that Japan forced this situation into being.

Until the latter half of the 1980s—be it in the scholarly world or in the realm of public opinion—China only became an issue from the time of the Marco Polo Bridge Incident of July 1937 forward. Even the Manchuria Incident of September 1931 was not accorded that much serious attention. Gradually, on the Japanese side the expression "Fifteen-Year War" (1931–45) for the Sino-Japanese War became increasingly used, and in China as well a consciousness developed to see the Manchurian Incident as the starting point of Japan's war of invasion. Thus, from the 1980s the relative weight placed on Manzhouguo has risen profoundly within Chinese research on the war of resistance against Japan. In many books until then, at least, only the period from the Marco Polo Bridge Incident was taken up for analysis.

In the Chinese system, it is Shanghai universities which deal with research on the Nanjing government and universities in the northeast which research topics concerned with Manchuria. While, on the whole, research findings concerning Manzhouguo are shared, this is not necessarily the case. Manzhouguo is written about in textbooks, and thus, as I noted earlier, the Chinese students who come to work with me have a deep sense of repudiation toward it.

The Responses of Other Countries

Kan: How was Manzhouguo perceived in other foreign countries?

Yamamuro: In France it was regarded as a "mannequin state" and dubbed "Mannequinchuria," indicating a view consistent with the idea of a "puppet state." One quite interesting response concerned Central and South American reactions to the Asian policy of the United States. In Panama there was a strong antipathy for the U.S., because it was believed that what the U.S. was doing in Panama was no different from Japanese policy in Manchuria. Had America not created a puppet regime so that it might use the Panama Canal? With this background, a number of countries in Central and South America recognized Manzhouguo at a rather early stage. Ordinarily, they would perforce have opposed what Japan had done, and this recognition was a refracted response: they were supporting Japan as a means of opposing the United States.

In the end, a good number of countries, including the Vatican, recognized Manzhouguo. Even Russia, in order to engage in negotaitions over the transfer of the North China Railway line, effectively recognized Manzhouguo as a state. Thus, it was accepted after a fashion as a sovereign state, although in substance it was seen as a puppet regime.

There is one further point of interest and this involves the view of such American magazines as *Fortune*, which claimed that Manzhouguo was an immense laboratory created by the Japanese army. The Japanese army would use the experiments carried out in Manchuria, it argued, in constructing a Japanese system for full national mobilization and a militarized state. This point is vital to understanding the link between Manzhouguo and Japan.

Manzhouguo and the Flow of Peoples in World History

Yamamuro: One additional issue is the existential importance of Manchuria for the Jewish people. Shanghai was the most important Jewish place of asylum in Asia, but second to it was Manchuria. Of course, once the Tripartite Alliance was signed among Japan, Germany, and Italy, they were to be expelled from Manchuria, too, but such schemes as the "Fugu Plan" conceived of a harmony of the six ethnicities—the five initially conjured up and the Jews—and military officers such as Yasue Norihiro (1888–1950) and Inuzuka Koreshige (1890–1965) were actively trying to realize it. "Fugu" or blowfish carried the meaning that, although this kind of fish is delectable, if it disagrees with you, its poison can be especially strong. If Jewish capital could be well used, this scheme envisioned, then it could be of great value. In the sense of using such a plan to control the Jews in the United States, this tactic was an extremely calculated political ploy.

Reading through the memoirs of people who actually lived in Manzhouguo, it appears that places such as Harbin were relatively easy for Jews and White Russians to live in. We know a bit about what happened to White Russian men who graduated from Kenkoku University. We thus need research which will examine what Manzhouguo, or the Kenkoku University, may have meant for White Russians. For not only Jews, but Muslims who had escaped from Central Asia as well, Manzhouguo provided a kind of asylum, as I describe it in my recent book, *Shisō kadai to shite no Ajia* (Asia as an intellectual task, published 2001), an important site where people who had escaped Soviet oppression could live. It is an undeniable irony of world history that, for people who escaped from Europe, Russia, and Central Asia, Manchuria bore importance as a space for survival. There were many more who traveled through Manchuria en route to the United States, and we need studies which examine this phenomenon.

Needless to say, there is as well the issue of how Manzhouguo tried to use the Jews and Muslims. Research on ethnic groups in Manzhouguo to this point has examined only the "five ethnicities," but we need to insert into our vision the flows of such world-historical peoples as the Jews and Muslims and consider the place of Manzhouguo in their migrations. We are collecting material in this area now. There is even a recent book about Poles in Manchuria, published in Poland, describing who was there and what they did.

Manzhouguo and Postwar East Asia

Kan: Finally, at the national level or at the individual level, how should we best understand Manchuria and Manzhouguo as a whole? What are your feelings on this topic?

Yamamuro: It is extremely difficult to try to generalize, but I think that we must consider this issue—including the problem of war responsibility—in a multilayered manner. I myself think that at present this is a theme for future research, not a time at which we can offer generalizations. Thus, let me just say a few words about the directions subsequent research might take and how we can try to place Manzhouguo in world history.

Although I have written about it in a number of articles, I think we need to reassess once more the meaning of Manzhouguo in postwar Asia. The legitimacy of the Chinese Communist Party derives at least one of its bases in the fact that it won the anti-Japanese war which began with the Manchurian Incident. In this way, the fact that some Japanese argue for the legitimacy of Manzhouguo thus denies the very legitimacy of the Chinese Communist Party. This dispute is unproductive, with a strong probability of the two sides following parallel tracks semipermanently.

Let me focus for a moment, though, on the importance of Manzhouguo on the Korean peninsula in postwar East Asia. First, in the Republic of Korea there were a number of men who were educated in Manzhouguo—such as Pak Chŏng-hŭi (1917–79) and Ch'oe Kyu-ha (b. 1919) who graduated from the Daidō Academy—and acquired power in postwar Korea. In this instance, Manzhouguo served as a supply base for human talent. We certainly cannot say this was always the case, for the debate continues over what the "pro-Japan faction" in Korea was. I have only introduced a very limited number of such men in my own work, but in fact there were a large number of them.

In North Korea as well, Kim Il-sŏng (1912–94) derived one of the bases of his legitimacy in the victory against Japan in Manchuria, and this legacy continues for North Korea today. There are pros and cons, but the postwar in East Asia cannot be understood without Manzhouguo.

By the same token, as concerns wartime and postwar Japan, Tōjō Hideki (1884–1948) came to amass such great power by virtue of the unification of the military police (*kenpei*) and the regular police in Manzhouguo. It was the first case he confronted as commanding officer of the Guandong Army's military police, when he was awakened to his administrative skills. Until that point, he had always been treated rather coldly in Japan, but in the process of his acquisition of power thereafter, the administrative experience tying him to the military police in Manchuria was to have critical importance.

Kishi Nobusuke spent only three years in Manchuria, but the money and personnel he put together at that time was to have a huge impact on postwar politics. Together with such men as Shiina Etsusaburō (1898–1979), Nemoto Ryūtarō (b. 1907), Hirashima Toshio (b. 1891), these mainstays of the Liberal Democratic Party all had Manchurian experience. At the time of the revision of the Japan-U.S. Security Treaty (Anpo) in 1960, Kishi made a trip to Southeast Asia before visiting the United States. The reason for this, in Kishi's words, was that, for Japan to cross swords as equals with the United States, it was best for it to assume a position as the leader of Asia. Only then, as he put it, would Japan be on an equal standing with the United States and thus be in a position to have the Anpo Treaty revised.

In reply to a question from an interviewer, Kishi noted: "My present feeling that Japan must become the leader of Asia is no different from the consciousness I had when I went to Manzhouguo. This has not changed in the least even in the postwar era. If indeed I possess a kind of pan-Asianism, then my present sense of things is completely linked to the time when I traveled to Manzhouguo." Thus, his Manzhouguo experience—including the money he amassed—played an extremely important role in his career. Although a well known story, Kishi told a fellow bureaucrat upon returning to Japan: "It's best to use money after filtering it." The effectively plutocratic essence of the Liberal Democratic Party as it has come down to us now may then be said to trace its roots back to Manchuria.

The Tactile Importance of the Experience of Having Known Asia

Yamamuro: The generation of Japanese prime ministers from Yoshida Shigeru (1878–1967), who was consul-general in Fengtian, and Kishi down to Fukuda Takeo (1905–95) and Ōhira Masayoshi (1910–80) all had Asian experience. When he was serving as a secretary in the Ministry of

Foreign Affairs, Fukuda spent over two years in Nanjing as an advisor on economic affairs to the government of the Republic of China. Ōhira worked in the Asian Development Board in Zhangjiakou and the liaison section of the Mengjiang regime.

Through the years of Fukuda and Ōhira, it was people who knew Asia as a tactile experience who served as prime ministers. Thereafter, Japanese policy toward Asia became thoroughly clumsy and unskilled. To be sure, the early men had stood on the side of the rulers, but they understood, as if it was experience acquired through their skin, about the vastness of the Asian mainland, the atmosphere prevailing there, and the enormity of the population. This also meant that they understood its formidable character. The prime ministers who followed them, however, lacked as a sense of touch this spatial understanding of Asia and China, and the influence exerted by this absence of experience on Japanese policy vis-à-vis Asia has been immense. In particular, from Hosokawa Morihiro (b. 1938) to the Koizumi Jun'ichirō (b. 1942) now, the continued blur of Japan's Asian policy is, I believe, linked to a lack of Asian experience. I would even go so far as to say that there is no remedy for this lack of sensibility.

I by no means want to leave the impression that their role in colonial rule was a good thing, but the fact that the policies of Japanese political figures, including diplomatic officials, toward Asia has now entered a dangerous stage is, in my view, heavily influenced by the lack of experience—including that acquired in Manzhouguo—gained through the senses and not simply having seen the place but having lived there. This will remain a problem for the future. I would argue for the need for men and women who wish to become politicians to spend two or three years wandering about various sites in Asia.

The Importance of a Spatial Consciousness

Yamamuro: In the cultural arena, Manchuria was at the vanguard in coming into contact with European civilization. This is something I would particularly wish to emphasize.[2]

Scholarship on Manchuria to this point has only addressed the issue of time. We also, I believe, need to address the issues of space and spatial consciousness. We need to consider how at different sites and different climes what sorts of ideas and thoughts people came up. This is particularly liable to be the case in the sealed-off space of Japan. In a poem by Anzai Fuyue (1898–1965), there is the line, "A butterfly flew across the Tatar Strait" (*Chōchō ga ippiki Dattan kaikyō o watatte itta*); if you do not actually know something of the space of Manchuria, this line makes no sense whatsoever. It evokes the sensation of a spatial differentiation among the expansive sky, the vast earth, and the diminutive place of mankind. In Japan, by contrast, everything is seen merely in life size. The sensibility cannot easily be expressed in words, but I believe it to be connected to many things. Thus, the sensibility which Gotō Shinpei experienced during his period of rule in Taiwan would have been altogether different from that experienced during his time in Manchuria.

How Shall We Think About the "Legacy" of Manzhouguo?

Yamamuro: There are as well issues concerned with Manzhouguo after the end of the war: the problem of withdrawal back to Japan and that of people who stayed behind in China to work at reviving various industries. For example, in the world of culture, there is the case of Uchida Tomu (1898–1970) who after the war filmed such movies as *Kiga no kaikyō* (literally, Straits of hunger, 1964; sometimes rendered into English as *A Fugitive from the Past*). He remained in China for several years after the end of the war and contributed to the revitalization of postwar Chinese cinema. The issue of "remaining behind" is itself extremely complicated. A man by the name of Yamamoto Shirō remained behind in China where he lived for half a century; I met him in Beijing in the last years of his life. A man such as he had effectively become Chinese. The issue of what relationship Japanese have to the problems of men such as Yamamoto and problems of the revival of postwar East Asia, leaving aside how this might be treated by Chinese, needs to be studied by Japanese.

Let me say a word about some recently discovered materials. In work to date on overseas students, there has been virtually nothing that deals with students in Japan from Manzhouguo. When we look at this new material, though, it is not the case at all that students coming from Manchuria meekly complied with Japanese rule. In Japan they had contacts with Taiwanese and Koreans and were active in the formation of the East Asian Anti-Japanese Youth League and the Salvation Association for Northeastern Youth. What these groups were exactly remains unclear now, but the issue of how young men and women who came to Japan from Manzhouguo lived their lives and what sorts of experiences and perceptions they had during the Manzhouguo era have been thoroughgoing blanks in our research work to date. This is another subject that we must address in future.

One Korean whom I had occasion to meet came to Japan as a student, studied sociology, went to the United States after the war, became a well-known scholar, and was invited to Stockholm. He had the following to say: "I never thought that control over Manzhouguo was a good thing, but for me in my life, being able to study there and travel to Japan was truly a savior. Had that not transpired, I would undoubtedly have spent my entire life as a peasant." There are, of course, a variety of problems here, for the same was true for Pak Chōng-hūi. He came from an impoverished family, and had he not been able to study at public expense at the army academy, he would not likely have subsequently risen to such a pivotal position in the army.

Thus, although it cannot be denied that "harmony of the five ethnicities" during the era of Japanese colonial rule was merely a slogan, by virtue of the existence of this slogan, it was decided that, for example, a certain number of Koreans would of necessity be admitted into certain schools. Of course, had there not been Japanese colonial rule, perhaps there would have been more and different possibilities for more people. However, amid all this, while Manzhouguo may have been an illusion, by raising such banners as "harmony of the five ethnicites" and "ethnic cooperation," clearly certain avenues were opened to people who would have been unable to rise to the surface under the previous warlord rule.

Even regarding problems on the postwar Korean peninsula, compared to those who have come to study in Japan, those who experienced Manzhouguo were better able to make the most of their abilities. Consideration of the formation of political spaces in postwar Asia, including such a comparative issue, offers us hints for future research on Manzhouguo. Needless to say, this is probably a bit of a self-serving conclusion for my part.

Ultimately, What Was Manzhouguo?

Yamamuro: When we contemplate just what Manzhouguo actually was, in the final analysis we come to relations between the nation and the people, between the state and the individual.

Abe Kōbō (1924–93) has a novel entitled *Kemonotachi wa kokyō o mezasu* (The beasts head for home). It takes place at a time when Manzhouguo has collapsed, and people cut off from and stripped of their state, their ethnic group, and their class wander about in search of a space to which they ought to return. The problem here is that the men who should have protected the state and its people—namely, the Guandong Army—were the first to flee the scene. What, then, was an army in the state? This is an issue that includes the problem of emergency laws. One has to write laws to plan for emergencies of state, but if one actually has to ask what ought be protected—the nation or the individual—the rights of the individual— the protection of individual rights is looked after only once obligations are defined. In the final analysis, an army protects itself; it is moved solely by what keeps injury to its own at a minimum.

How then in the case of Manzhouguo did the state and the military treat individuals who were abandoned or left behind? As to the issue of how the individual is tied to the state, this was one experience in which sacrifices called for were truly immense. If we include the over 600,000 Japanese who were interned in Siberia and the over 60,000 who died, this was too great a sacrifice. However, I think we must take account of Manchuria and

Manzhouguo, as food for thought, when we consider the issues surrounding coexistence within multiethnic societies, perhaps the most important question of the twenty-first century, and consider in this mix the import of Manzhouguo and the individuals within it in the history of the twentieth-century state, as well as the ideas of collaboration and harmony among peoples who transcended nationality.

In a sense, the issues of Manchuria and Manzhouguo may be seen as anachronistic, but they are topics that need to be examined further. To repay the excessively large sacrifices even a little, extract something human from them, and leave something behind, I believe this is something we have to do.

June 15, 2002

Appendix (2004)
On the Historical Significance
of Manchuria and Manzhouguo

As this book bears the subtitle "A Portrait of Manzhouguo," the discussion is aimed primarily at elucidating from the perspective of political science and legal history the historical process beginning with the state formation of Manzhouguo, proceeding to its transformation, and ultimately to its demise. Thus, for readers interested in the historical significance of Manchuria and Manzhouguo, including the state's prehistory, issues that occurred after the end of World War II, and images of Manchuria, this volume has been limited, perhaps even insufficient. In addition, it is in the nature of "new books" that they play a kind of guidance role concerning the issues dealt with, and this was a request I certainly sought to fulfill. In what follows, I have adopted a hypothetical question-and-answer format to address the topic of Manchuria's and Manzhouguo's historical importance. Let me now offer my views in response to questions which readers may have raised.

Question 1: The place name Manchuria and the ethnonym Manchu are the same in Japanese (*Manshū*), as they are in Chinese (*Manzhou*). What is the origin and meaning of this term?

   The people who lived on the territory which the Japanese dubbed Manshū (Manchuria) until 1945 were the Jurchens. They professed belief within the Buddhist faith in the bodhisattva Manju who revered Manjusri who was said to govern knowledge and to pacify and preserve a land in the East. Thus, after they adopted Chinese characters, they selected appropriate characters with pronunciation approximating Manju (or Manzhou). Early in the seventeenth century, the founder of the Jianzhou Jurchens, Nurhaci (1559–1626, surname Aisin Gioro), unified the entire body of Jurchens, who had been divided into Jianzhou, Haixi, and Yeman tribes, and created a state which was called in the Jurchen language "Manju gurun" (or Manzhouguo). For an ethnonym, they decided to use Jurchen. In interactions with the Ming dynasty and Korea, however, they used Aisin (meaning "gold" in their language, "Jin" in Chinese), and thus were called the Later Jin. But their original Jurchen-language state name was "Manju." In 1636 Hong Taiji (1592–1643), the second ruler of the Later Jin, changed the name of their state to the "Great Qing." Thus, "Manju" disappeared as a dynastic or state name, and thereafter came to be used as their ethnonym in place of Jurchen.

For these reasons, at the time of the 1911 Revolution which toppled the Qing dynasty of a non-Chinese people, *mie Man xing Han* ("destroy the Manchus, revive the Han") became a slogan aimed at returning sovereignty over China to the Han Chinese and annihilating the Manchus. The result was the establishment of the Republic of China in 1912. As a consequence, the Guandong Army created Manzhouguo and made Puyi (1906–67) chief executive of it on land on which a conquest dynasty had earlier arisen. This was difficult for the Han people, who comprised the great majority of the people of the Republic of China, to accept. Yet, in the world of Japanese scholarship at the time, the forgery theory of Professor Ichimura Sanjirō (1864–1947) became influential. He argued that, when Hong Taiji changed the dynastic name to "Great Qing," he erased all mention of the Later Jin, and he forged the name "Manju," the term so dear to his father, Nurhaci (who was seen as an incarnation of the bodhisattva Manjusri), and concocted the name "Manzhou" (with the water radical). With the establishment of the state of Manzhouguo in 1932, no one in Japan thought of it as a revival of the "Manju gurun" of the Jurchens.

Question 2: Despite the fact that in postwar Japan the character pronounced *shū* in *Manshū* (Manchuria) and *Manshūkoku* (Manzhouguo) is written without the water radical on the left, why in this volume is that older form of the character assiduously adhered to?

As we have seen in the previous question, the Chinese characters assigned to represent "Manju" were first affixed with the *shū* character written with the water radical. We must, nonetheless, consider the fact that attaching the water radical had a great deal of significance in terms of demonstrating the legitimacy of the Jurchen dynasty. Chinese dynasties indicated their own legitimacy on the basis of the five phases of "wood, fire, earth, gold, and water." The Ming dynasty which preceded the Qing took "fire" as its symbol, making it a dynasty of "fire morality." The Qing which toppled it took the symbol of "water" which transcends "fire" and thus became a dynasty of "water morality." Thus, both the dynasty name "Qing" and the ethnonym "Manzhou" (both characters) were written with the water radical. One theory has been put forward arguing that the attachment of the water radical to *shū* derived from a toponym, but it is worth noting here that, in the *Manzhou yuanliu kao* (Study of the origins of the Manchus, 1778) of A-gui (1717–97) and others, "Manzhou" is given as a tribal name, never as a place name. Although it has not been formalized in China, there were instances when the term was used as a toponym in the Qing period to indicate the area east of eastern Inner Mongolia, north of the Yalu and Tumen Rivers, and south of the Amur River.

At the end of the nineteenth century, this region we have just described was called by such names in China as Liaodong (East of the Liao River), Dongsansheng (Three Eastern Provinces), Dongbei (Northeast), and the like. A governor-general was assigned to the region in 1907, just as in China proper, and hence Dongbei or Dongsansheng—comprising the three provinces of Liaoning (depending on time frame, also known as Shengjing and Fengtian), Jilin, and Heilongjiang—became the generally used terms. Thus, in the twentieth century, the term "Manzhou" was used by the Japanese but not as a noun by the Chinese; employing the correct characters based on its origins and history, *Manzhou* (Manchuria, Japanese *Manshū*) and *Manzhouguo* (Manchukuo, Japanese *Manshūkoku*) should be written with the water radical.

Question 3: Historically what perceptions did the Japanese have of this region?

In antiquity, this region was known by such toponyms as Sushen, Koguryŏ, Liaodong, Mohe, and the like. With the founding of the kingdom of Bohai (Parhae) in 698 c.e., there began a period lasting some 190 years of intercourse with Japan in which emissaries from Bohai came to Japan thirty-four times. It was later understood to be terrain under the control of the (Khitan) Liao, (Jurchen) Jin, and (Mongol) Yuan dynasties. In the Edo period, Japanese referred to the region by such place names as Dattan (Tatar), Santan, Kokuryū, Oranke, and the like. Santan (Chinese, Shandan) comes from "Janta," what the Olcha people living in the Amur River region were called. In the language of the Ainu people, this is said to have become Santan, and thus the Santan people engaged in trade with Japan at Sakhalin. The Santan people received ancient Chinese ceremonial dress and embroidery from officials in Manchuria; they passed through the Ainu and traveled to Japan whence they became a treasured item known as "Ezo-nishiki" (Ainu or Hokkaido embroidery). Recognition of this terrain as "Dattan" (Tatar), however, seems clearly to have come later. A group of fifteen shipwrecked Japanese from Matsumae (in Hokkaido) visited Shengjing (now Shengyang) and Beijing, and after repatriation the the written statement they gave bore the title *Dattan hyōryū ki* (Chronicle of a Shipwreck in Tatary).

The circumstances surrounding the emergence of "Manshū" (*Manzhou*) as the toponym for the region can be seen in the changes in references in the *Ka'i hentai* (Tranformation from Civilized [Ming] to Barbaraian [Qing]) which the Tokugawa shogunate ordered Hayashi Gahō (Shunsai, 1618–80) to compile upon hearing the news from overseas that in 1644 the

Qing dynasty had replaced the Ming. After Gahō's death, his son Hayashi Hōkō (Nobuatsu, 1644–1732) continued his father's work until it was completed in 1724. Thus, initially they referred to the Jurchens as the "Tatar barbarians of the North" (*Dattan hokuryo*), and later they dubbed the Qing dynasty Tatars (*Dattan*) or Tatar barbarians (*Datsuryo*). Inasmuch as the Hayashi family revered the Zhu Xi School of Neo-Confucianism (Hayashi Hōkō was the first head of the imperial college), it was only natural that they looked down on the Qing as Tatar barbarians in contrast to the civilization of the Ming dynasty, which also revered the Zhu Xi School. However, when it became known in Japan through Chinese who from 1684 traveled to Nagasaki of the style of rulership of the Kangxi Emperor, we find the emergence of the expression, "the Kangxi Emperor's land of Tatary." This changed in 1687 to "the Kangxi Emperor's land of Manchuria" and "the Great Qing's land of Manchuria." Thus, in place of "Dattan," they began using "Manshū" for the place name of Manchuria, and this usage stuck thereafter.

Let me raise one example to illustrate in concrete terms what "Manshū" meant in the geographical understanding of the Japanese people. In his *Henyō bunkaizo kō* (Analysis of Maps from the Frontiers and Borders) of 1804, Kondō Seisai (Jūzō, 1771–1829) wrote: "The West moves from Karafuto [Sakhalin] to the border of Manshū Santan. The geography [of this region] has yet to have been investigated thoroughly. . . . We have yet to see or hear anything ordinary about the distant sea to the far north and the barbarians' dens." This would indicate that "Manshū" was thought of as an undeveloped border region, a "frontier" wherein one found "barbarians' dens." Prior to World War II, Kondō, though, was called the "founder of Manchurian geography" in Japan. In his "study of Manchuria" which this book brings together, he read and collected information in numerous Chinese and Japanese historical texts, and he clearly explained where "Dattan" and "Oranke" differed from Manchuria.

Later still, on a "Outline Map of Japan's Frontiers" prepared by Takahashi Kageyasu (1785–1829) around 1811, the region in question became "Manshū" and "Seikei" (Shengjing).[1] It was then reprinted in editions of Philipp Franz von Siebolt's (1796–1866) famous work, *Nippon*, from 1832, and transcribed there as "Mandscheu." Western geographical texts written by Europeans from the 1840s call this area "Manchuria," and when Japanese studied conditions in the West, they apparently came to accept Manshū (Manchuria) as a place name.

In the late Edo period when Russia and the United States, among others, sent vessels to Japan asking it to open its doors, "Manshū" (Manchuria) began to be seen as a place linked intimately with Japan's destiny. For example, Hashimoto Sanai (1834–59), who advocated a Russo-Japanese alliance, argued: "The border of Santan and Manshū links up with the state of Korea. Furthermore, it belongs territorially neither to an American state nor to

Indian territory, making it not very desirable." In observance of treaties with Russia and the United States, Yoshida Shōin (1830–59) once advocated: "We should nurture national strength and then cut off Korea, Manchuria, and China which should be easy enough to accomplish. What we will lose to Russia in trade will be made up for in land with Korea and Manchuria." This position of his is well known. Perhaps we can see a straight line from views of this sort as modern Japanese history moved from the late Edo period on to seek the territorial control over Korea and Manchuria. Of course, though, in the late Edo period this was no more in reality than an empty dream.

However, it is highly important for us to note that, at the end of the Edo period, the issue of Korea and Manchuria was conceived solely within the framework of relations with Russia and the United States already.

Question 4: From the middle of the nineteenth century when the Japanese began using the term *Manshū* (Manchuria, with the water radical), what condition was this terrain in?

After the Qing dynasty entered Beijing, it regarded the terrain on which it had arisen as sacred—the ancient land on which its ancestors had originated. With the aim of preserving it, the government adopted a policy known as the "closing off" of Manchuria. This entailed placing it under the jurisdiction of the special administration and military structure of the Manchu Eight Banners (resident on Manchurian soil to defend it), assigning men to such positions as Shengjing general and Jilin general, and prohibiting the entrance or relocation of Han or any ethnic group other than Manchus to the region. Because of this policy, however, the land became barren and the population plummeted. Therefore, they had no choice but to relax the policy, and in the first half of the nineteenth century a trickle of Han Chinese flowed into the area.

By the same token, from the middle of the seventeenth century, Russians had been moving South to the Amur River and putting pressure on the Qing's northern border. Thus, the Kangxi Emperor launched a counterattack, and on the basis of the Treaty of Nerchinsk of 1698, the border between the two countries was fixed at the Argun River at the Outer Xing'an Mountains. Later, however, the Russians returned to their policy of moving southward, and with the 1858 Treaty of Aigun, Russia gained recognition for its control over the left bank of the Amur River and the right to sail ships along the Sungari River. Although the Qing court rejected and fought against this, in the Treaty of Beijing in 1860 these rights were reaffirmed and the eastern bank of the Ussuri River was ceded to Russia as well. One fishing village by the name of Haicanwei acquired the name Vladivostok, which had the meaning "mastery over the East." The Maritime Province centered here was then developed as Russian terrain.

At the time of the Arrow Incident in 1858, the Qing signed the Treaty of

Tianjin with Great Britain, which compelled them to open the port of Niu-
zhuang. Foreign interests were now expanding all the way from the south.
At the end of the nineteenth century, one might say that the northeastern
part of China floated to the surface as the largest colony in Asia.

Question 5: In the era when Russia and Britain, among other foreign
powers, encroached upon China, what relations did Japan have with
Manchuria?

The Japanese began emigrating to Manchuria in the 1880s, and the
number of Japanese resident there in 1904, at the time of the commencement of the Russo-Japanese War, was on the order of 3,000. Its importance
at the time of the compulsory cession to Japan of the Liaodong Peninsula,
according to the terms of the Treaty of Shimonoseki concluding Japan's
victory in the Sino-Japanese War, was less the acquisition of land for Japanese emigrants than it was the geographical significance of protecting militarily strategic terrain, such as control over the port of Lüshun.

From the perspective of Japan, Manchuria was on the far side of the Korean Peninsula. It was less directly at issue. First was recognition of the geographic importance of Korea, and then, it would appear, the importance of
Manchuria surfaced as contiguous terrain. This was indicated symbolically
in the thinking of Prime Minister Yamagata Aritomo (1838–1922) who
gave a speech before the first Diet of 1890 in which he distinguished a "line
of sovereignty" and a "line of interest." Although Inoue Kowashi (1843–95)
drafted this, his was a statement of national defense based on a spatial perception: the line of sovereignty was the national border, and to protect it
Japan had to set up a zone in which it could exercise its own powers of influence before the frontier to stave off the incursions of foreign enemies,
and Japan had to protect the borderline of this zone's edges as a line of interest. From this perspective, given Japan's geopolitical conditions, it had
no choice but, as its line of interest, first to protect the Korean Peninsula
which was seen as a dagger that had been thrust into its flank, a particularly
weak point in the Japanese archipelago with its long national borderline. If
the countries that would penetrate this dagger were China and Russia, then
there was a certain inevitability that made the Sino-Japanese War and the
Russo-Japanese War all but impossible to avoid.

This all became linked to the view of a "Manchurian-Mongolian lifeline":
after having actually gone through these two wars and securing Korea,
then there was Manchuria beyond Korea to be controlled, and Mongolia
beyond Manchuria.

In this way, ideas about a line of interest ceaselessly appeared which argued for creating yet another sphere of influence before the border. People became captive to a near-persecution complex in which failure to do
so meant a lack of security. Of course, the year of 1890 in which Yamagata
delivered his speech at the first Diet lay behind the emergence of such an

understanding of things. Playing a major role here was the fact that in 1891 Russia started construction of the Trans-Siberian Railway. Already in 1887 plans for the construction of this rail line across Siberia were reported in the press. The *Chōya shinbun* for August 12 of that year noted perceptively: "This railway will pioneer Siberia. Even if we do not wait for the conclusion to this which will be a flourishing border region to the North of Manchuria and Mongolia, the principal objective lies not in this but in the ease of deploying troops." With construction on the railway, as everyone was able to surmise, imperial Russia was able to develop its military might to the Far East. Whereas Manchuria had hitherto been seen as a vast, undeveloped territory beyond the Sea of Japan on the other side of the Korean Peninsula, with the opening of traffic on the Trans-Siberian Railway, the possibility now opened up that a space linking it as far as mighty Europe to its rear might come bearing down directly on Japan. In roughly two weeks, Russia would have the capacity to transport as far as the Pacific Coast its army which boasted the largest force of men under arms stationed in Europe. The military importance of Manchuria soared dramatically.

Even after the Siberian Railway was completed, though, Vladivostok was still frozen throughout the winter; the menace was itself half-destroyed. An even greater threat now lay in the fact that Russia, having laid track for the Trans-Siberian Railway, was moving south into Manchuria seeking an ice-free port, was trying to secure effective controlling power over the Korean Peninsula and the Liaodong Peninsula, and would monopolize control of the seas at the Sea of Japan. As a result of the Tripartite Intervention, in 1898 Russia obtained leasing rights to Lüshun (Port Arthur) and Dalian (Russian *Dal'ny*, Japanese *Dairen*) in the Liaodong Peninsula which Japan was compelled to return, began to lay tracks linking Dalian with the Siberian rail line, and began construction on a major harbor there. As the advent of an urgent threat, these facts only increased the sense of emergency among Japanese. In 1898 Japan compelled Korea to build a railway linking Seoul and Pusan, a northern policy set to resist the southern policy of the Russian railway.

Question 6: How was Russian encroachment into Manchuria linked to the Russo-Japanese War?

The one event which turned Russia's place in Manchuria into a serious issue for the entire world of East Asia was the Boxer Uprising of 1900. When the Boxer movement spread into Manchuria, roughly two-thirds of the Russian railway linking Harbin with Dalian was destroyed; and calling for reconstruction of the railway and protection of its nationals living in the region, Russia dispatched troops. Despite the fact, though, that the protocol concluding the Boxer incident was signed in 1901 and should have resolved all issues, Russia ignored accords it had on three occasions concluded with the Qing court and continued to keep its troops in place, making no effort to withdraw them. For Japan which was obligated to protect Korea because of the Sino-Japanese War, this problem could simply not be overlooked, for it posed a dangerous forewarning as Russia had now moved troops as far as the Korean Peninsula with which Manchuria shared a frontier.

Instead of compelling Russia to recognize Japan's superior position in Korea, Itō Hirobumi (1841–1909) and Inoue Kaoru (1835–1915) both planned for joint Russo-Japanese influence by recognizing Russia's superior position in Manchuria and thus avoiding a clash. This stance was dubbed a Manchuria-Korea exchange or Russo-Japanese agreement. Katsura Tarō (1848–1913), Komura Jūtarō (1855–1911), and Hayashi Tadasu (1850–1913), by contrast, argued that, even if accord was reached with Russia, it was impossible to prevent its moving southward, and that it would thus be much more effective to forge a Anglo-Japanese alliance to oppose Russia in order to forestall this movement. At a meeting of Japan's senior leaders in December 1901, this latter position—moving toward signing a Anglo-Japanese Alliance—was endorsed. By the same token, in 1896 Korean King Kojong (1852–1919, r. 1864–1907) took refuge in the Russian Mission in Seoul, a move which not only made the Korean pro-Russian party more influential than before, but also meant there would be no advantage whatsoever in a Russo-Japanese trade-off, with Japan offering Russia in Korea what it sought in Manchuria; there was thus no way for a position advocating a Manchuria-Korea exchange to get off the ground.

Although Manchuria, which remained a pending issue, was ultimately Chinese territory, Russia provoked a great massacre of Chinese in the northern Manchuria border region when its troops were sent there. Also, after the incident was resolved the Russians continued to hold their position, which lit the flames of nationalism in China. Chinese studying in Japan at the time formed the nucleus in the creation of a Resist-Russia Volunteer Corps. This movement set its sights on physically removing Russian troops from the region. While the Empress Dowager (1835–1908) and the Guangxu Emperor (1871–1908) had escaped and remained in hiding in Xi'an, diplomatic anxieties led to an effort to quash this movement in the hope that Russia would on its own withdraw its troops. This only led to greater distrust of the Qing court and fanned the flames of a revolutionary anti-Qing movement. The Resist-Russia Volunteer Corps became the Militant People's Educational Association, and finally in 1905 it forged links with the Chinese Revolutionary Alliance of Sun Zhongshan (Sun Yat-sen, 1866–1925) and others in Tokyo. The fact that the Qing court erred in its manner of dealing with the Russian problem in Manchuria, this land on which it had arisen, led to its demise. For the Manchu people of the Qing, Manchuria was sacred ancestral terrain, but nearly 270 years had passed since the court had become separated from that terrain, as a process of Sinification had set in; for the Han Chinese, Manchuria evoked a place beyond the Great Wall, far from the heart of things. Thus, the Han did not assign much weight to defending the region, and hence an air pocket of sorts emerged in this area.

Russia moved in and sought to have its influence permeate Korea as well, events which caused Japanese sense of fears to heighten. With the opening of the Trans-Siberian Railway set for 1904, the transport of military goods from Europe to Dalian would become possible, and with possession of the two ice-free ports of Lüshun and Dalian, Russia would obtain control of the Sea of Japan. Even if this did not come to pass, the possibility remained low that Japan with its difference in quality in military might would be able to root Russia out of Manchuria. If it did come to pass, then despite the Japanese army's overwhelming inferiority of troops—240,000 men as compared to Russia's overall army with 2,070,000 men—Japan pushed off to commence hostilities with Russia before the completion of the Trans-Siberian Railway.

At the time of the departure for the front, the great novelist Mori Ōgai (1862–1922) tried to encourage the fighting morale of the troops: "On the day that the railway reaches Beijing, China's destruction will be directly before our eyes, and should the Korean Peninsula fall, will our land be safe? . . . We shall attack Russia which has for 300 years predominated. The time has come."[2] These lines realistically indicate the spiritual condition of how the encroachment of Russia into the world of East Asia by means of this railway were being handled.

Question 7: How did Japan's position in Manchuria change as a result of the Russo-Japanese War?

As a result of its victory in the Russo-Japanese War, Japan acquired from Russia a leasehold in the Guandong Territory (including Lüshun and Dalian) as well as management rights and a leasehold on the attached territory of the South Manchurian Railway (S.M.R.), by virtue of the Portsmouth Treaty of 1905 and the "Sino-Japanese Treaty Concerning Manchuria." This effectively laid the cornerstone for control over Manchuria.

Control over Manchuria, however, stoked the flames of a new international conflict. Japan had promised the Qing court, when it commenced hostilities with Russia, that after the war's conclusion it would return Manchuria to the Qing. Toward Europe, Japan had sought support for opening Manchuria for the purpose of freedom of commerce. Nonetheless, after the signing of the Portsmouth Treaty, Kodama Gentarō (1852–1907), chief of the general staff, among others, called for a military government on occupied Manchurian terrain and adopted a policy of the primacy of military objectives by establishing a Guandong Government-General which oversaw the office of the military government. In so doing, he elicited a confrontation with the authorities in the Three Eastern Provinces of Qing China, the United States, and Great Britain. By contrast, Resident-General in Korea Itō Hirobumi, who argued firmly to maintain cooperation with the Western powers and an open-door policy, proposed to Prime Minister Saionji Kinmochi (1849–1940) that he hold a conference in the Diet on the Manchurian issue with a resolution to gradually dismantle the military government there, open Dalian, and rename the Guandong governor-general, among other things. Kodama believed that "the sole key to managing Manchuria after the war was openly to adorn the mask of railway management and quietly put all manner of installations into place."[3] He and those of his ilk thus, naturally, held that management of Manchuria was Japan's exclusive and monopoly right. Hence, Itō argued: "Chief of Staff Kodama had apparently misunderstood Japan's position in Manchuria fundamentally. Japanese rights in Manchuria were ceded by Russia by virtue of a treaty. . . . Manchuria is not a subject state of Japan. It is purely a part of Qing terrain."[4] Prime Minister Saionji dealt with the issue along these lines.

The policy line of opening Manchuria by emphasizing Qing sovereignty there, however, was modified in 1907 when a treaty with Russia was concluded and moved further toward Russia and Japan planning together for joint expansion of their control in Manchuria and Mongolia and peace in the region. In other words, in the secret agreement of the first accords signed between Russia and Japan in July 1907, mutual recognition was reached for the special interests of Japan in Korea and Russia in Outer Mongolia. It was thus determined that southern Manchuria fell within Japan's range of interests and northern Manchuira within Russia's. With the second Russo-Japanese accords of 1910, the two countries sought to maintain the present situation in Manchuria by strengthening the preservation of railroad interests so as to forestall the encroachment into Manchuria of the United States.

This movement toward exclusive control over Manchuria by Russia and Japan was strongly resisted by Great Britain, which was trying to defend against Russia's move south through the conclusion of the Anglo-Japanese Alliance, and the United States, which had supported Japan in its war with Russia and sought to advance economically into Manchuria after the war. Immediately after the Russo-Japanese War, railway magnate E. H. Harriman (1848–1909) wanted to buy up the railway lines in Manchuria, and through this and similar ventures, the United States expected it would advance into Manchuria by using the open-door policy. When Japan linked arms with Russia and adopted a policy seeking to restrain this movement, the United States took it as an act of betrayal. Rebuffed by the governments of Russia and Japan for a 1909 neutrality plan with regard to the Manchurian railways, the United States moved in direction of infiltrating its economic might into the region by "smoking Japan out" of Manchuria, as Secretary of State Philander C. Knox (1853–1921) described it. Thus, Manchuria quickly became the focus of a U.S.-Japan confrontation. In 1909 an American military specialist by the name of Homer Lea (1876–1912) wrote a hypothetical novel about war between Japan and the United States entitled *The Valor of Ignorance*, translated into Japanese as *Nichi-Bei hissen ron* (Certain War between Japan and the United States).[5] Emerging from this particular historical stance was the conception raised by Ishiwara Kanji (1893–1981) of the necessity of gaining dominion over Manchuria to a decisive victory in Japan's war with the U.S.

When the Republic of China came into existence as a result of the Revolution of 1911, a strong reaction set in toward the fact that China's national sovereignty had been seriously infringed upon by the treaties the Qing court had signed. When the leasing terms were cut for Lüshun and Dalian where Russia continued to hold leaseholds in Manchuria, Japan in 1915 thrust a 99-year leasehold term in its Twenty-One Demands of the Chinese government. This action was seen as a national shame and gave rise to an anti-Japanese rights-recovery movement, and Sino-Japanese relations became dangerously strained. The response of the Guandong Army to this anti-Japanese movement would be linked to the Manchurian Incident.

Question 8: Despite signing a treaty with Russia, prior to the formation of the Soviet Union, and the decline of it as a threat, why was it necessary for Japan to remain so insistent in Manchuria, even in the face of ferocious Chinese opposition?

Until the fourth Russo-Japanese accords in 1916, Japan sought both cooperation with Russia and the expansion of its own control within Manchuria, but this did not mean that hostile relations with Russia had completely dissipated. Indicative of this was the "Imperial National Defense Plan" which Japan first drew up in 1907. Here we find for the first time clearly stated the great change from a defensive posture domestically, which had been the direction until then, to a more aggressive outward posture of foreign conquest: "As soon as some incident occurs, we shall not allow a national defense strategy to be taken within the island empire, but we can complete our national defenses only by taking an aggressive stance overseas."[6] What is especially important here is the fact that Manchuria was seen as the first line of national defense. The text goes on to illustrate a hypothetical enemy state: "The first potential future enemy is Russia, followed by the United States, Germany, and France."[7] A prowar stance over Manchuria is hypothesized here to ambush Russia, Japan's number-one enemy, and the view of America as an enemy state was also basic to the conflict over rights in Manchuria. "The standard for war preparations of the imperial army necessary for national defense follows the rule of being able to assume an attack posture in East Asia against the troops of Russia and the U.S. who most stress troop manipulation."[8] They thus set as their goal outfitting numbers of troops superior to Russia and the U. S., and thus the opening of Manchuria was an essential condition for preparing the necessary troop strength. In Japanese national defense plans, Manchuria was emphasized as an irreplaceable strategic necessity.

The crucial event which made the retention of Manchuria utterly essential in order for Japan to continue to exist, however, was World War I. It is incumbent upon us to consider the enormity of the impact on Japan of the fact that this great war changed all past understandings of warfare. For the first time in this war, humanity experienced the belligerent state of total war. Ishiwara Kanji, who prided himself on being the foremost student of the history of warfare, firmly believed that future wars would be wars of annihilation in which the "full capacity of all nations" was mobilized, and he stressed the need to maintain productive capacity for this fight to the finish. An absolute condition to this end was securing coal and steel, the most important natural resources to produce weaponry at that time, but these were precisely the items in which Japan was particularly lacking. Only Manchuria could provide a safe supply of them, and thus, as he saw it, it was essential for Japan to retain exclusive control over Manchuria.

In this sense, the shock which the total-war structure delivered to Japan was immense, and the meaning of Manchuria for Japan seems to have entered a different stage. After the Russo-Japanese War, in the era of Gotō Shinpei (1857–1929), the first president of the South Manchurian Railway (S.M.R.), Manchuria played an especially important function, for in order to achieve victory in the predicted second war between Russia and Japan, Japan needed to gain mastery of the Manchurian terrain through immigration. In 1906 Gotō called for 500,000 Japanese to be moved to Manchuria within the coming decade. The reason he managed the S.M.R. was to encourage migration there and militarily check Russian movements. For the same reasons, it would appear, Foreign Minister Komura Jūtarō in 1909 advocated a concentration of migrants in Manchuria and Korea and in 1910 called for the sending of one million Japanese over the subsequent twenty years to Manchuria and Mongolia. The S.M.R., of course, had the structure of a business enterprise and thus had to earn money. Therefore, Manchuria bore great significance to it as a production center of soybeans and sorghum, among other products. In addition, Manchuria with its Fushun coal mines and its Anshan iron works became following World War I a site that offered necessary strategic resources for the pursuit of total war. Already in 1918, in the midst of World War I, the War Industry Mobilization Law had been promulgated in which the Japanese government controlled war industries, taking as its premise the supply of war materials from Manchuria and elsewhere, and the Munitions Bureau was established.

While, to be sure, Manchuria was viewed as a base for the protection of strategic goods, this did not necessarily directly lead to the need for Japan to gain dominion over the region. Similarly, even if one stressed the importance of the natural resources of Manchuria, another perspective is conceivable. As Ishibashi Tanzan (1884–1973) argued, maintaining relations through commerce and trade, rather than outright seizing of control, would ultimately protect those resources more soundly, a position he articulated as relinquishing Manchuria. Perhaps, rather than incuring the heavy cost of continuing colonial control, Japan might participate in a cooperative international development of the area and thus through trade might protect better a cheaper flow of natural resources into it. By contrast, though, the opposing view was also conceivable; considering the economic domination of the West and the subsequent notions of the formation of economic blocs, such an optimistic view was not necessarily possible.

In fact, when Japan occupied the southern part of French Indochina in 1941, the United States cut off exports to Japan of oil and steel, and together with Great Britain and the Netherlands froze Japanese assets. These moves were economic sanctions for Japan's military actions, but whether or not it was possible it protect resources by means of free trade alone remained an open question. Considering this situation, the historical rationale postulated by Tanaka Giichi (1866–1949) and Ishiwara Kanji, who observed military operations in World War I, that if Manchuria were not seized as a colony then a secure source of steel and coal could not be preserved is not completely without basis. This is not at all to say that Japan had no choice other than dominion over Manchuria. Yet, we cannot properly discuss the issue of Manchuria if we overlook the fact that the idea that without holding onto Manchuria, Japan could not continue to exist, in the historical conditions of the post-World War I world, was a possibility hypothesized as one option from a purely military perspective.

Question 9: Was the impact of World War I on Japan and Manchuria only to be seen in the emergence of total war?

If we ignore the changes in the structural principles of international order after World War I, together with the sudden change warranting adoption of a total-war posture, then we may lose sight of the flow of world history in the twentieth century. This had decisive importance for Manchuria as well. That is, the principles of equality and self-determination of all peoples advocated by U. S. President Woodrow Wilson became the intellectual driving force of the anti-Japanese movement in Manchuria and the rights-recovery movement. As I have discussed in Chapter 2 of this book, the ideology of "ethnic harmony" was proposed to oppose Chinese nationalist thought from the May 4 Era (1919), which was itself aroused by the idea of ethnic self-determination called for by Wilson, and in particular the Three Principles of the People of the Chinese Nationalist Party.

There was as well from the time of the March First Independence Movement in Korea a sense of crisis that, if the Manchurian-Korean border zone, the base of operations for the anti-Japanese independence movement, was not suppressed in the face of the wave of ideas of self-determination following March 1, that control over Manchuria and Korea was threatened. Thus, at the time of the explosion of the Manchurian Incident, the Korea Army sent troops at its own initiative across the national frontier.

As a breakwater to the flooding into Korea and even Japan of Communist ideology from the newly-formed Soviet regime born during World War I, the role played by Manchuria as the front line against the spread of Communism was extremely important. Thus, World War I gave birth to the two pivotal ideologies in the history of the twentieth century. The impact exerted in Manchuria by World War I was huge even in the sense that Manchuria had to be built as the result of the sharpest confrontation between ethnic self-determination and Communism.

Despite the fact that it was predicted at the immediate outset that World War I would end within forty days, it was in the end a quagmire lasting four years. All manner of productive materials were poured into it, and women and children on the home front, too, were forced to shoulder a part in pursuance of the war. This is also of decisive importance when one considers the militarized state of Manzhouguo which adopted a structure of total mobilization.

Question 10: Aside from images of Manchuria seen from the perspective of government or military policy or from the perspective of world history, how did the image of Manchuria for the Japanese people take shape and how did it change?

Many Japanese who did resettle in Manchuria, starting in the 1880s, went from Vladivostok to Khabarovsk and then on into northern Manchuria. The majority of them were dubbed at the time "Amazonian troops," "prostitutes," and "harlots," among other things.

Manchuria caught the attention of many Japanese only in the 1890s, and the colonization of the region by Russia played a critical role. In 1898 Russia set to work on building the Chinese Eastern Railway linking Manzhouli to Harbin and the Suifen River (Pogranichnaya, which in Russian conveyed the meaning of a national frontier). In 1891 this rail line linked up with the Trans-Siberian Railway which was under construction and thus connected it to Vladivostok. By the leasehold treaty for Lüshun and Dalian of 1898, it was recognized that Russia would build a rail line from Harbin to Dalian. Together with construction on this railway, urban construction for the city of Harbin began in 1898; in 1899 construction commenced on a harbor of Dal'ny, meaning "far away" in Russian [more properly transcribed *dal'nyi*], in an area which the Russian leader Sakharov had called Qingniwa (literally, "green marsh"). In the end, from Russia Japan inherited Harbin, Dalian, and the South Manchurian Railway linking them, all the results of construction enterprises about which the Russians had boasted. As was said at the time: "By the grace of God, many sacrifices were made so that the emperor would bring civilization to this barbarous Manchuria."

As Russia commenced its full-fledged development of Manchuria as we have seen, the first Japanese work which drew attention there was entitled *Manshū ryokōki* (Travelogue of Manchuria, published in 1901) by Ogoshi Heiriku, a man who patterned himself after Katsu Kaishū (1823–99).[9] Ogoshi described on the basis of actual observation such things as urban construction in Harbin (a term which he claimed meant "a net to dry fish" in the Manchu language) and the state of Russian settlement along the Chinese Eastern Railway line. He thus informed his readers that a new universe for colonists was opening in Manchuria. In 1903 Tomizu Hirondo (1861–1935) published his *Tō-A ryokōdan* (Travel account of East Asia) in the form of a travel narrative.[10] Tomizu was one of the seven Tokyo University professors who had vociferously called for war in what led to the commencement of hostilities with Russia; a professor of Roman law, he had argued for forcing Russia to cede territory east of Lake Baikal and was thus bore the nickname of "Doctor Baikal." In this travel account, however, he wrote as follows about Manchuria: "Although there is much that remains undeveloped even today on the eastern plains, should it all be opened up, it is fit solely for agriculture. Manchuria is the world's great source of wealth. . . . In addition, because there are numerous coal mines there, he who occupies Manchuria will control a precious storehouse."[11] Views which saw Manchuria "the world's great source of wealth" and a "great storehouse of natural resources" and encouraged control over it were now beginning to circulate.

This image of an unopened treasure house commended Manchuria first and foremost to Japanese agricultural immigrants, and guidebooks for migrants soon began to appear. One among them was a volume published in 1919 entitled *Risshin chifū, kaigai tokō annai* (Advance in Life and Gain Wealth: Guide to Travel Overseas).[12] This book's purview covered the entire world, including South America, and advocated the possibility that Japanese could attain success through emigration. Using for one of its titles "Manchuria as a Place for Japanese to Develop," it forcefully made the case that Manchuria was itself the most appropriate site for Japanese emigration. Namely, "with its fertile soil and wide variety of produce, Manchuria is truly a great source of wealth for East Asia. It is a limitless treasure house of natural produce. As the number of Japanese increase each year by 500,000, they won't be going to far off South America and the Southeast Asian region, but to Manchuria which is close at hand. There is no one else to control the storehouse of Manchuria."[13] Thus, the book was also urging Japanese to move to Manchuria to relieve population pressure at home.

At the time of the Manchurian Incident in 1931, however, the total number of Japanese resident in Manchuria in the Guandong Leased Territory, the railway zone, and the treaty ports was between 20,000 and 30,000 with no more than one thousand in agriculture. This fact would tend to indicate that the image of "the world's great source of wealth" had not acquired the fascination to attract agricultural migrants. I do believe that this was in some manner intimately tied to the image that Japanese at the time held of Manchuria. For example, in 1909 Natsume Sōseki (1867–1916) was invited by S.M.R. President Nakamura Zekō (1867–1927) to travel through Manchuria, and in his travelogue of that trip, *Man-Kan tokorodokoro* (Here and There in Manchuria and Korea), Sōseki depicted Chinese coolies as swarming, wriggling ants, laboring silently as if "they were people without tongues," although overflowing with vitality; in Manchuria he observed perseverence and vigor forming "shadows of fate." In one of his works of fiction as well, Sōseki eerily portrays a person who has returned from Manchuria as a sort of broken man. Manchuria as a vast, desolate space into which he had poured all of his animal energies on the path to its development seems to have struck a sense difficult to describe that something was out of joint.

Looking at this image of an uncivilized space full of vitality from the other way around, we find a longing for Manchuria with its immense, free plains which did not exist in Japan, and this makes one think of a wilderness with bandits running around, pistols in hand. We find similar images evoked in Miyajima Ikuhō's musical composition "Bazoku no uta" (Song of the Bandits) which breaks out in song with: "I'm going, too, so you've gotta come!" It then goes on to loudly proclaim in song: "On thinking, now it's been over ten years and the big bandits in Manchuria and their followers drawn out from the great mountains of Asia number in the thousands." Similarly, the influence exerted by the illustrations of handsome young bandits by Takabatake Kashō (1888–1966) added to *Bazoku no uta* (Song of the Bandit), a juvenile novel written by Ikeda Kikan (1896–1956), a scholar of Japanese literature writing under the penname of Ikeda Fuyo, was powerful. Also, the first Japanese film shot on location in Manchuria was *Sekiyō no mura* (Village at Sunset) of 1921, in which Henry Kotani, recently returned from the United States, served as director, cinematographer, and star. This was an action drama with a love story in which, because of mountain bandits, Japanese travelers who directly faced such dangers are rescued by the bandit leader who is a young woman, and *Bazoku no uta*, which became extremely popular in 1925, was made into a film directed by Motoyama Yūji and starring Takata Minoru (1899–1977). In this action melodrama, when a handsome young Japanese is taken captive and his life threatened, he is saved by a female bandit leader who falls in love with him at first sight. In short, the image was conveyed of Manchuria as a dangerous wilderness where bandits roamed free but also a great open terrain where love, romance, and danger lurked, much as in the genre of American Westerns. It all nurtured and conveyed the dream of a continent of great ambitions.

There was another image of Manchuria as well, that of sacred terrain on which battles of the Russo-Japanese War had been fought in which Japan had risked the destiny of the nation. Already at the time of the Russo-Japanese War, soldiers recognized the Liaodong Peninsula as holy ground "purchased with the blood of Japanese men at that time" due to the earlier Sino-Japanese War, and they landed on the Mainland expecting to have it returned to them.[14] The bloody battle at Hill 203 in Lüshun during the Russo-Japanese War was dubbed *Nireisan* (Mountain of Souls) by General Nogi Maresuke (1849–1912) who caused the death in action of two of his own sons, Katsusuke (1879–1904) and Yasusuke (1881–1904). The area soon became a famous sight for tourism and study trips, together with the conference sight at the naval headquarters and monuments to war dead erected at a number of places. As this image permeated Japanese consciousness, we find Mashimo Hisen's (1878–1912) war song, "Sen'yū" (Comrade-in-arms), which had such lines as "Away from home by several hundred *ri*, in distant Manchuria, the red evening sun shining, my comrade lies beneath a rock in a corner of the field"; the Ministry of Education's song "Hirose chūsa" (Commander Hirose), which eulogized Hirose Takeo (1868–1904) of the navy as a war hero; Kagiya Tokusaburō's (1867–1924) song "Tachibana chūsa" (Lieutenant-Commander Tachibana) which sang the praises of Tachibana Shūta (1865–1904) of the army; and Sasaki Nobu-tsuna's (1872–1963) song "Suishiei no kaiken" (Conference at the Naval Station) which glorified the meeting between General Nogi and Russian General Anatoly Mikhailovich Stessel (1848–1915). These were all sung widely at the time. Thus, Sakurai Tadayoshi's (1879–1965) war novel *Niku-dan* (Human Bullets) of 1906 surely exerted a powerful influence at the time. This is clear as well from the "Manshū kōshin kyoku" (Song of the Advance into Manchuria), a work composed just after the Manchurian Incident which contained such lines as: "The bones of brave soldiers buried here during the bygone Russo-Japanese War, look up at the memorial to the war dead! Basking in the evening sun dyed in red blood, the vast sky soaring over the one thousand *ri* of wilderness." In the thirty years leading up to the Manchurian Incident, the sacrifices of the Russo-Japanese war had infiltrated the image of Manchuria as a "sacred site of the Yamato people" to the extent that soldiers could easily have imagined this space as such.

Nonetheless, as a result, in the face of Ishibashi Tanzan's argument in favor of relinquishing Manchuria, opposing heartfelt views which appealed to a tenacity of purpose—Can this sacred soil purchased with "100,000 souls and national expenditures of some two billion" yen be given up with no recompense?—were heard relentlessly. In the same way, the greatest element in the image of Manchuria as the greatest part of the "Meiji Emperor's morality" undeniably became a huge shackle on Japan's Manchurian policy.

Question 11: From the Russo-Japanese War until the founding of the state of Manzhouguo, by what mechanisms and institutions was Japanese participation in the region carried out?

Although there are differences depending on the time period and we can only offer an overview here, the first thing we need to recognize is that the rights Japan acquired as a result of the war with Russia were basically twofold: first, the leasehold in the Guandong Territory (Lüshun, Dalian, and the like); and second, management rights for the railway linking Changchun and Lüshun (the S.M.R.) and branch lines as well as the attached territory to those rail lines, and attached rights of such things as mining at the Fushun and Yantai mines.

How to maintain and expand these two became the principal question of what Japanese at the time called the "management of Manchuria." Supervision over the former fell to administrative offices from the Guandong Government-General straight through to the Guandong government and other bureaus. Responsibility for the latter fell to the South Manchurian Railway Company. Thus, consulates and sub-consulates set up in Andong, Shenyang, Jilin, and elsewhere dealt with such matters as overall diplomacy and the protection of Japanese nationals in Manchuria.

Among these, the Guandong Government-General, a military agency, after receiving the resolutions of the conference in the Diet on the Manchurian issue (mentioned above under Question 7), became in 1906 the Guandong Governor-General's Office, a peacetime organization. In addition to overseeing the Guandong Territory, the latter office had administrative and juridical rights in the areas attached to the railway lines, and it held the right to use force of arms to protect railway lines and supervisory authority over S.M.R. business. After the experience of the March First independence movement in Korea, the Guandong Governor-General's Office was discontinued in 1919, and its supervisory authority over the S.M.R., as well as its administrative and policing powers, passed to the Guandong government, while its military leadership authority fell to the newly established Guandong Army Headquarters. The head official of the Guandong Government was directly under the supervision of the Prime Minister (under the minister of colonial affairs from the time of the establishment of the Department of Colonial Affairs in 1929), and he was responsible for affairs of state, such as the management of business concerning the Guandong Territory and the S.M.R. The Guandong Army, which was in charge of military affairs, had earlier been garrison troops with a maximum of 14,419 men placed roughly fifteen every kilometer, as recognized by the supplementary articles of the Portsmouth Treaty in order to protect railway lines; with the creation of the Guandong Army Headquarters, it became independent of the Guandong Government, an administrative agency, and able to carry out operations under the command of the army.

The S.M.R. was basically a railway company, but it also had a research department, agricultural experimentation centers, a central laboratory, a geological survey institute, and the like, and developed a wide range of activities, such as mining and steel production in the attached territory, the management of hotels, hospitals, newspapers, and a movie studio, as well as educational institutions such as the Manchurian Medical University. In addition, with the land and markets on either side of its railway lines, the S.M.R. supervised institutions concerned with education, public works, and health and hygiene there. It had the power to levy and collect taxes and other fees from resident Japanese, and thus it functioned as well as an administrative agency. Its attached lands expanded from a total surface area of 150 square kilometers in 1907 when they were transferred from Russia to roughly 483 square kilometers at the time of the Manchurian Incident in 1931. Half the capital of the S.M.R. came from the government, making it a semi-official company acting as proxy state policy. Thus the Japanese government appointed its president and board of directors and carried out a strict direction of its management.

In the management of Manchuria, then, because there were four agencies—the Guandong Government, the Guandong Army Headquarters, the S.M.R., and the consulates—with different powers of supervision, rivalries and oppositions emerged, and the lack of unity was to become a problem.

Furthermore, when we examine the control over Manchuria, we need to keep in consideration the consulates which were under the jurisdiction of the Foreign Ministry and the Korean Government-General. Of course, the powers of the Korean Government-General did not extend to Manchuria, but there was an extremely complex web of power relations related to the issue of the Jiandao region—just across the Tumen River from eastern Jilin Province, facing what is today North Korea. Since the end of the Qing dynasty, there had been endless international disputes over control of this area as a colony for ethnic Koreans, and Japan, which held diplomatic rights here by virtue of the 1905 treaty with Korea, entered into negotiations with the Qing court; they signed the Jiandao accords which recognized Qing dominion in the region in 1909. These accords opened up for residence and trade for foreigners such sites as Longjing Village and Juzi Market, and there Japan established consulates and sub-consulates. Japanese consular officials and bureaucrats authorized by them attended to the civil and juridical affairs of locally resident Koreans. This very Jiandao region, however, is well known as the base of anti-Japanese, armed partisan activities of men such as Kim Il-sŏng (1912–94). The Korean Government-General was closely concerned with the exercise of a powerful police power in planning for control over Korea and stabilizing Manzhouguo. Also, because the Korean Government-General had long experience and information concerning control over Koreans—not only in Jiandao—even after the establishment of Manzhouguo until the abrogation of extraterritoriality in 1937, there was a complex problem with utilizing the three-tiered supervisory powers over ethnic Koreans in Manzhouguo of the Japanese consulates, the Korean Government-General, and the Manzhouguo government.

Question 12: From the formal coming into existence of the Guandong Army Headquarters in 1919 until the Manchurian Incident of 1931, how did the Guandong Army come to have controlling power in Manchuria for this short period of some twelve years?

As is often recounted anecdotally, before the establishment of the state of Manzhouguo, at banquets sponsored by the S.M.R. president, it was seen as perfectly natural for the commanding officers and commissioned officers of the Guandong Army to take up the lowest-ranking seats. Initially, the Guandong Army's only function was as guards along the S.M.R. lines, but after World War I in the process of setting up Manchuria as a supply base outfitted for Japan's posture of total war vis-à-vis the Soviet Union, the position of the Guandong Army gradually rose. In the midst of the international rise of the ideology of ethnic self-determination following the Great War, nationalism in China was also on the rise, and a national rights-recovery movement took shape in the form of boycotts of Japanese goods and disapproval of the Lüshun and Dalian leaseholds. To the extent that Japan responded with brute force to suppress them, anti-Japanese nationalism grew all the more, as did Japan's opposition and demands for extensions of its rights. Accompanying this geometric escalation, the Guandong Army's military preparedness continued to rise.

In addition, Japan's foremost hypothetical enemy, the Soviet Union, launched in 1928 its first Five-Year Plan, an event which became the basis for the Guandong Army, charged as it was with major responsibility for the Soviets, to expand. And, before the Five-Year Plan was even over, it was seen as substantiation for the view that Japan would not be able perpetually to confront the Soviet Union without gaining control over Manchuria.

In order to protect the rights and privileges associated with the S.M.R., Japan would not sanction China's laying tracks and building a rail line parallel to the S.M.R. With the support of Chinese nationalism, a movement developed for the Chinese to construct a railway that surrounded the S.M.R. line and sought to rival the S.M.R.'s monopoly control. Thus, to maintain its own rights and privileges as the S.M.R. with pressure on its management, the tendency developed for it to rely increasingly on the Guandong Army as a force which could fend off the regime of Zhang Zuolin (1873–1928) and his son Zhang Xueliang (1901–2001). As the imminent threat became more stringent, the Guandong Army put pressure with force to back it up on the Guandong Government and the consulates and began to take over leadership in Manchuria. Feeling the impact of the international panic from 1929, the S.M.R. fell into a sharp commercial depression, the arrangement of the four powers in Manchuria underwent a change at this point, as the S.M.R. came to the realization that, to plan for its revival, it had no choice but to support a military resolution of the problem by the Guandong Army.

When we understand this background, it is altogether clear why Ishiwara Kanji, Itagaki Seishirō, and others of the Guandong Army staff led the way in the Manchurian Incident, but we should not overlook the fact that the S.M.R. staff and the S.M.R. itself offered power support behind the scenes. The very fact that a force of a mere 14,000 men could gain supremacy over the entirety of Manchuria in a short period of time indicates that the S.M.R. was working at full blast at the time of an extraordinarily rapid movement of troops. Also, the knowledge and information collected by S.M.R. staff people, first and foremost those who were members of the Manchurian Youth League and the Majestic Peak Society who were the Japanese most conversant with local realities at the administrative sites of occupation, seems to have contributed greatly. In the establishment of a plan for the construction of the state of Manzhouguo, the Guandong Army had the S.M.R. organize the Economic Research Association, gave it the responsibility of an economic staff headquarters, and had it draft a plan entitled "Manshūkoku keizai kensetsu kōyō" (Outline for the Economic Construction of Manzhouguo). Without using the information and the Chinese human networks amassed by the S.M.R., the establishment of Manzhouguo would have undoubtedly ended a fiasco. Although the overall number of S.M.R. staff members at the time was roughly 39,000, the number of Japanese staffers who received commendations for services rendered in the Manchurian Incident was 15,884 and foreign staffers (including Chinese) was 6,370, including those who organized armed self-defense corps and supported the Guandong Army. With the establishment of the state, 244 staff members left their jobs and Japanese officials took over the essential posts. These facts, more than anything else, symbolize the change in ties between the S.M.R. and the Guandong Army over these years and clearly the depth of the mutual dependency.

After the founding of the state of Manzhouguo, the president of the S.M.R. remained as a post appointed by the Japanese government, but the powers of the plenipotentiary resident in Manchuria, whose function was to supervise Japan's foreign diplomacy there, and of the head of the Guandong Office, established in 1934 to replace the Guandong Government, fell within the hands of the Commander of the Guandong Army. The ill effects of a many-headed politics were continually a problem, and a plan was concocted for the centralization of power in the hands of the Guandong Army Commander, based on a system of "three posts, one system." Until the founding of Manzhouguo, Japanese control other than the Guandong Army was based in Siberia, but after the state came into existence this situation switched to a substantive military-government leadership.

Of course, there were concerns that acknowledging the Guandong

Army's exclusive control in the region would undermine the basis of Japan's own ruling structures. Thus, the Japanese government created an office to deal with Manchurian affairs, built up a variety of Japan-Manzhouguo associations, and sent home officials to man them, in an effort to come up with ways of strengthening its control. This political process was a history of the struggle for hegemony as to how Japan would regain the powers monopolized by the Guandong Army. It was manifest within Japan as a struggle for leadership among the military, the bureaucracy, and the Diet.

Question 13: How is it best to understand the historical significance of the Guandong Army's control of Manzhouguo?

Furumi Tadayuki (1900–83), assistant director of the Office of Administrative Affairs, regarded "Manzhouguo as immense installation built with top secret funds from the Guandong Army." Not only Manzhouguo, however, for the army was able to operate over a broad swath of terrain across Asia, because it invested the capital sucked out of Manzhouguo. The basic capital resource was opium. This issue is tied to the Japanese experience of overlordship in Taiwan. If a man's opium addiction ultimately leads to debility, then its abolition is only a natural demand. On the excuse, however, that if you eliminate the drug all at once, this may bring about social chaos, the Japanese adopted a policy of government monopoly and moved gradually to lessen the amount available. In Manzhouguo as well the same model was adopted, and Manzhouguo prided itself on being a good government as a result. Secretly sold opium, though, not only continued to provide Manzhouguo finances, but it became the principal capital source for a secret fund. The Japanese there not only saw to it that opium was cultivated at sites in Manchuria and Mongolia, and they used Satomi Hajime, head of the Manzhouguo News Agency, to spread the rumor that opium was flooding into Manzhouguo from Persia. This generated huge profits and provided a strategic fund for the China Expeditionary Army. Amakasu Masahiko (1890–1945) was able to exert his authority in Manzhouguo like a "shadow emperor" largely because of this slush fund. Amakasu created this fund by serving as an intermediary bringing Chinese laborers into Manchuria. Even Kishi Nobusuke (1896–1987), who was a minor official, made personal deliveries to Amakasu's special operation in the amount of ten million yen (comparable to between eight and nine billion yen today, given the rate of increase in wholesale commodity prices). Amakasu, though, did not embezzle this money, but used it for his special operation enabling Japan to encroach on North China and Mongolian borderlands from Manzhouguo. Thus, Manzhouguo was both a base of operations and a capital fund for an operation to create a "second Manzhouguo."

By its very nature, proving that the existence of a secret fund or slush fund on the basis of documents is exceedingly difficult. In the final analysis, it can only be corroborated by testimony, and we need to demonstrate it clearly.

By the same token, as we see in the editorial from the issue of *Fortune* magazine which I cited in Chapter 4, Manzhouguo might also be seen as one immense laboratory or training center of the Japanese army. By practicing control in Manchuria, the Japanese army used the frameworks of Japan's general mobilization structure and national-defense state structure. In creating these structures, not only the army but numerous reform bureaucrats—such as Kishi Nobusuke, Shiina Etsusaburō (1898–1979), and Minobe Yōji (1900–53)—were responsible. In this regard, then, we see the essential mutual bond linking Japan with Manzhouguo. Furthermore, with the subsequent formation of the Greater East Asia Coprosperity Sphere, Guandong Army staff officers were sent out to various sites as guidance officials and brain-trusters. Wachi Yōji (1893–1978), who supported Ishiwara Kanji at the time of the Manchurian Incident, was appointed to the highest post of commander of the military government of the Philippines; Iwakuro Hideo (1897–1970) supervised the General Affairs Department of Sumatra; Isogai Rensuke (1886–1967) became governor-general of the occupation of Hong Kong; and Imamura Hitoshi (1886–1968) became commanding officer of the front army at Java and later at Rabaul. It is thus undeniable that for Guandong Army staff officers to have had experience in colonial rule was of great importance to the Greater East Asia Coprosperity Sphere. Just as Ōdachi Shigeo (1892–1955), director-general for administrative affairs in Manzhouguo, became the mayor of Zhaonan City, created after the Japanese occupation of Singapore, many were the Japanese officials in Manzhouguo who went to serve at a wide variety of sites within the Greater East Asia Coprosperity Sphere.

In addition, Kanai Shōji (1886–1967), governor of Jiandao Province, Ōhashi Chūichi (b. 1893), vice-minister of foreign affairs, and Kanki Shōichi, director-general for administrative affairs, all served successively in Manzhouguo as directors-general for administrative affairs, the highest advisorial post, in the Mongolian Federated Autonomous Government, created by the Guandong Army to rule Inner Mongolia under Prince De (1902–66). We see here clearly that this Autonomous Government was a "second Manzhouguo" itself.

Question 14: What meaning did life in Manzhouguo hold for Japanese living back in the home islands?

When we think about the lives of Japanese in Manzhouguo, I think we need to divide the question into those living in the cities of the railway zone along the S.M.R. and those living in rural villages. Many of those in groups of colonists were situated in surroundings in which they had no opportunity to read a newspaper or magazine, while in the capital of Xinjing (Japanese Shinkyō, the former Changchun) which was intentionally built as a political symbol, capital was invested in infrastructure, sewer systems were fully put into place, and the percentage of land used for parks was 7.2% (compared with 2.8% for Tokyo). There was indeed much about this new city that made it more pleasant for urban life than Tokyo at the same time. Furthermore, Dalian—dubbed the "pearl of the North"—boasted the S.M.R. Hospital, the model for all East Asia, and areas of the city had various urban amenities such as asphalt pavement, flush toilets, and central heating.

We need recognize from the outset that the overall surface area of Manzhouguo was some 1,300,000 square kilometers; the overall Japanese empire at that time—including the 36,000 square kilometers of Taiwan and the 220,000 square kilometers of Korea—totaled 680,000 square kilometers. Manzhouguo thus was slightly less than twice the size of the rest of the Japanese empire at the time. Thus, as everything from agricultural panic to young women selling themselves into service and generational rifts became serious social problems of the day, people believed such startling lines as: "If you go to Manchuria, you can become landlord of ten hectares (roughly 24.5 acres) of land." And, if they settled as immigrants or as groups of colonists, their worries might be over. Ten hectares corresponded to 30,000 *tsubo* (each *tsubo* equaling roughly 36 square feet), and for people who had no land to till in impoverished villages, no doubt they conceived of this land as the earth of their aspirations, as an "Eden of the North." Of course, even among immigrants to Manchuria, there were a variety of cases—armed immigrant groups, collective immigrant groups, village immigrant groups, and the like—based on when and in what form they actually settled, circumstances might differ completely. In fact, though, they were not given that much land, and there were limitations to what they could themselves till in Manchuria with its different farming methods and climate. In the end, many hired local people to work the land.

The lands on which they settled were primarily in the northern and eastern parts of Manzhouguo, largely because they were situated before an attack from the Soviet Union. Army Colonel Tōmiya Kaneo (1892–1937) who was attached to the headquarters of the Guandong Army which was pushing the colonization of Manchuria called the colonial immigrants an "army of colonial development" (*tonkengun*), indicating clearly that the standard for the selection of settlement lands was strategic sites for a war with the Soviet Union. Despite the fact that a Soviet entrance into the war was imagined in June 1945, the Guandong Army did not allow the settlers to evacuate because it warned them that doing so would effectively invite the Soviet armies in. In this sense, colonization by armed groups of immigrants beginning in 1932 and by a Volunteer Army of Young Colonists in Manchuria and Mongolia who were known as the "Shōwa no sakimori" (frontier guardians of the Shōwa era) which reached 87,000 members between 1938 and war's end—in Manzhouguo, they frequently avoided the term "army," substituting volunteer "corps" in its stead—thereby preparing for the tragedy of 1945. In particular, from the time of the Nomonhan Incident of 1939, they moved to colonize with military installations to strengthen defenses against the Soviets, and "Mainland warriors of the plow" became scarecrow troops, as the Guandong Army transferred troop strength to the south, compelled to confront the Soviets' heavy tanks and machine guns with their plows. Writing in 1938, Yuasa Katsue (1910–82) noted of immigrants to Manchuria that they "fundamentally differed" from emigrants to Brazil, "literally sowing the populace as a shield for the nation."[15] The weakest people sowed in various places as shields for Manzhouguo would come to bear the most virulent censure of the state in the annihilation of that state.

Other cases of agricultural immigrants would also include members of religious sects and other religious groups, as well as merchants and industrialists from Tokyo, such as the Musashi-Koyama shopping street in Shinagawa Ward, who had to close down their stores and workshops due to shortages of material to sell and moved en masse to Manchuria. The arrangements for middle- and small-sized enterprises formed one link in the business of the control economy which Kishi Nobusuke promoted after returning to Japan from Manzhouguo. Numerous people with no agricultural experience who were ostracized in the process of the formation of the structure of total mobilization, however, also made their way to Manchuria. We must not forget that this included groups of immigrant *buraku* people who had been discriminated against. Despite the fact that immigrant groups flocked to Manzhouguo, seeking a new realm there to escape from disappointment in Japan, they still were discriminated against, were unable to settle down in Manchuria, and could only continue move from colonial site to site as if chased away. This fact would indicate that not only was the discriminatory structure of Japanese society not eliminated in the colonies, but was actually reproduced and expanded in Manchuria. Such discrimination and belittlement directed at people of the same ethnicity meant that an even colder gaze awaited people of other ethnic backgrounds.

In any event, there were many and sundry motives for people to move to Manchuria and equally many life experiences for them in Manzhouguo, making it all but impossible to generalize in simple terms. The terrain on which these colonists settled, however, was usually far from the railway lines in remote outposts where often there was not even a single radio in an entire colonial settlement. Cultural life there was extremely limited, with recreational diversions in festivals at Shinto shrines built by the settlements or in sports events. Thus, there was no end of people who suffered from homesickness and such neuroses as "colonial development sickness" and "nostalgia illness."

By the same token, in the main cities of Dalian, Fengtian (present-day Shenyang), Xinjing, Harbin, and the like, merchandise such as the leading fashions in the department stores, imported goods such as Western liquors unavailable back in Japan were overflowing, and Japanese-produced goods stood side-by-side them in Japanese shops. In Xinjing one found Yoshino-machi (known as the Ginza of Xinjing) and Nihonbashi Street; in Fengtian there was a Kasuga Street, and in Dalian a Naniwa-machi and a Yamagata Street; in Harbin there a site known as Yaponskaya ("Japanese" in Russian, indicating an area where Japanese lived and worked) for a marketplace where three streets intersected. These, as well as the many Japanese restaurants and amusements sites clearly indicated that life back in the home islands was being reproduced here. There were even sushi restaurants in Dalian. At hotels, halls exclusively for Japanese use, club houses, and the like, social dancing and musical performances were sponsored; there were theaters for which Japanese might dress up to watch plays and to mix socially. During the daytime, a distinctive colonial culture might be enjoyed with tennis, golf, and even hunting. In the wintertime, the more popular sports included skiing, skating, and hockey, and vacationers gathered at the hot springs in such places as Xiongyuecheng and Wulongbei. At Hoshigaura—dubbed the "Nice of the East"—in the outskirts of Dalian, there were villas lined up where one might enjoy sea-bathing. Furthermore, people gathered in the Balin area on the Binzhou rail line—known as the "Karuizawa of Manchuria"—to escape the heat; there was a yacht club at Zhongzhou and the Taiyang Islands in the Sungari River, and people (including Russians) thronged there to enjoy the brief period of summer to the fullest.

It was, I believe, in this distinctive colonial lifestyle that the image of Manchuria as a "Western cultural frontier" emerged. Even today when one walks the street of Dalian, in the residential streets in the southern foothills where elegant Western mansions remain, one senses the attachment concealing past times. In the stone pavement of Kitaiskaya Street of Harbin—known at the time as the "Little Paris of the East" and the "Moscow of the East"—I think the atmosphere of Europe floats thickly.

This was also a reason that during the Manzhouguo period the attachment to foreignness attracted Japanese to Manzhouguo. For example, Tachibana Sotoo (1894–1959), a writer who visited Harbin, noted in a piece published in 1940: "Harbin! It is Shanghai without the sea. . . . Here the bizarre, the romantic, and the adventurous come flowing together into a whirlpool, an international city in North Manchuria in which past and future play a zigzag symphony! Great princes and dukes of the Russian Tsar, reduced to poverty, polish the shoes of passers-by on the street corners, and leading dancers from the imperial opera company have grown old and sell matches on the roadside. What a terribly sad city!"[16] The "Russian" cities in Harbin and Dalian, as this citation indicates, were full of an atmosphere of what prevailed in Europe at the same time, and the closest thing to the West which Japanese were able to touch.

Question 15: Aside from the economic, what other reasons compelled Japanese to relocate to Manzhouguo, this frontier space where the wilderness met the West?

It is undeniable that many people went to Manchuria from Japan out of sympathy for the ideals of "a paradise of the kingly way" and "cooperation of the five ethnic groups." Also, we should not ignore the fact that, as Asahina Takashi (1908–2001) instructed with the Harbin Symphony Orchestra, Japanese society in wartime was shut off to the outside world, even foreign study, and Manchuria provided a window through which one could absorb Western culture. There were as well people who entered such institutions of higher learning as Harbin Gakuin, yearning to acquire knowledge of the Russian language and Russian literature. There were also people who entered the Manchurian Film Association (Man'ei) which had at its disposal abundant production funds to make movies that could not be produced in Japan, and there were many people, such as Fuchigami Hakuyō (1889–1960) and Unoki Satoshi (b. 1910) of the Manchurian Photographers Association, who were searching for a laboratory for the reform of the techniques of photography in Manzhouguo which was replete with objects for photographing not to be found in Japan.

When we consider its nature not only as a frontier space at which one might come into contact with Western culture but also as a political space in Japanese modernity, Manchuria clearly possesses distinctive meaning. Looking over modern Japanese history, one important fact worthy of consideration is the virtual absence—with the exception of a tiny minority, including Sano Seki (1905–66), Okada Yoshiko (1902–92), and Sugimoto Ryōkichi (1907–39)–of political refugees. The question itself of why there have been so few refugees provides a significant lesson to explaining Japan's modern history. And, given this history, Manchuria appears to have functioned as fictive space of refuge.

Numerous leftwingers who renounced their political views came to work for the S.M.R. and lived there in this space which approved of them. Man'ei also provided a place where men such as Ōtsuka Yūshō (b. 1897), who gained fame for his part in the Japan Communist Party's attack on the Ōmori Bank, could remain freely active. In this sense, Manchuria was perhaps modern Japan's sole asylum space. There was significance to "Manchuria" in the sense of asylum as a place to which one could escape the confined Japanese space and seek out in the broadest sense that which it was impossible to realize in Japan—including the political ideal of constructing a paradise of the kingly way—and in the sense that it was possible there even to study communism.

The polar images of Manzhouguo, then, coexisted: "Manchuria as a hell on earth" with the extremely dark image of a country in which men in desperate circumstances drifted about; and "Manchuria as asylum" in which one could escape traditional strictures and conventions and freely take flight. Depending on the person in question, the image of Manzhouguo split into these two poles. In short, while we would not want to deny that many people went to the space of Manchuria burning with idealism, it was also seen as a place people with nothing to count on in Japan might use to gamble on a new start, escaping from the realities of life in Japan, as such expressions of the time as Manchurian grotesque, Manchurian *rōnin*, and the like indicate. Even in the postwar era, it cast a flickering shadow and may have been the reason there developed a sense that something was awry, including a certain bias and a certain longing, with respect to people who were returning to Japan from Manchuria.

Question 16: As the contrary images of hellishness and asylum mixed, what sort of a space was Manzhouguo for women?

"Women are the pioneer developers of Japanese colonies" wrote Hirabayashi Hirondo (1886–1986) in an extremely apt view in 1934.[17] At the head of the Japanese entering Manchuria were the "Karayukisan of the North."[18] It has been said that even before the Russo-Japanese War there was not a city east of Lake Baikal that had no Japanese women in it. They sold their services to the Chinese and Koreans hired to work in the development of Siberia and on the construction of the railway and later for Russian soldiers, and together with the construction on the Chinese Eastern Railway they moved south into Manchuria. Men such as Ishimitsu Makiyo (1868–1942), who served as a military spy before the Russo-Japanese War from Vladivostok to Harbin, wrote in his autobiography, *Kōya no hana* (Flowers in the Wilderness), that he actively received both material and intellectual help from women who were "karayukisan" with such names as Okimi and Ohana who had been the common-law wives of bandits.[19]

After these women, their numbers increased with female employees of the S.M.R. or the wives of male employees who came to Manchuria following the Russo-Japanese War and whose number increased as the S.M.R. grew, women who were employed by civil-engineering and construction firms, patent-medicine companies, or by other companies and traders who moved into Manchuria, and finally women who worked as maids. With the founding of the state of Manzhouguo, opportunities opened up for women to work as clerks and typists in the Manzhouguo government and provincial governmental offices. This was, in effect, a fulfillment of the wishes of professional women who sought work, something extremely limited to them back home in Japan. Together with the growth in the Japanese population, there were as well people who became instructors at the primary and secondary levels and sought self-development as teachers. From the extant memoir literature, we can ascertain as well that there were women who went to Manchuria with the dream of realizing in practice ethnic harmony hand-in-hand with the education of children of other ethnicities.

The biggest reason that women went to Manzhouguo, however, was to accompany the pioneer immigrants there. Among them, in cases of immigrants who went as a family, they were fully aware of their roles as wives and mothers from the start. And, there were women dubbed "continental brides" (*tairiku hanayome*) who went to Manzhouguo as "the good wives of young settlers who had dedicated themselves to the sacred task of opening up lands."[20]

The first group of agricultural immigrants settled in Iyasaka village in 1932, and already the next year there was a stream of people leaving the group due to "colonial development sickness." Voices of doubt about the possibilities for immigration arose with such events as a movement to expel the leadership of the village. To this end Tōmiya Kaneo and Katō Kanji (1884–1967), among others, came to the belief that if they could marry off men who suffered from "colonial development sickness" and enable them to have the comforts of family life, they might settle down in Manchuria. They thus proposed a policy of "continental brides." In order to cope with the mass immigration policy which began in particular with the "Plan for the Settlement of One Million Households over Twenty Years" drawn up in 1936 and with the settling, beginning in 1938, of members of the Volunteer Army of Young Colonists in Manchuria and Mongolia after completing their training, the plan was for the organized dispatching of brides for them. In concrete terms, the women selected from participants in the Brides Training Institute and Brides Training School which the Manchuria Immigration Society set up at various sites within Japan, from participants in the Women's Colonization Training School sponsored by the Ministry of Overseas Affairs, and from participants in the Agricultural Brides School opened by the Ministry of Agriculture and Forestry would go to Manchuria after marrying on the basis of an interview with a man who was either a prospective emigrant to Manchuria or one who had made a brief trip home from the place on the continent where he lived to find a wife. There were cases as well of women who made the trip to Manchuria as prospective brides.

Additionally, from 1940 increasingly we find cases of women who, even before getting married, joined the Women's Volunteer Training Institute (dubbed the Colonial Women's Academy), and after receiving instruction in how to support themselves in Manchuria, they married on the scene. The great majority of these women who joined the Women's Volunteer Training Institute had responded to bridal recruitments in Japan, but despite coming to Manchuria after being told that the Colonial Women's Academy was a bridal school and an employment-training school, about halfway they were threatened that even if they did not marry, they could not return to Japan, they often pushed ahead with marriage on the basis of group interviews. Of course, many among them who harbored aspirations of escaping daily life in Japan which was plunged in war and poverty and that through their own efforts they might open up their own futures. In any event, given the limited options, one ought not gainsay the fact that for both men and women the notion was operative that marriage might not be decided solely on the basis of one's own volition.

Related to this issue of brides was a movie entitled *Kaitaku no hanayome* (Pioneer Bride), shot at the Man'ei studios in 1943 by Sakane Tazuko, who was known as "Japan's first woman film director" and "the sole female film director of the coprosperity sphere." It tells the story of a young wife who labors on an equal footing in Manzhouguo and rears the lives of those she loves and gives birth to. The movie itself clearly follows the prescriptions for national-policy films, but it places cooperation between the sexes as a prerequisite to ethnic cooperation. For Sakane, the first female director who after the war was unable to make movies in Japan solely because she lacked a university degree, the only space that afforded her the opportunity to make films as a director on a par with equally capable men was Man'ei located in Manzhouguo.

Thus, women were recruited to help develop Manchuria by a host of means. One document in which we find a clear expression of how the Japanese and Manzhouguo governments understood the distinctive importance of women in Manzhouguo was the *Joshi takushoku shidōsha teiyō* (Summary of the Women Leaders in Colonial Development), prepared by the Ministry of Overseas Affairs in 1942, the year in which "Joshi takushoku yōkō" (Outlines of Women in Colonial Development) was issued. This document offered the following as roles for women: "In order to secure the national resources, there is first the strengthening of the settledness of our pioneers"; "together with quantitative guarantee of the national resources, maintainance of the pure blood of the Yamato race"; "transplanting to the continent the Japanese duties of womanhood and creating a new Manchurian culture"; and "there are many areas in which women's cooperation is essential to the achievement of ethnic cooperation."[21] The tasks before women in Manzhouguo were clearly not the realization of their personal aspirations and self-fulfillment but ultimately seeing to it that pioneer immigrant males settled down in Manchuria and propagating the Yamato race through childbirth as the leading ethnic group in Manzhouguo.

To be sure, although "achievement of ethnic cooperation" was raised here, this was entirely ancillary and unautonomous. Furthermore, as preservation of the "pure blood of the Yamato race" was emphasized, they may have spoken of ethnic cooperation, "one drop of mixed blood was not allowed, and they had to become a blood defense corps,"[22] thereby strictly forbidding intermarriage with other ethnicities. In short, what was expected of women was neither the attainment of cooperation through interaction with other ethnic groups in Manzhouguo nor the building of a new Manchurian culture, but to function as a good mother who offered comfort to male pioneers and increased the race, while themselves being good workers within Japanese society in Manchuria, as: "good assistant tillers to the pioneer farmers"; "good comforters in the pioneer families"; and "good nurturers of the second generation."[23] The "Plan for the Settlement of One Million Households" was a plan to increase the population of Japanese in Manzhouguo over a twenty-year period to 5,000,000 by "giving birth, increasing in numbers, the august shield of the nation." The success or failure of this plan hung wholly on the childbearing capacities of "continental brides."

Inasmuch as life in these pioneer groups was a simple existence with little entertainment, given the severe weather conditions differing greatly from Japan, many were thus caught in a sense of disillusionment, and many were the women who, unable to accustom themselves to the communal lifestyle of the pioneer groups, were stricken with a feeling of alienation. No matter how disheartened or abhorrent they found it, however, they had married out to Manchuria and could not return to their parents' home. Lacking the necessary funds to return to Japan, the only reality before them to accomodating to life there.

There were, of course, women who deeply sympathized with the ideals of ethnic cooperation and a paradise of the kingly way, who sought to inculcate these ideals among Chinese women inside and outside the family, and who were conscious of a mission to realize Japanese-Manchurian friendship. One such was the writer Koizumi Kikue (1904–92), author of *Manshūjin no shōjo* (Manchurian Daughter), who believed that "Japanese sincerity" would achieve "Japanese-Manchurian friendship" and tried to inspire belief in "the benificence of the Japanese emperor" in her fourteen-year-old maid, Li Guiyu, who was protesting that those the Japanese dubbed "bandits" were in fact a "patriotic army" and "Manchurians were not dogs and cats."[24] Similarly, Mochizuki Yuriko (1900–2001) argued that the culture of the future would be created on the basis of cooperation between the sexes, and to that end she opened a Mainland Cultural Academy aimed at educating for their roles in the leading ethnic group Japanese women in Manchuria who would shoulder ethnic cooperation in Manzhouguo. Whether or not their activities were genuinely in accord with ethnic cooperation is certainly open to question, but at the least it is undeniable that they firmly believed and worked tirelessly in the belief that, in order to realize the ideal of ethnic cooperation, the very best plan was something they as Japanese women could devise.

And not only Koizumi and Mochizuki, for other women in Manchuria lacked the freedom from the strictures of total war and thus, like Japanese in the home islands, were mobilized in pursuance of the war effort. With the explosion of the Manchurian Incident, an All-Manchurian Federation of Women's Groups was organized at the suggestion of Mutō Nobuko, wife of the Guandong Army Commander Mutō Nobuyoshi (1868–1933).

"Participation as women in a great movement to build a utopia of peace and justice"[25] was to be enforced, and women were stirred up to take part in activities such as the opening of soldiers' homes and the sending to Japan of speaking groups. Also, requests were made by the Patriotic Women's Society and the Women's Association for the Defense of Japan, both based in Japan, for the establishment of Manchurian branches of their organizations. An important task for Japanese women in Manchuria in the realization of the ideals in the establishment of Manzhouguo lay in shouldering the task, with military support, of building the national defense family and advancing the "Japanization of Chinese women."

Question 17: What meaning did Manzhouguo have for peoples other than the Japanese?

I cannot answer this question completely, but one thing we need to recognize from the outset is that the thirteen and one-half years in the existence of the state of Manzhouguo is referred to in China as "fourteen years of enemy occupation in the Northeast." Given the implications of falling into "enemy occupation," there is clearly a sense of humiliation of being trampled under foot by the enemy which is attached to this expression. Also contained in this term is the difficult times endured until the anti-Japanese movement was victorious. In other words, even though there were collaborators who gained privileges with the formation of the state of Manzhouguo, most of the farmers had their land bought up cheaply and their basis for a livelihood stolen. Thus, whether they became tenant farmers or became coolies to sustain themselves or moved south of the Great Wall into China proper, they were compelled to make a choice. Shimaki Kensaku (1903–45), who witnessed the operations of a pioneer group in detail and returned to Japan, wrote: "The first of those men hired were the original residents who were still on the land to be colonized. With the arrival of the Japanese developers of the land, these [former residents] faced a fate of having no option save leaving this land sooner or later."[26] In such circumstances, the people the Japanese were calling "bandits" were devoting their lives to the anti-Japanese, anti-Manzhouguo movement and the Communist movement, or they were aiding those who were. There were among the Chinese women in the region some who were common-law wives or mistresses of Japanese, women known at the time as "Manchurian concubines" (*Mansai*), but they were not accepted in the society in which Japanese men moved. Of course, Chinese women in Manzhouguo were expected to be faithful to the state, and plans were organized by the Women's Association for Defense of the Manchurian Empire for military support and cooperation with Japan. The Women's Association for Defense of the Manchurian Empire was founded in 1938 in consolidation with the Manchurian branch of the Women's Association for the Defense of Japan, a Japanese group, and Xu Zhiqing, wife of Zhang Jinghui (1872–c. 1962), the prime minister of Manzhouguo, was made honorary chairwoman, as the process of organization advanced.

What do people placed in such circumstances think about? In Zhang Hanhui's (1902–46) musical composition and lyrics, *Sunghua jiang shang* (Along the Sungari River), which was widely read during the "enemy occupation" period, we hear of daily suffering as people chased away from their home villages and meandering over terrain they do not recognize swear earnestly that they will take back their former land holdings. This is also well known from the singing of Zhou Xuan (1918–57) in the 1937 film *Sanxing banyue* (Three Stars and the Moon), and the song "Heri jun zailai" (When Will You Return?), famous in Japan where it was performed by Watanabe Hamako (1910–99) and Li Xianglan (Ri Kōran, Yamaguchi Yoshiko, b. 1920), and the word *jun* (meaning "you") replaced the meaning of the word *jun* (meaning "army"), pronounced in precisely the same way. It became popular as an anti-Japanese ballad of waiting expectantly for that day when the Chinese army would return to expel the Japanese in Manzhouguo.

As for Koreans living in the area, from before the founding of Manzhouguo, there were people working on paddy lands who had their lands bought up for Japanese agricultural immigrants and had no choice but to become their tenant farmers. After the founding of the state as well, in semi-compulsory fashion, the Korean Government-General moved farmers from the southern part of Korea where there was little arable soil by means of the Korea-Manzhouguo Colonial Company; from 60,000–70,000 persons at the time of the founding of Manzhouguo, the numbers of ethnic Koreans thus rose to 2,160,000 by 1945. Corresponding to this, the number of ethnic Korean officials in the Manzhouguo government rose to 2,300 in 1940. Furthermore, from 1940 a Young Korean Volunteer Army was mobilized to settle in the region. During the Manzhouguo period, Japanese were dubbed "Eastern devils" (*Dongyang guizi*) by the Chinese, and ethnic Koreans in Manchuria occupied a subordinate position, dubbed "secondary devils" (*er guizi*). After the war, they found themselves in extremely straightened circumstances; for economic reasons, they could not return home to Korea, and nearly 1,120,000 were, perforce, left behind. Although the Koreans discharged their obligation to national defense as "important structural elements in Manzhouguo,"[27] second only to Japanese, at the same time they were taxed and drafted as "citizens of the empire," mobilized to fight on the front in China and Southeast Asia, and suspected of war crimes; many were interned in Siberia. After the war, though, they lost their Japanese citizenship, and they were thus excluded from protection and compensation.

A Korean man who came from Manchuria whom I once met had come to Japan to study sociology. After the war, he earned a reputation in the United States as a scholar and was invited to Europe. "I never thought that rulership in Manzhouguo was a good thing," he explained to me. "However, the opportunity in my life to study in Japan was certainly a good thing. Had I not had that opportunity, I would probably have spent my entire life working as a farmer." Had Japan not taken control over Manchuria, of course, altogether different possibilities might also have opened up, so I would not want to generalize on the basis of this man's experience. However, take the case of Pak Chŏng-hŭi (Park Chung-hee, 1917–79), the former president of the Republic of Korea who came from a poor rural family; had he not studied at the Japanese Army School in Manzhouguo and at the Army Cadet School at state expense, he would probably not have risen to a central position in the military and taken over the reins of government.

In this highly limited sense, the very existence of such slogans as "ethnic cooperation" or "cooperation among the five ethnicities" in Manzhouguo—even if agree that there were simply slogans—nonetheless effectively set standards which necessitated the inclusion of a certain number of Chinese and Koreans in schools and other public institutions. Of course, without Japanese colonial control, there might have been opportunities for even more people to easily rise to positions of prominence. However, even if it was simply a fabrication, it is also a fact that Manzhouguo had perforce to open doors in government offices and in educational institutions, even if only on a small scale, to peoples other than the Japanese, insofar as ethnic cooperation was being offered up as a national plan.

As concerns these other ethnic groups, there were people among the minority ethnicities who had been repressed until then and who placed their hopes for ethnic autonomy in this purported Manzhouguo state-founding ideal of ethnic cooperation.

Take the example of a Buryat Mongol by the name of Garmaev Urzhin. Born in the Siberian city of Chita, Urzhin became a professional soldier in the Russian army. At the time of the Russian Revolution, he joined the Cossack forces of the Grigori Semenov (1891–1946) then being supported by the Japanese military which was engaged in the Siberian Expedition. After being routed at Xinihe in Inner Mongolia, he entered Manzhouguo and became the key man among Mongol forces in its Xing'an provincial garrison army. After the collapse of Manzhouguo, he surrendered to the Soviets, and on suspicion by a military tribunal of having worked for Japanese Special Services, he was shot and so ended his career. How genuine the ideal of ethnic cooperation in Manzhouguo was for Urzhin is unknown, but he remained to the very end duty-bound as president of the Xing'an Provincial Military School in an uprising of Mongolian forces apparently tinged with a fierce anti-Communism. Semenov himself assembled in Manzhouguo the White Russians opposed to the Russian Revolution and inquired about the opportunity of launching a counteroffensive against the Soviet Union, but he was caught and executed by a military court after the collapse of Manzhouguo.

Manzhouguo with its rich mixture of over thirty ethnicities was home to White Russians, Jews, Poles, and others. In order to get information on the Soviet Union in Manzhouguo, they adopted a policy of protecting the fiercely anti-Communist White Russians as well as Muslims who had escaped from Central Asia. There were White Russians among the students at the State-Founding University of Manzhouguo. Thus, for White Russians and Muslims, Manzhouguo was a kind of safe haven offering to people who lived under Soviet oppression a place to live, but this also became the reason they were further oppressed when the Soviets counterattacked when the war ended. To be sure, it was not that the Manzhouguo government actively sought to offer these people a place to live in peace, but rather Manzhouguo situated as it was amid the flow of world historical peoples through the Trans-Siberian Railway was preparing to pursue war against the Soviet Union and against the United States and was trying to make use of Jews and Muslims and Poles.

Question 18: It has been said that Manzhouguo had plans to settle Jews and come up with a "cooperation among the *six* ethnic groups," but what actually was the Jewish policy of the Japanese and Manzhouguo governments?

In addition to Russian Jews who fled after the Russian Revolution as well as Polish Jews, Manzhouguo provided a place for Jews fleeing Nazi persecution in Europe on a scope second only to Shanghai. However, in places like Harbin, many Jews were thought to be among the leaders of the Soviet Communist Party leadership, which fueled the anti-Semitic sentiment of principally the White Russians there. Thus, rather than settling in Manzhouguo, many Jews transited through Manzhouguo with the hope of making their way overseas to the United States or elsewhere.

Given this experience, S.M.R. President Matsuoka Yōsuke (1880–1946) and Chairman of the Manchurian Heavy Industry Company Ayukawa Yoshisuke (1880–1967) looked into devising a plan for settling on the order of 50,000 Jews in Manzhouguo. Among those involved in developing an implementation design were such military men as Higuchi Kiichirō (1888–1970) of the Harbin Special Services Agency, Yasue Norihiro (1888–1950) of the army, and Inuzuka Koreshige (1890–1945) of the navy, as well as the private scholar of Jewish studies, Kotsuji Setsuzō (Abraham Kotsuji, 1899–1973). While the settlement plan looked forward to the influx of capital from the United States and effected the transmigration of the Nissan Corporation to Manzhouguo, Ayukawa Yoshisuke, whose supply of needed goods had been cut off, and Matsuoka Yōsuke, who had sought to activate the sluggish Manchurian economy, had come with the idea that, if their plans materialized, then as a result they would be able to make use of Jewish capital and technical skills. At the same time, their aim was to use the influence of Jews in American mass media and politics to be in a position to encourage a change of policy in the U.S. government which had adopted a stance of non-recognition toward Manzhouguo. Meanwhile, in places such as Harbin, there were repeated acts of kidnapping Jews and attacks on them, and international suspicions were strong that the Manzhouguo government was behind these acts. Thus, should a "cooperation of the six ethnic groups" ever materialize by virtue of a settlement, it was hoped that this might be effective propaganda.

With these ulterior aims, Jewish policy in Manzhouguo went through these confused machinations, and in December of 1937 the First Conference of Far Eastern Jewry convened in Harbin. A manifesto of "no coercion of small or weak peoples between Japan and Manzhouguo" was adopted, and the following March 1938 somewhat fewer than 20,000 Jews, who had escaped from Europe and been refused entrance into Manzhouguo and forced into a refugee existence at Otopol in Soviet terrain, were given permission to transit. Higuchi Kiichirō, who worked hard to get the Manzhouguo government to accept this transit arrangement, though, criticized "the attitude of Manzhouguo which was espousing the motto of 'cooperation of the five ethnic groups' and appealling for 'all peoples to live in peace and prosperity' as completely incomprehensible"—despite both Poland and the Soviet Union having already given transit permission.[28] The Manzhouguo foreign ministry nonetheless continued throughout to take a passive stance on accepting these Jewish refugees out of concern for the German government.

By the same token, the Japanese government in December 1938 convened the Five Ministers Conference at the behest of Prime Minister Konoe Fumimaro (1891–1945), and on the basis of the principle that the expulsion of the Jews violated the equality of the races, from "the necessity of attracting foreign capital to pursue the war and especially for economic construction as well as from the viewpoint of wishing to avoid the deterioration of ties with the United States,"[29] a decision was reached concerning Jews resident in Japan, Manzhouguo, and China that they would be treated fairly just as any other nationality and that no active policy of expulsion or invitation levied toward them. There was the proviso, however, that "there would no such limitation imposed on individuals with use value such as capitalists and technicians," and thus it was clear that they were adopting a plan that would, in fact, actively invite Jews with "use value."[30]

Japan, Germany, and Italy signed the Tripartite Alliance in September 1940, and circumstances were then such that expectation of a favorable turn in relations with Great Britain and the United States which could make use of the Jews could no longer be wished for, and thus for Japan and Manzhouguo, the "Jewish card" lost its effectiveness. Thus, the Fourth Conference of Far Eastern Jewry scheduled to convene in December 1940 in Dalian was canceled just prior to its planned opening. Yasue Norihiro was dismissed from his position as head of the Dalian Special Services Agency, and Higuchi and Inuzuka Koreshige were cut off from any further role in maneuvers involving Jews.

In a decision reached by a liaison committee of the Japanese government in March 1942, after the commencement of the U.S.-Japan war, it was deemed unnecessary to be concerned with public opinion in Britain, the U.S., or elsewhere in the world, and in Manzhouguo or in territory occupied by Japan "there will be no special conditions allowing for Jews to come, this now being completely prohibited"; "close scrutiny is to be exercised of their residences and businesses, and any enemy machinations are to be eliminated and suppressed"; and "we shall no longer do anything to support the Jewish people's movement."[31] With this decision, establishment of a Jewish settlement area or autonomous zone in Manzhouguo ended without realization. The very conception of this was extremely instrumental. From the 1930s in Japan as well, men such as Shiōden Nobutaka (1879–1962) and Sakai Katsutoki (1874–1940) were claiming that most of the leaders of the Soviet Communist Party were Jews and that Jews were "red devils" who plotted to infiltrate Communist thought into Japan. Such anti-Semitic propaganda was loudly raised as a part of anti-Communism, and thus there were clearly limits to the realization of "cooperation among the six ethnic groups" in Manzhouguo.

Question 19: With the Soviet entry into the war against Japan on August 9, 1945, the Japanese living in Manzhouguo found themselves in tragic circumstances, but was the Japanese settlement when defeat was imminent problematic?

With the acceptance and notification of the Potsdam Declaration on August 14, 1945, the war did not automatically come to an end, but negotiations became necessary for how best to disarm the Japanese military and execute the conditions of surrender. To that end, Lieutenant General Kawabe Torashirō (1890–1960) was sent as plenipotentiary to draw up the armistice agreement in Manila at the headquarters of General Douglas MacArthur, the allied commander. On August 20 the documents of surrender were accepted. Despite the fact that at that time they received notification from SCAP that the Soviet Army was not under the control of the allied armed forces, Japan entrusted the fate of the Guandong Army on the scene to negotiation with the Soviets, ultimately not sending a plenipotentiary delegate to General Rodion Malinovskii (b. 1898), supreme commander of the Soviet Far Eastern Army. Because the expected cease-fire negotiations were not carried out, military actions by the Soviet army which did not recognize the Guandong Army as the formal representative of the Japanese government continued, and Japanese and Koreans remaining in not only the former Manzhouguo but Korea, Sakhalin, and the Kurile Islands were forced into an extremely difficult situation.

The problem was that, with the adoption of the principle of territorial occupation by which the U.S. and the Soviet Union decided areas under their respective control by virtue of the terrain they occupied at the conclusion of the war in Europe, the Soviets demanded of the U.S., given the actual results of occupation, the northern part of Hokkaido. Thus, even with cease-fire negotiations and cease-fire accords in place, the Soviets ignored this and proceeded with fighting with the plan of possibly extending the area under their occupation. Having entrusted negotiations to the Guandong Army, however, the Japanese government did not clearly express its intentions, and this afforded the Soviet Union an extraordinary pretext. Soviet strategic invasions continued until August 20 in the former Manzhouguo, until August 26 in Sakhalin, and until October 5 in the Kuriles, all increasing the numbers of dead and interned.

Question 20: What sort of situation did Japanese face after the collapse of Manzhouguo?

There were some 230,000 Japanese living in Manchuria in September 1931 at the time of the outbreak of the Manchurian Incident; in August 1945 their numbers had swelled to 6.7 times that number, or 1,550,000. Compared to the 400,000 Japanese in Taiwan, which they ruled for fifty years, and the 900,000 in Korea, which they controlled for thirty-five years, their numbers had risen greatly in a much shorter period of time. Perhaps there was something in the catchphrase—"Fertile soil for one thousand *ri* beckons you, warriors of the soil, to that hybrid, Manchuria"—which appealed to the sensibilities of Japanese who were worried about population increase and loss of employment. The pioneer immigrants among them numbered roughly 270,000, and during the period of withdrawal some 80,000 lost their lives in a tragic conclusion.

There were, indeed, mistakes made in the cease-fire negotiations and in the disarming of Japanese soldiers, which led to tragedy of over 600,000 being interned in Siberia, of whom over 60,000 perished. Of course, internment itself was in clear violation of the Potsdam Declaration, which stated: "The Japanese military forces, after being completely disarmed, shall be permitted to return to their homes with the opportunity to lead peaceful and productive lives." Nonetheless, Japanese detainees under this violation of international law remained, in the most extreme instance, held until 1956 or for eleven years.

Following the collapse of Manzhouguo, not only did the Guomindang (Nationalist Party) and the Chinese Communists return to a state of civil war in the region, with advances and retreats going back and forth, but the Soviet army remained in a complex position of power with considerable influence. In the midst of this, Japanese, citizens of a defeated state, were subject to forced repatriation as "Japanese prisoners" who bore responsibility for the invasion of China. There were repatriation vessels, and people were compelled to live in camps. Suicides and massacres during escapes as well as the spread of infectious diseases and malnutrition cruelly took the lives of 180,000 of the 1,550,000 Japanese who remained in Manchuria at the time of the defeat.

In order to eke out a bare existence under these circumstances, many worked for agencies of the Guomindang or the Communists or were employed by companies at the scene. Also, there were people out of a sense of individual atonement for the actions perpetrated by Japan who sought independently to offer their specialized knowledge and technical skills to China. Responding to invitation or recruitment to participate in building the new China, technicians, soldiers, doctors, nurses, and others voluntarily chose to remain in China. Such men and women were dubbed people who were "retained in employment" (*liuyong*); their numbers have been estimated at roughly 20,000, including family members, in the area of the former Manzhouguo. In the field of cinema, for example, Sakane Tazuko, the woman movie director mentioned above, Uchida Tomu (1898–1970) who made such films as *Kiga kaikyū* (Straits of Hunger, 1964) and *Miyamoto Musashi* (1961) after returning to Japan, and Kimura Sotoji (1903–88) who promoted the peace movie with such anti-A-bomb films as *Senbazuru* (A Thousand Cranes, 1958) all were retained for employment by the Northeast Film Company, led by the Chinese Communist Party. Mochinaga Tadahiko (1919–99) produced the first Chinese doll animation here, later moving to Shanghai, where he contributed to the reconstruction of Chinese animated films. The issue of "retained in employment" was itself an exceedingly complicated one in which many people found themselves compelled to do things contrary to their desires, but the issue of the ways in which Japanese were involved in the reconstruction of the postwar Asian world in areas outside Manchuria needs to be considered in conjunction to any evaluation leveled at it from our present perspective.

Question 21: Although Manzhouguo ceased to exist on August 18, 1945, how is it best to conceive the importance of Manzhouguo for the postwar Asian world?

First of all, we cannot forget the importance of the fact that the destruction of Manzhouguo meant that a new international order in the East Asian world came into existence. The legitimacy of the Chinese Communists laid emphasis on the facts that, ever since the Manchurian Incident, it had consistently resisted the Japanese invasion, that it brought about the demise of Manzhouguo as a "bogus state" which had denied Chinese sovereignty in the region, and that it won the anti-Japanese war which extended from 1931 through 1945. In these senses, we need to consider that Japanese who supported the view that Manzhouguo was not a bogus regime and that it did have sovereignty were immediately linked to a denial of the legitimacy of the Chinese Communists, namely the basis for the establishment of the new China.

By the same token, although filled with subtle questions concerning the legitimacy of the regime and the state, when we look at the postwar in East Asia, we cannot overlook the meaning of Manzhouguo on the Korean peninsula.

In the Republic of Korea, aside from Pak Chŏng-hŭi, there was indeed an era when talented men educated in Manzhouguo—former students from the Datong Academy such as President Ch'oe Kyu-ha (b. 1919) and graduates of State-Founding University such as Prime Minister Kang Yŏng-hun and Chief of the Army General Staff Min Ki-sik—became the principal actors in the postwar South Korean political arena. This issue is linked in a complex manner to how we evaluate the historical meaning of the "pro-Japanese faction." While this continues to be a point of discussion in Korea, compared to those who were educated in Japan, those Koreans who passed through Manzhouguo seem to have made the most of their capacities and taken free stances on issues. In the Democratic People's Republic of Korea (North Korea), the legitimacy of the Kim Il-sŏng (1912–94) regime owes its foundations, more than anything else, to its leadership and victory in the anti-Manzhouguo, anti-Japanese war as partisans in Manchuria. The name Kim Il-sŏng itself was, in the first instance, that of a legendary ethnic hero spread among Korean society in the Jiandao region. Its linkage to Manchuria is thus deeply rooted in Korean ethnic sensibilities.

Hence, we need to consider postwar politics in China and on the Korean peninsula in connection to Manzhouguo and in the overall linkage to Manzhouguo as a political space.

Question 22: I believe that Japanese bureaucrats and politicians were sent not only to Manzhouguo but to numerous sites throughout China. How should we view their relations with postwar politics?

During his years as a diplomat, Yoshida Shigeru (1878–1967) worked as consul-general in Tianjin and Fengtian. Shigemitsu Mamoru (1887–1957), who as plenipotentiary signed the documents of surrender aboard the U.S.S. *Missouri* and in the postwar years was active as Minister of Foreign Affairs, served in the Chinese wartime capital of Nanjing as resident ambassador plenipotentiary to the Republic of China. While speaking of those who served as prime minister, in addition to Kishi Nobusuke, Fukuda Takeo (1905–95) spent over two years in Nanjing as a secretary on foreign affairs and as an economic advisor to the Republic of China; Ōhira Masayoshi (1910–80) served for one and one-half years in the Mengjiang (Mongolian borderlands) liaison section of the China Development Board in Zhangjiakou and took part in a household investigation in Inner Mongolia. In the case of Kishi Nobusuke, he worked in Manzhouguo for only three years, but the personal and capital networks he built had extraordinary importance in the postwar political realm. Many men whose experience in Manzhouguo was similar to Kishi's—such as Shiina Etsusaburō, Nemoto

Ryūtarō (b. 1907), Hirashima Toshio (b. 1891), and Shiseki Ihei (1907–91), among others—served postwar governments. Men such as Hoshino Naoki (1892–1978), Matsuda Reisuke (1900–84), Furumi Tadayuki (1900–83), and Ayukawa Yoshisuke formed a mutually supportive structure in the postwar economic world. Although a well known story, when Kishi described his return to Japan from Manzhouguo, he claimed: "It would best for us to use money that is filtered" (in modern parlance, laundered funds). This way of thinking determined his subsequent stance on political funds, and what enabled Class A war criminal Kishi within a mere eight years after being released from Sugamo Prison to push his way back to the pinnacle of power was these personal connections and capital resources from Manchuria. In this important sense, the plutocratic essence of political parties in Japan to this day owes its origins to Manzhouguo. In addition, Kinoshita Shigeru of the Kinoshita Corporation, whose ties to Kishi in the postwar period involving reparations to Indonesia ran deep, set out immediately after the outbreak of the Manchurian Incident to handle dealings in iron materials and scrap metal.

At the time of the Anpo Treaty revisions in 1960, before traveling to the United States, Kishi visited Southeast Asia first. In his own words, his reason was none other than, if Japan was to associate with and cross swords with the United States, it would assume the position as leader of Asia. Then, he argued, the Anpō Treaty could be revised from a position of equality with the U.S. We see here a world view permeated by the notion of a U.S.-Japan face-off as representatives of Western and Eastern civilizations, respectively, of Ishiwara Kanji. In responding to an interviewer's question, Kishi explained: "When I say that Japan must be the leader of Asia, my consciousness now is in fact the same as it was when I went to Manzhouguo. It has remained the same without interruption into the postwar era. If we are to say that I am a pan-Asianist, then my present consciousness is completely in accord with what it was when I went to Manzhouguo."[32]

Putting the question of whether or not Kishi's pan-Asianism was in fact fully consistent with his views when he took up his post in Manzhouguo, it seems clearly to be the case that, to go on living in international society, Japan thought that it had to fix itself firmly in Asia. Thus, prime ministers from Yoshida Shigeru through the era of Kishi, Fukuda, and Ōhira knew Asia to their skin, and because of this they sought in Asia a place for Japan which did not simply follow in the footsteps of the United States. In 1977 Fukuda Takeo proposed what would be called the Fukuda Doctrine: "As a true friend of the countries of Asia, Japan shall build lasting, heart-to-heart relations of mutual trust."[33] In 1980 Ōhira Masayoshi offered a plan for Pacific Rim solidarity to "enable the Pacific region to become one regional society."[34] Furthermore, Ōhira worked tirelessly as foreign minister in the cabinet of Tanaka Kakuei (1918–93) for the revival of Sino-Japanese diplomatic relations, and the "All-China Japanese Teacher-Training Institute" (known popularly as the "Ōhira School") which he created in Beijing in 1980 succeeded on many fronts in fostering "pro-Japanese elements" among those connected to its successor, the Beijing Center for Japanese Studies, as well as Japanese language teachers, scholars of Japanology, and those in the media.

To be sure, Kishi and others were inclined toward colonial control, but they knew only too well from personal experience the vastness of the Asian mainland, its atmosphere, its multiplicity of ethnic groups, and its immense population; and they sensed the difficulty of controlling peoples who feared their control and who were of different cultures. Of course, this is undoubtedly the very same reason they could not escape from a sense of leadership vis-à-vis Asia.

Taking a broad overview of the influence of Manchukuo on postwar Japanese politics, we find Nemoto Ryūtarō (graduate of Daidō Academy) serving as minister of agriculture and forestry, and Ōdachi Shigeo (former director-general for administrative affairs in Manzhouguo) and Araki Masuo (1901–73, former head of the personnel desk in the office of administrative affairs) both serving as ministers of education. In addition to these politicians in the Liberal Democratic Party, Kan Tarō, Susukida Yoshitomo (1897–1963), and Shiobara Tokisaburō, among others, served in the upper house of the Japanese Diet, while Kishi Ryōichi, Kusumi Yoshio, and others served in the lower house. In local administrations, Matsuki Tamotsu (1898–1962, former vice-director for administrative affairs) served as mayor of Tsuruoka in Yamagata Prefecture; Kida Kiyoshi (1900–93, former head of the personnel desk in the office of administrative affairs) served as mayor of Jinjō in Yamagata Prefecture as well; Hoshiko Toshio (1905–95, former director of overall police affairs) served as mayor of Kumamoto City; and Genda Matsuzō (former head of the personnel desk in the office of administrative affairs) served as mayor of Kake Township in Hiroshima Prefecture. It is surely no exaggeration to say that Manzhouguo bequeathed a great many persons to postwar Japanese politics. Of course, the historical importance of this heritage remains for future scholars to investigate.

Question 23: What perspectives are there for studying Manzhouguo, and how would it be best to think about its historical significance?

Naturally, it is essential that the issue of Manzhouguo be understood first and foremost within the historical context that unfolded in that space of China's Northeast. An essential task is for us to relativize and reassess it within the modern history of China, including the era after Manzhouguo's collapse. Such a perspective will henceforth become, I believe, the main current in Chinese scholarship.

Now, when we look solely at Manchuria or Manzhouguo as a historical subject—namely, when we raise the problem as "Manzhouguo history" as a

topic unto itself—it has little meaning. Thus, it is of fundamental importance to stress this phenomenon as one link in modern world history or
modern East Asian history. That I have basically been concerned with
Manzhouguo as a research topic emerged as an "intellectual chain reaction" in the process of collecting historical materials to place modern
Asian history within the flow of world history.

At the same time, it needs to be placed within modern Japanese history
as well; that is, we need to situate Manzhouguo as a principal constituent
element within the overall structure of the colonial, imperial Japanese
regime. The meaning that Manchuria or Manzhouguo possess for modern
Japan is as the axis of colonial control in planning for self-expansion within
an environment of international confrontation. Thus, studies lacking this
perspective will conceal the factual core.

On second thought, looking back over scholarship on the Japanese empire to date, Taiwan, Korea, and the Greater East Asia Coprosperity Sphere
have each been studied separately, but a perspective which involves the
linkages with Manzhouguo has been rare. What we need is a fresh viewpoint to understand how Japan as a colonial empire formed a system
linked with Asia—by seeing Manzhouguo's import as fixed, the flow of
forms of control and the people involved in Taiwan and Korea which preceded it, and the flow of forms of control and personnel from Manzhouguo
to various sites within the Coprosperity Sphere.

In addition, together with the issue of perspective and methodological
framework, I think that one issue which Manzhouguo studies can raise
which will become important in future research is how we incorporate the
viewpoint of space.

In humanistic and social-science research to date, time has been the only
coordinate used as a object. In contrast, I have come to the view that a re-
structuring of humanistic and social-science scholarship from the viewpoint
of space itself and the perception of space will emerge as vital tasks in the
twenty-first century. What sorts of ideas and conceptions do people in different natural environments and different topographies have? It is essential
that we fundamentally rethink just what space means for human beings.

Returning to this issue of Manzhouguo, let us hypothesize that one is apt
to be caught in the closed space in Japan and thus that there are spatial
sensibilities and spatial dispositions which cannot be understood from this
conception of things. Such a hypothesis would became a necessary presup-
position in the case of Manzhouguo as a topic for scholarship, above all,
for Japanese spiritual history or the life record of the Japanese people.

While this is ultimately just one example, the poet Anzai Fuyue
(1898–1965) has a one-line poem entitled *Haru* (Spring) which reads: "A
single butterfly flew across the Straits of Tartary." The spatial sense cap-
tured here is that, if you do not know the space of Manchuria as a real,
bodily sensation, you cannot possibly comprehend it. This was the sense

that I had the first time I stood on the vast terrain of Manchuria; it made me reflect on the absence of a sense of pain in the absolute differential of spatial sensibities in the immensity of the sky and the land and the extraordinary dwarfishness of humanity. In this space where the deep crimson evening sun sets beyond the great prairie one looks out over, beyond the limitless horizon, one senses in a tactile manner the breadth of this space which while living in Japan one cannot possibly experience. It is entirely possible, hence, that one stands in a phase—in terms both of temporal and spatial sensibilities—in which the common sense nurtured in Japan does not hold true. This world in which one is wrapped up in and absorbing the sensations of a different dimension can be articulated in words.

Perhaps, by the same token, this is only a personal impression, but in Japan there is the sense that all space including nature is an extension of one's own body and one can only see what is as large as life. One should not think that the disparity in this sense of distance born between nature and the body is itself related to various aspects of the manner in which Japanese related to Manchuria and Manzhouguo. This question of space is not limited, of course, to research on Manzhouguo, but following the lead of Manzhouguo studies, my hunch is that a new approach in which comprehending space as a key coordinate in humanistic and social science research will be opening up.

Furthermore, taking Manzhouguo as a topic for study is decisely different from research on other historical topics, in that the relative importance of the dimensions of ideology and morality is considerable higher. In humanistic and social-science research generally, objectivity and value-neutrality are essential. By not mixing research with subjective value judgments, one avoids arbitrariness, and insofar as this constitutes scholarship it is a prerequisite naturally demanded of us. Insofar as this concerns Manzhouguo, however, I believe that the need to avoid all value judgments concerning ideals and ideologies does not hold. At least, because Manzhouguo is a historical entity in which, raising such ideals as paradise of the kingly way and cooperation of the five ethnic groups, people were attracted and many lives were plundered, it is impermissable to ignore pressing this issue home. Because people were moved by words and ideals, insofar as we overlook the issue of how people were captivated and how, by the same token, they were fooled, might the same thing be repeated? For, more than anything else, how we are to understand the nature of the human endeavor of ideology is an utterly indispensable task.

As concerns my evaluation in this book of the historical significance of Manzhouguo, I acknowledge that there have been some extremely strong criticisms levelled, some just and some not. In newspaper reviews of this book, in fact, it has been noted that Manzhouguo was colonial rule and thus the existence of ethnic discrimination and exploitation are to be expected—one can't make these into issues; on the other hand, I was criticized for failing to assess the Japanese investment of capital in the region and the development of industry as a result. If I accept that Manzhouguo practiced ethnic discrimination and exploitation without mentioning the ethnic cooperation it advocated, then perhaps I offered an assessment of one who clearly understands that this is elemental to colonial control. By contrast, however, you soon come to see that anyone who boasts that we are all equals and that he will work hard and sacrifice on another's behalf is someone who doubts his own speech; such a person will likely trample under foot his counterpart's aspirations and desires; and despite this, there is no breach of faith harmful to one's counterparts to the extent that one fails to be attentive to said person, is there? This is casuistry, false disinterest, only intended to ring in one's counterparts' ears. Once we recognize that there is an inconsistency of interests here, rather than restrain our response emotionally, surmising logically how long we can coexist does not incur resentment. This is not only a problem related to Japan's colonial rule, but is an issue examined in post-colonial studies of Western colonial rule where it is raised as "civilizing mission" and "white man's burden." While it is easy to parry ideals and ideologies at face value, the more lofty those ideals are at first glace, the more attractive they are to people, the more necessary it is for us to closely interrogate their logical structure and their actual content. This, I believe, is a core task which historical studies simply cannot ignore. This is by no means to stand at some Olympian height and judge the past, questioning others' ethical responsibilities; there is, in fact, no reason to entertain such a perspective.

While I was reading through documents and essays concerned with Manzhouguo, I could not suppress a certain recurrent sense that something was awry: the sense that there was something that might be called "a surplus of lack of consciousness of the other" forming a pair with "an addition to good intentions" or "a surplus of consciousness of the self" lurking concealed within this conviction, a sense that I alone believed and doubtless practiced the ideal of ethnic cooperation. As I continued to be conscious of this, because it left me with a sense of something being out of kilter, in my interactions with foreign scholars and students, it was as if there was a mirror into which I was staring to see if such "a surplus of lack of consciousness of the other" was hidden within me.

Needless to say, what I was most attentive to in the writing of this book was to depict a "portrait of Manzhouguo," as my subtitle reads, from my own perspective in as objective a manner as possible. Before I am a scholar, however, I am a human being, and as such I felt it a more important task to elucidate the nature of the rhetoric by which the ideology and ideals of Manzhouguo became a mechanism giving birth to self-deception and where to locate the ethical and moral qualities in Manzhouguo itself which run through world history. I still firmly believe, irrespective of the criticisms I have received, that there is no need to deny the importance of such items in Manzhouguo studies of the future. But, I have no intention whatsoever of demanding this of others.

Question 24: Finally, then, what importance can we assign to the fact that we are thinking about Manzhouguo at a time over half a century after it ceased to exist?

Yes, to be sure, in the sense of the passage of physical time, over one-half century has elapsed since the collapse of Manzhouguo. Nonetheless, the issues that Manzhouguo raised have not disappeared in the least as issues of the past. Not only the still-unresolved questions of women and orphans abandoned in China at the end of the war, but also the problem of how to deal with such things as the chemical weapons (estimated at 700,000 shells or rounds by the Japanese and at 1,800,000 by the Chinese) abandoned at numerous sites, first and foremost the Chinese Northeast, by the Japanese military; and the issues thrust before us as lawsuits for state reparations in the cases of the Unit 731's germ warfare and the Pindingshan Incident in which some 3,000 Chinese villagers were said to have been massacred by the Japanese army in September 1932. For the women and orphans abandoned on the mainland, returning to Japan has not resolved their problems. Callous everyday issues stand in the way such as: returning together as family groups, how are they going to be able to adapt to Japanese society; without the safety net of a pension and the like and without people with whom to talk, how will they support themselves in retirement? The number of those who have returned to Japan permanently has already reached roughly 20,000, but about 60 percent of the returning orphans have commenced litigation seeking state reparations for livelihood guarantees in retirement. Thus, such issues concerning Manzhouguo remain a "present reality" forming a mountainous pile—including war responsibility and issues deriving from it—which must be considered at a variety of levels.

At present, people who actually lived in and experienced Manzhouguo at first hand are becoming fewer not only in Japan, but in China, Korea, and Taiwan as well, and all manner of alumni associations of schools and military groups from those years continue to be quite active in many places. Efforts in a variety of ways to create people-to-people interactions have emerged in which colleagues in the future will mix so that children and grandchildren born in postwar Japan can revive and relive the experiences of their forefathers who played some role in Manzhouguo, such as by participating in reforestation programs in China, or by requestioning the experience of Manzhouguo in the form of providing assistance to students in Japan from China or Korea.

Thus, consideration of what Manzhouguo was together with such substantive tasks ultimately, I believe, leads to the question of consideration of "now" for us: what is the relationship between the state and its people, between the state and the individual?

For example, let us look momentarily at the novel entitled *Kemonotachi wa kokyō o mezasu* (The beasts head for home) by Abe Kōbō (1924–93) who lived in Shenyang for over eighteen months after the fall of Manzhouguo. From his experience amid the collapse of this entity called Manzhouguo, Abe in this novel focuses squarely on the reality of the "state as a ruined phenomenon" in which, more than anything else, it is always the state that is in collapse. More than this, though, human beings in utter destitution, cut off from their state, their people, and their class, wander about seeking a space to which they can appropriately return; in the end, it seems to me, the novel thrusts before us the realistic reflection that theirs is an existence with a place to go, for which there is no relief. In a state in which all the standards of life have been completely overturned and those constant things in life have ceased to exist, every single day exposes one to the dangers to life itself. Under such circumstances, we are faced with questions such as what are people capable of and what sort of social forms will they forge. For the first time in their history, these are just the kinds of issues Japanese faced so urgently and imminently after the collapse of Manzhouguo when they confronted how to think about a state vis-à-vis the state of nature in which "all men are wolves to one another," which Thomas Hobbes took to be the highest task of the science of governance. Is it not a genuine feeling that one needs to be deeply skeptical when coming out with a response that accords with reality and is appropriate to the weightiness of the sacrifice such an issue necessarily gives rise to? The state and society for us Japanese have been conceptualized solely as givens already and always, but this is surely pregnant with the potential for have originally been "created" or "invented." Manzhouguo was created and it collapsed. I have stuck consistently to the artificiality of Manzhouguo because it is tied to this very issue.

Even if we do not return to this question as an issue of political philosophy, of course, it is still possible for us to recall and consider it in the mix of our own reality as an issue born of the fact that people connected to the Guandong Army who bore responsibility for protecting the state and its people were, in fact, the first to run away. Concealed here is a hint concerning the issue of just what constituted a state's soldiers in the first instance. Just as the selection of the Guandong Army which boasted such elite capacity clearly indicates, a soldier is someone whose continued existence is predicated on the highest task before him of winning in battle; his ultimate essence moves only in the direction of making himself the object to be saved in the final analysis and of minimizing all personal harm.

Of course, although this is only one perspective. It is not merely a question of how the state and its soldiers in Manzhouguo treated individuals or how the individual was linked to the state. It began with the artificial founding of a state by a foreign people, introduced large numbers of immigrants, and brought about its destruction by the armed forces of a foreign people. In this sense, it was an unprecedented historical experience in human history surrounding the state. It was also a historical experience accompanied by far too great a sacrifice—including the 180,000 after the collapse of Manzhouguo and over 60,000 from the over 600,000 detainees in Siberia. Yet, I cannot help but remain convinced that we need to understand Manchuria and Manzhouguo as intellectual sustenance which enable us to contemplate the issue we are facing of multi-ethnic coexistence with people who transcend nationality in the twenty-first century, including the issue of the importance attached to the state among people in the twentieth century and hence the status of the individual within all this.

Dealing with the space of Manchuria and the state of Manzhouguo which have now ceased to exist as such may seem anachronistic, but in order to repay even a little the excessively cruel sacrifices incurred, to bring out and convey some human wisdom even a small amount, we can never relegate this experience to the past and forget it.

Insofar as Manzhouguo remains pregnant with such intellectual tasks, it must remain our "perennial present."

Chronology of the Modern History of Manchuria and East Asia

DATE	EVENTS[1]
1840	Opium War erupts
1842	Treaty of Nanjing: Qing dynasty opens five ports and cedes Hong Kong to Great Britain
1851	Taiping Rebellion begins
1853	arrival of Commodore Perry in Japan; Crimean War breaks out
1854	Kanagawa Treaty (peace treaty between U.S. and Japan)
1855	Shimoda Treaty (commercial treaty between Japan and Russia)
1856	eruption of Arrow War in which Britain and France invade China
1858	Great Britain commences direct rule in India; Britain, France, the U.S., and Russian conclude Treaty of Tianjin with the Qing; Japan and U.S. conclude treaty of amity and commerce; Aigun Treaty between Russia and China concluded
1860	Treaty of Beijing concluded, ceding part of Kowloon peninsula to Britain and giving Russia possession of the Maritime Province
1864	squadron of British, French, American, and Dutch battleships fire on Shimonoseki
1868	Meiji Restoration
1871	seeking commerce, U.S. occupies Korean stronghold at Kanghwa Island; Sino-Japanese Friendship Treaty concluded
1874	Japanese military expedition to Taiwan
1875	treaty exchanging Sakhalin and the Kurile Islands; Unyō Incident at Kanghwa Island
1876	Treaty of Friendship (Treaty of Kanghwa) between Japan and Korea concluded
1879	Japanese seizure of Ryukyu Islands
1882	Imo Incident (military mutiny) in Korea

1884	Kapsin Incident (coup d'état) in Korea; Sino-French War erupts; Russia and Korea establish diplomatic ties
1885	Tianjin Treaty concluded: Qing relinquishes suzerainty over Vietnam, which become protectorate of France
1887	French Indochinese Union formed
1891	Ōtsu Incident in which there is attempted assassination of Russian Crown Prince Nikolai Aleksandrovitch; Russia begins laying track for Trans-Siberian Railway
1894	rebellion of Tonghak Party in Korea; Sino-Japanese War commences
1895	Treaty of Shimonoseki signed and China cedes Liaodong peninsula, Taiwan, and Penghu Islands to Japan; Tripartite Intervention and Liaodong peninsula restored to China
1898	Russia leases Lüshun and Dalian and acquires rights to build Chinese Eastern Railway (Harbin-Lüshun-Dalian); Germany leases Jiaozhouwan; Great Britain leases Weihaiwei
1899	U.S. announces Open Door policy for China; France leases Guangzhouwan
1900	Boxer Rebellion erupts; Joint Expeditionary Forces led by Japan and Russia sent to suppress it
1901	Beijing Protocol signed in which Qing agrees to pay huge indemnities to the powers and allow their armies residence in Beijing; Chinese Eastern Railway opened to traffic
1902	Trans-Siberian Railway between Vladivostok and Khabarovsk opened to traffic; Chinese Eastern Railway between Harbin and Manzhouli opened to traffic; Anglo-Japanese Alliance concluded
1903	Chinese Eastern Railway between Harbin and Lüshun and Yingkou branch line opened to traffic
1904	Russo-Japanese War erupts; Japan-Korea Protocol signed giving Japanese freedom of movement within Korea; first Japan-Korea agreement concluded placing those recommended by the Japanese government as advisors to Korea on finance and foreign affairs
1905	Portsmouth Treaty signed in which Japan acquires protectorate rights in Korea, subsidiary rights to the Chinese Eastern Railway south of Chang'an, and leasing rights to southern Sakhalin and the Liaodong peninsula; second Japan-Korea agreement concluded in which diplomacy passes to Japan, Korea becomes a protectorate, the Residency-General system established, and Itō Hirobumi becomes first resident-general; Hibiya Park riots erupt; notes drawn up between Katsura and Harriman over management of the South Manchurian Railway (later abrogated by Japan)

1906   South Manchurian Railway Company founded (first president, Gotō Shinpei); Guandong Governor-General's office established in Lüshun (army general appointed governor-general)

1907   Secret messenger sent to the Hague by Korean King Kojong; third Japan-Korea agreement concluded in which Korean military disbanded and Japan gains control over Korean domestic political affairs; first Russo-Japanese treaty secretly concluded giving sphere of interest in southern Manchuria to Japan, and in northern Manchuria to Russia, as well as mutual recognition of Japan's special interests in Korea and Russia's in Outer Mongolia

1909   Jiandao Treaty between Japan and China signed establishing a national frontier between Qing China and Korea, regulation over the anti-Japanese movement of Koreans in the region, and the like; Itō Hirobumi assassinated by An Chung-gŭn in Harbin; U.S. proposes neutrality over Manchurian railways (later rejected by Japan and Russia)

1910   Japanese annexation of Korea: "Hanguk" (Japanese *Kankoku*) is abandoned in favor of "Chōsen" (from Korean *Chosŏn*); the Government-General of Korea (*Chōsen sōtokufu*) is established with Terauchi Masatake as its first Resident-General

1911   1911 Revolution in China; return of tariff autonomy to Japan; Mongolia declares independence

1912   downfall of the Qing dynasty and founding of the Republic of China; third Russo-Japanese accords—with the issues raised by the 1911 Revolution and Mongolian independence, Japan and Russia extended the line dividing their spheres of influence to the border between Inner and Outer Mongolia and Inner Mongolia was newly divided east and west

1913   treaty between Mongolia and Tibet mutually recognizing independence; Sino-Russian declaration of Mongolian autonomy (Chinese sovereignty)

1914   start of World War I; Japanese occupation of Qingdao

1915   Japan presents Twenty-One Demands to China (extention to ninety-nine years of Japanese leasehold over the Guandong Territory); Treaty of Kiakhta among China, Russia, and Mongolia (with Outer Mongolia an autonomous state under Chinese suzerainty)

1916   death of Yuan Shikai, followed by warlord regimes; fourth Russo-Japanese accords—a military alliance vis-à-vis a third party in China

1917   Russian Revolution; Ishii-Lansing Agreement; formation of a Soviet government

1918   Siberian Expedition

1919	March First Independence Movement (Korea); reorganization of the Guandong Governor-General's office and the establishment of a Guandong Government and the (independent) Guandong Army; May Fourth Movement; China forces Mongolia to abandon autonomy
1920	League of Nations is launched
1921	formation of the Guangdong military government; Chinese Communist Party founded in Shanghai
1922	Sun Zhongshan (Sun Yat-sen) launches Northern Expedition; Zhang Zuolin announces independence of the Three Eastern Provinces (Manchuria); Washington Naval Limitations Treaty signed; Nine-Power Treaty concluded—U.S. advocacy on behalf of China passes and Japanese interests regress
1924	First United Front between the Chinese Communists and Nationalists (Guomindang); declaration of independence by the People's Republic of Mongolia
1925	Sun Zhongshan and Jiang Jieshi (Chiang Kai-shek) commence Northern Expedition; May 30 Incident, an anti-imperialist movement of workers in Shanghai
1926	Zhang Zuolin organizes military government in Beijing and becomes generalissimo
1927	first Japanese dispatch of troops to Shandong; Far Eastern Conference convened in Japan (decision reached on the severance of Manchuria-Mongolia and to support the Guomindang); Jiang Jieshi's coup d'état and the end of the First United Front; Mao Zedong and the Red Army commence struggle for armed, liberated areas
1928	Guomindang government recommences Northern Expedition; second Shandong expedition by Japan; murder of Zhang Zuolin; Zhang Xueliang unites forces with Nationalist government; Ishiwara Kanji becomes staff officer with Guandong Army
1929	beginning of Great Depression
1930	May 30 uprising in Jiandao led by Korean Communists resident in Jiandao
1931	Liutiaohu Incident; occupation of Fengtian and Chichihar by the Guandong Army
1932	Guandong Army occupies Harbin; State-Founding Proclamation of Manzhouguo; Lytton Commission comes to Manchuria; Japan-Manzhouguo Protocol
1933	Guandong Army occupies Shanhaiguan and invades Rehe Province; Japan secedes from the League of Nations; Tanggu Truce concluded
1934	monarchy instituted in Manzhouguo with Puyi as emperor

1935	Japan, Manzhouguo, and Soviet Union conclude transfer of the North Manchurian Railway (formerly, Chinese Eastern Railway)
1936	Japan and Germany conclude Anti-Comintern Pact; Xi'an Incident occurs in which Jiang Jieshi imprisoned by Zhang Xueliang and Zhou Enlai's reasoning prevails
1937	Marco Polo Bridge Incident; Second United Front; Nationalist government moves its capital to Chongqing
1938	first Konoe statement abrogating diplomatic relations with China; second Konoe statement announcing the New Order in East Asia
1939	clash between Outer Mongolian Army and Manzhouguo Army at Nomonhan, leading to a battle between Soviet and Japanese forces; Germany invades Poland and World War II breaks out
1940	Axis Alliance (Germany, Japan, Italy) concluded
1941	neutrality treaty between Japan and Soviet Union; Japan attacks Pearl Harbor, leading to war with the United States and Great Britain
1944	first air raids of U.S. B-29 bombers on Anshan, Fengtian, and Dalian
1945	Soviet Union declares war on Japan; Sino-Soviet treaty of friendship concluded with accords on Manchurian Railways, Lüshun, and Dalian; Japan issues unconditional surrender; U.S. and Soviet Union divide the Korean peninsula north and south; Emperor Puyi of Manzhouguo deposed
1946	Nationalist government recognizes People's Republic of Mongolia; Soviet Army withdraws from northeast China; Nationalist-Communist civil war grows serious
1948	Republic of Korea founded; People's Democratic Republic of Korea founded
1949	People's Republic of China founded

Notes

Introduction

1. In Manshūkoku shi hensan kankōkai, ed., *Manshūkoku shi sōron* (History of Manzhouguo, an overall view) (Tokyo: Man-Mō dōhō engokai, 1970), 5.

2. In Manshū kaikōshū kankōkai, ed., *Aa Manshū, kunitsukuri sangyō kaihatsusha no shuki* (Ah, Manchuria, notes of an industrial developer for state-formation) (Tokyo: Manshū kaikōshū kankōkai, 1965), 302.

3. Furumi Tadayuki, "Manshūkoku no yume wa kienai" (My dream of Manzhouguo will never be extinguished), in Furumi and Katakura Tadashi, *Zasetsu shita risōkoku, Manshūkoku kōbō no shinsō* (An ideal state frustrated, the truth about the rise and fall of Manzhouguo) (Tokyo: Gendai bukkusha, 1967), 2.

4. Katakura Tadashi, *Kaisō no Manshūkoku* (Reminiscences of Manzhouguo) (Tokyo: Keizai ōraisha, 1978), 325.

5. Hoshino Naoki, *Mihatenu yume, Manshūkoku gaishi* (An unfinished dream, an unofficial history of Manzhouguo) (Tokyo: Daiyamondosha, 1963), 66–67.

6. In *Aa Manshū*, 325.

7. Hoshino Naoki, *Mihatenu yume*, 12.

8. In Mutō Tomio, *Watakushi to Manshūkoku* (Manzhouguo and me) (Tokyo: Bungei shunjū, 1987), 12.

9. I should note in advance several points that emerge in the narrative of this volume. First, the name "Manzhouguo" was not a term initially agreed upon by the people who lived there, and to that extent it lacked popular legitimacy as a state. Second, in China the region in which Manzhouguo was founded was called at the time "Dongsansheng" (Three Eastern Provinces) or "Dongbei" (the Northeast), "Manzhou" or "Manshū" (Manchuria) in Japanese being a Japanese appellation. Similarly, there were the two names of "Manzhouguo" and "Manzhou diguo" (Empire of Manchuria) used at different times when the state system was a republican one and when it was a constitutional monarchy. These and similar issues reveal that even today there is not necessarily an established historical vocabulary.

Chapter 1. Japan's "Sole Road for Survival"

1. Translator's note. The term "Man-Mō" (translated simply as "Manchuria-Mongolia") was frequently used in prewar Japanese writings, popular and scholarly, to designate a vaguely defined area north and east of the Great Wall.

2. This and the previous quotation in this paragraph were common expressions from this time.

3. Tō-A keizai chōsakyoku, comp., *Sanminshugi shōka kahon* (Textbook of songs for the Three People's Principles) (1929), number 9, 62–63.

4. Itō Musojirō, *Manshū mondai no rekishi* (History of the Manchurian problem), two volumes (Tokyo: Hara shobō, 1983–84), 875.

5. "Kokuun tenkai no konpon kokusaku taru Man-Mō mondai kaiketsusaku" (Policy to resolve the Manchuria-Mongolia issue, basic national policy in the evolution of the fate of the nation), dated July 5, 1929; hereafter, "Kaiketsusaku." Citations to Ishiwara's discussion of policy are drawn primarily from Tsunoda Jun, ed., *Ishiwara Kanji shiryō, kokubō ronsaku* (Materials on Ishiwara Kanji, issues of national defense) (Tokyo: Hara shobō, 1967), 40.

6. Ishiwara, "Genzai oyobi shōrai ni okeru Nihon no kokubō" (Japan's national defense at present and in the future) (hereafter, "Kokubō"), in Tsunoda Jun, 65.

7. "Kokubō," 63.

8. "Kokubō," 63.

9. "Kaiketsusaku," 40.

10. "Man-Mō mondai shiken" (Personal views on the Manchuria-Mongolia issue) (May 1931), in Tsunoda Jun, ed., *Ishiwara Kanji shiryō, kokubō ronsaku*, 77.

11. "Man-Mō mondai shiken," 76.

12. Ishibashi Tanzan, "Man-Mō mondai kaiketsu no konpon hōshin ikan" (What should the basic plan be for resolution of the Manchuria-Mongolia issue?), *Tōyō keizai shinpō* (October 10, 1931), 13.

13. "Kaiketsusaku," 40.

14. Chiga Tsurutarō, "Nihon no Ōshū senran ni taisuru chii" (Japan's position toward the European war), *Taiyō* (September 27, 1917), 12.

15. Ibid.

16. *Teikoku kokubō shigen* (Resources for the defense of the empire) (1917), in Koiso Kuniaki, *Katsuzan sōkō* (self-published, 1963), 343.

17. *Ugaki Kazushige nikki* (Diary of Ugaki Kazushige) (entry dated January 1918), ed. Tsunoda Jun (Tokyo: Misuzu shobō, 1968), 150.

18. "Kaiketsusaku," 40.

19. "Kaiketsusaku," 41.

20. Itagaki Seishirō, "Gunjijō yori mitaru Man-Mō ni tsuite" (On Manchuria and Mongolia as seen from the military) (March 1931), in Kobayashi Tatsuo and Shimada Toshihiko, eds., *Gendai shi shiryō 7: Manshū jihen* (Materials on contemporary history, volume 7: The Manchurian Incident) (Tokyo: Misuzu shobō, 1964), 142.

21. "Man-Mō mondai shiken," 76.

22. "Man-Mō mondai shiken," 78.

23. "Gunjijō yori mitaru Man-Mō ni tsuite," 140.

24. "Man-Mō mondai shiken," 77.

25. Satō Yasunosuke, "Manshū mondai" (The Manchuria issue), in Nasu Akira, ed., *Shanhai ni okeru Taiheiyō kaigi* (The Pacific Conference in Shanghai) (1932).

26. Minami Manshū tetsudō kabushiki gaisha shachōshitsu jinjika (Personnel office of the office of the president of the S.M.R.), ed., *Zai-Man Senjin appaku jijō* (Situation concerning pressures on Koreans in Manchuria) (Dalian: Minami Manshū tetsudō kabushiki gaisha, 1928), 50.

27. "Kantō shuppei seimei" (Declaration of sending troops to Jiandao), in *Nihon gaikō nenpyō narabi ni shuyō monjo* (Chronology of Japan diplomacy and principal documents), ed. Gaimushō (Tokyo: Nihon kokusai rengō kyōkai, 1955), vol. 1, 517.

28. Toyoshima Fusatarō, "Chōsengun ekkyō shingeki su" (The Korea Army attacks across the border), *Bessatsu chisei* 5 (December 1956), 58.

29. Ibid.

30. "Man-Mō mondai ni tsuite" (On the Manchuria-Mongolia issue) (May 1932),

in Inaba Masao and Kobayashi Tatsuo, eds., *Taiheiyō sensō e no michi, bekkan, shiryōhen* (The road to the Pacific War, additional volume, documents) (Tokyo: Asahi shinbun sha, 1963), 106.

31. Gaimushō (Ministry of Foreign Affairs), ed., *Nihon to Man-Mō* (Japan and Manchuria-Mongolia) (Tokyo: Kokusai renmei Shina chōsa Gaimushō junbi iinkai, 1932), 34–35.

32. "Kantōgun sanbō [hon]bu iken" (Views of the General Staff Headquarters of the Guandong Army) (1931), in Kobayashi Tatsuo and Shimada Toshihiko, eds., *Gendai shi shiryō, 7: Manshū jihen*, 162.

33. Itagaki Seishirō, "Gunjijō yori mitaru Man-Mō ni tsuite," 140.

34. Itagaki Seishirō, "Man-Mō mondai ni tsuite," 107.

35. Itagaki Seishirō, "Man-Mō mondai ni tsuite," 102.

36. Ishiwara Kanji, "Man-Mō mondai shiken," 77.

37. "Man-Mō mondai kaiketsu no tame no sensō keikaku taikō" (Outlines of a war plan for the resolution of the Manchuria-Mongolia issue) (April 1931), in Tsunoda Jun, ed., *Ishiwara Kanji shiryō, kokubō ronsaku*, 70

38. "Kaiketsusaku," 40.

39. "Gunjijō yori mitaru Man-Mō ni tsuite," 142–43.

40. "Man-Mō mondai shiken," 78.

41. "Kaiketsusaku," 40.

42. "Kokubō," 60.

43. "Kokubō," 59.

44. "Gunjijō yori mitaru Nichi-Bei sensō" (The Japan-United States war from a military perspective) (May 20, 1930), in Tsunoda Jun, ed., *Ishiwara Kanji shiryō, kokubō ronsaku*, p. 49.

45. Ishiwara Kanji, *Shin Nihon no kensetsu* (Construction of the new Japan) (Tō-A renmei dōshikai, Kansai jimusho, 1945), 39.

46. "Kaiketsusaku," 40.

47. In Japanese: "Seigi no shihai suru tokoro, buki wa muyō de aru."

48. Translator's note. The reference here is to *Livy*, Book 9.1.10: "Iustum est bellum, Samnites, quibus necessarium, et pia arma, quibus nulla nisi in armis relinquitur spes." The reference is to the Samnites talking about what monsters the Romans are (ca. 4th century B.C.E.). Many thanks to Christina Kraus of Yale University for tracking down this reference, apparently the only conjunction in Livy of war, justice, and necessity.

49. "Man-Mō mondai shiken," 77.

50. "Manshū kenkoku zenya no shinkyō" (My state of mind on the eve of the founding of the Manchurian state) (1942), 90.

51. "Man-Mō mondai ni tsuite," 103.

52. "Man-Mō mondai shiken," 77.

53. Kantōgun sanbōbu, "Man-Mō ni okeru senryōchi tōji ni kansuru kenkyū" (Study of controlling occupied terrain in Manchuria and Mongolia) (September 1930), in Tsunoda Jun, ed., *Ishiwara Kanji shiryō, kokubō ronsaku*, 53

54. "Man-Mō mondai kaiketsu no tame no sensō keikaku taikō," 71.

55. "Man-Mō mondai shiken," 77.

56. "Kokubō," 63.

57. (Beiping: Guoli zhongyang yanjiuyuan, lishi yu yuyan yanjiusuo, 1932), frontispiece.

58. Speech of February 19, 1932, Council of the League of Nations, in *Nihon gaikō nenpyō narabi ni shuyō monjo*, vol. 2, 202.

59. "Kokubō," 59.

60. "Kokubō," 60.

Chapter 2. Transforming Manchuria-Mongolia into a Paradise for its Inhabitants

1. Translator's note. The term translated here, "rikugun chūō," refers to the backbone of decision-making in the army centering in the Army Ministry and the Army General Staff Headquarters, both based in Tokyo.

2. "Man-Mō mondai kaiketsusaku an" (Plan for the resolution of the Manchuria-Mongolia problem), in Kobayashi Tatsuo and Shimada Toshihiko, eds., *Gendai shi shiryō, 7: Manshū jihen* (Materials on contemporary history, volume 7: The Manchurian Incident) (Tokyo: Misuzu shobō, 1964), 189.

3. "Manshū jihen kimitsu seiryaku nisshi," in Kobayashi Tatsuo and Shimada Toshihiko, eds., *Gendai shi shiryō, 7: Manshū jihen*, 189. Hereafter "Katakura Diary."

4. "Katakura Diary," 189.

5. "Katakura Diary," 187.

6. "Katakura Diary," 199.

7. "Katakura Diary," 199.

8. "Sentōtei o yōritsu shite dokuritsu kokka kensetsu ka. Tōhoku kakushō no rekei naru," *Manshū nippō*, October 16, 1931.

9. "Man-Mō mondai no konpon hōsaku" (Basic plan for the resolution of the Manchuria-Mongolia problem), in Kobayashi Tatsuo and Shimada Toshihiko, eds., *Gendai shi shiryō, 7: Manshū jihen*, 233.

10. Tachibana Shiraki, *Manshū to Nihon* (Manchuria and Japan) (Tokyo: Kaizōsha, 1931), 169.

11. Tachibana Shiraki, *Manshū to Nihon*, 171.

12. Hayashi Kyūjirō, *Manshū jihen to Hōten sōryōji, Hayashi Kyūjirō ikō* (The Manchurian Incident and the Fengtian Consul-General, the papers of Hayashi Kyūjirō) (Tokyo: Hara shobō, 1978), 94.

13. "Katakura Diary," 332.

14. Gaimushō, ed., *Nihon gaikō monjo, Manshū jihen* (Documents of Japanese diplomacy, the Manchurian Incident) (Tokyo: Gaimushō, 1977), vol. 1.1, 321.

15. Cable from Jilin Consul-General Ishii to Foreign Minister Shidehara (October 7, 1931) in *Nihon gaikō monjo, Manshū jihen*, vol. 1.1, 329.

16. Cable from Fengtian Consul-General Hayashi to Foreign Minister Shidehara (October 3, 1931), in *Nihon gaikō monjo, Manshū jihen*, vol. 1.1, 316.

17. Cable from Fengtian Consul-General Hayashi to Foreign Minister Shidehara (September 30, 1931), in *Nihon gaikō monjo, Manshū jihen*, vol. 1.1, 309.

18. Cable from Fengtian Consul-General Hayashi to Foreign Minister Shidehara (October 3, 1931), in *Nihon gaikō monjo, Manshū jihen*, vol. 1.1, 316.

19. Cable from Fengtian Consul-General Hayashi to Foreign Minister Shidehara (November 6, 1931), in *Nihon gaikō monjo, Manshū jihen*, vol. 1.1, 371.

20. Cable from Fengtian Consul-General Hayashi to Foreign Minister Shidehara (November 7, 1931), in *Nihon gaikō monjo, Manshū jihen*, vol. 1.1, 372.

21. "Katakura Diary," 247.

22. In Kobayashi Tatsuo, Shimada Toshihiko, and Inaba Masao, *Gendai shi shiryō, 11: Zoku Manshū jihen* (Materials on contemporary history, volume 11: The Manchurian Incident, continued) (Tokyo: Misuzu shobō, 1965), 411.

23. Ibid., 411–12.

24. Edgar Snow, *Far Eastern Front* (New York: Harrison Smith & Robert Haas, 1933), 94; Japanese translation: *Kyokutō sensen* by Kajiya Yoshihisa (Tokyo: Chikuma shobō, 1987).

25. Cable from Fengtian Consular Agent Morishima to Foreign Minister Shidehara (November 20, 1931), in *Nihon gaikō monjo, Manshū jihen*, vol. 1.1, 396.

26. Cable from Consul-General Hayashi to Foreign Minister Inukai (December 15, 1931), in *Nihon gaikō monjo, Manshū jihen,* vol. 1.1, 380.

27. "Zang Shiyi bigong" (Deposition of Zang Shiyi, dated August 9, 1954), in Zhongyang dang'anguan et al., eds., *Riben diguozhuyi qin-Hua dang'an ziliao xuanbian, jiuyiba shibian* (Selected archival materials on the Japanese imperialistic invasion of China, the Manchurian Incident) (Beijing: Zhonghua shuju, 1988), 389–93.

28. Zhou Junshi, *Higeki no Kōtei, Fugi: Gi Manshūkoku kyūtei hishi* (Puyi, the tragic emperor: History of the bogus Manzhouguo court), Japanese translation by Tei Zenken (Tokyo: Kōbunsha, 1984), 153–54.

29. In Kobayashi Tatsuo and Shimada Toshihiko, eds., *Gendai shi shiryō, 7: Manshū jihen,* 316.

30. In Tsunoda Jun, ed., *Ishiwara Kanji shiryō, kokubō ronsaku* (Materials on Ishiwara Kanji, issues of national defense) (Tokyo: Hara shobō, 1967), 87.

31. In Tsunoda Jun, ed., *Ishiwara Kanji shiryō, kokubō ronsaku,* 88.

32. Ishiwara, "Manshū kenkoku zen'ya no shinkyō" (My state of mind on the eve of the establishment of Manzhouguo) (1942), in *Ishiwara Kanji shiryō, kokubō ronsaku,* 91. Hereafter "Shinkyō." (Originally appeared in the March 1942 issue of *Tō-A renmei.*)

33. Included in the "Katakura Diary," 333.

34. "Shinkyō," 91.

35. "Shinkyō," 92.

36. In Ishiwara Kanji zenshū kankōkai (Committee for the publication of the collected works of Ishiwara Kanji), ed., *Ishiwara Kanji zenshū* (Collected works of Ishiwara Kanji) (Chiba Prefecture: Ishiwara Kanji kankōkai, 1977), vol. 7, 115.

37. Ishiwara Kanji, *Manshū kenkoku to Shina jihen* (The establishment of the state of Manzhouguo and the China Incident) (Kyoto: Tō-A renmei kyōkai, Kansai jimusho, 1940), 78–79.

38. "Manshū jihen shi, Manshū jihen ni okeru gun no tōsui (an)," 411.

39. "Manshū jihen shi, Manshū jihen ni okeru gun no tōsui (an)," 411.

40. "U Chūkan no shutsuro to sono seiken" (Yu Chonghan's coming out of retirement and his political views) (November 22, 1931), in Kobayashi, Shimada, and Inaba, *Gendai shi shiryō, 11: Zoku Manshū jihen,* 569.

41. "Yo no risō" (My ideals), *Manshū nippō,* January 1, 1932.

42. "Tairiku seisaku jūnen no kentō" (Discussion of ten years of mainland policies), *Manshū hyōron* 21.17 (October 25, 1941), 30.

43. "Manshū kokumin kara mita Manshū mondai" (The Manchuria issue as seen from the perspective of the Manchurian people), *Manshū hyōron* 2 (June 4, 1932), 2–3.

44. *Manshū kenkoku to Shina jihen,* 72.

45. "U Chūkan no shutsuro to sono seiken," in Kobayashi, Shimada, and Inaba, *Gendai shi shiryō, 11: Zoku Manshū jihen,* 570.

46. "Katakura Diary," 313.

47. *Manshū jihen shi,* 412.

48. "Katakura Diary," 237.

49. "Katakura Diary," 213.

50. Manshū seinen renmei shi kankō iinkai, ed., *Manshū seinen renmei shi* (A history of the Manchurian Youth League) (Tokyo: Hara shobō, 1968 reprint; 1933 original), 35.

51. Greetings from the Kobiyama Naoto, chairman of the board, at the first meeting of branch heads of the Manchurian Youth League. In *Manshū seinen renmei shi,* 73.

52. *Manshū seinen renmei shi,* 456.

53. (Dairen: Manshū seinen renmei honbu, June 1931).

54. *Manshū seinen renmei shi*, 455–56.

55. In Japanese, respectively: "Nik-Ka wagō," "Nik-Ka seinen kyōwa," and "Nik-ka kyōson kyōei."

56. Itō Musojirō, *Manshū mondai no rekishi* (History of the Manchuria problem) (Tokyo: Hara shobō, 1983), vol. 2, 1008.

57. Kanai Shōji, "Manshū kenkoku to seinen renmei no katsuyaku" (The establishment of a state in Manchuria and the activities of the Youth League), in *Manshū kenkoku sokumen shi* (A history of one side of the establishment of a state in Manchuria), ed. Miyauchi Isamu (Tokyo: Shin keizai sha, 1942), 36.

58. *Kyōwa* (June 1, 1927), 148.

59. *Manshū seinen renmei shi*, 99.

60. *Manshū seinen renmei shi*, 156.

61. Hirashima Toshio, "Seinen renmei tōji no kokusai kankyō" (The Youth League in the present international environment), in *Manshū kenkoku sokumen shi*, 58.

62. *Manshū seinen renmei shi*, 535.

63. *Manshū seinen renmei shi*, 520.

64. "Ryōnei shō seiji kikan fukkatsu yōryō" (Outlines of the revival of political agencies in Liaoning Province), in *Manshū jihen chokugo ni okeru Hōtenshō gyōzaisei ni kansuru shōhō* (Full report on the administration and finances of Fengtian Province in the immediate aftermath of the Manchurian Incident), ed. Guandong Army (self-published, 1932), 11.

65. Ōkawa Shūmei, "Chō Gakuryō shi o toburau no ki" (Account of a visit to Mr. Zhang Xueliang), *Gekkan Nihon* (November 1928), in Ōkawa Shūmei zenshū kankōkai (Committee for the publication of the collected works of Ōkawa Shūmei) *Ōkawa Shūmei zenshū* (Collected works of Ōkawa Shūmei) (Tokyo: Iwanami shoten, 1962), vol. 4, 599.

66. "Aikokusha no yūitsu ro" (The only road for patriots), *Gekkan Nihon* 4 (August 1925), 26.

67. Ibid., 31.

68. In Kinoshita Hanji, *Nihon kokkashugi undō shi* (A history of the nationalist movement in Japan) (Tokyo: Fukutake shuppan, 1971), vol. 1, 59.

69. In Kobayashi and Shimada, eds., *Gendai shi shiryō, 7: Manshū jihen*, 237.

70. Manshūkoku shi hensan kankōkai, ed., *Manshūkoku shi sōron* (History of Manzhouguo, an overall view) (Tokyo: Man-Mō dōhō engokai, 1970), 153.

71. "Chihō jichi shidō ni kansuru shian" (Our plan concerning the local self-government guidance board), in *Manshūkoku shi kakuron* (History of Manzhouguo, detailed exposition) (Tokyo: Man-Mō dōhō engokai, 1971), 1971, 160.

72. In Kobayashi, Shimada, and Inaba, *Gendai shi shiryō, 11: Zoku Manshū jihen*, 571.

73. Kasagi Yoshiaki, "Manshūkoku kenki sanjikan no dai shimei" (The great mission of county-level counselors in Manzhouguo), *Dai Ajia* (October 1933), 5.

74. Kasagi Yoshiaki, "Manshūkoku ken sanjikan seido no jūyōsei" (The importance of the system of county advisors in Manzhouguo), *Kaizō* (June 1933), 77.

75. Kasagi Yoshiaki, "Manshūkoku ken sanjikan seido no jūyōsei," 77.

76. "Jichi shidōin fukumu kokoroe" (Rules of service for the members of the Self-Government Guidance Board), in Manshūkoku shi hensan kankōkai, ed., *Manshūkoku shi sōron*, 158.

77. Ibid., 158.

78. Kasagi Yoshiaki, "Manshūkoku kenki sanjikan no dai shimei," 5.

79. Masuda Wataru, *Ro Jin no inshō* (Impressions of Lu Xun) (Tokyo: Kōdansha, 1966), 42.

80. Both volumes were published by Nihon hyōronsha, in Tokyo.

81. Tachibana Shiraki, *Shokuiki hōkō ron* (On service in one's post) (Tokyo: Nihon hyōronsha, 1942), 1.

82. Tachibana Shiraki, "Shina wa dō naru ka" (Whither China?), *Gekkan Shina kenkyū* 1.3 (February 1925), 8.

83. Tachibana Shiraki, "Shina o shiru no michi" (How to understand China), *Gekkan Shina kenkyū* 1.1 (December 1924), 7.

84. Tachibana Shiraki, "Shina kinji no minzoku undō oyobi Shanhai jiken no shisō teki haikei" (The recent popular movement in China and the intellectual background to the Shanghai incident), *Gekkan Shina kenkyū* 2.3 (August 1925), 104.

85. Ibid., 106.

86. Tachibana Shiraki, "Shina hihan no shin kichō" (The new basis to criticism of China), *Dokushokai zasshi* (November 1926), as cited in Yamamoto Hideo, *Tachibana Shiraki* (Tokyo: Chūō kōronsha, 1977), 183–84.

87. *Manshū hyōron* 7.6 (August 11, 1934), 33.

88. Ibid., 33.

89. In *Rikukaigun bunsho* (Documents of the army and navy) 816 (November 10, 1931), n.p.; also cited in *Manshūkoku shi kakuron*, 162.

90. Tachibana Shiraki, "Manshū shin kokka kenkoku taikō shian" (My plan of an outline for the establishment of a new state in Manchuria), *Manshū hyōron* 2.1 (January 12, 1932), 31.

91. Tachibana Shiraki, "Henshū no ato ni" (After editing), *Gekkan Shina kenkyū* 1.4 (March 1925), 202.

92. Tachibana Shiraki, "Ōdō no jissen to shite no jichi" (Self-government as the implementation of the Kingly Way), *Manshū hyōron* 1.15 (December 5, 1931), 2.

93. Tachibana Shiraki, "Jichi shidōbu no gyōseki" (The achievements of the Self-Government Guidance Board), *Manshū hyōron* 3.4 (July 23, 1932), 6.

94. Tachibana Shiraki, "Ōdō riron no kaiten" (The development of the theory of the Kingly Way), *Manshū hyōron* 3.7 (August 13, 1932), 11–14.

95. Tachibana Shiraki, "Ōdō riron no kaiten," *Manshū hyōron* 3.7 (August 13, 1932), 14.

96. "Kenkokusha sengen" (Manifesto of the State-Founding Society), in Tachibana Shiraki, "Ōdō riron no kaiten," *Manshū hyōron* 3.7 (August 13, 1932), 14.

97. In Kobayashi Tatsuo and Shimada Toshihiko, eds., *Gendai shi shiryō*, 7, 117.

98. Tachibana Shiraki, "Jichi shidōbu no gyōseki," 2–3.

99. "Tōhoku shishō sanzenman minshū ni tsuguru no sho," in *Kenkoku no seishin* (The spirit of state-building) (Xinjing: Manshū teikoku Kyōwakai chūō honbu, 1940), 40.

100. "Zen-Man kenkoku sokushin rengō taikai sengen ketsugibun"(Text of a resolution of the entire confederation sponsoring state-building throughout Manchuria), in *Kenkoku no seishin*, 16.

Chapter 3. Toward a Model of Politics for the World

1. *Manshūkoku seifu kōhō* 1 (April 1, 1932), 2.

2. Manshūkoku kokumuin sōmuchō kōhōsho, ed., *Senden no kenkyū* (Propaganda research) (n.p., 1937), vol. 1, 1.

3. "Manshūkoku kenkoku sengen" (State-founding proclamation of Manzhouguo), in Kobayashi Tatsuo, Shimada Toshihiko, and Inaba Masao, *Gendai shi shiryō, 11: Zoku Manshū jihen* (Materials on contemporary history, volume 11: The Manchurian Incident, continued) (Tokyo: Misuzu shobō, 1965), 524.

4. Yanaihara Tadao, *Manshū mondai* (The issue of Manchuria) (Tokyo: Iwanami shoten, 1934), 87.

5. "Manshūkoku kenkoku sengen," 524.

6. "Manshūkoku kenkoku sengen," 524.

7. "Manshūkoku kenkoku sengen," 525.

8. "Kenkoku ni kansuru taigai tsūkoku" (Announcement to foreign nations on the founding of the state), in *Manshūkoku hōrei shūran* (Collection of laws and ordinances of Manzhouguo), ed. Manshūkoku hōrei shūran kankōkai (Tokyo: Manshūkoku hōrei shūran kankōkai, 1932), 8

9. "Manshūkoku kenkoku sengen," 525.

10. Hayashi Kimihiko, "Ōdō no jissen to shite no kan no kaizen" (Improving officials as a practical aplication of the Kingly Way), *Manshū hyōron* 3.7 (August 13, 1932), 25.

11. "Manshūkoku kenkoku sengen," 525.

12. "Shissei sengen" (Administrative proclamation), in Tsunoda Jun, ed., *Ishiwara Kanji shiryō, kokubō ronsaku* (Materials on Ishiwara Kanji, issues of national defense) (Tokyo: Hara shobō, 1967), 526.

13. *Manshū tōchi ron* (On ruling Manchuria) (Tokyo: Nihon hyōronsha, 1934), 137.

14. In Takasu Yūzō, ed., *Manshū jihen to Manshū seinen renmei* (The Manchurian Incident and the Manchurian Youth League) (Tokyo: Manshū seinen renmei konwakai, 1973), 2.

15. Katakura Tadashi, *Tengyō, Manshūkoku no kensetsu* (The emperor's work, the founding of Manzhouguo) (Dalian: Manshū hyōronsha, 1932), 179.

16. *Manshū hyōron* 21.17 (October 25, 1941), 31.

17. "Manshū kokka no soshiki" (The structure of the state of Manzhouguo), in Chūma Teruhisa, ed., *Manshūkoku no kaibō* (An analysis of Manzhouguo) (Tokyo: Shinkōsha, 1932), 7.

18. "Manshūkoku kongo no hōshin ni tsukite" (On the future direction of Manzhouguo), *Dai Ajia* 1.3 (July 1933), in *Naitō Konan zenshū* (Complete works of Naitō Konan), ed. Naitō Kenkichi and Kanda Kiichirō (Tokyo: Chikuma shobō, 1972), vol. 5, 182.

19. This translation is based on the original, *Wo de qianbansheng* (The first half of my life), and the Japanese translation by Ono Shinobu, Nohara Shirō, et al., *Waga hansei: "Manshūkoku" kōtei no jiden* (Half of my life, an autobiography of the emperor of "Manzhouguo") (Tokyo: Chikuma shobō, 1977), vol. 2, 5–6. The English translation by Kuo Ying Paul Tsai conveys the flavor of the original, but takes many liberties: *The Last Manchu: The Autobiography of Henry Pu Yi, Last Emperor of China* (New York: Pocket Books, 1987), 162. See also the translation by W. J. F. Jenner, *From Emperor to Citizen: The Autobiography of Aisin-Gioro Pu Yi* (Beijing: Foreign Languages Press, 1989), 254.

20. "Katakura Diary," 187.

21. Hirano Reiji, *Manshū no inbōsha* (The conspirator of Manchuria) (Tokyo: Jiyū kokuminsha, 1959), 127.

22. Literally, "it's as if we were able to do this in an alcove" (*tokonoma*), implying that they had successfully created the leader of a state propped up for external consumption. Hirano Reiji, *Manshū no inbōsha*, 130.

23. Luo Zhenyu, "Jilu bian" (Encountering hardship) (1932), in *Xuetang zishu* (Autobiography of Luo Zhenyu) (Nanjing: Jiangsu renmin chubanshe, 1999), 4–5.

24. "Katakura Diary," 189.

25. Translator's note. Many thanks to Christopher Atwood for the correct romanizations of the Mongolian names in this paragraph and for other information on Mongolian participation in the events described herein.

26. In Kobayashi Tatsuo and Shimada Toshihiko, eds., *Gendai shi shiryō, 7: Man-shū jihen* (Materials on contemporary history, volume 7: The Manchurian Incident) (Tokyo: Misuzu shobō, 1964), 389.

27. "Katakura Diary," 204.

28. Reginald F. Johnston, *Twilight in the Forbidden City* (1934; Oxford: Oxford University Press, 1989), 450–51.

29. *Waga hansei*, 302.

30. *Waga hansei*, 302.

31. *Ugaki Kazushige nikki* (Diary of Ugaki Kazushige), ed. Tsunoda Jun (Tokyo: Misuzu shobō, 1970) (entry for October 10, 1931), 813.

32. Banzai Rihachirō, *Man-Mō mondai no jūten* (The importance of the Manchuria-Mongolia issue) (Tokyo: Shin Nihon dōmei, 1931), 3.

33. Cable from Shidehara to Kuwashima, in *Nihon gaikō nenpyō narabi ni shuyō monjo* (Chronology of Japanese diplomacy and principal documents), ed. Gaimushō (Tokyo: Nihon kokusai rengō kyōkai, 1955), vol. 2, 187.

34. Shidehara, in *Nihon gaikō nenpyō narabi ni shuyō monjo*, vol. 2, 187.

35. Cable from Minami Jirō to Honjō Shigeru, in *Nihon gaikō nenpyō narabi ni shuyō monjo*, vol. 2, 187–88.

36. "Jihen zengo no Tōhoku jinbutsu no bunya" (The respective spheres of per-sonages in the Northeast at the time of the Manchurian Incident) (December 1931), 52.

37. *Jijū bukan Nara Takeji nikki, kaikoroku* (Diary and reminiscences of Nara Takeji, the emperor's aide-de-camp) (Tokyo: Kashiwa shobō, 2000), entry for Octo-ber 8, 1931, vol. 4, 366.

38. Rescript of the Shōwa emperor, as cited in Kobayashi and Shimada, eds., *Gendai shi shiryō, 7: Manshū jihen*, 337.

39. *Nara Takeji nikki*, vol. 4, 409.

40. "Man-Mō jiyūkoku kensetsu an taikō" (Outline of a plan for the establish-ment of a free state of Manchuria-Mongolia), in Kobayashi and Shimada, eds., *Gendai shi shiryō, 7: Manshū jihen*, 251–54.

41. In Kobayashi and Shimada, eds., *Gendai shi shiryō, 7: Manshū jihen*, 333.

42. Tachibana Shiraki, "Ōdō seiji" (Government based on the Kingly Way), *Man-shū hyōron* 2.21 (May 28, 1932), 3.

43. Komai Tokuzō, *Dai Manshūkoku kensetsu roku* (Chronicle of the founding of the great state of Manzhouguo) (Tokyo: Chūō kōronsha, 1933), 113.

44. "Manshū kokka no soshiki," in Chūma Teruhisa, ed., *Manshūkoku no kaibō*, 11.

45. Komai Tokuzō, *Dai Manshūkoku kensetsu roku*, 125.

46. Katakura Takashi, *Kaisō no Manshūkoku* (Reminiscences of Manzhouguo) (Tokyo: Keizai ōraisha, 1978), 149.

47. Ishii Itarō, *Gaikōkan no isshō* (The life of a diplomat) (Tokyo: Yomiuri shin-bunsha, 1950), 195.

48. Ishii Itarō, *Gaikōkan no isshō*, 193.

49. *Waga hansei*, vol. 2, 7; English translation, 164–65.

50. *Waga hansei*, vol. 2, 15; English translation, 169–70.

51. *Manshūkoku seifu kōhō* 1 (April 1, 1932), 6.

52. Kishida Eiji, "Manshūkoku kenpō sūgi" (A humble opinion of the constitu-tion of Manzhouguo), *Manshū hyōron* 7.19 (November 10, 1934), 14–15.

53. "Kenkoku isshūnen kinen kyōsho" (Message on the first anniversary of the founding of the state), *Manshūkoku seifu kōhō* (March 1, 1933), 1; reprinted in *Kenkoku no seishin* (The spirit of state-building) (Xinjing: Manshū teikoku Kyōwakai chūō honbu, 1940).

54. *Manshūkoku seiritsu no keii to sono kokka kikō ni tsuite* (Tokyo: Rikugunshō chōsahan, 1932), 26.

55. Article 29, Organizational Law of the Nationalist Government, 1931.

56. "Katakura Diary," 253.

57. Matsuki Tamotsu, "Manshūkoku kenkoku no rinen to sore o meguru hito-bito" (The ideals for establishing a state of Manzhouguo and the people involved), *Gaikō jihō* (September 1961), 53.

58. Matsuki, "Man-Mō jiyūkoku kensetsu an taikō," 249.

59. In Kobayashi and Shimada, eds., *Gendai shi shiryō, 7: Manshū jihen,* 189.

60. Gaimushō, ed., *Nihon gaikō shuyō nenpyō narabi ni shuyō monjo,* vol. 2, 216.

61. "Katakura Diary," 356.

62. Telegram from Morishima to Yoshizawa, dated February 13, 1932, in Gaimushō, ed., *Nihon gaikō monjo, Manshū jihen* (Documents of Japanese diplomacy, the Manchurian Incident) (Tokyo: Gaimushō, 1979), vol. 2.1, 367.

63. "Manshūkoku tetsudō kōwan kasen ni kansuru shori hōshin," in Gaimushō, ed., *Nihon gaikō shuyō nenpyō narabi ni shuyō monjo,* vol. 2, 217–20.

64. In Kobayashi and Shimada, eds., *Gendai shi shiryō, 7: Manshū jihen,* 499.

65. "Katakura Diary," 356.

66. "Katakura Diary," 392.

67. "Man-Mō mondai zengo shori yōkō," in Kobayashi and Shimada, eds., *Gendai shi shiryō, 7: Manshū jihen,* 361.

68. "Man-Mō mondai shori hōshin yōkō," in *Nihon gaikō nenpyō narabi ni shuyō monjo,* vol. 2, 204–05.

69. "Man-Mō mondai shori hōshin yōkō," in *Nihon gaikō nenpyō narabi ni shuyō monjo,* vol. 2, 205.

70. *Extracts from the Lytton Report, Extraits du Rapport Lytton* (Geneva: Press Bureau of the Chinese Delegation, 1932), 52. Japanese edition: Gaimushō, transl., *Ritton hōkokusho, kokusai renmei Shina chōsa iinkai hōkokusho zenbun* (Report of the Lytton Commission: Full text of the League of Nations China Investigative Committee) (Tokyo: Tōji shoin, 1932), 235.

71. Ishiwara Kanji, "Itagaki shōshō ni kōji o takusuru shuki" (Memorandum entrusting affairs to Major General Itagaki) (dated August 12, 1932), in Tsunoda Jun, ed., *Ishiwara Kanji shiryō, kokubō ronsaku,* 105.

72. "Kanai, Minagawa, Ōtsu no tanpyō" (A short critique of Kanai, Minagawa, and Ōtsu), *Manshū gyōsei* 3.9 (September 1936), 69.

73. Tokuda Chūjirō, "Manshū kanryōjin gunzō" (A group picture of officials in Manchuria), *Sōzō* 9.11 (October 1939), 36. This issue was entitled "Yakushin Manshūkoku no zenbō" (A full view of Manzhouguo making rapid progress).

74. See, for example, Furumi Tadayuki, *Wasureenu Manshūkoku* (Unforgettable Manzhouguo) (Tokyo: Keizai ōraisha, 1978), 10.

75. Kantōgun shireibu (Guandong Army headquarters), "Tai-Man-Mō hōsaku" (A policy for Manchuria and Mongolia) (dated May 1932), in Kobayashi, Shimada, and Inaba, eds., *Gendai shi shiryō, 11: Zoku Manshū jihen,* 638.

76. "Manshūkoku jinji gyōsei shidō hōshin yōkō" (Outline of a plan for leadership in the personnel administration of Manzhouguo), in Kobayashi, Shimada, and Inaba, eds., *Gendai shi shiryō, 11: Zoku Manshū jihen,* 923.

77. Telegram from the Commander of the Guandong Army to the Director of the Military Bureau (dated May 14, 1935), in Kobayashi, Shimada, and Inaba, eds., *Gendai shi shiryō, 11: Zoku Manshū jihen,* 927.

78. "Man-Mō mondai zengo shori yōkō," in Kobayashi and Shimada, eds., *Gendai shi shiryō, 7: Manshū jihen,* 316.

79. "Man-Mō kyōwakoku tōji taikō an" (Draft plan for ruling the Manchurian-Mongolia republic), in Kobayashi and Shimada, eds., *Gendai shi shiryō, 7: Manshū jihen,* 228.

80. "Man-Mō jiyūkoku kensetsu kōryō," in Manshū seinen renmei shi kankō

iinkai, ed., *Manshū seinen renmei shi* (A history of the Manchurian Youth League) (Tokyo: Hara shobō, 1968 reprint; 1933 original), 659.

81. "Shin kokka nai ni okeru Nihonjin no chii ni tsuite" (On the position of Japanese within the new state) (dated January 25, 1931), in Tsunoda Jun, ed., *Ishiwara Kanji shiryō, kokubō ronsaku*, 93.

82. "Katakura Diary," 356.

83. "Katakura Diary," 356.

84. Manshū teikoku seifu (Manchurian imperial government), ed., *Manshū kenkoku jūnen shi* (History of the ten years since the founding of Manzhouguo) (Tokyo reprint: Hara shobō, 1969), 118.

85. Manshūkoku tsūshinsha, ed., *Manshūkoku gensei* (The present situation in Manzhouguo) (Tokyo reprint: Hōwa shuppan, 1986; original: Manshūkoku tsūshinsha, 1935), 145.

86. Yorinaga Gorō, "Kokumuin to kakubu o kataru" (On the State Council and the various ministries), *Sōzō* 9.11 (October 1939), 386. "Yakushin Manshūkoku no zenbō" issue.

87. Ibid., 386.

88. *Manshūkoku gensei*, 136.

89. Bureaucratic Organization of the State Council, Items 8, 10, and 18, respectively, in Kobayashi and Shimada, eds., *Gendai shi shiryō, 7: Manshū jihen*, 414–15.

90. "Manshū jikyoku ni kansuru kansatsu" (Observations on the situation in Manchuria), *Shin tenchi* 12.2 (February 1932), 18.

91. Tachibana Shiraki, "Dokusai ka minshu ka" (Autocracy or democracy?), *Manshū hyōron* 2.8 (February 27, 1932), 7.

92. Furumi, "Manshūkoku to Nihonjin" (Manzhouguo and the Japanese), in *Manshū kenkoku no yume to genjitsu* (Dream and reality in founding a state in Manchuria), ed. Kokusai zenrin kyōkai (Tokyo: Kokusai zenrin kyōkai, 1975), 105.

93. Ibid., 105.

94. "Manzhouguo shidō hōjin yōkō," in Kobayashi and Shimada, eds., *Gendai shi shiryō, 7: Manshū jihen*, 589.

95. From the "Manshūkoku shidō yōryō" (Summary of guidance over Manzhouguo), a plan drawn up by Hashimoto Toranosuke, in Kobayashi, Shimada, and Inaba, eds., *Gendai shi shiryō, 11: Zoku Manshū jihen*, 640.

96. Kantōgun shireibu, "Tai-Man-Mō hōsaku," in Kobayashi, Shimada, and Inaba, eds., *Gendai shi shiryō, 11: Zoku Manshū jihen*, 636.

Chapter 4. "The Long-Term Policy for National Management Will Always Be in Unison with the Japanese Empire"

1. *Kyūshū nichinichi shinbun*, January 22, 1932.

2. *Ōsaka asahi shinbun*, March 2, 1932.

3. Yanaihara Tadao, "Manshū kenbun dan" (Talk on a visit to Manchuria), *Kaizō* (November 1932), 106.

4. Ibid., 107.

5. Ibid., 110–11.

6. Ibid., 113.

7. Yanaihara Tadao, "Manshū shin kokka ron" (On the new state in Manchuria), *Kaizō* (April 1932), 29.

8. "Tōhoku shishō sanzenman minshū ni tsuguru no sho" (A letter to the 30 million people of the four provinces of the northeast), in *Kenkoku no seishin* (The spirit of state-building) (Xinjing: Manshū teikoku Kyōwakai chūō honbu, 1940), 8.

9. For statements to this effect, see Kasagi Yoshiaki, *Kasagi Yoshiaki ihōroku* (Memoirs of Kasagi Yoshiaki) (n.p.: Kasagi Yoshiaki ihōroku kankōkai, 1960), 331–32, 340–41.

10. Komai Tokuzō, *Dai Manshūkoku kensetsu roku* (Chronicle of the founding of the great state of Manzhouguo) (Tokyo: Chūō kōronsha, 1933), 144.

11. Tachibana Shiraki, "Dokusai seitō ron" (On autocratic political parties), *Manshū hyōron* 5.9 (August 26, 1933), 13.

12. Yasuda Yojūrō, " 'Manshūkoku kōteiki ni sasaguru kyoku' ni tsuite" (On the "Melody to Lift up the Imperial Flag of Manzhouguo"), *Kogito* 102 (December 1940), 26.

13. Yasuda Yojūrō, " 'Manshūkoku kōteiki ni sasaguru kyoku' ni tsuite," 26.

14. "Katakura Diary," 199.

15. "Katakura Diary," 409.

16. "Katakura Diary," 409.

17. "Katakura Diary," 410.

18. "Katakura Diary," 410.

19. Ishiwara Kanji, "Man-Mō mondai no yukikata" (Treatment of the Manchuria-Mongolia issue) (dated December 2, 1931), in Tsunoda Jun, ed., *Ishiwara Kanji shiryō, kokubō ronsaku* (Materials on Ishiwara Kanji, issues of national defense) (Tokyo: Hara shobō, 1967), 88.

20. Ishiwara Kanji, "Shin kokka nai ni okeru Nihonjin no chii ni tsuite" (On the position of Japanese within the new state) (dated January 25, 1932), in *Ishiwara Kanji shiryō, kokubō ronsaku*, 93.

21. Ishiwara Kanji, "Shin kokka nai ni okeru Nihonjin no chii ni tsuite," 93

22. Ishiwara Kanji, "Shin kokka nai ni okeru Nihonjin no chii ni tsuite," 99.

23. "Man-Mō mondai zengo shori yōkō" (dated January 27, 1932), in *Ishiwara Kanji shiryō, kokubō ronsaku*, 365.

24. Memorandum to Isogai Rensuke, dated June 25, 1932, in *Ishiwara Kanji shiryō, kokubō ronsaku*, 100–02.

25. Yamaguchi Jūji, *Manshū kenkoku no rekishi: Manshūkoku Kyōwakai shi* (A history of state-founding in Manchuria: A history of the Concordia Association of Manzhouguo) (Tokyo: Eikō shuppansha, 1973), 19

26. Yamaguchi Jūji, *Manshū kenkoku no rekishi*, 26.

27. Ishiwara, as cited in Yamaguchi Jūji, *Manshū kenkoku no rekishi*, 29.

28. Katakura Tadashi, *Kaisō no Manshūkoku* (Reminiscences of Manzhouguo) (Tokyo: Keizai ōraisha, 1978), 184.

29. In Kobayashi Tatsuo, Shimada Toshihiko, and Inaba Masao, *Gendai shi shiryō, 11: Zoku Manshū jihen* (Materials on contemporary history, volume 11: The Manchurian Incident, Continued) (Tokyo: Misuzu shobō, 1965), 844.

30. Ishiwara, Memorandum to Isogai Rensuke, in *Ishiwara Kanji shiryō, kokubō ronsaku*, 101.

31. Ishiwara, Memorandum to Isogai Rensuke, in *Ishiwara Kanji shiryō, kokubō ronsaku*, 100.

32. S.M.R. Economic Research Association, *Manshū keizai nenpō* (Manchurian economic yearbook) (Tokyo: Kaizōsha, 1934), 151.

33. "Katakura Diary," 386.

34. Sasa Hiroo, "Manshū seisaku no setsudanmen" (A section of Manchurian policy), *Kaizō* (September 1932), 100.

35. *Manshū keizai nenpō* (1934), 151.

36. Koiso Kuniaki, *Katsuzan kōsō* (Footprints of a white bird in the mountains) (Tokyo: Chūō kōronsha, 1963), 584.

37. Ishiwara, "Man-Mō ni kansuru shiken" (August 1932), in *Ishiwara Kanji shiryō, kokubō ronsaku*, 107.

38. Yamaguchi Jūji, *Kieta teikoku Manshū* (The vanished empire of Manchuria) (Tokyo: Mainichi shinbunsha, 1967), 238.

39. Yamaguchi Jūji, *Manshū kenkoku no rekishi*, 267.

40. Katakura Tadashi, *Chikusui no hengen* (Just a few words) (1933), as cited in *Kasagi sanbō no shōen hanran to chin'atsu* (Staff Officer Katakura's deposition, rebellion, and suppression) (Tokyo: Fuyō shobō, 1981), 112.

41. Tachibana Shiraki, "Jichi kara ōdō e" (From autonomy to the Kingly Way), *Manshū hyōron* 6.12 (March 24, 1934), 2

42. Tachibana Shiraki, "Den'enri no Nikkei kanri" (Japanese officials out in the rural districts), *Manshū hyōron* 6.10 (March 10, 1934), 5.

43. Ikegami Teihachi, "Kishi Kishirō ron" (On Kishi Kishirō), *Manshū hyōron* 6.4 (January 27, 1934), 29.

44. *Shūin gijiroku sokkiroku* (Stenographic record of the proceedings of the Diet) 3 (August 25, 1932), 13.

45. Ibid., 18.

46. "Nichi-Man giteisho" (Japan-Manzhouguo Protocol), in *Gendai shi shiryō 7: Manshū jihen*, 496–97.

47. *Tōkyō mainichi shinbun*, September 16, 1932.

48. *Extracts from the Lytton Report, Extraits du Rapport Lytton* (Geneva: Press Bureau of the Chinese Delegation, 1932), 50.

49. *Hōchi shinbun* (September 16, 1933).

50. Yonezawa Kikuji, "Nichi-Man giteisho chōin kiroku" (Record of the signing of the Japan-Manzhouguo Protocol), *Kakankai kaihō* 285 (1933), 16.

51. "Hata Shunroku nisshi," in *Zoku gendai shi shiryō 4: Rikugun, Hata Shunroku nisshi* (Documents on modern history, continued, volume 4: The army, diary of Hata Shunroku) (Tokyo: Misuzu shobō, 1983), 50.

52. Yonezawa Kikuji, "Nichi-Man giteisho chōin kiroku," 16.

53. Ibid.

54. Kikuchi Sadaji, *Shūpū sanzen ri: Chūgoku yonjūnen no kaiko* (Three thousand ri of an autumn breeze, memories of forty years in China) (Tokyo: Nanbokusha, 1966), 8 (of introduction).

55. Usui Yasushi, "Sōri daijin ni tsukaete" (Working for the prime minister), *Manshū gyōsei* (April 1935), 75–77.

56. "Bohyō ni kaete" (In place of a tombstone), reprinted in *Ozaki Gakudō zenshū* (Collected works of Ozaki Yukio), ed. Ozaki Gakudō zenshū hansan iinkai (Tokyo: Kōronsha, 1955), vol. 8, 9.

57. *Ozaki Gakudō zenshū*, vol. 8, 10–11.
Translator's note. This essay bore the title, "Bohyō no kawari ni," when it appeared initially in *Kaizō* (January 1933), but was changed for reprinting in Ozaki's collected works.

58. Masaki Naohiko, *Jūsanshōdō nikki* (Diary from the Hall of Thirteen Pine Trees) (entry for September 25, 1934), 4 volumes (Tokyo: Chūō kōron bijutsu shuppan, 1965–66), 1179.

59. Nagao Uzan, "Tei Sokan sensei" (Mr. Zheng Xiaoxu), *Kaizō* (September 1934), 33.

60. Hatano Sumio and Kurosawa Fumitaka, eds., *Jijū Bukanchō Nara Takeji nikki kaikoroku* (The diaries and memoirs of Chamberlain Hara Takeji) (Tokyo: Kashiwa shobō, 2000), vol. 3, 458.

61. In *Manshūkoku gun shi* (Military history of Manzhouguo) (Tokyo: Ranseikai, 1970), 130.

62. *NHK shuzaihan dokyumento Shōwa 7: Kōtei no mitsuyaku* (NHK assignment documentary, 1932: The secret agreement of the [Manchu] emperor) (Tokyo: Kadogawa shoten, 1987), 162.

63. Hoshino Naoki, *Mihatenu yume, Manshūkoku gaishi* (An unfinished dream, an unofficial history of Manzhouguo) (Tokyo: Daiyamondosha, 1963), 157.

64. Zhou Junshi, *Higeki no Kōtei, Fugi: Gi Manshūkoku kyūtei hishi* (Puyi, the tragic emperor: History of the bogus Manzhouguo court), Japanese translation by Tei Zenken (Tokyo: Kōbunsha, 1984), 226.

65. "Ishimaru Shizuma nikki" (Diary of Ishimaru Shizuma), in *Manshūkoku gun shi*, 137.

66. Edgar Snow, *Far Eastern Front* (London: Jarrolds Publishers, 1934), 278–79; Japanese translation by Kajitani Yoshihisa, *Kyokutō sensen* (Tokyo: Chikuma shobō, 1973), 236–37.

67. "Teisei jisshi sōri seimei" (Prime minister's announcement on the implementation of the imperial system) (dated January 24, 1934), in *Kenkoku no seishin*, 44. There was also a Chinese version of this text which the same title, pronounced "Dizheng shishi zongli shengming," published at the time.

68. Ibid., 45.

69. In ibid., 61.

70. Koiso Kuniaki, *Katsuzan kōsō* (Footprints of a white bird in the mountains) (Tokyo: Chūō kōronsha, 1963), 591.

71. *Riku-Man dai nikki* 249 (February 27, 1933), 1.

72. "Manshūkoku shidō hōjin yōkō," in *Gendai shi shiryō* 7, 589.

73. *Wei-Man kuilei zhengquan* (The bogus Manzhouguo regime) (Beijing: Zhonghua shuju, 1994), 152.

74. *Wei-Man kuilei zhengquan*, 152.

75. *Wei-Man kuilei zhengquan*, 152.

76. Tsukushi Kumashichi, "Manshūkoku kenpō seitei ni tsuite" (On the enactment of the Manzhouguo constitution), manuscript, August 1933, 1.

77. "Manshūkoku kōtei suitai chūbi ni kansuru ken" (Item concerning preparations for the installation of the emperor of Manzhouguo) (dated October 18, 1933), document held in the National Documents Center, Tokyo.

78. Snow, *Far Eastern Front*, 276; Japanese translation, 235.

79. Tanabe Harumitsu, "Teisei jisshi to ōdō seiji no yōtei" (The implementation of an imperial system and the secret of government by the kingly way), in *Manshū kenkoku sokumen shi* (Bypaths of the history of the founding of Manzhouguo), ed. Miyauchi Isamu (Tokyo: Shin keizaisha, 1942), 103.

80. Rōyama Masamichi, "Teisei Manshūkoku no sekai seiji teki igi" (The international political significance of a monarchical Manzhouguo), *Kaizō* (April 1934), 260.

81. Sasaki Tōichi, *Aru gunjin no jiden* (Autobiography of a soldier) (Tokyo: Keisō shobō, 1967), revised edition, 243.

82. *Waga hansei*, vol. 2, 46.

83. Ibid., 36.

84. Puyi, "Huiluan xunmin zhaoshu," in *Kenkoku no seishin*, 62. A slightly different translation of this passage from the text may be found in *From Emperor to Citizen: The Autobiography of Aisin Gioro* (Beijing: Foreign Languages Press, 1965), 296–97.

85. *Waga hansei*, vol. 2, 36.

86. Ibid.

87. Guandong Army Headquarters, "Manshūkoku no konpon rinen to Kyōwakai no seishitsu" (The fundamental ideals of Manzhouguo and the nature of the Concordia Society) (dated September 18, 1936), in *Gendai shi shiryō 11: Manshū jihen*, 909.

88. Ibid.

89. A slightly different translation of these passages from the text may be found in *From Emperor to Citizen*, 301.

90. Katakura Tadashi, *Kaisō no Manshūkoku* (entry for July 7, 1940), 242.

91. *Waga hansei,* vol. 2, 56. A slightly different translation of this passage from the text may be found in *From Emperor to Citizen,* 300.

92. *Waga hansei,* vol. 2, 55. A slightly different translation of this passage from the text may be found in *From Emperor to Citizen,* 300.

93. Cited in Li Nianci, *Manzhouguo jishi* (A true account of Manzhouguo) (Taibei: Jindai Zhongguo shiliao congkan xubian, vol. 82, 1954), 290.

94. *Waga hansei,* vol. 2, 60. A slightly different translation of this passage from the text may be found in *From Emperor to Citizen,* 304: "Apart from eating and sleeping, my life could be summarized as consisting of floggings, curses, divination, medicine, and fear."

95. Tachibana Shiraki, "Jakushō minzoku no shomondai" (Problems of the minor ethnicities), *Manshū hyōron* 6.22 (November 26, 1934), 2.

96. Tachibana Shiraki, "Jakushō minzoku no shomondai," 2.

97. Tachibana Shiraki, "Jakushō minzoku no shomondai," 2.

98. Edgar Snow, *Far Eastern Front,* 269 (Japanese translation, 228): "Don't think that all Chinese in government offices are here because they like it. They can be divided into four classes. First, those working frankly to make money, with the cynical philosophy that somebody will make it, why not they? Second, those like *Wang Tao Cheng,* who long for a Confucian revival, and think the Japanese are going to give it to them. Third, those who become puppets as alternative to losing their property—and their heads. Fourth, those who stay because, if they fled, their families would be massacred. Only a few of us are in the first two classes. Most of the puppets are here for reasons not their own."

99. Kikuchi Teiji, *Shūpū sanzen ri,* 8 (of introduction).

100. Kikuchi Teiji, *Shūpū sanzen ri,* 8 (of introduction).

101. Joseph C. Grew, *Ten Years in Japan: A Contemporary Record Drawn from the Diaries and Private and Official Papers of Joseph C. Grew, United States Ambassador to Japan, 1939–1942* (New York: Simon and Schuster, 1944), 30.

102. Edgar Snow, *Far Eastern Front,* 268; Japanese translation, 227.

103. Yamaguchi Jūji, *Kieta teikoku Manshū,* 237.

104. Ōkura Kinmochi, "Saikin no Manshū jijō" (The recent state of affairs in Manchuria), in *Kido Kōichi kankei bunsho* (Documents concerning Kido Kōichi), ed. Kido nikki kenkyūkai (Tokyo: Tokyo University Press, 1966), 190–91.

105. Ōkura Kinmochi, "Saikin no Manshū jijō," 190–91.

106. *Waga hansei,* vol. 2, 11.

107. "Daidō gakuin to Furumi san" (The Great Harmony Academy and Mr. Furumi), in *Kaisō Furumi Tadayuki* (Memoirs of Furumi Tadayuki) (Tokyo: Furumi Tadayuki kaisōroku kankōkai, 1984), 154.

108. Shiina Etsusaburō, *Watakushi no rirekisho* (My history) (Tokyo: Nihon keizai shinbunsha, 1970), 198.

109. Kamio Kazuharu, *Maboroshi no Manshūkoku* (The phantom Manzhouguo) (Tokyo: Nit-Chū shuppan, 1983), 45.

110. Hoshino Naoki, *Mihatenu yume,* 194.

111. Matsumoto Masuo, "Chō Keikei sōri to no jūnenkan" (Ten years with Prime Minister Zhang Jinghui), in *Mokugekisha no kataru Shōwa shi, 3: Manshū jihen* (Shōwa history as told by witnesses, vol. 3: The Manchurian Incident), ed. Hiratsuka Masao (Tokyo: Shin jinbutsu ōraisha, 1989), 165–66.

112. Matsumoto Masuo, "Chō Keikei sōri to no jūnenkan," 165.

113. Kishida Eiji, "Manshūkoku kenpō sui" (My humble views on the constitution of Manzhouguo), *Manshū hyōron* 7.19 (November 10, 1934), 16.

114. Hoshino Naoki, *Mihatenu yume,* 265.

115. *Waga hansei,* vol. 2, 39.

116. Manshūkoku tsūshinsha, ed., *Manshūkoku gensei* (The present situation in Manzhouguo) (Manshūkoku tsūshinsha, 1943), 677.

117. Manshūkoku tsūshinsha, ed., *Manshūkoku gensei*, 69.

118. Matsumoto Masuo, "Chō Keikei sōri to no jūnenkan," 167.

119. Matsumoto Masuo, "Chō Keikei sōri to no jūnenkan," 166, 167.

120. Matsumoto Masuo, "Chō Keikei sōri to no jūnenkan," 163.

121. Hoshino Naoki, *Mihatenu yume*, 199.

122. Daihon'ei rikugun kenkyūhan, comp., *Kaigaichi hōjin no gendō yori mitaru kokumin kyōiku shiryō (an)* (May 1940), 34.

123. Katakura Tadashi, "Mayuru seika" (The sacred torch burning), in *Manshūkoku to Kyōwakai* (Manzhouguo and the Concordia Association), ed. Koyama Sadatomo (Dairen: Manshū kyōronsha, 1935), 129–30.

124. "Kensetsu jūnen no kaiko to shōrai e no tenbō" (Reflections on the ten years of state-building and prospects for the future), in *Manshū kenkoku sokumen shi*, 396.

125. "Kensetsu jūnen no kaiko to shōrai e no tenbō," 397–98.

126. Translator's note. This pun is based on two homophonous terms, written of course with different characters and bearing radically different denotations.

127. Okamoto Eiji, "Yogen" (Forecasts), in *Ishiwara Kanji kenkyū* (Studies of Ishiwara Kanji), ed. Hosaka Fujio (Osaka: Seikakai chūō jimusho, 1950), 83.

128. Yokoyama Shinpei, *Hiroku Ishiwara Kanji* (The secret record of Ishiwara Kanji) (Tokyo: Fuyō shobō, 1971), 305.

129. In *Ishiwara Kanji shiryō*, vol. 2, 235–38.

130. Cited in Mutō Tomio, *Amakasu Masahiko no shōgai: Manshūkoku no danmen* (The career of Amakasu Masahiko, a phase to Manzhouguo) (Tokyo: Seihoku shōji kabushiki gaisha, 1956), 140.

131. *Manshū kenkoku jūnen shi* (Ten-year history of Manzhouguo) (Tokyo: Hara shobō, 1969), 78.

132. *Manshūkoku seifu kōhō* 668 (June 11, 1936), 174.

133. Tsukushi Kumashichi, "Manshū kenkoku no kaiko" (Memories of the founding of Manzhouguo), *Sōzō* (November 1942), issue on "Manshū genjō hōkō" (Reports on the present state of affairs in Manzhouguo), n.p.

134. Morishima Morindo, *Inbō, ansatsu, guntō* (Plots, murder, sabres) (Tokyo: Iwanami shoten, 1950), 81.

135. Kishi Nobusuke, Yatsugi Kazuo, and Itō Takashi, *Kishi Nobusuke no kaisō* (Memories of Kishi Nobusuke) (Tokyo: Bungei shunjū, 1981), 22.

136. Minobe Yōji tsuitōroku (Account of the eulogies for Minobe Yōji), *Yōyōka* (Tokyo: Nihon hyōron shinsha, 1954), 43.

137. *Nihon keizai nenpō, dai 18 shū* (Japan economic annual, No. 18) (Tokyo: Tōyō keizai shinpōsha, 1934), 42.

138. Naisei shi kenkyūkai, ed., *Kurihara Minoru shi danwa sokkiroku* (Notes from a conversation with Mr. Kurihara Minoru) (Tokyo: Naisei shi kenkyūkai, 1977), 84.

139. Katakura Tadashi, *Kaisō no Manshūkoku*, 198.

140. Furumi Tadayuki, "Manshūkoku no yume wa kienai" (My dream of Manzhouguo will never be extinguished), in *Zasetsu shita risōkoku Manshūkoku kōbō no shinsō* (An ideal state frustrated, the truth about the rise and fall of Manzhouguo) (Tokyo: Gendai bukkusha, 1967), 210.

141. Baba Akira, *Nit-Chū kankei to gaisei kikō no kenkyū* (Studies in the diplomatic machinery in Sino-Japanese relations) (Tokyo: Hara shobō, 1983), 441.

142. Kantōgun sanbōbu, ed., *Shi no Nichi-Man* (Japan and Manzhouguo in history) (Guandong Army, 1937), 67.

143. Maki Kenji, "Manshūkoku no tōchi ni tsuite" (On ruling Manzhouguo), *Hōaku ronsō* 31.1 (July 1934), 57.

144. C. K. Sei, "Manjin wa kaku sakebu" (Manchurians call out in this manner), *Tesshin* (journal of the Manshūkoku chianbu) (May 1938), 197.

145. "Manshūkoku no konpon rinen to Kyōwakai no honshitsu" (The basic ideals of Manzhouguo and the essence of the Concordia Association) (September 18, 1936), in *Gendai shi shiryō 11*, 909.

146. "Warera wa kaku kensetsu seri" (We have laid the foundation in this way), *Sōzō* (November 1942), "Manshū genjō hōkoku" issue.

147. *Manshū kenkoku jūnen shi*, 23.

148. *Manshū kenkoku jūnen shi*, 21.

149. C. K. Sei, "Manjin wa kaku sakebu," *Tesshin* (June 1938), 197.

150. "Who Runs the Emperor," *Fortune* 29.4 (April 1944), 285.

151. "Who Runs the Emperor," *Fortune* 29.4 (April 1944), 280, 283.

152. Aritake Shūji, *Shōwa Ōkurashō gaishi* (An informal history of the Finance Ministry during Shōwa), vol. 2 (Tokyo: Shōwa Ōkurashō gaishi kankōkai, 1969), 26.

153. "Man-Mō mondai shiken" (dated May 1931), in *Ishiwara Kanji shiryō*, 78.

154. Sasaki Tōichi, "Manshū tōchi ni okeru yūkan" (Troubles in the rule over Manchuria) (dated May 1933), in *Gendai shi shiryō 11*, 855.

155. "Manshūkoku seiji kōsei kikō kaikaku taikō" (Outline for the reform of the structure of the political administration of Manzhouguo) (dated May 1937), in *Seiji gyōsei kikō kaikaku ni tsuite* (On the adminstrative reform of politics), "Manshūkoku kokusei panfuretto 3" (Pamphlet on national conditions in Manzhouguo 3) (Xinjing: Manshū teikoku kokumuin sōmuchū jōhōsho, 1937), 4–6.

156. *Manshūkoku gensei* (The present state of Manzhouguo) (Xinjing: Manshū kōhō kyōkai, 1932), 217.

157. "Manshū ni okeru shokuryō shūka kikō to shūka taisaku" (The structure of food collection in Manchuria and a policy for collection), 1943.

158. "Manshūkoku no konpon rinen to Kyōwakai no honshitsu," in *Gendai shi shiryō 11*, 909–10.

159. In *Shūiin sokkiroku 3* (January 22, 1937), 40.

160. Koyama Sadatomo, *Manshū Kyōwakai no hattatsu* (The development of the Concordia Association of Manchuria) (Tokyo: Chūō kōronsha, 1941), 92.

161. "Zenren kyōgikai yōkō" (Main principles of the national conference), in Koyama Sadatomo, *Manshū Kyōwakai no hattatsu*, 56.

162. Koyama, *Manshū Kyōwakai no hattatsu*, 91

163. Koyama, *Manshū Kyōwakai no hattatsu*, 93.

164. Liu Huiwu and Liu Xuezhao, eds., *Riben diguozhuyi qin-Hua shilüe* (Shanghai: Huadong shifan daxue chubanshe, 1987), 95–96.

165. Puyi, "Jikyoku ni kansuru shōsho," special issue of *Manshūkoku seifu kōhō* (December 8, 1941), 1.

166. *Waga hansei*, vol. 2, 77. In the official English translation (*From Emperor to Citizen*, 319): "I have forgotten the wording of the sixth rescript, but I do remember that the indispensable references to the 'Divine Blessing of the Heavenly Shinning [*sic.*] Bright Deity and the Protection of His Imperial Majesty the Emperor of Japan' were struck out by Hashimoto with a wry smile."

167. Matsumoto Masuo, "Chō sōri to Manshūkoku" (Premier Zheng and Manzhouguo), in *Aa Manshū, kunizukuri sangyō kaihatsusha no shuki* (Aa, Manchuria, notes of a industrial developer involved in nation-building), ed. Manshū kaikoshū kankōkai (Tokyo: Nōrin shuppan, 1965), 92.

168. Mutō Tomio, "Manshū kenkoku no kuromaku, Amakasu Masahiko" (Mastermind of the establishment of the state of Manzhouguo, Amakasu Masahiko), in *Mokugekisha no kataru Shōwa shi*, ed. Hiratsuka Masao, 183.

169. Mutō Tomio, "Manshū kenkoku no kuromaku, Amakasu Masahiko," 175.

Chapter 5. Conclusion

1. Furumi Tadayuki, "Manshūkoku no yume wa kienai" (The dream of Manzhouguo cannot be extinguished), in *Zasetsu shita risōkoku Manshūkoku kōbō no shinsō* (The frustrated ideal state: The truth about the rise and fall of Manzhouguo) (Tokyo: Gendai bukkusha, 1967), 302.

2. Yamaguchi Yoshiko and Fujiwara Sakuya, *Ri Kōran, watakushi no hansei* (Li Xianglan, half of my life) (Tokyo: Shinchōsha, 1987), 110.

3. Translator's note. Yamamuro is playing on the expression "*nichijō sahan*" (everyday occurrence, ordinary affair) which usually has nothing directly to do with the tea and rice in it; in this instance, it is precisely the foodstuffs ("ordinary?") to which he is pointing.

4. Testimony of Zhu Haide, as cited in Andō Hikotarō, "Enpen kikō" (Travels to Yanbian), *Tōyō bunka* 36 (March 1964), 38–39.

5. Furumi, "Manshūkoku no yume wa kienai," 270.

6. Gao Shan, "Manshūkoku gunkan gakkō" (The cadet school of Manzhouguo), in *Chūgoku shōnen no mita Nihon gun* (The Japanese army as seen by Chinese youth), ed. Lin Huaiqiu and Ishikami Masao (Tokyo: Aoki shoten, 1985), 58–59.

7. Sakuda Shōichi, "Manshū kenkoku no kaiko" (Memories of the founding of Manzhouguo), in *Aa Manshū, kunizukuri sangyō kaihatsusha no shuki* (Aa, Manchuria: notes of a industrial developer involved in nation-building), ed. Manshū kaikoshū kankōkai (Tokyo: Nōrin shuppan, 1965), 65.

8. Li Zhandong, "Kokoro ni nokoru uta" (A song left in my heart), in *Chūgoku shōnen no mita Nihon gun*, 28.

9. "Manshūkoku to Nihonjin" (Manzhouguo and the Japanese), in *Manshū kenkoku no yume to genjitsu* (Dream and reality in founding a state in Manchuria), ed. Kokusai zenrin kyōkai (Tokyo: Kokusai zenrin kyōkai, 1975), 108.

10. Wang Ziheng, "Wei-Man guanli de mimi shouce" (Secret pamphlet for officials in the bogus state of Manzhouguo), in *Wenshi ziliao xuanji* (Selection of literary and historical documents), ed. Wenshi ziliao yanjiu weiyuanhui, vol. 39 (Beijing: Zhongguo wenshi chubanshe, 1963), 57, 59, 60.

11. Zenkoku ken'yūkai rengōkai, ed., *Nihon kenpei gaishi* (Unofficial history of the military police) (Tokyo: Kenbun shoin, 1983), 297.

12. Kantōgun shireibu, "Manshūkoku no konpon rinen to Kyōwakai no honshitsu" (The fundamental ideals of Manzhouguo and the essence of the Concordia Association) (dated September 18, 1936), in *Gendai shi shiryō 11: Manshū jiden*, 908. Emphasis in original.

13. Translator's note. This is an untranslatable play on words. The term for harmony in Japanese is *kyōwa*, and the author here has split it into *kyō* which he identifies with "assistance, help" and *wa* which he identifies with "Yamato."

14. Kantōgun sanbōbu (Operations Section, Guandong Army), "Man-Mō ni okeru sanryōchi tōji ni kansuru kenkyū" (Study of controlling occupied terrain in Manchuria and Mongolia) (dated May 1930), in *Ishiwara Kanji shiryō, kokubō ronsaku*, 53.

15. Itagaki Seishirō, "Man-Mō mondai ni tsuite" (On the problem of Manchuria and Mongolia) (dated May 1931), in *Taiheiyō sensō e no michi* (The road to the Pacific War), ed. Nihon kokusai seiji gakkai Taiheiyō sensō gen'in kenkyūbu (Tokyo: Asaha shinbunsha, 1963), additional volume, 104.

16. Manshūkoku saikō kensatsuchō, *Manshūkoku kaitakuchi hanzai gaiyō* (1941), in Yamada Shōji, ed., *Kindai minshū no kiroku 6: Manshū imin* (Records of the people in the modern era, vol. 6, migrants to Manchuria) (Tokyo: Shinjinbutsu ōraisha, 1978), 455.

17. Tsukui Shin'ya, "Aa 'muga shijun'" (Alas, "selflessness and purity"), *Henkyō* 9 (November 1972), 228.

18. Nasu Shiroshi et al., "Man-Mō kaitaku seishōnen giyūgun hensei ni kansuru kenpakusho" (Petition concerning the formation of a youth volunteer brigade for Manchurian and Mongolian colonization) (dated November 1937), 3.

19. Tsukui Shin'ya, "Aa 'muga shijun,'" 228.

20. In *Kikigaki, aru kenpei no kiroku* (Verbatim notes, account of a military policeman), ed. Asahi shinbun Yamagata shikyoku (Yamagata branch of the Asahi newspaper) (Tokyo: Asahi bunko, 1991), 187.

21. Ibid., 190.

22. Ibid., 192.

23. *Bayue de xiangcun* (Shanghai: Rongguang shuju, 1935), 3 (introduction).

24. Manshikai (Society for Manchurian history), *Manshū kaihatsu yonjū nen shi* (History of forty years of Manchurian development) (Tokyo: self-publ., 1964), vol. 1, 1 (introduction).

25. Ōta Seikyū et al., eds., *Shōwa Manyōshū* (Ten thousand leaves for the Shōwa period), vol. 3 (Tokyo: Kōdansha, 1979), 124–26.

26. Manshūkoku gunseibu gunji chōsabu (Military research bureau of the military administration of Manzhouguo), ed., *Manshū kyōsan hi no kenkyū* (Studies of the Communist bandits in Manchuria) (n.p.: Gunseibu komonbu, 1937), vol. 1, 730.

27. Ed. Manshūkoku shi hensan kankōkai (Committee for the editing and publishing of the history of Manzhouguo), *Manshūkoku shi, sōron kakuron* (Tokyo: Man-Mō dōhō engokai, 1971), vol. 2 ("kakuron"), 199.

28. Minseibu keisatsushi (Office of Police Affairs, Ministry of Civil Affairs), *Hōkō seido ron* (On the *baojia* system) (self-publ., 1936), 22.

29. Nagai Sadamu, "Hōkō seido no genzai to shōrai" (The present and future of the *baojia* system), *Manshū gyōsei* 3.11 (November 1936), 16.

30. "Zanji chōji tōhihō" (Provisional law for the punishment of bandits), *Manshūkoku seifu kōhō* 44 (September 10, 1932), 3.

31. Guandong Army, *Shōwa jūni nendo yori jūroku nendo ni itaru Manshūkoku sensō junbi shidō keikaku* (Guiding plan for war preparations in Manzhouguo from 1937 through 1941). N.p.

32. Kokuheihō jimukyoku, *Kokuheihō yōran* (Overview of the National Troop Law) (1940), as cited in *Kokuheihō wa nani ka* (What is the National Troop Law?) (Shinkyō [Changchun]: Kokuheihō shikkō chūō iinkai jimukyoku, 1940), 18.

33. Item 1, National Labor Service Law (Kokumin kinrō hōkō hō).

34. Takahashi Gen'ichi, *Daigun jushō Manshūkoku* (Manzhouguo, a great army and supply factory) (Osaka: Asahi shinbunsha, 1944), 63.

35. Item 1, Populace Registers Law (Kokumin techō hō).

36. Manshū nichinichi shinbunsha, *Shōwa jūonen han, Manshū nenkan* (The Manchurian Yearbook for 1940) (Dairen: Manshū nichinichi shinbunsha, 1939), 365.

37. "Kokumuin fukoku daijūnangō" (Proclamation No. 17 of the State Council), *Manshū teikoku seifu kōhō* (December 8, 1942), 1.

38. Cited in Aisin Gioro Hao, *"Ruten no ōhi" no Shōwa shi* (History of the Shōwa era, itinerant queen) (Tokyo: Shufu to seikatsusha, 1984), 69.

39. Andō Hikotarō, "Tōhoku kikō" (Trip the the Northeast), *Chūgoku tsūshin, 1964–1966* (Dispatches from China, 1964–1966) (Tokyo: Daiyasu, 1966), 480.

40. Yuji Manzō, ed., *Kenkoku daigaku nenpyō* (Chronology of Kenkoku University) (Tokyo: Kenkoku daigaku dōsōkai, 1981), 554–55.

41. Ibid., 555.

42. "Kenkoku daigaku ni tamawaritaru chokusho" (Imperial rescript on Kenkoku University, May 1938), *Manshūkoku seifu kōhō* (May 2, 1938), 1.

43. "Kenkoku daigaku rei daiichijō" (Law on Kenkoku University, Item Number 1), *Manshūkoku seifu kōhō* 1006 (August 5, 1937), 65.

44. *Manshūkoku shi, sōron*, 5.

45. Kanasaki Ken, "Sanritsu ittai sei ni kawaru mono" (In place of the system of three posts in one), *Gaikō jihō* 713 (August 15, 1934), 89.

46. Ibid., 93.

47. Komai Tokuzō, *Dai Manshūkoku kensetsu roku* (Chronicle of the founding of the great state of Manzhouguo) (Tokyo: Chūō kōronsha, 1933), 124.

48. Furumi Tadayuki, "Kenkoku jūnen no kaiko to shōrai e no tenbō (Recollections on the ten years since state-founding and prospects for the future), in *Manshū kenkoku sokumen shi* (Bypaths of the history of the founding of Manzhouguo), ed. Miyauchi Isamu (Tokyo: Shin keizaisha, 1942), 398.

49. Takamiya, *Jungyaku no Shōwa shi* (Loyalty and treason in Shōwa history) (Tokyo: Hara shobō, 1971), 147.

50. Ibid., 147.

51. Translator's note. Or, as we say in English, the path to hell is paved with good intentions.

52. Mutō Tomio, "Manshūkoku ni kaketa yume" (Dreams pinned on Manzhouguo), *Shisō no kagaku* 21 (December 1963), 36.

Conclusion

1. Kasagi Yoshiaki, *Kasagi Yoshiaki ihōroku* (Tokyo: Kasagi Yoshiaki ihōroku kankōkai, 1960).

Interview

1. In Peter Duus and Kobayashi Hideo, eds., *Teikoku to iu gensō: "Dai tō-A kyōeiken no shisō to genjitsu* (The illusion of empire: Ideology and practice in the Greater East Asia Co-prosperity Sphere) (Tokyo: Aoki shoten, 1998).

2. In the special issue of *Kan* in which this interview initially appeared, there are essays on the Manchurian Film Company as well as on Fuchigami Hakuyō (1889–1960) and the Manchurian Photographers' Association. The issues involved with photography, graphics, and film-making are all very important.

Appendix

1. Translator's note. Takahashi Kageyasu also studied the Manchu language and was the author of *Manbun shūin* (Collected rhymes in Manchu). In 1826 he met Siebold and the two men exchanged scholarly materials. For the serious infraction of giving the foreigner a map of Japan, the Tokugawa shogunate imprisoned Takahashi and he died in prison.

2. Mori Ōai, "Daini gun" (Second army), *Uta nikki* (Poetry diary), *in Ōgai zenshū* (Collected Works of Mori Ōgai) (Tokyo: Iwanami shoten, 1973), vol. 19, 107, 110. Compare to the translation by the Rev. A. Lloyd:

When her railway came to Pekin, the threatened woe began,
For China and the Hermit Kingdom, and our own beloved Japan.
. . . .
Three centuries of Russian greed must now come to an end.

See "Our Second Army," in *The Russo-Japanese War Fully Illustrated* 2 (June 1904), 214.

3. From Kodama Gentarō, *Manshū keizaisaku kōai* (Summary of an economic plan for Manchuria), as cited in Tsurumi Yūsuke, *Gotō Shinpei* (Tokyo: Keisō shobō, 1965), vol. 2, 651.

4. Hiratsuka Atsushi, *Itō Hirobumi hiroku* (The confidential memoirs of Itō Hirobumi) (Tokyo: Shunjūsha, 1929), 408.

5. (New York: Harper, 1909); Japanese translation by Mochizuki Kotarō (1865–1927), *Nichi-Bei hissen ron: genmei muchi no yūki* (Certain war between Japan and the U.S.: original title, *The Valor of Ignorance*) (Tokyo: Hara shobō, 1982 rpt.).

6. Shimanuki Takeji, "Nichi-Ro sensō igo ni okeru kokubō hōshin, shoyō heiryoku, yōhei kōryō no hensen (jō)" (Changes in defense directions, necessary military force, and tactical plans after the Russo-Japanese War, part 1), *Gunji shigaku* 32 (March 1973), 3.

7. Shimanuki, "Nichi-Ro sensō," 6.

8. Shimanuki, "Nichi-Ro sensō," 6.

9. *Manshū ryokōki: ichimei, hakusan kokusui roku* (Travelogue of Manchuria, or a chronicle of white mountains and black rivers) (Tokyo: Zenrin shobō, 1901).

10. *Tō-A ryokōdan* (Tokyo: Egusa Onotarō, 1903). The text was reprinted recently in a collection entitled *Bakumatsu Meiji kenbunroku shūsei* (Collection of travelogues from the bakumatsu and Meiji eras), ed. Kojima Shinji (Tokyo: Yumani shobō, 1997 rpt.), vol. 14.

11. Tomizu Hirondo, *Tō-A ryokōdan* (Tokyo: Yūhikaku shobō, 1905 rpt.), 127.

12. Chōhōsha, *Risshin chifū, kaigai tokō annai* (Tokyo: Rakuseisha, 1911), reprinted in the series *Kindai Ō-Bei tokō annaiki shūsei* (Collection of modern travel guides to the West) (Tokyo: Yumani shobō, 2000), volume 5.

13. Chōhōsha, *Risshin chifū, kaigai tokō annai*, 11–12.

14. Sakurai Tadayoshi, *Nikudan* (Human bullets) (Tokyo: Eibun shinshisha, 1906), 36; translated into English by Masujiro Honda and Alice M. Bacon as *Human Bullets (Niku-dan): A Soldier's Story of Port Arthur* (Tokyo: Teibi Pub. Co, 1906).

15. Yuasa Katsue, *Senku imin* (Pioneer immigrants) (Tokyo: Shinchōsha, 1939).

16. Tachibana Sotoo, "Harbin no yūutsu" (The melancholy of Harbin), *Bungei shunjū* 18.8 (1940), 264.

17. Hirabayashi Hirondo, *Manshū ni okeru hōjin sekkyakufu no seiryoku* (The influence of Japanese hostesses in Manchuria) (n.p., 1934), frontispiece.

18. Translator's note. The literature on *karayukisan* is as voluminous as it contentious. They were women who who left Japan to work, more often than not as prostitutes, overseas. Some argue that they were tricked into forced servitude by labor racketeers who took advantage of the fact that many young women had to leave Japan's rural areas because of widespread poverty and that many died in the process of going to their places of work or on the job. Others argue that these women were fully aware of what they were doing and, remaining ahead of the curve, sought to carve out a productive niche for their own security.

19. Ishimitsu Makiyo, *Kōya no hana* (Tokyo: Ryūseikaku, 1958); (Tokyo: Chūō kōronsha, 1978 rpt.).

20. Words from a propaganda poster of the time.

21. *Joshi takushoku shidōsha teiyō* (Summary of the women's colonization leadership) (Tokyo: Takushokushō takuhokukyoku hodō, 1942), 124.

22. *Joshi takushoku shidōsha teiyō*, 126–27.

23. *Joshi takushoku shidōsha teiyō*, 124.

24. Koizumi Mikue, *Manshūjin no shōjo* (Xinjing: Gekkan Manshūsha, 1938); (Tokyo: Zenkoku shobō, 1942 rpt.; Seikakai, 1945 rpt.). Citation from *Gaichi bungaku*

zenshū (Collected literary writing from the overseas territories) (Tokyo: Ōzorasha, 2000), vol. 19, 78, 115, 125.

25. Manshū shakai jigyō kyōkai, *Manshū shakai jigyō nenpō 1935 nenkan* (Manchurian social enterprises, 1935 edition) (n.p.), 125.

26. Shimaki Kensaku, *Manshū kikō* (Travelogue of Manchuria) (Tokyo: Sōensha, 1940), 26.

27. Kantōgun shireibu (Guandong Army Headquarters), "Zai-Man Chōsenjin shidō yōkō" (Summary of Korean leaders in Manchuria) (July 25, 1938), in Kobayashi Tatsuo, Shimada Toshihiko, and Inaba Masao, ed., *Gendai shi shiryō, 11: Zoku Manshū jihen* (Materials on contemporary history, volume 11: The Manchurian Incident, continued) (Tokyo: Misuzu shobō, 1965), 956.

28. Higuchi Kiichirō, *Attsu Kisuka gunshireikan no kaisōroku* (Memoirs of the army commander at [the islands of] Attu and Kiska [in the Aleutians]) (Tokyo: Fuyō shobō, 1971, 1999 rpt.), 352.

29. *Yudayajin taisaku yōkō* (Summary of the Jewish policy) (1938), in Ajia rekishi shiryō sentaa, reel A-0217, 1.

30. *Yudayajin taisaku yōkō*, in Ajia rekishi shiryō sentaa, reel A-0217, 2.

31. *Jikyoku ni tomonau Yudayajin taisaku* (Jewish policy accompanying the present situation) (1942), in Ajia rekishi shiryō sentaa, reel A-1214, 1.

32. In Hara Yoshihisa, ed., *Kishi Nobusuke shōenroku* (Testimony of Kishi Nobusuke) (Tokyo: Asahi shinbunsha, 2003), 355.

33. Fukuda Takeo, "Waga kuni no Tōnan Ajia seisaku" (Japanese policy in Southeast Asia), in *Waga gaikō no kinkyō* (The recent scene in Japanese relations), no. 22 (Tokyo: Gaimushō, 1978), 328.

34. Ōhira Masayoshi kaisōroku kankōkai, ed., *Ōhira Masayoshi kaisōroku* (Memoirs of Ōhira Masayoshi) (Tokyo: Kashima shuppankai, 1983), 571.

Chronology

1. *Kan: rekishi, kankyō, bunmei* 10 (Summer 2002), 36–37.

Index